SELLING TO
THE AFFLUENT

The Professional's Guide to
Closing the Sales that Count

D1016771

SELLING TO THE AFFLUENT

The Professional's Guide to Closing the Sales that Count

Thomas J. Stanley, Ph.D.

McGraw-Hill

New York San Francisco Washington, D.C. Auckland Bogotá
Caracas Lisbon London Madrid Mexico City Milan
Montreal New Delhi San Juan Singapore
Sydney Tokyo Toronto

McGraw-Hill

A Division of The McGraw-Hill Companies

Library of Congress Cataloging-in-Publication Data

Stanley, Thomas J.
    Selling to the affluent : the professional's guide to closing the sales that count / Thomas J. Stanley, Ph.D.
       p. cm.
    ISBN 0-07-061049-5
    1. Selling.   2. Rich as consumers–United States.   I. Title.
HF5438.25.S73   1991
658.8'5—dc20   90–45154

Printed in the United States of America
    4 5 6 7 8 9 0 BKP/BKP 9 0 2 1 0 9

For Janet, Sarah, and Brad

PREFACE

Why would anyone want to sell to the affluent? Many factors suggest that a career in this discipline can, in fact, be a rewarding one. The affluent population, whether measured in terms of a minimum annual household income of $100,000 or a net worth of $1 million or more, is far outpacing the growth of the household population. In recent years, both categories have grown at a rate of more than 20 percent per year. Interestingly, the number of households in America is increasing at a rate of less than 2 percent.

But growth is not the only factor which makes the concept of selling to the affluent so attractive. The affluent market in this country is a very resilient one. In the last 20 years, has there even been a single year when the number of high-income households declined? No. In each and every year since 1970, the number of households in the $100,000 or more annual income category has increased. The affluent population seems to have an uncanny ability to generate high incomes in spite of downturns in the broader economy. Most of the members of the affluent population are responsive to changes in the economy. Most are sellers in one way or another of a product or service. Most generate incomes from well-defined market niches or subsegments that are more insulated from the trends that significantly influence our general population. They are typically proactive in regard to capitalizing upon trends which may provide important opportunities in the market.

The cost of personal selling in the context of the typical individual target is often prohibitively expensive given modest revenue potential. However, affluent targets have greater promise. For example, households in America that have annual incomes of $1 million or more on average spend nearly $100,000 annually on interest on personal loans. Compare this form of behavior with the average household's credit/consumption habits. The typical American household spends less than $1,000 per year for interest on personal loans. Yes, personal selling of credit services is better suited for the affluent. The same applies to expensive homes, luxury automobiles, and investment services. Remember that the wealthiest 5 percent of American families hold 58 percent of the wealth and nearly 20 percent of the income.

There is yet another compelling reason to consider a career in selling to the affluent. Only a minority of sales professionals who target the affluent have yet to acquire the skills necessary to do it effectively. Many of those professionals who are highly successful in this arena tell their stories in *Selling to the Affluent*. Almost all of these sales professionals earn more than $100,000 per year via the affluent market. Several contributors to this book make in excess of $1 million annually by addressing the needs of the affluent.

ACKNOWLEDGMENTS

The genesis of this book comes from conversations, interviews, and the case studies of hundreds of sales professionals who target the affluent. Many of these marketers are truly extraordinary people. Their willingness to share strategic information is greatly appreciated.

I am indebted to my wife, Janet, for her guidance, patience, and assistance in the development of the manuscript.

Special thanks are accorded to Kay Campbell, Ruth Tiller, and Sharon Weaver for their help in editing and word processing. I owe a deep debt of gratitude to Susan Glinert for her sage editorial comments.

Finally, I wish to acknowledge the contribution of Sarah and Brad Stanley, who always gave "their candid insights about the true value of countless concepts and case scenarios."

Thomas J. Stanley

CONTENTS

PART 1
INTRODUCTION

1   WHAT THIS BOOK IS ABOUT   3

What Do the Affluent Need?   3

Two of America's Most Extraordinary Sales Professionals   6

Identifying and Conditioning Affluent Business Owners   7

Prospecting Affluent Sales Professionals   11

Prospecting Affluent Women   13

Prospecting Asian Americans: Becoming an Advocate for Affluent Affiliation Groups   14

Prospecting Successful Authors   14

Selling to Targets on the Move   15

Influencing People Who Influence the Affluent   16

Selling Luxury Automobiles to High-Income Consumers   18

Selling Real Estate to the Affluent   19

Are You an Apostle or Antagonist to the Affluent?   20

2   TWO OF AMERICA'S MOST EXTRAORDINARY SALES PROFESSIONALS   21

Daniel F. Kirk: Profile of a Most Extraordinary Sales Professional   21

Two Roads to Expertise   34

When Prospects Are Far from Being Euphoric   38

PART 2
TARGETING THE AFFLUENT:
SOME OVERLOOKED MARKETS

3   IDENTIFYING AND CONDITIONING AFFLUENT BUSINESS OWNERS   53

Finding Big Ships that Wear Blue Collars   53
The National Fisherman   65

4   PROSPECTING THE SALES PROFESSIONAL   69
Introduction   69
Capitalize on the Real Needs of High-Income Sales Professionals   70
Pro Forma Prospecting   76
"So, It's Not a Good Time to Talk"   86

5   PROSPECTING AFFLUENT WOMEN   91
Affluent Women in America: At Least Two Distinct Segments   91
Esther M. Berger Becomes a Recognized Authority on
Women and Money   101
An Encore Performance by Roger Thomas   119

6   PROSPECTING ASIAN AMERICANS: BECOMING
AN ADVOCATE FOR AFFLUENT AFFILIATION GROUPS   129
Introduction   129
Understanding the Affluent Asian American Market   132
On Becoming an Advocate of Affluent Affinity Groups   143
A Letter to a Frustrated Financial Consultant   146
Pro Forma Postcard Providing Evidence of
Being an Advocate   148
Pro Forma News Release Providing Evidence of
Being an Advocate   149

7   PROSPECTING SUCCESSFUL AUTHORS   152
Introduction   152
Robert Read   154
Suggestions for Mr. Young   173
Keith Called While You Were Out of Town   177
Prospecting for a Special Form of Tuition Refund   183
I Will Miss Him, and Sales Professionals, You Overlooked Him   196

8   ALARM: RETIRED AND OTHER TYPES OF MILLIONAIRES
ARE MOVING INTO YOUR MARKET AREA   200
The Bismarck Example   200
Be There First and Be Armed With the Right Message   201
Targeting Affluent Movers Even Before They Move:
Greetings from Rancho Mirage   212
Temporarily in Your Neighborhood: Mr. D. Cheers
Just Surfaced inside an NBA Convoy   214
Even Superstar Athletes Pay for These Shoes   217

PART 3
INFLUENCING PEOPLE WHO INFLUENCE THE AFFLUENT

	INTRODUCTION	221
	Ted's Pro Forma Dialogue	222
	Conditioning for the Future	227
	Ted Is a Mentor and Promoter	233
9	ENDORSED BY THE MEDIA	235
	So, You Want to Be a Talk-show Host	235
	Fred, Can You Send Us One More Article?	236
	Follow Fred's Footsteps	242
	Addendum to Chapter 9	255
10	LEVERAGE YOUR AFFLUENT TARGETS' NEED FOR SEMINARS AND SPEAKERS	262
	No, You're Not Too Young to Persuade the Affluent	262
	Susan's Special Brand of Telephone Conditioning	270
	More Than Just Speaking about Selling Exclusive Travel Services	276

PART 4
SELLING TANGIBLES TO THE AFFLUENT

	INTRODUCTION: A MASTERPIECE OF PERSONAL SELLING	285
11	SELLING LUXURY AUTOMOBILES TO HIGH-INCOME CONSUMERS	297
	Introduction	297
	Hungry Fish and Euphoric Prospects	298
	The Spending Frenzy	299
	Obsolete Theories of Marketing	300
	ESPs Are Proactive	301
	Jack, You'll Never Own Another Dinosaur	302
	Exploit Their Need to Affiliate	304
	An Interview with Mr. Gerhardt Blendstru	305
	An Interview with an Ordinary Sales Professional	308
	Share This Letter With Your Luxury Automobile Dealers	312
	Proactive versus Reactive Selling	328
	No Calls for Hungry Fish	330
	Public Information	331

Develop Your Own List   333
The Big League Orientation   333
The Low Cost of High Productivity   335
Target by Industry   336
A Winning Portfolio of Sales Professionals   337
Be Perceived as an Expert   339
They Make House Calls!   341
Selling Luxury Cars by the Parade Method   344
John Sells More than Luxury Automobiles   347
Exploiting His List of Targets   355
Focus on the Needs of the Target   358
Conditioning the Prospect   358
Ask for Help from a Ghost   368
Condition Your Manager   369
Follow John's Proactive Methods   372

12   SELLING REAL ESTATE TO THE AFFLUENT   374

Jackie Spota: A Most Extraordinary Sales Professional of
Extraordinary Real Estate   374
How the Affluent Make Decisions   383
Luxury Real Estate for Yachting, Golfing, or
as a Reward for Succeeding   395
Communicating with Affluent Prospects Who Are Euphoric
because of Recent Recognition by Their Industry   402
Fieldston Confessions   404

PART 5
CASE STUDIES: THE SELLING OF SERVICES
TO THE AFFLUENT

13   APOSTLES VERSUS ANTAGONISTS OF THE AFFLUENT   409
Introduction   409
Contrasts in Atmospheres   411
A Bank that Wins versus One that Loses an Affluent Client   417
Timing the Sales Pitch   420
Prospecting CEOs   427
Two Different Orientations toward the Children of the Affluent   430
Variations in Service among Providers of Surface
Transportation   435

Antagonist versus Apostle of a Researcher Who Studies the
Affluent Market   449

Swamp Land or Luxury Home Sites:
Differences of Perceptions   451

The Real Needs of an Extraordinary Saleswoman   453

What the Affluent Really Need   454

Opportunities among the Blue-Collar Affluent   457

Patronage Opinion Leaders: Responding to
Centers of Influence   459

Conditioning Patronage Opinion Leaders   462

Conditioning Those Who Influence Affluent Readers   464

The Spalding School's Country Fair   466

INDEX   469

PART 1

INTRODUCTION

CHAPTER 1

WHAT THIS BOOK IS ABOUT

WHAT DO THE AFFLUENT NEED?

Take a moment to visualize 100,000 sales professionals who target the affluent all seated in a large enclosed stadium. A picture of an affluent prospect appears on a huge overhead screen. A brief biographical sketch of the prospect is distributed to each of the sales professionals. The information includes the prospect's occupation, social and professional affiliations, annual income ($183,350), net worth ($2.3 million), and achievements and/or awards. Also enclosed is an examination that contains only one essay question. The question asks the following: What does this affluent prospect need?

The majority of the sales professionals, more than 90,000, respond in a very similar way.

- Financial consultants indicate that the prospect needs their specific brand of financial advice and investment products.
- Life insurance agents state that the fellow on the screen needs a seven-figure face value life insurance product and estate planning.
- Real estate agents state that this target needs the home on the third fairway that they just listed two days ago.
- Jewelry sales professionals write that the prospect needs the $11,000 master timepiece and the prospect's wife desperately needs the diamond encrusted woman's version.
- Luxury car sales professionals unequivocally pronounce that "Mr. Affluent needs our top-of-the-line two-door while his wife would likely need the four-door touring sedan."
- Clothing sales professionals are certain that this prospect needs a complete wardrobe overhaul given the picture dis-

played on the screen. They stipulate that he desperately needs their special-fabric, hand-tailored, custom-fitted, executive series of suits.
* Travel consultants feel that Mr. Affluent and his family need the 24-day world cruise at the super-class level which includes a helicopter tour of the Great Wall of China.

But a minority of the sales professionals, fewer than 1 in 10, submit a completely different essay. Interestingly, this minority group contains America's most successful marketers. How do they sell to the affluent? How do they influence people who influence the affluent? How do they find prospects when they are most vulnerable to solicitations? What themes do they use to encourage prospects to say yes to solicitations? How do they time solicitations to enhance the probability of closing the sale? How can their selling skills be acquired by others who wish to target the affluent? These are only a few of the questions that are answered in this book. As an introduction to the topic, examine several of these prototypical responses. "Mr. Smart" earned over $400,000 in net commissions last year by selling to the affluent. His exam reads as follows:

> William Manchester, the author of the best-selling biography of Winston Churchill, once stated, "Men who think of themselves as indispensable are almost always wrong." I fully realize that most affluent people can live and succeed in life without my basic product. There are thousands of people who sell identical or similar products. Thus, I always attempt to appeal to a higher need. Most of my clients and prospects in the affluent category are, in one way or another, selling something. They are business owners, attorneys, physicians, accountants, and sales and marketing professionals who happen to make extremely high incomes. More often than not, they buy from me because of something more than product and excellent service. I always attempt to help clients and prospects with that ever important need of increasing their revenue. I make referrals on behalf of all my clients who have something to sell. I also recognize their achievements both in conversations and in letters and cards that I send. Often, significant career achievements precipitate the need for my offerings. I pay special attention to determining the cash flow changes that are specific to the industries of which my clients and prospects are a part. Many of my clients

receive up to two-thirds of their annual incomes during one or two months of the year. Calling upon them at other times shows gross insensitivity on the part of the sales professional. I am also actively involved in five trade/professional organizations that represent the segments of the affluent population that I have targeted. I specifically targeted the senior officers of several of these organizations. Some have purchased from me; others have not. But I have done many favors for all of them such as developing programs and seminars for their demanding members. I have also used my marketing expertise to further the causes of some of these organizations. I was instrumental in initiating a letter-writing campaign designed to influence selected lawmakers in opposing proposed legislation that would adversely affect the industry of which many of my clients are members. They have often reciprocated by asking me to give important speeches at major gatherings. Several have also published my ideas in their national trade publications. The affluent have a very strong need to affiliate with others within their same discipline. All things being equal, they prefer or need to patronize those sales professionals, as in my case, who are perceived as integral parts of these affiliation groups. I never take my clients for granted. Their careers, their revenue, and their achievements are significantly more important to them than whether or not they buy my product at all or purchase one from me or from someone else. However, I do my very best to associate my product and my form of service with these career-related needs.

Another respondent to the exam told of his commitment to affluent fishermen and fishing fleet owners. He insists this commitment is why many prospects from this industry seek him out as opposed to him "chasing the fish." Recently, when several owners of fishing fleets received substantial compensation (more than $1 million each) from an oil company for damage to their fishing grounds, why did they entrust it to this particular financial advisor? Because he is viewed as an expert in helping solve the investment problems of people who fish for a living.

One of the most productive marketers of luxury automobiles also had a unique response.

How do I target the affluent? I do it by focusing on affinity groups that contain high concentrations of high-income prospects. Many of my best customers are surgeons. They don't make house calls. They are too busy. So I make "house calls." I tell them loud and clear that I cater to surgeons. I also target very high income producing sales professionals. I know when they are making money, but they never get enough recognition. So I give them my sales professional recognition package. It comes complete with a plaque and letter.

One of the essays from a super producer from the life insurance/financial planning industry told of his special brand of selling to the affluent. He is considered by many in his trade area to be the foremost source of financial wisdom for physicians. He has a genuine passion for helping doctors achieve financial independence. This commitment extends to his co-signing loans for young medical students to open professional practices. And this help is given without any promise on the part of the physician to become a client of this extraordinary financial planner. But many do become clients for life. Many refer their colleagues to him, and most brush off others who attempt to solicit their financial-planning business.

TWO OF AMERICA'S MOST EXTRAORDINARY SALES PROFESSIONALS

As an introduction and orientation to the topics covered in this book, profiles of two top performing sales professionals are given in Chapter 2. Both Dan and Gene are excellent role models for those who aspire to become quality professionals as well as balanced human beings. They were selected for the "most extraordinary" designation not only because they generate very high levels of sales commissions. Both have also adopted the whole life concept. In other words, they both have full control of their careers. Their careers do not control them. Both have fully balanced their family and career responsibilities, and both have achieved greatness by their own hard work, discipline, intellect, and tenacity. We can learn a great deal from Dan and Gene about how to sell to the affluent and also how to enjoy life.

IDENTIFYING AND CONDITIONING AFFLUENT BUSINESS OWNERS

Why target affluent business owners? Approximately 80 percent of the millionaires in this country work for a living. And 80 percent of these own their own businesses. Members of this segment are more likely than any other group to have high levels of income. This applies to the $100,000 and over annual income category as well as to the $1 million and above designation. Taken as a percentage of income, this group does have a lower propensity to purchase so-called status products. However, since many of its members generate extremely high incomes, even a small portion allocated to consumer products makes this group important to marketers. Also, the growth of privately held businesses in this country exceeds the rate of population growth by three to four times. Affluent business owners, as an occupational category, have the highest propensity to accumulate wealth. They should be a primary target for those who sell investment- and insurance-related products and services. Yet there is another reason why this segment is important. Only a small minority of sales professionals are truly proficient at selling to the affluent business owner.

What do affluent business owners want from sales professionals who target the affluent? Their needs are similar to those of affluent members in other occupational categories. There is an important difference, however, which sales professionals should recognize. Affluent business owners place a higher priority on their achievements within the context of their chosen industry than they do upon status or social class membership. The enlightened sales professional looks for opportunities to associate his product or service with the career achievements of the prospect. Some of the more innovative marketers of expensive products have discovered the value of the affluent business owner's need to own the symbols of achievement. A manufacturer of expensive watches gives the Rolex Spirit of Enterprise award each year to those whose accomplishments deserve special recognition. Most recently it gave the awards in the categories related to applied science and invention, exploration and discovery, and the environment.

Over- or Underprospected?

A national trade publication recently presented a list of what it considered to be the top 100 contracting firms in America. The list contained the names, addresses, and telephone numbers of the three top executives in each firm. How many sales professionals called these executives in an effort to recognize their achievements? How many sales professionals wrote a letter to these euphoric executives stating that it is only appropriate for a top executive with a top-ranked firm to purchase the best product, to get the best service, and to patronize the best supplier? ZERO! Why ZERO? Because most people who attempt to sell to the affluent never make unsolicited calls upon prospects, and those that do never read any material about successful people who exist outside their own industry!

A multimillionaire recently asked me an interesting question. "Tom, is it true that most wealthy people are not called on by salesmen?" My response was given as a question. "Robert, how often are you called on by sellers of anything?" His answer was predictable. "Tom, the only guy who ever called me is the owner of a Rolls Royce dealership, and he was smart to do so. But you would think that people would call. I'm not hard to find. I just gave $200,000 to a local charity. They put my name on a bronze plaque so everybody in town could see it. But nobody selling anything called. You would think they would realize that I have money."

An owner of a small fleet of fishing boats recently received a check from an oil company for over $1 million. This money was intended to compensate the owner for damages to his fishing grounds. How many sales professionals called this affluent prospect? One and only one. The sales professional in this case is a specialist. He focuses upon selling to affluent fishermen, suppliers to this industry, and buyers of their harvest. He also reads "the journal of affluent fishing," *The National Fisherman.*

Fifty top-ranked sales professionals spent an entire day together at a seminar. The seminar was held in a room within 100 feet of a doll auction. The auction was attended by hundreds of affluent prospects. Many dollars changed hands that day. Several attendees paid up to $40,000 for one doll. The auctioneers received between 10 and 35 percent of the sale price. Not one top-ranked sales professional who targets the affluent attended the auction. These sales professionals need to ask themselves, "Is it more productive to cluster with high concentrations of my competitors or with high concentrations of prospects?"

A three-day conference was recently held in Hawaii. The average annual income of the attendees was $750,000. How many sales professionals were even aware of this target of affluent market opportunity?

Some of the Themes the Affluent Business Owner May Wish to Hear

"The feature article in *Waste Age* is about you. Your achievements in the industry are legendary."

"Many of my clients are also business owners. I'm sure that a lot of them would be interested in learning about the services your firm offers."

"I have several contacts who are business writers. I'm sure that they would love to tell their readers about your operation."

"Your industry has been very good to me. Most of my best clients own restaurants within the same chain that you do. You probably have come into contact with a few of them."

"The article in *Pizza Today* said that you were one of the top independents in the country. You may want to reward yourself for your achievements by trading up to one of our top-of-the-line models. After all, you are the best in your industry. It's only logical that you should own the best product offered from my industry."

"Would it be all right to mention your company's products when my clients ask me about where they should go to buy something like this?"

"You are an important role model for a lot of people in your industry."

"Tell me how you made this operation so successful."

"We have selected you as entrepreneur of the month. It is a statewide award. Here is your plaque that salutes your outstanding achievements. Would you mind if we told the local business press about your award?"

"Here's a copy of the speech that I gave at your industry's international convention. It contained several of your ideas. Would it be all right if I mention you as the source of my inspiration? This material will be published in next month's issue of your association trade journal.''

''Many of my clients sold their businesses. It's not easy to turn over the keys to someone else. Some of my clients told me that it took over a year before they got over their withdrawal symptoms. You may want to talk to some of them. I'm sure that they could be of some assistance to you.''

''I just wanted to call to congratulate you on your selection as businesswoman of the year. Would you be willing to come by our office sometime and give an informal speech about how you succeeded in a very competitive industry. Many of the young women in our department are struggling. They could benefit from your insights. They need a strong female role model. Will you come by Friday morning? I will buy breakfast.''

''Congratulations on winning your latest contract. It's not every day that a locally based firm takes on the international big boys and wins. You are probably very much involved with keeping this operation on track right now. But when you want a bit of diversion, please review the video tape I have enclosed. The program will give you the highlights of the finest residential living in this region.''

''I am just starting out in sales. Do you think it would be a good strategy to focus on the successful business owners in your industry?''

''When is the best time during the year to contact people in your industry? In other words, is there a time when cash flow is at a peak?''

''Why do you think that targeting your industry would be productive?''

''There are hundreds of ways that a sales professional could attempt to market to you. Tell me how you would like to be approached. In other words, would you prefer to be telephoned, paid a personal visit via a cold call at your office, or contacted by mail? What do you prefer? You now have an opportunity to design a tailor-made sales approach.''

Suggestions about how to identify as well as how to condition affluent business owners are given in Chapter 3.

PROSPECTING AFFLUENT
SALES PROFESSIONALS

For many aspiring sales professionals who target the affluent, one target in particular will likely bear fruit. There are more than 300,000 high income producing sales and marketing professionals in the United States. Members of this segment are among the most sensitive to persuasive communications. Interestingly, they are among the least prospected affluent groups in this country. The key to selling these prospects is to understand their needs and changes in their cash flow. Many of these prospects are so physically and/or psychologically close to the sales professional that they constantly look beyond them for new business. In fact, I recently asked more than 1,000 high-income sales professionals an important question. How many had ever received an unsolicited telephone or in-person sales call from anyone marketing any type of tangible luxury product such as automobiles, boats, or residential real estate? Not one respondent recalled ever being prospected in the context of the proactive manner described in the question!

Only a minority of sales professionals have even begun to penetrate this lucrative market. Those who have communicate the precise message that these high-income prospects wish to hear. These messages are directly associated with the product or service that is offered. Few, if any, affluent occupational groups need more status recognition than sales professionals. Our society ascribes middle to low status to those individuals in the profession called selling. How do these prospects balance their low- or middle-level occupational status with their extremely high annual incomes? They purchase many of the artifacts which are often associated with high status. Such behavior includes purchasing top-of-the-line luxury automobiles, the largest home in a so-called prestige neighborhood, expensive watches and jewelry, and custom-made clothing.

In addition to their status needs, high-income sales professionals often seek to reward themselves for superior performance. Those marketers who position their product and/or service offerings as rewards for extraordinary achievements in sales are likely to succeed in penetrating this segment. Surprisingly, many employers of high-income sales professionals do not provide symbols of significant achievement other than cash payments. The enlightened sales professional can capitalize on this oversight. In essence, he can provide the achievement recognition that these affluent prospects desire. It is not unusual for high-income sales professionals to receive one-half or more of their income during a single month. Those marketers who blend their message in the context of status, achievement recognition, and high positive cash flow will greatly enhance their chances of capturing a significant portion of the patronage habits of affluent sales professionals.

This segment is an ideal target for marketers of tangible status products. However, there are significant opportunities within this target group for those who sell such services as big-ticket life insurance, financial planning, credit vehicles, and investments. As a prototypical example, consider the circumstances under which a top saleswoman recently purchased a big-league life insurance policy from, in her own words, "a nice young man." Her accomplishments, including being the number one saleswoman within a major metropolitan area, were prominently displayed in a widely distributed newspaper. How many sales professionals attempted to capitalize upon this "saleswoman of the year's" euphoria? Only one sales professional called her and made an appointment to visit this top producer in person. When the caller arrived at this prospect's office, he was armed with one of the most potent weapons in the so-called arsenal of selling to the affluent. He presented his prospect with a laminated copy of the newspaper article acknowledging her achievements mounted on a walnut plaque. The prospect was grateful for the gift she received and reciprocated eventually by purchasing a large-denomination life insurance policy from Mr. Acknowledgement. It is interesting to note that several of this prospect's relatives also sell life insurance. But not one of her relatives, not one of her colleagues, not even her manager congratulated her for being recognized as the "saleswoman of the year."

Recognition of achievements strongly influenced the prospect's purchase behavior in this case. Remember that there are many first-rate insurance companies with high-quality products and hundreds of thousands of insurance agents that an affluent prospect can patronize. But the saleswoman discussed above chose to deal with the sales professional who focused on a need that went beyond the intrinsic qualities of insurance. Just when the prospect was beginning to believe that no one read about her achievements, she was given a lasting symbol of achievement to hang on her wall. Lack of recognition of one's accomplishments is a perception that many outstanding sales professionals share. Capitalize upon this issue but keep in mind that not every euphoric prospect many feel the need for a top-of-the-line product. However, in this case, the prospect was told by Mr. Acknowledgement that "it would be incongruent for the saleswoman of the year to have anything but major-league coverage via our top-of-the-line policy."

Recognition of achievement is only one way to address the affluent sales professional's needs. Some clever marketers provide such prospects increases in sales via referrals, affiliation group marketing, access to new market opportunities, and press coverage (see Chapter 4).

PROSPECTING AFFLUENT WOMEN

A young woman recently gave up a promising career in advertising for a position as a financial consultant with an investment company. From the first day on the job, she used innovative selling methods. Cold calling/smiling and dialing, she reasoned, were not congruent with her personality. Nor were they the most productive methods of selling for someone who was an outstanding public speaker and excellent writer. This young woman also had a passion for helping women gain economic and psychological independence. From day one as a financial consultant, she began giving speeches to groups that contained high concentrations of affluent women. She also co-founded an affluent women's affiliation group. Recently, her ideas appeared in a leading national news magazine with 3 million subscribers. And most recently, her views about women and money were given more than a one-half page in *USA Today*. Today, at the age of 37, she is considered to be the leading authority/expert on women and money. She is also an advocate of important issues regarding this segment. And this young financial consultant is an information conduit for the women's affinity group she helped es-tablish. No wonder so many wealthy women take the initiative to seek her advice. And how did she gain a national reputation in such a relatively short period of time? She asked the fundamental question of editors, that is, "Would you be interested in publishing some of my ideas about women and money?" (See Chapter 5.)

PROSPECTING ASIAN AMERICANS: BECOMING AN ADVOCATE FOR AFFLUENT AFFILIATION GROUPS

Affluent prospects do have a choice. There are thousands of sales professionals whose solicitations can be accepted or rejected by the affluent. Many sales professionals sell the same or similar products or services. What can enlightened sales professionals do to enhance their chances of being selected as a supplier by high concentrations of the affluent? What can they do to encourage members of affluent affinity groups to seek them out to purchase their offerings? Sales professionals, you can become a recognized expert in a specific segment of the affluent population. Why not consider becoming an advocate of important causes that are shared by affluent Asian Americans? Several segments of this population have significant concentrations of high-income households. Becoming an advocate will assure that you are an information conduit for strategic intelligence regarding economic changes among your membership (see Chapter 6).

PROSPECTING SUCCESSFUL AUTHORS

The typical affluent prospect has a strong need to be on offense. In other words, most affluent prospects have one or more products or services that they sell. The bulk of the affluent market is composed of business owners, self-employed professionals, commissioned sales professionals, and even successful authors. One extraordinary sales professional focuses upon the need of affluent prospects to "play offense" (i.e., to sell their product). In Chapter 7, you will be introduced to Robert Read and his method of prospecting the affluent by "playing defense." He plays this game better than anyone I know. How did I find Robert Read? I did not find him. He found me. He targets authors, publishers, and owners of bookstores. He knows more about the publishing business than most authors. He is a sales professional. He is not an author. But he fully understands when a prospect in my chosen field is euphoric about positive changes in his cash flow.

SELLING TO TARGETS ON THE MOVE

When are the affluent likely to be most vulnerable to solicitations? There are several critical situations when they are extremely sensitive to promotional messages. Geographic movement is one of these important events. Nearly 20 percent of the population of the United States moves each year, and this geographical movement is associated with many types of consumer behavior. There is a strong, positive relationship between the geographical movement of the affluent and changes in patronage habits. When the affluent move, the probability lessens that they will continue to patronize the same product/service providers.

The key issues in capitalizing upon geographic movement include: (1) identifying the affluent prospects just prior to, during, or shortly after they have moved; (2) conditioning them to recognize the value of adopting new patronage habits; and (3) providing them with important benefits that go beyond core products or services.

Early in his career, David Cariseo (see Chapter 8) developed an ingenious system that addressed all three of these important issues. As a result, almost overnight he became the number one sales professional in his branch office. He determined the identities of retiring and other types of millionaires who were moving into his market area. The source he used was both timely and accurate. But it is also interesting to note that the information he gathered was available free of charge.

David's marketing genius extended beyond merely identifying affluent movers. He offered more than a product, more than just a mundane service. David essentially provided an orientation program for his targeted audience. Part of his orientation program was the offer to provide new residents with the names of David's recommended physicians, dentists, accountants, attorneys, and other product and service providers. It is no wonder that so many movers as well as long-time residents in the affluent category wanted to deal with David.

Many affluent prospects are also vulnerable to solicitations when their geographic movement is only temporary. Take, for example, when highly paid professional athletes are "on the road." Often, these affluent prospects have a habit of spending significant numbers of dollars when they are away from home. Many can be classified as recreational shoppers. In reality, shopping is a diversion from the pressures of competing professionally at the very highest levels. And of course, many like to dress well. One sales professional is especially adept at selling visiting teams when they are in his town. It is not unusual for him to sell 30 pairs of $400 dress shoes at one time to one superstar athlete. He is considered by many all-pro athletes to be the number one supplier of fashion footwear to America's best paid sports figures. For the details on how this image was developed, please see Chapter 8.

INFLUENCING PEOPLE WHO INFLUENCE THE AFFLUENT

Most sales professionals who are proficient at identifying, conditioning, and closing affluent prospects never fully leverage their relationships with clients. They fail to realize that some clients have significant influence upon the patronage habits of many other affluent prospects. Take, for example, the case of Mr. Rock. He is a young and relatively successful marketer of investment products. But until recently he has used only conventional, if not obsolete, sales techniques and strategies.

What happened to Mr. Rock's sales productivity, however, when he adopted an innovative method of leveraging his relationship with affluent clients? Mr. Rock's number one client was a surgeon in a very high paying, specialized discipline. Interestingly, Mr. Rock had only this one surgeon as a client and had never asked this client the fundamental selling-to-the-affluent question: "Do you know any other surgeons in your field who might benefit from the services I offer?" However, once this simple question was asked, it resulted in a referral to another surgeon in the same discipline. This surgeon who is now a client of Mr. Rock earned over $10 million last year. I understand that this eight-figure-income-producing physician is considered to be the top surgeon in his field. Having a client of this stature makes it appreciably easier to penetrate the affluent surgeon market. Most affluent prospects place significant value upon endorsements from industry-specific opinion leaders. For Mr. Rock, the opportunity to sell within this field of medicine is almost unlimited.

But the depth of Mr. Rock's sales aptitude can be more fully appreciated by reflecting upon his latest marketing coup. Mr. Rock asked his new client (a top ranked surgeon) for the name of the number one supplier of surgical equipment in his field. His client gave him the name of the head of the firm from which he bought most of his surgical equipment. This executive invited Mr. Rock to provide a "courtesy service" for prospects and clients of the surgical equipment firm. Mr. Rock will provide complementary investment/pension advice from one of the surgical company's booths at the international convention of specialty surgeons! Thus, Mr. Rock is designated as the expert financial advisor for surgeons. He clearly has emerged in the middle of a very large convoy of affluent prospects. In addition, the surgical equipment company provided Mr. Rock with this unusual sales opportunity free of any fees or charges of any type.

Mr. Rock's case provides a pro forma method of developing a symbiotic relationship with influential people. His "free advice" to surgeons is effective in attracting prospects for the surgical equipment company. And in turn, he is positioned as an expert and is exposed to thousands of affluent prospects. It would likely take several years of prospecting with conventional methods to generate the same potential exposure. And what does Mr. Rock say when surgeons ask about his offerings? "I'm also a specialist. My best clients are surgeons. Perhaps you know Drs. _____, _____, and _____ ?"

The material in Chapters 9 and 10 details other methods of influencing people who influence the affluent. The information in Chapter 9 includes discussions on how to sell one's ideas to both broadcast and print media. It also illustrates how sales professionals can translate the publicity they generate into actual sales revenue. Chapter 10 provides the reader with recommendations and actual dialogues on how to leverage the need that affluent targets have for seminars and speakers.

SELLING LUXURY AUTOMOBILES TO HIGH-INCOME CONSUMERS

Sales professionals who market durable goods to the affluent can benefit from leveraging relationships with patronage opinion leaders. It is not unusual for sales professionals to ask satisfied customers for referrals. But often, calling upon these so-called prospects results in little new business. In too many cases, those who are contacted have little interest in the offerings and have little or no influence on the product as well as patronage habits of significant numbers of affluent prospects.

Sales professionals should target important opinion leaders. One referral from a customer who is part of an influential, affluent network can be more valuable than 100 referrals to lukewarm prospects. For example, take the case of a family-owned European luxury car dealership. Several of the managers of this organization recently attended one of our seminars on how to identify, condition, and capitalize upon patronage opinion leaders. During the seminar, the topic of referral was discussed. The attendees were told about the benefits of networking with the officers of trade and/or professional organizations that contain high concentrations of affluent prospects.

Had anyone at this dealership ever asked a current customer if he was a member of an affluent affiliation group? No. But even more important, the dealer never asked any customers if they were officials of such groups. This dealer, like most others, is very democratic in asking for referrals. He indiscriminately asks every customer to recommend friends, relatives, and/or business associates. But this system has been only marginally successful. And in terms of sales force resources, the dealer seriously questioned the efficacy of using referrals as a method of prospecting for new customers. The dealer's attitude about networking, however, recently changed dramatically.

This attitude change was the direct result of the dealer's use of targeting opinion leaders. Sales professionals and managers at the dealership began a campaign of asking current customers about their occupations and affluent affiliation group activities. Almost immediately after this program was initiated, it began to bear fruit. The dealer discovered that one of its "most satisfied" current customers was the secretary of the state medical association. As part of her official responsibilities, the secretary has personal contact with thousands of physicians each year. Her name has strong recognition among the membership. In addition, she responded in a very favorable way when asked if she would recommend that her colleagues patronize the dealer. The secretary of the medical association told the dealer, "Call my colleagues; mention my name. Tell them I am a very happy customer. Have them call me if they want the full story about customer satisfaction!" The dealer took her advice and immediately launched a sales campaign directed at physicians. As a result, sales at the dealership increased significantly. The dealership management is now considering tapping into other affluent affinity groups which contain attorneys, senior corporate executives, and advertising/public relations professionals. Attorneys and accountants are especially important targets. They have a higher-than-average propensity to purchase luxury automobiles. But also they often influence the dealership patronage habits of their clients. Selling luxury automobiles to high-income consumers is the topic of Chapter 11.

SELLING REAL ESTATE TO THE AFFLUENT

How did Jackie become the top-ranked sales professional at one of America's truly outstanding residential developments? The material in Chapter 12 provides a detailed profile of a most extraordinary sales professional. The factors that underlie her enormous and rapid success provide a template for those who dream of reaching the highest levels of both professional and personal success. Jackie's achievements are legendary in spite of having no previous formal training in selling. Interestingly, she is fairly new to the sales profession. She was a housewife for more than 20 years before she entered the real estate sales arena.

ARE YOU AN APOSTLE OR ANTAGONIST TO THE AFFLUENT?

Chapter 13 contains numerous case studies about two contrasting orientations toward the affluent. An apostle to the affluent is a sales professional whose mission is to serve this target market. Sales professionals in this category are advocates and ardent supporters of the affluent they serve. Apostles spend considerable time identifying affluent opportunities. They also are proficient at attracting, conditioning, and retaining the affluent as clients.

Antagonists, more often than not, show more concern for their own needs or the needs of their friends and associates than for those of the affluent. Antagonists typically ignore important affluent market opportunities. They often repel as opposed to attract the affluent as clients. Their egocentric orientation antagonizes both prospects and clients. However, even the most antagonistic sales professionals who wish to serve the affluent can be converted and transformed into apostles.

CHAPTER 2

TWO OF AMERICA'S MOST EXTRAORDINARY SALES PROFESSIONALS

DANIEL F. KIRK: PROFILE OF A MOST EXTRAORDINARY SALES PROFESSIONAL[1]

Midway through the spring semester, a student asked me if I would be interested in having a guest speaker address our personal selling class at the university. The student told me that the sales professional he had in mind was a top producer in the insurance industry. My student asked, "Dr. Stanley, why don't you call him? I am sure if you ask him, he will agree to share some of his ideas with our class."

I did call Dan Kirk, one of America's top agents. He agreed to share his selling methods during the very next class meeting. Shortly into our telephone discussion, I realized that Dan was not a complete stranger to me. He had called me two years ago and asked me about my need for life insurance. This fact by itself is not indicative of Dan's marketing prowess. The circumstances under which Dan Kirk targeted me and many other prospects are important in understanding his success.

How did Dan Kirk find Tom Stanley? On July 1, 1986, I delivered a speech to an audience of 10,000 of the world's best insurance sales professionals. Dan was part of this audience, the 59th

---

[1] The most Extraordinary Sales Professional designation is given to those individuals that generate annual incomes from selling which place them in the top one-half of one percent of the income distribution in America and who have adopted the whole person concept.

annual meeting of the Million Dollar Round Table. The following week, Dan called me and congratulated me on my performance. Dan was the only one out of 10,000 who prospected me.

Dan's method is based on two fundamental targeting questions: the identity of the target (the "who" question) and the issue of need or question of timing (the "when" question). Dan is an active reader as well as observer of events that take place in the lives of the affluent.

Dan observed from my presentation that I had a family and would probably be in demand as a speaker after the Million Dollar Round Table main platform endorsement. Many of Dan's prospects are identified and their needs defined in this manner. Along these lines, the second chapter of my book, *Marketing to the Affluent* (Homewood, Ill.: Dow Jones-Irwin, 1988) reflects upon an extraordinary sales professional (ESP) who markets expensive clothing for men. Both Dan and this apparel salesman prospect those they observe or read about who have a major event/affluent situation take place in their lives (see "Somewhere in the Middle of Six Figures," pp. 114–17). I have often stated that affluent prospects are more likely to be sold when they are encountering euphoria. But how can the marketer tell when such prospects are in this mind set? Both Dan and the apparel salesman consume news stories about affluent events. A news story that praises the owner of a very profitable firm as an enlightened leader and manager is a clue. The typical affluent business owner greatly appreciates recognition and has a positive feeling toward those who provide such accolades.

But Dan does it one better. Not only does he congratulate those whom he predicts are euphoric about a news story, he presents a "very special" copy of the material in person to the affluent prospect. Dan's technique includes calling the prospect's secretary and asking for an appointment to see her boss. He first explains that he is in the insurance business. In 9 out of 10 situations, the secretary grants Dan's request for a specific time appointment to make his presentation.

The key to gaining an appointment with a prospect is the support of his or her secretary. When she is told that a bronze "recognition" plaque will be presented to her employer, her complete support in most cases is given to Dan's request for an appointment. This probability is enhanced when Dan explains that the plaque contains a bronzed copy of a recent news story/article in which the targeted prospect's achievements were recognized.

Why does Dan's "prospecting with plaque" help him gain the business of many very affluent prospects? Most affluent people have a strong need to have their achievements recognized. When a news story or article about their successes appears in the press, the prospects are typically euphoric. This mood is not only a function of public recognition but also of real positive changes in their career and cash flow. It is during this time that affluent prospects are most sensitive to solicitations by those selling products and services which involve significant cash outlays. One of these outlays, of course, includes seven- or eight-figure face value life insurance policies.

A lasting memento of publicized recognition is very valuable to high achievers. The plaque is an important vehicle which enables Dan to meet very affluent prospects at a time when they are euphoric. Prospects are often responsive to Dan's ideas because he has immortalized their achievements "in bronze." Dan contends that a bronze plaque is more effective than plastic or wooden models. It is likely to be perceived as an expensive gift. Thus, Dan not only conditions prospects by achievement recognition but also by the concept of indebtedness. Many prospects feel an obligation to reciprocate by patronizing Dan and his company's offerings.

Dan has given away many plaques during his career. One would think that the growing number of articles about the successes of decamillionaires would be good for the companies that produce plaques. However, this is not the case. Dan told me that not once during all of his prospecting did he encounter a sales professional from any category of business who used the same plaque technique as he did on targeted affluent prospects.

His First Big Sale

How did Dan identify his first major league client (a client who purchased over $5 million of life insurance from him)? Was it from some exotic form of intelligence data or from some expensive list of "hot prospects"? The answer is none of the above. His first $5 million plus policy was sold to a prospect who held an orphan policy. An orphan policy in this situation refers to one left by an agent who originally serviced the policy and has since resigned from the firm.

Dan took the initiative of looking over a complete list of his firm's orphan policies for those who lived in his self-designated trade area. One of the names on the list seemed to ring a bell in Dan's mind. Although this particular holder had only a $100,000 policy, Dan was sure from news reports and articles that this individual was very wealthy. Dan telephoned the holder and was promised an audience with him. However, upon his arrival, the gentleman told Dan that he did not care to speak with him. Dan always believed that you cannot change people's minds so he stood up, thanked the gentleman and began to walk out the door. His exit, however, was interrupted. In the course of a few seconds, Dan Kirk learned something about the affluent market that most other sales professionals never discover. He learned that the fabric of the affluent market is held together by what I call the "affiliation need." The affluent have a very strong need to associate with those who share common goals, experiences, hardships, triumphs, and so forth.

The prospect noticed Dan's tie pin had the Marine Corps emblem on it. "Wait a minute, young man," he said. "Were you in the Marine Corps?" Dan replied that he had been a captain in the Corps. With that response, the multimillionaire told Dan that he also proudly served in the Corps. He asked Dan to sit down and then ordered his personal secretary to "bring every life insurance policy that I own." Dan's prospect then instructed him to examine all the policies and figure out a way to consolidate all the coverage. Dan told me that there were so many policies he literally could not put his arms around them.

Dan did exactly as he was told and returned to the prospect's office with a proposal for consolidating the smaller policies into one large one. The gentleman accepted Dan's proposal then as well as several other proposals since that time.

Those who read about Dan's successes may wish they could turn the clock back (i.e., become 20 years of age again and join the Marine Corps). You cannot change time, but you can provide affluent prospects with fulfillment of their affiliation need in another way. Remember that most affluent prospects are successful business owners. Most successful business owners are active members of one or more trade associations. Also, they are likely to attend trade association meetings and to read trade journals. In essence, they have a need to associate and affiliate with people that have a sincere interest in their business, their industry, and their livelihood.

Sales professionals who affiliate with the trade associations of the targeted affluent segments can reap many benefits. One of the most important is credibility with prospects. The affluent recognize that sales professionals who take the time and interest in aligning themselves with affiliation groups have a sincere interest in them.

But Dan's affiliation with the Marine Corps was not the reason that he called upon this prospect.

Why was Dan the only sales professional to call upon a multi-millionaire who had an orphan policy? Where were the other insurance product/service providers? More than two dozen sales professionals had sold this gentleman at least one life insurance policy that was still in force when Dan Kirk arrived on the scene. There are many possible explanations for the development of this situation. Most sales professionals spend too much time prospecting for new clients and too little time selling more of their current products to their current clients. The "more current products to current clients" is the first theorem of strategic marketing. Dan's marketing strategy is fundamentally sound. He reasoned that even someone in the orphan account category with a net worth in the mid-eight-figure range might be interested in at least talking about trading up and/or consolidating. Dan was absolutely correct.

But there are other compelling hypotheses as to why so many sales professionals fail to fully exploit market opportunities among their current client base. Conversely, for every one of these rationales, there are many more compelling arguments supporting the concept of full penetration within one's customer base. It is important to reflect upon several of these points.

Many sales professionals who market life and related insurance products ignore the "grey haired," older prospect. Marketers often reason that older targets do not need life insurance. As one sales professional told me at a sales seminar, "Those with big incomes who have not accumulated wealth are my major target. Older affluent folks just don't need insurance." Most millionaires are over 55 years of age. And many need major-league life insurance. Along these lines, Dan Kirk actually targets, not avoids, the "grey hairs." Dan told me, "I like to prospect people whom I recognize as being affluent and who are also in their late 50s into their 60s. Look at this fellow right here; he was born in 1927. He's a very successful attorney. He needed a big policy."

Dan provided another example of his successes in grey-hair targeting. Just a week before this interview took place, he sold a mature prospect a $5 million policy. Why would a multimillionaire who was nearing retirement age need life insurance? Originally, Dan had proposed a $2.5 million dollar policy. When the prospect, his wife, and their attorney sat down to sign the necessary papers, an interesting thing happened. The prospect, who had already verbally agreed to buy, suddenly stated, "I don't need $2.5 million worth of life insurance." Dan had anticipated this response. "You're right," said Dan. "You need $5 million! Given the size of the estate your two sons will receive, do you think they will be able to write checks to the IRS for $2.5 million each?" The prospect became a client within minutes. The prospect's sons became the beneficiaries. All this took place because Dan asked the $5 million question that reflects the needs of older affluent targets.

Many sales professionals theorize that any good policy holder would not be an orphan. Many an extraordinary sales professional cut their teeth via the orphan route. Dan Kirk's success can certainly be partially explained by orphan prospecting. If most sales professionals ignore these types of holders, this should be a sign of opportunity. The old axiom in marketing holds true in this context, that is, "Never follow the crowd." If you can head the pack, then take a counter route to ESP status. Most ESP's like Dan travel the path much less traveled. That is precisely why they are successful.

Akin to the "that's why they are orphans philosophy" is the face value hypothesis. Just because someone has a small face value policy does not mean that he is not an affluent prospect. About a month before I conducted this interview with Dan, a gentleman called me with a request. This ESP from the life insurance industry wanted a list of decamillionaires. I explained that I did not have such a list. Why did he want a list of people who had a net worth of $10 million or more? He had just sold his first $10 million policy to a decamillionaire. The first year's premium was $385,000. He felt so good about his success that he wanted to focus on the very big league targets.

The circumstances surrounding this ESP's success in selling an eight-figure policy are noteworthy. He wrote letters to the CEO's of the Fortune 500 corporations. One letter translated into a personal call and eventually a sale. The CEO that he sold was worth over $35 million. "He had a $10 million CD!" But up until the time that he purchased the $10 million policy he had only one $100,000 face value coverage. Also interesting is the fact that this client "was on the board of directors of another life insurance company." Remember, never judge the level of one's net worth by the home they live in, the car they drive, or the current face value of their life insurance. Also never assume that millionaires, even decamillionaires, have one tenth the coverage they really need.

Courage

Dan believes in two axioms: "If you associate with the affluent, you're likely to become affluent" and "if you are trained by people with courage, you will likely be courageous." But Dan was not always a person of great courage. He was a "tall, lanky and timid" youngster in grammar school "so the bullies always picked on me . . . always got beat up . . . lost a lot of my lunch money." After several encounters of that type, Dan related his lunch money problem to his dad. "Dan," his father said, "I need to tell you how it was on Okinawa beach when we first assaulted it." With that statement as a lead-in, he took Dan into the basement and gave him boxing lessons. He let Dan hit him with full force, all the time assuring his student, "If you can hit me this hard you can whip any bully in your class." After several lessons, a bully once again attempted to take Dan's lunch money. But this time "I ate the bully's lunch." He was never threatened by another school yard bully.

Dan also feels that the courage he possesses to approach very affluent targets comes in part from his Marine Corps experience. One of his instructors was Col. Oliver North. Col. North was respected and revered by his men because he always volunteered first for the most dangerous task, such as walking the point on patrols. His students were inspired by his example.

Dan defines leadership as doing things that others don't wish to do or are frightened to do. Dan Kirk "walks the point" every day in the context of selling to the affluent. The single most frightening event in marketing to the affluent is asking very wealthy strangers to do business with you. Dan attributes much of his success to his ability to ask prospects for their business. "Anybody can do what I do if they would just do it." But most sales professionals lack the courage to ask major league affluent targets to do business with them.

Dan pointed out that his courage was tested when he first applied for a sales position. His first job after leaving the Marine Corps was in sales with a major corporation that produced building materials. Generally, the firm only hired people with previous sales experience. Dan, who had no previous sales experience, insisted on an interview. How did he convince a skeptical sales manager to hire someone other than a seasoned professional?

When Dan entered the sales manager's office, the gentleman had his back to Dan and his feet propped up on the window sill. Dan tried to introduce himself several times, but the sales manager would not turn and face him. In complete accord with Dan's brand of courage, he told the sales manager, "If you don't have the courtesy to turn around and face me, I'll never work for you." How did the sales manager respond to Dan's threat? The sales manager gave Dan two choices in his immediate response—"Do you want the Philadelphia or Miami territory? You're hired." What Dan and many other extraordinary sales professionals have discovered is that most sales managers would prefer to hire men and women with courage than experienced sales professionals who have little or none of this trait.

Dan accepted the sales position offered. He was an almost instant success, bringing in many new seven- and eight-figure accounts. But he stayed with the firm for only one year. At the end of this most productive period, Dan was given some bad news by his sales manager. He told Dan that in spite of his top production record, his end-of-the-year bonus would only be $70. Others in the sales force, however, who were not nearly as productive were given major sized bonuses. Dan inquired about the obvious lack of correlation between sales productivity and compensation. The sales manager told him that he placed more weight on seniority than on sales productivity. "After all," he said, "many of the other salesmen in this branch have been with me for years." Dan disagreed with this logic and left the company.

But adversity, such as a loss of employment position, often has an important bearing on one's career in sales. So it was with Dan Kirk. He could have stayed in his position with the building supply company and on a good year perhaps broken into the very low six-figure annual income category. He was eventually rewarded for his strength of character in challenging an unfair compensation policy. He would not only become one of the top sales professionals among a firm's sales force of over 16,000, but he would be well rewarded for his enormous level of production.

Dan did not find a new sales position immediately upon departing from the building supply company. With his income stream shut off, he contemplated the sale of his home and even his "new bean bag chairs and everything else just to pay bills." His brother recognized the seriousness of Dan's economic dilemma by offering the return of his $300 wedding gift. Dan refused the offer.

Dan's job search was not immediately successful because few companies were hiring sales professionals during a recessionary period. One of his friends suggested that he apply for a position with an insurance company. Dan applied, but the manager at the insurance company made the same emphatic statement that others did (i.e., "We are not hiring at this time."). About one week later, Dan called up the manager for the second time and received the same negative response. But Dan Kirk is a man not easily discouraged. He called upon his target a third time in as many weeks. This time the sales manager was so impressed with Dan's special brand of courage that he hired him. He told Dan that if he was as persistent in selling life insurance as he was in selling himself, he would achieve top performance status. It was fortuitous for both Dan and the company that the sales manager was a good judge of variations in courage and determination. Dan was a natural for insurance sales. He welcomed the challenge of selling an intangible and being evaluated totally on an objective criterion. Dan has ranked among the top 10 producers nationwide since 1982.

Dan as Mentor

A young sales professional told me of his frustration in gaining only one sale from an average of 176 telephone solicitations and sought my advice about improving his productivity. I noted with interest that his office was in the same complex as Dan Kirk's. I suggested that he visit with Dan in order to gain insight about prospecting and targeting.

Dan told the young man that he only spoke to three prospects on average each day. The response to Dan's comment was anticipated. "Well, that works for you, Dan, because you are a top producer now." Actually, the converse is true. Dan dramatically increased his productivity when he reduced his number of daily solicitations and focused his energy on the most lucrative targets.

Dan not only advised his young student about the importance of concentrating one's firepower. He shared his wisdom about his philosophy concerning the "whole person concept." According to Dan, "A big income is meaningless if you don't have time to enjoy your success with your family. Many times I see kids of top producing sales professionals who refuse to follow in their father's footsteps. They don't want to sell because they see how miserable it makes their father in his relationship with his family." He mentioned as an example a sales professional who earns over $300,000 per year selling residential real estate. But Dan pointed out that the high income in this case is a substitute for close interaction with family members. "Working seven days a week from 10:00 A.M. to 8:00 P.M. and eating crackers in one's car is not a good job, no matter how much you are making."

Dan Kirk's Views about the Whole Person Concept

The whole person concept is an idea coined by the Million Dollar Round Table but practiced by many individuals long before it was named. The Million Dollar Round Table discovered that for some among its 15,000 members worldwide, the life expectancy was less than that of the general population. Members were their own best customers, filing death claims on themselves because they were working day and night.

The whole person concept to me is built around the "Ideal Day." Each morning when I arrive at the office at 7:30 A.M., I write "Ideal Day" on my calendar and list the people I want to talk with that day. I do my best to talk with three people about life insurance each day. If I miss somebody, I move him to tomorrow until we can talk. I circle 3:30 on the calendar at which time I plan to leave. It often takes me until 3:45, and sometimes 4 o'clock, then I go to the high school track and run five miles. My goal this year is a simple 1 + 1 = 2 goal. One thousand miles running, 1,000 life insurance policies sold, and 2,000 hours spent with my family. You can't be a slob and run five miles each day and 1,000 miles each year, which is my goal. I keep a log. If you serve 1,000 families as life insurance agent, you will provide a great service and make enough money to buy all the things you need. If you spend 2,000 hours with your family, you're not an absentee dad. The Department of Labor says a full-time employee is one who works 1,000 hours per year. If you put in 2,000 hours (about 5 hours per day average), you are going to be there for the quality time and the happy accidents which occur whether or not you're there to declare this "quality time."

Which is the best career? The one which pays $800,000 per year and you work till 8:00 P.M., or the one which pays $350,000 and you go home at 3:30? That's my job, the 3:30 one. In the last three years, I've made about a million dollars. Folks, you can't spend a million dollars in three years. My wife and I have paid off our home on 15 acres and built a "go to hell fund." We have zero marital/financial stress. We have won the lottery a day at a time. I took off from life insurance sales five weeks last year for vacations and conventions. So far this year, I have taken off every Friday afternoon, so it seems like each weekend is a three-day weekend. I work no evenings, and I go to no one's home to sell life insurance. I'm overpaid. I overmarried. My wife is a Ph.D. chemist who worked as a scientist, and she now elects to stay home with our three children. I have a $4 million universal life insurance policy on my own life. Every night by 6:00 I'm home from running and rolling around on the floor with our three children. My wife is the same bride I married 12 years ago. After the children are in bed, we usually watch public TV at night or read until about 10:00 P.M.; then it's lights out until 5:30 A.M.

Last year, I went salmon fishing in Alaska, ran the Marine Corps Marathon with a time of 8:22 per mile, and I swung on the flying trapeze at the Florida State University circus. I always want to be in the arena.

Each night I say a prayer to my kids: "God bless Mommy, God bless Daddy, God bless Heidi, God bless Benjamin, God bless Matthew. Keep us all healthy and happy and safe and strong. Help us grow in love for each other, and be good people, and do Your will, and serve our neighbor."

When my five year old daughter, Heidi, draws with chalk on our driveway, she writes Mommy, Daddy, Heidi, and love, so I think the whole person concept is working.

Dan's definition of a good job is one that allows enough time and energy for developing a close relationship with one's family. Dan puts a priority on his family life. He works five days a week. His day starts at 7:30 A.M., and he is out of the office by 3:30 P.M. He never works on weekends and never brings work home. And when he is at home, he does not talk shop. As Dan has told many young students, "You have 1 billion heartbeats in a lifetime. You can use up your supply in a short time by calling on 176 prospects each day." Dan contends that a person can balance his family life and professional sales career by focusing on the task at hand and never letting either one interfere with the other.

Dan Inside the Retail Convoy

Dan's marketing strategy of exploiting clusters of affluent opportunities can be appreciated by reflecting upon some of his recent successes. A few years ago, Dan entered a store that greatly impressed him. He noticed that the employees were very efficient and that the store was extremely well laid out and clean. He reasoned that someone at the top of this business must really understand how to operate a retail chain. As a logical progression of this thought, Dan speculated that the executive who managed this company might likely be affluent and, correspondingly, in need of life insurance.

Dan decided that he would identify and solicit the business of the retail chain's chief executive officer, and he asked the store manager for the CEO's name. Dan was successful in transforming his prospect into a client. Interestingly, after Dan procured this business, he recognized in essence that his work had just begun. While other sales professionals might have had a celebration party in recognition of their success in closing a big target, Dan was not ready to pat himself on the back.

The chief executive officer/owner of the retail chain told Dan that there were more than 90 stores within the organization. The managers of each of the stores received personal annual incomes in excess of $100,000. Dan had discovered yet another affluent convoy containing over 90 affluent prospects. Most sales professionals ignore managers of retail stores. This is likely to be the case because retailing as well as retail positions are not perceived by people in our society as high-status occupations. Interestingly, while all of these store managers had incomes in excess of $100,000, only about one-half of the physicians in America have attained this level. Dan was right in his assumption that no other life insurance sales professional had ever attempted to solicit business among these store managers. What Dan had discovered is that the most difficult sale is the initial one in an affluent trade or other affiliation group. Other, less experienced sales professionals in Dan's industry exhaust themselves by attempting to have one client from each of 500, 600, or even 700 different affiliation groups. Not long after Dan sold a policy to the chief executive officer, he contacted all the store managers that operated within his self-designated trade area. In short order, Dan converted 23 prospects into clients. His success, he points out, is directly attributable to marketing by affiliation. The affluent place significant importance on the endorsements of those people who share their career experiences. Successful people constantly seek information about the approved patronage habits that others in their industry have adopted. In this specific situation, store managers responded to Dan because he was essentially endorsed by their chairman as well as other managers.

How long would it take for a sales professional to identify and close 23 prospects from 23 different industries? It would take significantly more time and energy than it took Dan to penetrate this one affiliation group of retail store managers. But Dan does not limit his strategy of targeting clusters of wealth to just one industry. Dan recently sold a life insurance policy to a gentleman who owned several fast-food restaurants within one franchise operation. At the time of this writing, Dan has as clients 17 franchise operators from the same chain.

Dan told me that one of his most productive prospecting statements begins with, "Several of my clients also own stores within your franchise. I believe you know John Doe and Bill Smith. They both run great operations down here. So, I thought you might be interested in speaking with me. When can we get together?"

Dan's success in prospecting various affluent convoys is based on his ability to recognize affluent affiliations and where these affiliations are strongest. Dan has also found affiliation marketing to be equally productive among members of such diverse groups as senior partners in large law firms to owners of dry cleaners, laundries, forest farms, and restaurants. Affiliation marketing, as a general rule, is most successful when applied to cohort groups which contain self-employed professionals and/or business owners/managers. These broad categories account for approximately four of the five self-made millionaires in this country who are currently employed. Marketing by capitalizing on affiliation needs will account for a significant portion of the more than 100 life insurance policies Dan will sell this year with face values of $1 million or more.

TWO ROADS TO EXPERTISE

Dan is perceived as a life insurance expert by a growing number of people in the affluent population. His image in this regard has been enhanced by two methods. First, Dan generates considerable amounts of new business from the referrals made on his behalf by current clients. Gaining referrals is commonplace among good sales professionals. But Dan's method is much more productive than conventional types. Dan targets aggressively via the "deep and narrow" within selected affluent industries/occupations.

Prospects that are referred are often presold because Dan is viewed as the industry-specific life insurance expert. He has found that endorsements from industry-specific cohorts are among the most powerful. For example, affluent attorneys respect the judgments of their peers when it comes to selecting life insurance professionals. The same applies to franchisees, contractors, and other industry groupings of entrepreneurs.

Dan's other method of achieving the image of expert relates to publishing. But you most likely will not read about him in the popular press. While the popular press may give a person visibility and exposure, it is much less likely to condition affluent prospects to view Dan as an expert. Dan chose a much less traveled road. As an example, he used a more innovative approach to enhance his visibility and credibility among forest farmers—a $9 billion industry in his state, 70 percent of which is family owned.

Step One: Gain the Endorsement of Important Industry Opinion Leaders

Dan's first step in his image-building campaign was to telephone the editor of the number one trade journal in the industry. He asked the editor if he would be interested in publishing an article about the opinions of several key members (owners of family forest farms) about financial and estate planning. The editor agreed almost immediately to publish the article. Dan then contacted several important forest farmers and interviewed them. The comments and suggestions from both the editor and the respondents helped Dan conceptualize his ideas about the insurance needs of the industry's membership.

Why was Dan's proposal for publishing so readily accepted by the trade journal editor? Dan clearly identified himself as a sales professional from the life insurance industry. This revelation did not provide any real leverage with the editor. However, Dan's ideas were approved because he focused on the needs of the editors and the readers of the trade journal.

More than 20,000 trade journals and related periodicals are published in America. Often an editor of one of these journals must make certain that upwards of 100 articles are contained in the journal each year. It may be relatively easy for some of the popular consumer magazines such as *Newsweek, Time, People,* and so forth to attract unsolicited manuscripts (articles). This is not the case for most trade journals. Thus, most editors of trade journals welcome, even solicit, manuscripts of articles they can publish. Consider the time pressures that editors are under when they must make certain each and every month that 5, 6, even 10 articles are available by the deadline.

Many trade journal editors actually go out of their way to facilitate the publishing of unsolicited manuscripts. Certainly this was the situation when Dan took the initiative of calling the editor of the targeted trade journal. The key word here is initiative. Very, very few sales professionals have even asked for the endorsement of an editor. Even though the editor in Dan's case is not a prospect for insurance services, he is likely to be the single most important opinion leader in the industry. By accepting Dan's article for publication, the editor in essence is giving Dan an endorsement. Also, Dan will be given exposure and credibility in terms of thousands of readers of this journal.

There are two other reasons why Dan's manuscript was accepted. A major concern that many entrepreneurs in this country must face is keeping the family business in the family. Dan's article focused on how insurance products could be used to offset the significant estate tax liability that many sons and daughters will have to pay. Often, this liability is so large that the family business must be liquidated to pay the estate taxes. Thus, the editor was delighted to accept Dan's proposal because it provided a solution to the problem that many readers of the trade journal had to address.

Dan also increased the probability of "being published" by mentioning one other theme for his article. His article contained the comments and opinions of three of the industry's most respected forest farmers. Most editors of trade journals realize that an article which contains the thoughts of industry leaders will be well read by subscribers.

Step Two: Publish Your Endorsements and Ideas in the Targeted Industry's Trade Journal

Dan's article "Free Enterprise and the Georgia Forestry Family" appeared in the official publication of the Georgia Forestry Association. Several years of traditional prospecting and client/prospect referring would have been required to gain the same exposure that Dan received from one published article. The article contained several comments from industry experts. Associating his name and publication with those industry leaders enhanced his credibility. The content of Dan's article was of considerable interest to those who owned family forest farms. It dealt with the "common misconceptions which some intelligent, yet uninformed people have about passing property on to their children." Dan's article discussed the federal estate taxes that would have to be paid when sons and daughters inherited their parents' property. In turn, the article sensitized the reader to the need for having life insurance as a way of paying for the estate tax liability. Thus, with the proper life insurance coverage, the land would "remain in family hands."

Step Three: Coordinate Personal Interaction with Target Audience with the Publication Date of Article Published in Trade Journal

Some sales professionals think that one published article will result in prospects jumping into their boats. While there may have been occasions when this has happened, they are the exceptional cases. A published article should be perceived as the point of entry into a targeted affluent convoy. Dan viewed his first success in publishing as a foundation for his promotional strategy.

One week after Dan's article was published, he capitalized on his publicity. He attended the annual trade conference for forest farmers and rented a booth at the meeting. Dan manned the booth himself and provided 1,000 reprints of his article from the forest farmer's journal (with 1,000 business cards attached). Also, Dan sweetened the attractiveness of the booth with 500 Hershey bars! All the reprints as well as the chocolate bars were distributed to prospects before the end of the conference.

How many other suppliers of life insurance were involved in prospecting at this convention? Where was the highest concentration of affluent prospects for two and one-half days in May? Dan was the only insurance sales professional at a convention which was attended by the highest concentration of wealth in the state. While other sales professionals were prospecting individual targets, Dan concentrated his marketing firepower on a convoy of capital ships. In just two and one-half days, Dan shook hands with hundreds of affluent prospects. If he had used normal, traditional prospecting methods, it would likely have taken Dan more than a year to personally interact with the same number of affluent individuals.

In addition to attending the conference, Dan joined the trade association. This also demonstrated his commitment and interest in serving the industry. And "membership has its privileges." Through the industry's trade publications, Dan has access to information about important events that take place among the membership.

**Step Four: Follow up Trade Conference Activities by
Contacting Prospects. Offer to Quote Insurance Rates
on Large Face Value Policies**

At the time of this writing Dan is preparing a direct-mail campaign.
Those prospects that Dan came into contact with will receive a
personalized letter from him. The letter will contain Dan's biographical sketch and an offer to provide quotes on various levels of
life insurance coverage. Dan intends to personally deliver life insurance quotes to all those who respond. This same simple "quote
system" has been very productive for Dan in other affluent industries. But Dan will generate an even higher number of responses and
eventual closes in this industry. This can be explained by the marketing foundation that Dan laid down. A published article, personal
interactions with large numbers of prospects, as well as related
trade association activities will condition prospects to respond
more favorably to his solicitations.

Dan has an extraordinary aptitude for positioning himself as an
industry-specific expert and supplier of life insurance services and
information. This special brand of conditioning coupled with his
discipline to seek endorsements from industry opinion leaders/
industry-specific clients are the hallmarks of Dan's success in penetrating the affluent market.

**WHEN PROSPECTS ARE FAR FROM
BEING EUPHORIC**

Matt Dawson, one of my best marketing students, recently interviewed a truly extraordinary sales professional. This sales professional markets recognition products to corporations. These
products are usually bought by corporations and then given to
employees in recognition of superior performance. The artifacts of
recognition include crest rings, plaques, belt buckles, and watches.
According to Mr. Dawson, great sales professionals are strategic
consumers of information. In order to succeed in selling recognition
products, one must time his solicitation according to the most sa-
lient need of the target. Often mediocre sales professionals ignore
the time issue when soliciting new business. Others fail to recognize

that the needs of a prospect can be discovered via news stories in business periodicals, company annual reports, and even company-specific newsletters.

But what types of information are indicative of the need for recognition products? Many less seasoned sales professionals would prospect only companies that they read about who are enjoying very favorable economic and performance conditions. However, the really exceptional sales professional understands that unfavorable conditions can precipitate the need for their product

> strategically reads the newspaper for idea leads . . . he reads that insurance premiums (for truck drivers) are going up. He would in turn solicit major trucking firms with proposals for safe driving programs and awards. He sells the service as self-liquidating in terms of cost to their insurance premiums . . . carefully watches the demographic taste of his clients' employees . . . then is able to suggest appropriate elements of a customized (meritorious employee recognition) program. A truck driver with a superior driving record doesn't want to be recognized with cuff links; he wants a belt buckle.

The key to superior selling is to provide solutions to the most critical and most current problems the prospect is facing. In the case of the recognition program discussed, the proposed solution is intended to pay for itself via improved driving records which translate into reduced insurance premiums.

An Interview with Gene Naparst: Marketing Genius and Most Extraordinary Sales Professional

MR. NAPARST:

> Gene Naparst.

DR. STANLEY:

> Gene, my name is Tom Stanley. I don't know if you remember me. I was the speaker at your meeting.

MR. NAPARST:

> Yes, I remember you.

DR. STANLEY:

I'm working on my next book, and I wanted to include you.

MR. NAPARST:

Right, you're from Georgia—and a professor, too, right? I was a professor, too.

DR. STANLEY:

Really!

MR. NAPARST:

Yes, I taught astronomy, geology, mathematics.

DR. STANLEY:

But you didn't make any money, right?

MR. NAPARST:

I was misguided as a youth, you see. Then I taught school. Then I got to the top of the salary schedule, and I saw all the other deadbeats making the same amount of money as me. Then I said, wait a second, there's something wrong with this. I want to do something with my earnings. Last year I made $400,000 —that was net, not gross. That's a nice number.

DR. STANLEY:

Gene, I have a section in the book about a fellow who writes letters. Letter writing seems to be a dead art, so that's why I focused on you.

MR. NAPARST:

Basically, it's all a game. The game is that you write to any identifiable segment in a language that they can understand. So, for example, when I write to automobile dealers, I tell them I know them; I understand them; and I love them. A lot of people don't understand the following: When you go in and buy a car and you pay $20,000 for that car, that car has been floor planned. In other words, he [the dealer] went to the bank and borrowed to put that car on the floor. Let's say the car cost him $19,000. He sells it for $20,000 and makes $1,000. Let's say at the same time you brought in a used car. He's going to give you $15,000 for the used car. So now he's going to give you $15,000, he owes the bank $19,000, you're paying $20,000, so you only write him a check for $5,000. As soon as he sells that car, he has got to pay the bank $19,000. He only took in $5,000. That's called holdback or whatever the term is. A lot of people don't understand that. Really, the place that the guy in a car dealership makes the most money is in parts and service. So you got to talk to them about holdback, floor planning, and so forth.

DR. STANLEY:

So you tell him all his problems, right?

MR. NAPARST:

Yes, and that I work with other automobile dealers and that I understand the needs and the cash flow of auto dealers. Then I write to attorneys. By the way, you have to do research. How do you do that? Well, you read articles in *Newsweek* and *The Wall Street Journal* and *Barron's* about how lawyers are taking it in the neck, liability insurance is going up—you write the same letters to doctors, by the way. On how they are being squeezed, their expenses are increasing. I read an article that their expenses increased 60 percent over the last five years and their revenue only went up 38 percent. So, they're making less money in real terms today than they were five years ago. The starting salaries of young attorneys coming out of school are astronomical, and I understand the needs of lawyers and law firms.I work with them and help plan their cash flow.

DR. STANLEY:

You're different from other people. You're a strategic reader.

MR. NAPARST:

You send out two or three letters a day, and you follow up a week later.

DR. STANLEY:

So you just call them?

MR. NAPARST:

Yes, call them and set up an appointment. When I came into business over 20 years ago, there was a mutual funds salesman, God bless that guy. He taught me a lot. He lectured us in New York. He said, "You know, when a guy gives you an objection, you have to remember the three fs." Dr. Stanley, you give me an objection. I say, "Dr. Stanley, I know how you feel. Many of my clients have felt the same way. They found that by following this investment course—they found that they got financial success." Three fs—it's wonderful. I use it all the time. In other words, you tell the guy, let me hold your hand and tell you I love you. I care about you.

DR. STANLEY:

Well, Gene, are you now marketing a lot of managed money accounts? Do you think that's a good niche for you?

MR. NAPARST:

Yes, yesterday I had lunch with a Mr. and Mrs. _____ . He was the founder and chairman of the board of a major company. He sold the company and has $40 million to spend. So, I take them to lunch yesterday. We met at 11:30, and at 2 o'clock we're still talking. He says to me, "Okay, Gene, let's say I give you a million dollars." Of course, I've done my homework. He's about to ask me something, and I know what's coming. I look him straight in the eye and I say, "Mr. Prospect, I don't take $1 million accounts." He says, "Let's just use that as an example." He got defensive. I had him where I wanted him.

DR. STANLEY:

As a kid, did you like to hunt or fish?

MR. NAPARST:

No, I didn't do any of that. My father was a businessman who owned—he was an immigrant and ended up with a chain of 32 dry cleaning stores and his own cleaning factory.

DR. STANLEY:

You must have loved the dry cleaning.

MR. NAPARST:

I have a few dry cleaners as clients; I understand their business. It's profitable if you can afford the lawsuits. Everybody comes in and tells you, "You ruined my new suit. I only wore it one time." I started out with that when I was five or six years old—in my father's first store. He had a tailor at the back, and people used to come in and take off their pants in the little booths; they'd have their pants pressed or a cuff done or a zipper replaced. They'd sit in the little booths while they waited. I'd see them sitting there with the garters holding up the socks. He had a wooden floor back there. Before stapling machines, you put the ticket on the clothes with a straight pin. My job as a five year old was to drag a big horseshoe magnet over the floor at the back of the store and remove the pins—the steel pins—and put them in a box. For every box I filled up, I got 10 cents.

DR. STANLEY:

Was that your first job?

MR. NAPARST:

Yes.

DR. STANLEY:

How did you get into astronomy? When did you decide you wanted to be a college professor or a high school teacher?

MR. NAPARST:

I decided that I was really interested in science. I was a fairly good student and was also fairly popular. I was elected president of my high school, and my school had 5,000 students. Big political campaign. I liked the sciences because things were pretty much fixed. I didn't learn too many emotions in my family. The law of gravity was the law of gravity. One and one was two. We had our own home there after the war. My father made a lot of money in the cleaning business. He had contracts to clean army uniforms. He'd charge them 10 cents a uniform or something like that. The trucks would come up, and on Sundays, the factory would be burning.

DR. STANLEY:

So then you went to college?

MR. NAPARST:

I went to college, got my bachelors and masters. I was a hard worker. While I was getting my masters degree, I was teaching junior high school. I'd then get right on a trolley car and go down to school. I had five part-time jobs. I worked in the seismograph station at the City College. That was a job I had for five years, seven days a week, 365 days a year. I never missed a day.

The records were 24-hour records. They had to be recorded daily and sent to the U.S. Coast Guard and Geodetic Survey. At a buck and half an hour for five years. It took me about an hour and a half, but I got paid for four hours, and that was compensation for coming in Christmas, July 4th, Saturdays and Sundays.

DR. STANLEY:

How long did you teach before you got into this business?

MR. NAPARST:

I taught for seven years and then was a pilot for Pan Am. I did that for just two years and really didn't like it. I'm a family guy, love my wife and kids. It was during the Vietnam War and I'd put in bids to fly from San Francisco to Honolulu—it was a beautiful bid line and I'd win the bid, but then we'd get to Honolulu—they'd say your flight was cancelled. You'd go into Clark in the Philippines and then on to Cam Ranh Bay in the Nam, then Saigon. One day we landed with 16 bullet holes in the starboard wing and gas was dripping. We hadn't caught on fire, but I said to the captain, "Captain, I quit." I quit right on the spot. That's when I came home and sat down and did an analysis. My degrees were in geology and geophysics. I'd never practiced. I said I was going to get into that business and got hired by a company in L.A. I stayed in that business for about three years. Got to the top of the salary schedule; it was very hard work. I worked in R&D and did mostly development. For example, I won a prize in 1968 for inventing one of the top 100 developments in the United States. I'm also an explosives expert. I developed a new seismic tool used to prospect for oil offshore. They made millions with that, but after three years, I got to the top of the salary scale. I go in to see my boss (I usually got big raises). He said, "Gene, you're at the top of the schedule. You're making the same as some of our executive vice presidents." I said, "Hey, that's their problem." I said, "Look, I have a solution. Set up a separate corporation. Put all the development projects in that corporation. I'll own 49 percent of the stock. You'll own 51 or let me own 25 percent." "No, we can't do that," he said. I quit. He said, "You have a job here for life. Stay as long as you want to." I found myself another job. That's when I came into this industry. When I left, it was such shock in the company.

DR. STANLEY:

You went to work for the brokerage firm?

MR. NAPARST:

Yes. I've been here 22 years.

DR. STANLEY:

When you write these letters, are these people you really don't know?

MR. NAPARST:

I don't know these people.

DR. STANLEY:

But why would you target them? Did you just pick any automobile dealer? Or do you read about them in the newspaper, or what?

MR. NAPARST:

There's a finite number of dealers. Lawyers, I went ahead and got the Legal Directory and went through there and picked out the ones. Names I recognized. I try not to go to the big ones—I don't go to those. I go to the smaller ones.

DR. STANLEY:

People must be shocked when they get a letter that says you understand their problems.

MR. NAPARST:

I've had people call me and say they've never gotten a letter like this. You're the first son of a bitch that understands my concerns. They say, I don't know if I want to do any business with you, but I'd sure like to meet you. It costs me 25 cents and I get an appointment with a guy—automobile dealers are very wealthy guys. The ones that really make it are like this fellow. He sold out his business, and he's a very wealthy guy. What happened is he started selling used cars and got cash flow and started financing the cars. Then you can do your own financing and don't have to go to the banks.

DR. STANLEY:

Did you start out writing letters, or did you start out wandering in the wilderness for a while?

MR. NAPARST:

No, I didn't wander in the wilderness. I came into the business over 20 years ago. I was 32 years old. I had always been successful at what I did and knew this business very well. So, I really got started in this business as an avocation when I was 15 years old. You asked if I hunted, fished—really, I did a lot of reading and got started—you probably heard this story 100 times. But I really took a course in economics in high school, and the teacher made us pick 10 stocks and was going to give a prize. Of course, I wanted to win the prize. I won the prize, and I did it diligently. It was in summer school. All the kids were going to the beach and I'm home. I was a little chunky, didn't like myself in a bathing suit. I compensated by getting an A in the course and getting the prize.

DR. STANLEY:

It seems that there is always an early experience that influences successful people.

MR. NAPARST:

I'm somewhat of a student of that, and I think you're right. I've read a lot of biographies. I see successful people, and there is always something that turns them on. When I started the business, I decided that I was going to do face-to-face prospecting. Everybody else was on the telephone. I put on my suit, and you know, in a suit you have at least four pockets. I put about 10 cards in each pocket so it didn't look bulky. Nothing in my hand. And I'd pick out an office building on a freeway and get there 7:00–7:30 in the morning because the bosses all arrived then. I'd go up on the top floor, start there, and go into the offices and say, "I want to see the boss. I want to see the manager." I'd say, "I'm Gene and I'm with so and so. I happen to be in the building visiting one of my other clients early this morning, and I've always made it a practice to make a cold call before I leave the building. And Mr. Manager, you've won the prize today—the cold call prize today."

DR. STANLEY:

And it worked?

MR. NAPARST:

It worked. Some days I'd spend the whole day there. Like 4:30 in the afternoon I'd get a little cocky. I'd be on the bottom floor and stop in to see a secretary. I'd say, "I'd like to talk to the guy with the most money." She said, "Oh, that's John." John comes out. It's a drafting company. He comes out—about 6 foot 5, weighs about 280 pounds, huge, barrel-chested—takes me into his office and says, "Well, I deal with your competition." I said, "Well, do you have your statement here? Let me take a look at it. I'll take it back with me and send it to our people in New York. We'll analyze it and get back to you." Turns out the company was just sold to a big company in Florida, and the guy had 3.5 million in cash. I always ask for referrals. I started by knocking on doors at 7:00 in the morning and ended at about 5:30 in the afternoon. Then I'd go back to the office. Everybody was gone and it was quiet. I'd write handwritten thank-you notes to all the people I'd met that day.

DR. STANLEY:

So you might be in one building all day?

MR. NAPARST:

Oh, yes. Sure. I'd pick a 10- to 12-story office building and be in there all day. Go and eat lunch in the cafeteria. The secretaries would recognize me and speak to me—how's it going, howya doing. I'd say, well, I'm down to number four. Then I had so many prospects—I'd filled the pipeline—that I couldn't afford to go out anymore. I started servicing them and then selling. I broke a 40-year record. Actually, I started in the business with another firm; they trained me. I broke a 40-year record in opening up new accounts with them. I opened up 338 accounts my first year in the business and did $122,000 gross. Other people beat me in first year gross, and of course, I'm talking 20 years ago. That was a lot of money back then. But the reason I left is everybody got the same payout. My boss told me you're better than O.J. Simpson. You're breaking all records. At the end of the year, it didn't matter. I said if I'm so good, you need to reward me. An extra percent—nothing—I said, I quit.

DR. STANLEY:

I just got off the phone with a young guy in Boston who says he just spent $10,000 doing direct mail. He doesn't have one lead, and he's just really upset.

MR. NAPARST:

Tell him to send out 10 letters a day and a week later, make 10 follow-up calls.

DR. STANLEY:

I appreciate your time.

MR. NAPARST:

You've got to understand I'm not busy and I'm not because the money is managed. I have the time to talk to guys like you. My business is being done. I have 13 money managers that I use, and they're taking care of my clients' business so I get additional clients, additional prospects. And it just keeps growing. Another area I've become expert in is the use of computers in the business. A lot of guys just don't know how to use them efficiently.

DR. STANLEY:

Did you receive that training through the company?

MR. NAPARST:

Computers? I've been into computers. I built my first one out of a kit about 25 years ago. If I had it today, I could sell it for a fortune. I have three computers here. They can talk to each other. All my prospecting, all my clients are on the computer.

DR. STANLEY:

Can you remember your first sales job?

MR. NAPARST:

I had a job selling Knapp Shoes from door to door, and in three months, I was the top salesman in California.

DR. STANLEY:

Well, where did you prospect for shoes?

MR. NAPARST:

Door to door. I had a little kit, about four or five shoes. I remember the number of the one I sold more of—the K88. It was a great shoe. I sold them for $14 and made about $2 a pair. It was terrific.

DR. STANLEY:

You carried them or shipped them later.

MR. NAPARST:

We took orders and shipped them.

DR. STANLEY:

You're an ambitious guy.

MR. NAPARST:

I always liked money. I never wanted to be poor. I love opera, ballet, and symphony and always liked to sit in the orchestra. Fortunately, now I'm on the board of trustees of the Grand Opera, and I give them a lot of money.

DR. STANLEY:

Well, is there something about your New York experience and background that helped you raise your kids?

MR. NAPARST:

I pushed a little bit of that on my kids. I didn't give them an allowance. Told them, if you want money, get out there and hustle for it. I mean, my son, while he was a senior in high school—by the way, he has a Ph.D. in mathematics. He's a brilliant kid. My daughter is finishing her Ph.D. in clinical psychology. He was working 50 hours a week as an assistant general manager at Popeye's Fried Chicken and put away about $7,000 during his senior year of high school. He'd go to school and sleep in class. He was so brilliant in high school, he graduated third in the class. And his father? I still make 10 cold calls a day. I tell them I try to enhance what they already own, and I try and reduce taxes. That's something they might be interested in.

DR. STANLEY:

Cold calls. Gene, I appreciate your help.

MR. NAPARST:

I like to do cold calls. Thank you. It's very flattering that you called.

DR. STANLEY:

Thank you, Gene. Good-bye.

How to win friends and influence people—talk in terms of the other person's interests.

Dale Carnegie

PART 2

TARGETING THE AFFLUENT: SOME OVERLOOKED MARKETS

CHAPTER 3

IDENTIFYING AND CONDITIONING AFFLUENT BUSINESS OWNERS

FINDING BIG SHIPS THAT WEAR BLUE COLLARS

Naval Intelligence

The strategies and tactics used in penetrating the affluent market are often closely related to those of military science. A military decision maker must allocate his resources so as to maximize their effectiveness in achieving certain objectives. For example, he may place a disproportionately high number of troops in a position from which they will be able to inflict maximum damage on the enemy's resources. Before doing this, however, he must determine where the enemy is weak and strong, where its troops will be deployed, why they will be deployed in that way, the composition of those troops, and how they should be attacked. Above all, the military strategist must obtain accurate and timely information about his targets without alerting the enemy. The military strategist, much like his marketing counterpart, must be able to predict the actions and whereabouts of his quarry.

Finding the affluent is often as difficult as finding an enemy whose aim is not to be found. Such an enemy uses camouflage and other means of disguising its strength and intentions. Similarly, many affluent consumers in America disguise themselves as people of modest financial means. Many affluent people feel that it is in bad taste to display symbols of superficial success. The marketer's job is thus made doubly difficult. First, his affluent targets may not demonstrate their wealth by the prestige of their occupations, the size of their homes, their areas of residence, or jewelry, clothing, and other conspicuous artifacts. Second, many affluent people are receptive to solicitations for major financial allocations only during brief periods in the fiscal cycle, and, in some cases, their life cycle.

The marketer to the affluent can often identify his targets in the same way that naval intelligence located its targets. Local, regional, and national newspapers carry hundreds of clues to the affluent each day. In addition, trade publications list businesses for sale within their industry. Oftentimes the appearance of an advertisement in a trade journal indicates a certain level of success in regard to an entrepreneurial business. For many entrepreneurs, advertising is an expense that is to be incurred only after a certain level of success has been achieved! Identifying affluent targets via trade advertising can be very productive. A good example of how affluent business owners can be identified in this manner relates to an affluent revelation that Mr. Gregory of Texas recently experienced.

A Legend in Rock and Dirt

On March 9, I delivered a speech entitled, "Reaching Out to the Affluent." Much of the material in this speech related to the concept of identifying affluent business owners and other prospects when they are euphoric. The 400 attendees at this program at the Wharton School of Business in Philadelphia were managers of sales professionals who target the affluent.

On the following morning, Friday, March 10, I received a telephone call from a young vice president/sales manager, Mr. Gregory, who had attended my program the day before. Mr. Gregory stated the following. "I heard you speak yesterday. I only have one question. Can you really find wealthy people in America?" I said, "That's how we have found affluent people to interview." His response, "Well, that's great, Dr. Stanley, because I have a room filled with our sales professionals here in the conference room, and you are on a conference call. Tell us, Dr. Stanley, why should we invite you to our office so that you can share your ideas about finding wealth in America?"

Anyone who has attempted to sell would likely agree that it is most difficult when you are talking to a committee of 50 strangers via the telephone. After about 10 minutes of Dr. Tom Stanley slipping beneath the waves, I said to Mr. Gregory, "I have another proposal for you." The day before our conversation, the mailman delivered one of the more important and what I consider to be one of the fundamental affluent trade journals in America, *Rock and Dirt*. What is *Rock and Dirt?* I consider *Rock and Dirt* to be the premier trade publication that lists new and used earth-moving equipment as well as mining equipment that will be sold and/or auctioned off in the near future. While I was sinking beneath the waves, I began flipping through my copy of *Rock and Dirt*. I did not have to go deeply into the publication before I said to myself, "Thank you, Lord." What I found was a full-page advertisement for a company that was selling reconditioned diesel engines.

Interestingly, this company was in the same town in which Mr. Gregory was located. Shortly after I discovered this information, I said to Mr. Gregory, "Mr. Gregory, I'm going to give you the name of a business and its telephone number and address in your community. You will drive down five blocks in perhaps an industrial-type neighborhood. Don't be thrown off by it. You will probably visit a plant, and you will probably meet a man who does not wear a suit. He may look like someone that does not have money, but it is likely that this prospect will turn out to be a great client."

A Letter from a Convert

March 21

Dear Tom:

    I decided that I would make a cold call (the first in 10 years). Upon arriving at the location of the business, I felt better about my decision to call personally on this prospect. Even though the company was located in a very bad area of town, it was housed in a fairly neat, older, concrete structure on about four acres sur-

(continued)

rounded by a chain link fence adjacent to a railroad track. The cars parked in front were all recent vintage of mostly U.S. manufacture.

Upon entering, the first thing I saw to my left was a "boiler room" where two salesmen were telephoning. Behind them was a blackboard on which items wanted were written. I could "feel" business taking place and started to get excited. I asked the receptionist to see the owner. She took my card back to him and, upon returning, asked me to take a seat while he finished his call to Australia. (I got more excited and continued to rehearse my opening comments in my mind.)

A young gentleman neatly dressed in boots, jeans, and a western shirt stopped by to tell me that the owner was still on his international call and would be with me shortly. Soon the receptionist took me back to meet the owner.

The owner was a tall, well-groomed, bearded chap, slightly overweight. He was dressed in jeans and a pullover shirt. I told him who I was and that I was not there to sell him anything; I just wanted information on his industry. He relaxed. He asked where I obtained his name. I explained that . . . his industry was an extremely profitable one. . . . I told him that it was a result of his advertisement in *Rock and Dirt*.

He proceeded to explain his industry and his company in great detail. (I took notes.) He talked about his future plans, which included an increase in sales followed by a public offering. Following his description of his company's needs, I asked him if he would be interested in our ideas. He indicated he would and asked me to follow up the next day (which I did). The conversation continued. He described in detail his business: its history, sales history, profits, customers, financing, philosophy, and so on. An hour and a half later, he said,

(concluded)

"If you think this is good, I want to show you something."

We went to the gravel parking lot. Standing next to the chain link fence, he started telling me about the business on the other side of the tracks. (You could not see it, because a train was passing). He said, "A year ago that site was a field; now it's a building. This guy fries okra and other vegetables for the restaurant industry. You should meet him." Was this ever exciting. Two live prospects with big business potential from a cold call that started at 4:45 P.M. on a day when I had not planned to leave the office.

All of this made me feel great about the experience and the common sense you bring us.

Just so you know, I subscribed to *Rock and Dirt* yesterday, and I'm going to see the "okra guy" next week.

Best regards,

Mr. Gregory
Vice President

That very day Mr. Gregory, wearing an expensive top-of-the-line Brooks Brothers suit and driving his Turbo-charged Mercedes, drove into an industrial strength neighborhood. As he was ushered into the business by the secretary of the owner, he sat there in amazement and looked at the high level of business activity that was taking place. Shortly thereafter, he was introduced to the owner of the company. The owner asked Mr. Gregory how he discovered him. This is a critical question when prospecting affluent business owners. But Mr. Gregory had anticipated this question. His response was clear and certain. He said, "I saw your advertisement in *Rock and Dirt*." Upon hearing that, the owner of the business immediately responded in a positive manner to Mr. Gregory's presence.

What Mr. Gregory has discovered is that identifying and prospecting affluent business owners via trade journals can be extremely productive. (See Table 3–1.) Most people who advertise in trade journals are proud of their advertisements and businesses. And very often, just the presence of advertisements indicates some level of business success. And Mr. Gregory was correct in his assessment. For the business that he visited on this day was a top-10 small business exporter in the state of Texas.

Mr. Gregory called me on the telephone the following Monday. He was noticeably excited. He explained that he took my advice and visited the business owner who had an advertisement in *Rock and Dirt*. He also invited me to spend a day at his office discussing marketing to the affluent.

I agreed to do so. I also asked Mr. Gregory if he would be kind enough to introduce me personally to the business owner that he just prospected.

Several weeks later, I had the privilege of interviewing this successful man. I found him to be an intelligent, perceptive, and very interesting young man. When I entered his office, I was somewhat embarrassed because I interrupted his lunch, a triple-patty Wendy burger. I asked if we could come back at some other time. But he insisted, and in an excited way, he said, "Sit down and I'll tell you about my business."

I told Mr. Gregory that I was going to ask what I consider to be the ballistic question in prospecting affluent business owners. I did. And I quote: "Young man, please tell me how you became so successful at such an early age." The answer to that question took nearly two hours with a personal tour of the business owner's plant. It also included Dr. Thomas J. Stanley, father of two, new suit, standing next to the business owner's acid bath! The acid bath that washed all the dirt and grime off of these large diesel motors.

As we walked out into the yard, the young man explained that he did not believe in spending money on frills—just on the things that are important in making the business highly productive. He explained that he did not change his personal appearance for anyone. He did not try to impress anyone. And he did not believe in the concept of having a "big hat and no cattle." In sharp contrast, this

TABLE 3–1
The Big 10 Versus The Really Big 36 Trade Journals/
Magazines in the Cahners Network[1]

	Circulation
Building Design & Construction	80,000
Consulting/Specifying Engineer	50,000
Construction Equipment	80,200
Contractor	50,400
Highway & Heavy Construction	78,000
Professional Builder	148,500
Building Supply Home Centers	51,300
CPI Purchasing	40,000
Industrial Distribution	41,500
Modern Materials Handling	106,000
Plant Engineering	128,800
Plastic World	63,500
Purchasing	100,000
Traffic Management	73,300
Physicians Travel & Meeting Guide	225,000
Packaging	107,500
Control Engineering	100,100
Design News	170,000
Research & Development	120,100
EDN	139,600
Electronic Business	73,700
Electronic Packaging & Production	46,000
Electronics Purchasing	56,000
Semiconductor International	41,700
Test & Measurement World	68,000
Security	40,700
Security Distributing & Marketing	25,500
Interior Design	59,600
Datamation	162,200
Systems Integration	110,250
Foodservice Equipment Specialist	20,300
Hotels	41,000
Restaurants & Institutions	143,200
Graphic Arts Monthly	94,000
Publishers Weekly	36,300
Power and Motoryacht	136,000
Total Circulation	3,068,250

[1] According to Cahners, 60.1 percent of recipients of at least one of their trade publications in the Cahners Network do not subscribe to any of the 10 popular magazines listed below. Data published with the permission of Cahners Publishing Company, 1989.

young man was the epitome of a successful entrepreneur. No hat, but lots of cattle. And many cattle will bear fruit in the future.

Magazines Subscribed to by Network Recipient
(respondents currently subscribe to)

Popular News and General Interest Magazines	Percentages
Business Week	10.0%
Forbes	4.4
Fortune	4.4
INC	4.5
Money	7.5
Newsweek	12.1
Sports Illustrated	7.7
Time	9.8
US News	4.9
The Wall Street Journal	11.4
Do not subscribe to any of above	60.1

He pointed out several of the products that he produced, and he stated: "You see over there? There are 100 reconditioned, re-manufactured diesel engines that will be shipped to Venezuela to-day. They are prepaid for, by the way. Over here you will see another 100 motors. They are destined for Argentina. Yesterday we sent out a hundred motors—destination Australia."

After our plant tour, we reconvened in the owner's office. I then asked the young owner, "Tell me, young man, do you have an accountant?" "No, I don't have an accountant; I have a bookkeeper, but I guess I do need an accountant." In essence, what the young man was saying is, since I have publicly announced my success, it is incongruent that I am still using a bookkeeper and not a certified public accountant.

My next question: "Young man, tell me, do you have a finan-cial consultant?" His response, "No, I do not have a financial consultant." It is incongruent that a young business owner, who is so very successful, does not have a professional financial consul-tant. Interestingly, Mr. Gregory is the manager of a large office that is filled with financial consultants. When the young owner told me that he did not have a financial consultant, I turned to Mr. Gregory and said, "I'll leave you two alone to discuss this matter."

In reality, Mr. Gregory and the young business owner developed an affinity for each other. This is particularly interesting given the fact that Mr. Gregory is a member of what I consider to be the upper-middle-class segment of the American population while the business owner is in the category I refer to as the upper part of the lower- or blue-collar category in America. How can it be possible that two people from two distinct social classes, with two distinct backgrounds, can become affiliated with one another?

The answer to this lies in Mr. Gregory's approach to the prospect. Mr. Gregory was wise enough to read information in *Rock and Dirt* about the owner's business prior to making his initial sales call. Mr. Gregory was also wise enough to ask important questions about the young man's business and to praise and pay homage to the successes that this entrepreneur had experienced.

What Mr. Gregory has discovered is that it is possible to have clients that are members of various social classes, to have clients that drive different types of automobiles, and to have clients that live in different types of neighborhoods. In reality, Mr. Gregory has discovered that by demonstrating his interest and affinity for a prospect's business, he is able to bridge sociological and status-related barriers.

The value of identifying and prospecting affluent business owners via information in trade journals cannot be overstated. The young entrepreneur that Mr. Gregory visited had a business which experienced more than a 100 percent increase in revenue in the year prior to our interview. His advertisement that appeared in a trade journal preceded by one year an article that featured the entrepreneur and his business in a popular national business periodical.

In essence, you would have to wait 12 months to find out about the success of this entrepreneur if you read only the national press and not the trade press. Very often the trade press provides the identities of successful business owners long before their achievements are recognized by national publications.

Rock and Dirt can be ordered by contacting TAP Publishing Company, Crossville, Tennessee 38557; telephone 615-484-5139; telex 325-815. One full year subscription of *Rock and Dirt* sent third-class mail is $24.00. Or you can have UPS second day air deliver your copies for one year for $196.00. I consider the price of *Rock and Dirt* to be quite reasonable in terms of the value of information provided in this periodical. It not only indicates the identities of sellers, but it also provides some indication of the amount of sales dollars that will be generated by these individuals in the near future. It is not unusual for auctioneers to list millions of dollars worth of equipment that will be sold at auction within several weeks or months of the publication date. Certainly, auctioneers, who in some cases receive between 10 and 35 percent of the sales price of the equipment they sell, are in a favorable cash position. In other words, they are likely to be euphoric immediately following the sale of this merchandise.

The Access to People Is through Their Concerns
(Werner Erhard)

It was just before dawn on a rainy Monday morning when Richard entered his office. He was the first person to arrive for work at the automobile dealership that he owns and manages. It was his first day back after attending a national trade conference for auto dealers. The information disseminated at the conference was still vivid in his mind, especially the negative trends for auto dealers. Richard thought that by sorting through the stacks of mail that had accumulated during his absence he would be able to take his mind off the harsh realities of his industry.

Richard and his wife took off four days to attend the national trade conference and then five more for a brief vacation. During this period, more than 300 pieces of mail addressed to him had arrived at the office. Nearly 100 pieces were solicitations. Also, there were nearly 100 telephone messages awaiting his response. A significant portion of these were from sales professionals who were attempting to solicit his business in regard to everything from lubricants to investment services and executive search programs to exotic travel packages. Richard thought to himself that these solicitors were wasting their time. He was not in the mood to buy. Who would want to buy, he reasoned, after taking an objective look at the negative factors influencing auto dealers?

During Richard's absence, his trusted assistant placed all of his mail in three separate piles. The first pile was for mail categorized as "probably worthwhile to read and respond to." The second pile was for mail categorized for "quick scanning." The third pile was designated as "suggested for circular file!" His assistant placed one letter at the very top of the first pile with a note stating, "Richard, read this first."

While Richard was attending the conference, he had several telephone conversations with his assistant. He informed her of the major topics discussed at the conference. These included: (1) major automobile producers selling automobiles to rent-a-car companies at prices below what dealers pay for them, which significantly increases competition when these cars are eventually sold in the consumer market; (2) the rapid increase in expenses that greatly exceeds increases in revenue; and (3) the increased difficulty in obtaining and maintaining preferred credit.

These factors were directly related to why Richard's assistant placed one letter ahead of all the others. The letter was from a financial consultant who markets the services of professional money managers. But the letter was completely unique in that it

---

Ron Tonkin left the National Automobile Dealers Association presidency the same way he came in a year ago—with six-guns blasting at the factories.

Tonkin received a thunderous standing ovation when he climaxed his 50-minute opening speech by announcing that he has filed a fleet subsidy lawsuit against four automakers in his home state, Oregon.

Edward Lapham, "Tough Tonkin Steps Down to Applause," *Automotive News* February 19, 1990, p. 24.

The suit said his dealerships compete with the rental companies, which sell recent-model cars to the public. Because rental companies purchase cars at a lower wholesale price than Tonkin can buy them, he is at a disadvantage when they are resold.

Charles M. Thomas, "Year of Words Ends; Tonkin Sues Big 3," *Automotive News* February 19, 1990, p. 3.

addressed the specific problems that Richard was pondering. Three of the four paragraphs in the letter essentially condensed each of the three negative trends that Richard had become sensitized to during the trade conference.

Paragraph 1 included quotes from the speech delivered by the president of Richard's trade association. This information reflected the growing concern among auto dealers that producers of cars were using alternative distribution methods that favored rent-a-car companies over traditional retailers. The second paragraph included precise statistics about the increase in the expenses incurred by auto dealers and the negative trend with regard to revenue. The third paragraph addressed the issues of the credit squeeze facing a growing number of automobile dealers. As Richard was reading this letter, he felt that the author was reading his mind! How perceptive he thought the author was. But what solutions, if any, might be proposed?

The fourth and final paragraph simply stated that given these significant downtrends, it was more important than ever to seek professional management of one's financial investments. The information also pointed out that many auto dealers were looking for alternative ways of enhancing their financial position given the lagging performance in their industry.

> More than ever, auto dealers must have a realistic and disciplined approach that will enhance their economic future. In this regard, I have helped many of my clients access the services of some of America's most highly qualified investment managers. I will call you next week to determine if we can set up a meeting to discuss these issues.

After reading this letter, Richard wrote a note on the top instructing his assistant as follows: "When he calls, set up an appointment ASAP!" Richard responded to only this solicitation out of nearly 100 received by mail during his absence. He did so because the author was clever enough to demonstrate how forecasted changes in his main source of income necessitated the utilization of professional investment managers.

THE NATIONAL FISHERMAN

Dear Marketer:

The classified advertisement that you placed in the current issue of *National Fisherman* is outstanding. In fact, it is the best that I have seen this year. Congratulations! Your message meets all of the Affluent Market Institute's criteria for effective communications with the affluent market.

With respect to this market, the best message is one that is targeted. Communicating in an industry-specific trade journal is a brilliant strategy. This is especially true in your situation. According to our studies of the affluent population, captains and other officers of commercial fishing vessels are among the top 10 high income occupational categories. High income, in this situation, refers to the $100,000 and above level distributed on an annual basis.

Another criterion that we use to judge promotional messages and strategies relates to the level of competition that is associated with the targeted segment. Captains/owners of commercial fishing vessels are one of the least prospected affluent groups in America. Mistaking status for money in America is a tradition among those who fail in their attempt to penetrate the affluent market. Our society does not give fishermen high status rankings. But as you have apparently discovered, many commercial fishermen are very affluent. This includes both income and net worth. Only extraordinary marketers such as yourself have the uncanny ability to look beyond social status when targeting the affluent.

About two years ago, I gave a speech in Seattle on marketing to the affluent. Over 100 sales professionals who target the affluent were in attendance. All of the attendees were based in the Seattle area. Most had at least five years of experience in targeting the affluent. And many were at least moderately successful in penetrating this market.

I was advised by the sponsors of the program that the attendees sought new methods as well as motivation to reach new heights of productivity. Many had reached but never exceeded the low six-figure income plateau. So I spoke of unconventional ways of finding affluent prospects, timing one's solicitations to match upswings in cash flow, and the anatomy of wealth via geography.

During the question-and-answer period, a member of the audience asked me about affluent opportunities in the Seattle area. I responded by asking, "How many of you have any customers who are in the fishing industry?" Not one person in the room raised his hand. What could I judge from all the blank stares and opened mouths? I was convinced that no one had ever considered the fishing industry as the economic base for many affluent prospects in the area. Apparently, many of the attendees had forgotten the lessons learned from their freshman course in economic geography. Seattle is a major fishing center in America.

The most productive advertisements are those that are not surrounded by competing messages. By competing messages, I refer to themes designed to sell the same product or similar products. Your advertisement is the only one in the classified section that addresses the financial planning needs of the commercial fisherman. In fact, your message is the only one in the entire issue that relates to the financial service needs of this affluent segment. It seems that you alone have surfaced in the middle of a very large convoy of affluent prospects.

According to my calculation, a classified advertisement such as yours costs approximately $250. What an extraordinarily efficient way to communicate with your target audience. I understand that the *National Fisherman* has a primary readership of over 50,000. The pass-along consumption must be several times higher. So, for $250 you have the potential of exposing your message to

200,000 readers. Even at the primary readership estimates, your advertisement cost you only one-half a cent per reader. This is by far one of the very most economical and productive ways of soliciting business. Too often those who attempt to target the affluent feel that they must spend large sums of dollars to attract prospects. Your strategy is testimony to the value of quality media selection. In dollar terms, quality is more important than quantity for those who target the affluent.

Timing is another criterion that is important in our evaluation of advertisements. The October issue was the ideal place for you to capitalize upon critical events in the industry. As you know, the highest concentration of affluent commercial fishermen as well as suppliers to the industry can be found at FISH EXPO on October 18–21 in the Seattle Center. I understand that upwards of 25,000 people will attend this year's event. The October issue of *National Fisherman* will be very heavily distributed/read before, during and even after this event. Thus, you should anticipate a surge in inquiries from your advertisement. Even referring to it when you are at the meeting should enhance your credibility with prospects. Of course, October is also the time when much of your target audience is in home port. Thus, they have both the time and resources to contemplate their financial futures.

The theme used in advertisements is yet another dimension with which to judge commercial messages. Again, your message is ideally suited to the needs of your target market. Too often, marketers use a generic theme and attempt to sell generic products to a multitude of affluent segments. This wide and shallow/shotgun approach is rarely, if ever, successful in attracting wealthy targets.

In sharp contrast, your theme hits the target in the "industry-specific bull's-eye." You have publicized your interest and dedication to helping the affluent fisherman solve his specific financial service problems. Interestingly, those sales professionals who reach the highest levels of production do so by specializing. Specialization, in terms of category of product, is not uncommon even among marginally successful sales professionals who target the affluent. However, many of the very best go one step further. They specialize in terms of target market. Obviously, you have developed a unique product as well as target theme.

Investing today for the purchase of a fishing vessel tomorrow is an issue that most of your prospects must resolve. Your advertisement informs prospects that you not only have empathy for this problem; you are the source of industry-specific solutions to it. Your message is truly remarkable because most affluent prospects feel that their "currency" is industry-specific. In other words, money generated by fishing is a unique currency. Thus, they prefer to deal with providers who share their values, speak their language, and understand the "currency requirement." You clearly communicated that you are the preferred provider.

Your choice of target, media, and message should provide an important template for those who hope to penetrate other affluent industries. I wish you all the best of success. May you always be in the middle of large and affluent fishing fleets.

Regards,

Thomas J. Stanley, Ph.D.
Chairman, Affluent Market Institute

CHAPTER 4

PROSPECTING THE SALES PROFESSIONAL

INTRODUCTION

One of the most underprospected high-income segments is the sales/marketing occupational category. In terms of the total number of households that generate annual incomes of $100,000 or more, 6 of the top 11 are headed by those in the sales/marketing occupational category. These occupations include:

- Sales managers/executives.
- Sales agents/manufacturers representatives.
- Real estate sales professionals.
- Commercial product/service sales professionals.
- Marketing/advertising/public relations managers/executives.
- Insurance sales professionals.
- Securities sales professionals.

The material in this chapter contains several suggested methods for selling to affluent sellers. The information provided, however, is not limited to the seven occupational categories listed above. There are hundreds of categories of sales professionals. The role of those who target the high-income sales professional encompasses going beyond merely identifying specific prospects. The superior sales professional understands the importance of conditioning the prospect with the correct message delivered at the most appropriate time. Remember that the effectiveness of any commercial message directed at the affluent sales professional varies according to the prospect's economic situation. Time your solicitations in harmony with your target's economic triumphs. What does the high-income-producing sales professional need? The answer to this question goes beyond anyone's core product or service. Affluent sales professionals need their achievements to be recognized. Blend the prospect's need for recognition of his achievements with your product or service offering. This is the golden rule for those who wish to succeed in selling to the affluent seller.

The relationship between occupation and sensitivity to solicitations is among the most consistent research findings. High-income sales professionals (those with annual incomes of $100,000 or more) are among the most likely to respond positively to persuasive communications. This is especially true when such messages are present in harmony with positive changes in cash flow.

Many top-producing sales professionals who target the affluent "cut their teeth" by initially soliciting business from high-income sales and/or marketing professionals. Few affluent segments, if any, have more empathy for the needs of those in their own profession. Why not consider prospecting the successful seller?

CAPITALIZE ON THE REAL NEEDS OF HIGH-INCOME SALES PROFESSIONALS

He was nearly finished dressing for the awards dinner when the telephone rang. The president of the company was calling Larry to ask for a special favor. Larry netted well over $200,000 this year solely from commissions on the sales he generated. Along these lines, he was scheduled to receive 8 of the 12 awards for superior selling that would be given out by the president at this evening's banquet.

Larry suspected that the president was calling to give a one-on-one congratulatory message. But that was not why he was calling. The president asked Larry if he would mind receiving all eight of his awards at one time. Otherwise, Larry would have to walk to and from the podium eight times and give eight different thank you addresses. The program was jam packed with various events. The president realized that the ceremonies could easily run into the early morning hours. So he sought to avoid exceeding the original planned time for the ending of the program. Anything past 11 o'clock in the evening, he reasoned, would turn the audience off in terms of future events of this type.

Larry's response was quick and precisely to the point. "I will sit at the very back of the banquet room. When you call my name, I will stand up slowly and walk slowly up to the podium. I will graciously accept my award. I will make a short speech. Then, I will slowly remove myself from the platform and walk slowly back to my seat. I want to and I will do this eight different times tonight."

Why did Larry insist on participating in eight separate processions? Because he needs to have all his achievements as the top-performing sales professional within the firm recognized. He competed against and defeated over 400 other sales professionals. In terms of selling, Larry has performed and will continue to perform in an extraordinary manner as long as he knows his achievements will be recognized.

All top-performing sales professionals have this need. And there are more than 300,000 sales professionals in America in the affluent income category (annual incomes of $100,000 or more). Thus, marketers who target affluent sales professionals can capitalize on this need. Providing recognition to high-performing sales professionals is certainly one way of gaining both their attention and appreciation.

Carlton's Request

"Tom, can you wait 60 more minutes before you speak? It takes a long time to give out these plaques." This was the question posed to me by Carlton, the national sales manager of a group of over 100 high-performing sales professionals. I told Carl that I had no objection to waiting for my part of the program to begin. Carl was kind enough, in spite of his very tight schedule, to tell me why the program was running late. Apparently, during the previous year's awards trip, many attendees wrote on their program evaluation sheet that one thing was lacking. The expensive watches, golf clubs, and warm-up suits were rated as great awards. The food, recreation, and lodging were consistently checked as being first rate. But these top-performing sales professionals felt that "not enough award plaques were given out." The previous year, each sales person received one plaque even though many were top performers in terms of a variety of product areas. In essence, they wanted multiple plaques. They demanded multiple plaques, and they received multiple plaques. And as I expected, the program ran beyond the 60-minute delay that was anticipated by my host. But the insight which I discovered that day was well worth the wait. In this instance and in many others subsequent to it, I have developed an appreciation for the needs of top-performing sales professionals. The need to have their superior performance recognized is among the very strongest. Compensation in dollars and gifts is not enough to satisfy most top performing sales professionals.

Typically, the real estate, insurance, and securities industries are quite sensitive to the recognition needs of their top performers. Major corporations in many other industries provide such awards. However, most sales professionals in the six-figure annual income category do not work for firms that give awards for superior performance. Most high-income sales professionals are employed by small- to medium-sized firms. Most of these organizations pay cash, not homage, to even the very highest performing sales professionals.

There are many reasons for this oversight. Some of these organizations are just not sophisticated in their understanding of the needs of sales professionals. Others view the superior performing sales professional with envy, even distrust. To recognize superior performance, they feel, would encourage the sales professional to demand higher commissions. Still others never fully appreciate the value of having great sales people supporting their offerings. But for whatever reason, most high-income sales professionals feel that their superior performance is not being given recognition beyond cash incentives.

Our society often ascribes only middle or low status to sales professionals. Conversely, a college professor may have a status ranking in America of 90 on a 100-point scale (100 being the highest level of status). Ninety is quite high, almost as high as a U.S. Senator. But most college professors never make more than $60,000 per year. Many sales professionals may have an annual income in the six-figure category. Some have incomes that exceed many times those of people with very high status.

But status in America is not the same as income. Status relates to occupation and not to the size of one's paycheck. Top-performing sales professionals often feel that they are not given their proper status rank by our society. They have a strong need to separate themselves from the low status ranking given them in stereotypical fashion by their neighbors, colleagues, and society.

As one high-income sales professional recently told me, "I have enough money to buy just about anything that I want, but nobody in my neighborhood has any idea about how productive I am." In another interview, a top-performing sales professional based in California told me he had everything that he ever wanted. With an income in excess of $500,000, he could buy many artifacts of wealth. But I suggested to this fellow that he still needed one thing. "One thing—what one thing do I need?" asked the top producer. I replied, "You need to be recognized. You need to be famous. You need people to know how good you are. And you need to communicate your achievements to people beyond the firm that employs you." With this statement, the top-producing sales professional smiled, nodded his head, and said, "Yes, you're right."

His response should provide much food for thought for those who wish to target the affluent. Any sales professional who sells products or services designed for the affluent can capitalize upon the achievement and recognition needs of high-income sales professionals. Help the highly paid sales professional satisfy his need for recognition, and you will likely be rewarded. The consumer patronage habits of the affluent sales professional are much more likely to be awarded to those who offer something beyond the core product and service. The very best professionals who sell to the affluent first make their prospects feel good about themselves and their achievements. They do this by providing a "recognition service" for the prospect. These types of services run from "getting good press" for the prospect to bestowing upon him a recognition plaque for extraordinary sales performance.

I'm Gonna Hire D. Caller

How can the marketer of affluent offerings capitalize upon the achievement/recognition needs of the high-income sales professional? One suggested method is discussed below. But before outlining this tactic, it is important to reflect on a recent episode in the life of an extraordinary sales professional. In *Marketing to the Affluent* (Homewood, Ill.: Dow Jones-Irwin, 1988), pp. 26–27, I discussed the courage of William D. Caller, a highly paid apparel sales professional.

> He is the number one, by far, sales professional for a modest-sized U.S. producer of apparel . . . in my fall 1971 class . . . he received the lowest grade. What did William do about his F? At 5:30 P.M. that afternoon there was a knock at the front door of my home. . . . My wife answered the door. I told [my wife] to get rid of [D. Caller]. But [she] invited him to stay to dinner. He had enough . . . brass to go to a professor's home—not only my home but to the homes of other professors as well. "I do it all the time. About half the time they throw me out; half the time I come in and we have dinner."

Immediately after *Marketing to the Affluent* was published, I sent a copy to William D. Caller. After he read the book, he passed it along to his boss who also owned the apparel company for which he worked. One morning a few weeks later, Mr. D. Caller received a telephone call from his employer. "Bill, get your posterior lobes in my office." According to Mr. D. Caller, the term *posterior lobes* was not exactly how his boss referred to this delicate part of his anatomy!

William D. Caller immediately jumped to his feet, ran down the hallway, and went into his employer's office.

EMPLOYER:

> Billy, I finished reading that book about great sales people. It's full of them. Know what I mean?

WILLIAM D. CALLER:

> Yes, sir. They are all great.

EMPLOYER:

> They are the kind of people we need around here. In fact, I want you to help me. I was really impressed by the apparel salesman . . . you know, D. Caller.

WILLIAM D. CALLER:

> Ah, D. Caller, sir?

EMPLOYER:

Yes, D. Caller. I want you to find this D. Caller guy. Get him on the phone for me. I'm gonna hire D. Caller.

WILLIAM D. CALLER:

But, sir, I'm William D. Caller.

EMPLOYER:

You're not D. Caller. You work for me. You can't be D. Caller.

WILLIAM D. CALLER:

But, sir, I am D. Caller. Dr. Stanley did not use my real name because he thought that you would be offended if a bunch of head hunters were crawling all over our offices.

EMPLOYER:

You are William D. Caller?

WILLIAM D. CALLER:

Yes, sir. I'm D. Caller.

Often, great achievements in sales go unrecognized. How many truly extraordinary sales professionals such as William D. Caller never receive recognition for their achievements? Most of them only receive cash. Often their employers do not realize how exceptional some of these people are.

What if you wanted to sell William D. Caller a luxury automobile, fine watch, or even a top-of-the-line cabin cruiser? How could you help condition him to become euphoric? Remember, affluent prospects who are euphoric about their achievements are very susceptible to solicitations. Recognizing the achievement of William D. Caller will generate euphoria. And if you are the generator of this recognition and subsequent euphoria, William D. Caller will be in your debt.

While there are many ways in which to recognize greatness, one unique method is highlighted. William D. Caller desperately wants to separate himself and his self-image from the stereotypical hawker image given by society to sales professionals. He also wants to affiliate with other extraordinary performers. Such support groups do not currently exist for William D. Caller. So, why not start one? Remember that William D. Caller, like many of his peers, has a high propensity to spend money on conspicuously consumed luxury items such as expensive watches, automobiles, boats, clothing, and residential real estate. One of the key elements in selling to high-performing sales professionals is timing one's solicitations. There is one disadvantage of identifying and prospecting via news stories. What if, for example, William D. Caller was recognized in his industry's trade journal as being a top-ranked sales professional? William D. Caller may be excited about having his name published in a trade journal. However, this event may not coincide with upswings in his cash flow. He told me that:

> My biggest sales are in November, December, and January. That is when my customers place orders for the upcoming fall season. We ship the fall merchandise in June, July, August, September, and part of October. My biggest month (in terms of income) is August. That is why I just bought a boat in September. . . at the end of the boating season. Everybody buys boats in the spring. I buy according to my own season . . . when the paymaster shows up.

William D. Caller is most susceptible to solicitations during August of each year. Conversely, he may not appreciate high-pressure solicitations during the months when he is aggressively selling but not receiving actual dollar income (November, December and January).

PRO FORMA PROSPECTING

D. Caller Dialogue, Wednesday August 3, 10:15 A.M.

MS. BARBARA McNASTY: (secretary of defense)

Good morning, Alpha-Omega Apparel sales department.

MS. SUSAN WHITE:

Good morning, I wish to speak with a sales professional.

MS. BARBARA McNASTY:

Anyone in particular?

Pro Forma Letter Asking An Extraordinary Sales Professional to Join the Society of Extraordinary Sales Professionals

Mr. William D. Caller
Alpha-Omega Apparel
1360 Western Avenue
Hometown, GA 37308

Dear Mr. D. Caller:

Enclosed is a copy of a letter written on your behalf by Mr. Arthur Difford, CPA. Mr. Difford has nominated you for membership in the Society of Extraordinary Sales Professionals. A copy of the nomination letter should come in handy since you will probably wish to share this good news with your colleagues and clients. I have also sent a copy to your employer.

I am also involved in sales as a profession. Over the past few years, it's become obvious to me that there is a need for outstanding sales professionals to share ideas and interests with one another. Along these lines, two months ago I proposed to establish the Society of Extraordinary Sales Professionals. Last Thursday, seven extraordinary sales professionals met during breakfast to discuss the goals, objectives, and membership parameters for the Society. We define an extraordinary sales professional as someone who generates a minimum of $100,000 net annual income from commissions and/or ranks in the top 5 percent of the sales force. The top 5 percent criterion assumes a sales force size of at least 1,000 and a minimum annual net income from selling of $75,000.

Some may argue that the $100,000 income threshold is not extraordinary. However, only 1.5 percent of all households in America have annual income of $100,000 or more.

Why form the Society of Extraordinary Sales Professionals? Dr. Thomas J. Stanley stated in his best selling book, *Marketing to the Affluent,*

. . . there is tremendous ignorance . . . about the relationship between wealth and occupation. Sales and marketing positions, according to my estimates, account for 5 of the top

(continued)
10 occupations in America in the generation of six-figure incomes.

. . . this market is highly fragmented. Extraordinary sales professionals are found in a very wide variety of industries. They are typically the cream of their industries' crop of thousands of sales professionals. You are not likely to find large numbers of ESPs working for the same firm. Most ESPs are employed by small and medium-sized firms. . . . Typically, they . . . are not supported by advertising, sales promotion, or even public relations dollars (pp. 156–159).

In talking with many extraordinary sales professionals, I have found that most have little in common with the others in their firm's sales force. However, all agreed that they have more in common with other super producers from diverse fields. As one top ranked sales professional recently told me, "I can't learn anything about selling from the folks in my office . . . they are really at a different mind set when it comes to setting sales objectives—for themselves."

Others have told me that sometimes they feel lonely and that they are misunderstood by colleagues, employers, and even by family members. They strongly feel a need to interact with other superachievers in a noncompetitive environment. Also, one of the goals of the Society is to have our members share their selling methods with students who major in marketing at our area colleges and universities. Eventually, we hope to help fund college scholarships to young people interested in a career in selling.

A list of our first seven charter members is enclosed. All of these members, except yours truly, generated annual net incomes in excess of $200,000 last year. I just broke into six figures for the first time last year. But this is not so bad for a 31-year-old fellow who has been selling residential real estate for only three and one-half years.

The Society plans on meeting every third Thursday of the month at 7:00 A.M. Our meetings will take place at different locations. We hope that each month a different member will host a coffee and bagel/doughnut breakfast at his office. Our next meeting is scheduled to take place on the 21st of March at 7:00

(continued)

A.M. in the conference room of my office suite. It is located in Hometown at 4110 Commercial Plaza, Suite 1220. All of our members would be delighted if you would consider our offer to become a permanent member of the Society of Extraordinary Sales Professionals.

I will call you early next week to answer any questions about the Society. Please make every effort to join us. We plan on finishing breakfast by 7:30 A.M. At that time, we would like you to take the podium for 15 or 20 minutes and informally comment on the factors that contributed to your extraordinary success in the profession of selling. Alternatively, you may wish to comment on some of the most memorable experiences you have encountered in your career. Following your presentation, you will be given an engraved plaque which acknowledges your extraordinary achievements in the profession of selling. A reporter and photographer from the local newspaper will be attending the meeting. I hope you would not object to having a news story published about your achievements. News releases about your award will also be sent to all local area newspapers, to business journals, and to your industry's trade journals.

I am looking forward to speaking with you next week.

Sincerely,

Bruce D. Representative
Vice President

CHARTER MEMBERS
THE SOCIETY OF EXTRAORDINARY SALES PROFESSIONALS
(HOMETOWN, GEORGIA)

Joel Adams
Extraordinary Sales Professional
Smyth Industrial Equipment Company

David Black
Extraordinary Sales Professional
Ultra Promotions

(concluded)

Carl J. Simmons
Extraordinary Sales Professional
Johnson Computers

John C. Hall
Extraordinary Sales Professional
American International Insurance

Greg B. Higgins
Extraordinary Sales Professional
World Media Sales

Bruce D. Representative
Extraordinary Sales Professional
Southern Luxury Homes

Richard W. Wilson
Extraordinary Sales Professional
Davis Weapons Systems

MS. SUSAN WHITE:

Yes. I wish to speak with your top sales professional. This is too important to discuss with anyone else.

MS. BARBARA McNASTY:

Well, then, you want to speak with Mr. D. Caller.

MS. SUSAN WHITE:

Are you certain that he is your top salesman?

MS. BARBARA McNASTY:

Oh, absolutely. We call him "Mr. Flashlight" because he can find business even with the lights out.

MS. SUSAN WHITE:

But does he handle the most important accounts?

MS. BARBARA McNASTY:

He brought in five of our biggest accounts.

MS. SUSAN WHITE:

Does he still maintain these accounts?

MS. BARBARA McNASTY:

Oh, yes, and several other important ones.

MS. SUSAN WHITE:

All right, you convinced me. Can I speak with him?

MS. BARBARA McNASTY:

Yes. His line is open.

MR. D. CALLER:

Hello.

MS. SUSAN WHITE:

Hello, is this Mr. D. Caller?

MR. D. CALLER:

Yes, I am William D. Caller.

MS. SUSAN WHITE:

Mr. D. Caller, do you know what your receptionist, Ms. Mc-Nasty, just told me about you?

MR. D. CALLER:

What did she say?

MS. SUSAN WHITE:

She told me that you were the top salesman in the company. Is she telling me the truth?

MR. D. CALLER:

I am number one. I have been number one every year for 10 years. What else did she tell you?

MS. SUSAN WHITE:

That you handle the most important accounts. Is it true?

MR. D. CALLER:

You better believe it. I am Mr. Apparel.

MS. SUSAN WHITE:

Well, what I want to know is how you became number one and how you sell to the biggest retailers in the business?

MR. D. CALLER:

[What followed was an eight minute dialogue about courage, superior product knowledge, superior service, reliability, and the personality of D. Caller.]

MS. SUSAN WHITE:

Your boss must really appreciate what you are doing for the company. I'll bet your wall is filled with those plaques that say "Top Sales Professional." How many top producer trips have you won so far?

MR. D. CALLER:

I have never received one plaque or even one trip. Our company does not give a whole lot of that type of recognition.

MS. SUSAN WHITE:

You're kidding! Our company gives recognition to all of its top sales professionals.

MR. D. CALLER:

Who do you work for?

MS. SUSAN WHITE:

Imported Performance Motor Vehicles. Our firm offers top-of-the-line high performance imported automobiles. I'm in the same profession that you are. I sell. I am successful because I make an effort to focus on really successful clients like you. Other people sometimes really don't appreciate the need for our product.

MR. D. CALLER:

I like fast cars. What I have now is still fast, but it's getting a bit sluggish.

MS. SUSAN WHITE:

I believe that the best sales professionals share a common affection for high-performance automobiles. I would be delighted to stop by your office and take you for a demonstration tour. Am I calling at the wrong time?

MR. D. CALLER:

When can you come by? What are you doing for lunch? This is my best month of the year in terms of payout.

MS. SUSAN WHITE:

Today?

MR. D. CALLER:

Today. I'm more serious than a train wreck. What about noon?

MS. SUSAN WHITE:

I can be there with our latest model. But I will not be able to have the plaque prepared by that time.

MR. D. CALLER:

What plaque?

MS. SUSAN WHITE:

We give a laminated walnut plaque to the very top rated sales professionals who test drive one of our "missiles."

MR. D. CALLER:

What does it say on the plaque? Will it have my name on it? How big is it?

MS. SUSAN WHITE:

Well, it's hard to describe it over the phone. It's 10 1/2 by 13, and it designates you as an extraordinary sales professional. At the bottom it states that our manufacturer salutes your success and achievements.

MR. D. CALLER:

Do you have one that I could look at?

MS. SUSAN WHITE:

Oh, yes. I'll have it with me when I come by at noon.

MR. D. CALLER:

I'll be standing outside the building at the main entrance. By the way, what size jeans and jacket do you wear?

MS. SUSAN WHITE:

Eight jacket, seven in jeans. Why do you ask?

MR. D. CALLER:

I'll have a denim recognition outfit made for you as an award for your creativity.

MS. SUSAN WHITE:

See you at noon.

MR. D. CALLER:

In front of the building. I'm wearing a blazer, khakis, Patek Phillipe watch, Cole-Hahn tassel loafers, and a pink shirt!

The other problem with prospecting via news stories is that you cannot control the news. You wait and hope that key pieces of information about prospects will appear frequently in selected publications. Thus, it may be useful to supplement this source of information with others. Accountants can supply information about the identities of their clients who are high-income sales professionals. How can this be tied into the material given in the letter above about the Society of Extraordinary Sales Professionals? It may be useful to ask selected accountants to nominate one or more of their clients for membership in this prestigious organization. But don't forget another important source in the context of professionals. Some of the highest paid professionals in America are in the occupational category called Partner in Charge of New Business Development. These types of sales professionals can be found in top-performing accounting firms, law firms, engineering design organizations, executive recruiting companies, and advertising and public relations firms.

Other sources that can be useful in identifying high-income sales professionals include:

1. *Purchasing agents.*   The National Association of Purchasing Management has nearly 30,000 members. Its members are responsible for buying goods and services for organizations in industries that range from chemical producers to educational and training services. There are more than 150 local chapters of this affiliation group. Why not ask some of its members in your community to identify/nominate the "best sales professional they have ever encountered"?

2. *Major corporations.*   Many large corporations in America give awards each year to their best suppliers. It is not unusual for these types of corporations to purchase goods and services from thousands of suppliers in the course of one year. However, only 10 of these suppliers may be given the "outstanding supplier of the year award." Surprisingly, many of these award winners are small- to medium-sized entrepreneurial firms—yes, the same types of firms that often employ the "unrecognized, affluent sales professional." Call or write the public relations or corporate information department of the major corporations in your designated trade area. Ask them for their list of award-winning suppliers. Once this list is procured, you can contact the winning firms and ask for the names of their top sales professionals. Interestingly, some of these are owners/partners of their respective firms.

3. *Self designates.*   The business press, whether it be local, state, regional or national, loves to publish articles about top-performing sales professionals. Send out simple, one- or two-page news releases to the press about the Society of Extraordinary Sales Professionals. Your concept is almost assured of coverage in the press. Even a brief telephone conversation about the topic with selected business writers and editors should generate considerable press coverage. How will top-performing sales professionals in your trade area react when they read about an organization that recognizes their achievement? Some are likely to take the initiative to contact and petition the members of the nominating board of the Society in terms of being selected. *Remember:* No matter how fine a researcher you are in uncovering

affluent sales professionals, no one will ever be able to find all of them. Thus, this method of encouraging the target to find you provides a supplement to the more conventional methods outlined.

"SO, IT'S NOT A GOOD TIME TO TALK"

The higher one's annual income, the more likely it is to vary considerably from month to month. Thus, timing one's solicitations should be based upon the prospect's cash flow. Most sales professionals who target the affluent have little or no understanding of the concept of cash flow and, correspondingly, euphoria. When the affluent prospect encounters a significant upswing in his cash flow, he is likely to be euphoric. People with large sums of cash who are euphoric are most susceptible to solicitations. But sometimes this euphoria lasts only for a few short weeks during the year. In some cases, real euphoria only comes a few times during the entire adult life of the affluent prospect.

But most sales professionals never take the time to discover if the prospect is euphoric. Some never ask the critical questions of their targeted prospect or even their current clients (e.g., "Is this a good time to talk to you about _____ ?").

How do clients and prospects view sales professionals who attempt to solicit their business when they are cash poor, distracted with other events, and anything but euphoric? They categorize them as grossly insensitive, ignorant, and even uncaring. The timing of solicitations explains much of the variation in sales performance. Improper timing also accounts for why so many affluent clients change their patronage habits so often.

The issue of improper timing can be readily appreciated by the case of Mr. Steward. He is the part owner and sales manager of a small container company. And the call he received from a "sales professional" could not have been more poorly timed. During our interview, Mr. Steward paraphrased his encounter with Mr. Insensitive.

MR. STEWARD:

     Hello, this is Steward.

MR. INSENSITIVE:

Mr. Steward, congratulations. I saw your daughter's picture in the _____ . She looks beautiful.

MR. STEWARD:

We are very pleased with the picture and our daughter.

MR. INSENSITIVE:

I'm glad you're pleased. Why I'm calling. I have some important ideas about how to provide for her college education. Are you familiar with some of the advantages of high-quality annuity products?

MR. STEWARD:

Well, I have some understanding. But we do have money set aside for our children. They should be able to pay for their college education even if we stopped adding funds today.

MR. INSENSITIVE:

Excellent. Most people never plan so well in advance. But do you think you're getting the best return on these _____ accounts?

MR. STEWARD:

They are in quality zero coupons. We like the product and are very satisfied with our account executive. But I appreciate your interest. Thanks for calling.

MR. INSENSITIVE:

Well, even more important are your own investments. Your kids have their entire lives ahead of them. But I'm sure you realize the importance of investing now for your golden years. We have a new issue coming out this week. It's going to be big . . . probably sell out in short order. I would like to suggest that you initially buy 10,000 shares.

MR. STEWARD:

Well, I have had a lot of expenses lately.

MR. INSENSITIVE:

And that is exactly why you need to invest today.

MR. STEWARD:

Well, how much will it cost to buy 10,000 shares?

MR. INSENSITIVE:

Less than $100,000.

MR. STEWARD:

Well, my business is off a bit this quarter.

MR. INSENSITIVE:

And that is exactly why you need to invest today. Aren't you the owner of an important container company?

MR. STEWARD:

Who told you that?

MR. INSENSITIVE:

Well, the newspaper article about your daughter's bat mitzvah spoke of your business. I assumed that you were an astute business person who could recognize a bargain when he sees one. You are a major force in the container business, aren't you?

MR. STEWARD:

Well, not this quarter. But thanks for calling.

MR. INSENSITIVE:

Well, are you interested in investing some of your business profits?

MR. STEWARD:

Profits are down.

MR. INSENSITIVE:

Well, I just figured that anyone who ran a successful business would be serious about investing in a quality offering.

MR. STEWARD:

Business is off somewhat and. . . .

MR. INSENSITIVE:

> I thought that anyone who had the kind of bat mitzvah that the newspaper mentioned would be a big player. OK. Is this not a good time to talk?

MR. STEWARD:

> Not a good time to talk. Business is off. . . . I have bills all over my desk.

MR. INSENSITIVE:

> So, it's not a good time to chat? I'll call you next week. What is a good time for you? I can even stop by.

MR. STEWARD:

> If you were in my office right now and I had a pistol in my hand, you would be in grave danger!

MR. INSENSITIVE:

> So, it's not a good time to talk. How about. . . .

MR. STEWARD:

> Not day time, not night time, not any time [Hangs up phone.]

Mr. Steward is normally mild mannered. However, insensitive people can provoke even the most even tempered prospects. No, it is not a good time to call someone who just purchased nearly $50,000 worth of products and services for a family celebration.

You cannot always predict a prospect's level of euphoria. But you can always ask about it early in your conversation. Most often, a prospect will tell you if and when it is a good time to call. Why not transform Mr. Insensitive into Mr. Empathy. Mr. Empathy would not call Mr. Steward on the Monday following a major social and consumption event. He may, however, cut out the article about Mr. Steward's daughter and mail it to him. Mr. Empathy would enclose his card with a brief handwritten message (always in black ink).

> Mr. Steward, you will probably never have enough copies of this news story about your lovely daughter. Congratulations. Enclosed is an extra copy. I hope we will have the chance to talk about business in a month or so. I am sure

you're feeling a bit exhausted from all the festivities. Rest up. You deserve it. Well done.

All the best,

Mr. Empathy

Mr. Empathy has just impressed a stranger. Mr. Steward has to be impressed. For Mr. Empathy just demonstrated his uncanny ability to read Mr. Steward's mind. Yes, Mr. Steward thinks to himself: (1) I wish I had another copy to send to the grandparents; (2) Yes, I'm exhausted; (3) Yes, I want to rest; and (4) Yes, I admire people with empathy for my mood, my situation, and my needs.

CHAPTER 5

PROSPECTING AFFLUENT WOMEN

AFFLUENT WOMEN IN AMERICA: AT LEAST TWO DISTINCT SEGMENTS

I was recently contacted by a young woman who had just become a security broker and was confident that a strategic market plan she had already written would enable her to become a top producer in a short time. What was Dorothy's plan? Upon what segment was she about to place her bets? Aggressively, she stated, "I'm going after the affluent women in this town!"

I asked, "Why the women's market?" Dorothy responded by reporting what the popular press had been touting for the last decade, namely, that the market of female executives and entrepreneurially oriented women was large, untapped, and growing rapidly. I then asked, "Where do you get your market facts?" Dorothy could not recall the exact sources of her information but said that some of the regional and local press had provided strong evidence about the so-called women's market.

The hard data about the women's market for investment services and what one reads in the newspaper are at odds. I advised Dorothy to consider placing a hold on her strategy until she had reviewed some of the available data. First, I discussed the downside of the women's market. Among the highlights of my findings on this market are the following:

1. There is no such thing as a *women's market* for financial services. There are several distinct segments among the women who require financial services. Each of these seg-

ments has significantly different needs, and each requires a completely different marketing approach.

2. Each of these segments is appreciably smaller than the casual observer might think. This is the case despite the significant educational and occupational changes that the women's movement has created.

3. More often than not, women who have made their own fortunes have the same needs and patronage intentions as their male counterparts.

4. Among the affluent producers of six-figure incomes, men outnumber women 10 to 1. Why should one ignore 10 out of 11 prospects?

5. About one-half of the women in this country with annual incomes of $75,000 or more are married. Often, their husbands make or significantly influence their financial decisions.

6. Of these affluent women, 35 percent are 65 years of age or older, and 70 percent are 55 years of age or older. People in these age categories have often already established a relationship with a financial adviser. However, there is a growth market among younger affluent females.

7. Most of the women who have a personal (as opposed to household) net worth of $1 million or more inherited their wealth.

8. Statistics on the affluent market in America strongly suggest that the typical affluent household is a traditional one. In fact, a highly significant relationship exists between the level of affluence (measured in terms of income and/or net worth) and the level of family traditionalism. These findings are supported by several independent research studies. For example, the latest IRS figures show that well over 90 percent of all returns with adjusted gross incomes of $50,000 or more were filed by married persons. These figures also show successively smaller proportions of returns filed by those who are married at the successively lower adjusted gross income levels.

9. In a recent study of millionaires, I found that 86.5 percent of them were married and that in 95 percent of these cases, the male head of household made the major financial deci-

sions. Approximately two-thirds of the millionaires had two or more children. According to census reports, over 90 percent of the households that are in the top 5 percent in terms of income are headed by a male (householder), and in 83.1 percent of these households, the wife is present.

10. Although many wives in affluent families work, the main financial contribution in such families is generally made by the husband. In a recent Federal Reserve report, it was stated, "Families in the highest income category (those with annual incomes of $280,000 or more) are most likely to have a household with a working husband and a non-working wife . . . only 21 percent of the wives are employed full-time" (Robert B. Avery and Gregory E. Elliehausen, "Financial Characteristics of High-Income Families," *Federal Reserve Bulletin,* March 1986, pp. 163–77). Also, the male partner is generally the dominant economic force within such families. My research studies indicate that if 100 affluent married couple households respond to a survey that requests that the household's financial decision maker complete the questionnaire, over 90 of the questionnaires will be completed by males.

Opportunities for Affluent Women

In spite of these comments about the realities of the affluent women's market for financial services, Dorothy still wished to pursue her strategy. Toward that end, she asked me to detail where the opportunities were among affluent women.

Women have made some progress in becoming affluent on their own. However, accumulating wealth takes a considerable number of years, so that often references to the affluent women's market actually should be recast as references to the future affluent women's market. What are the qualities of the affluent women's market? The following pieces of documentation testify to the growth of that market:

1. According to the American Assembly of Collegiate Schools of Business (AACSB), approximately one in three of the individuals who received graduate business and manage-

ment degrees in 1987 were women, whereas only 3 percent of the 1972 graduates were female. Education, however, is not the only tool needed to attain high corporate positions. Today, a typical CEO of a major corporation will have an advanced degree along with 20 to 30 years of relevant working experience. This is one of the main reasons why *Forbes* magazine's research found the "797 Most Powerful Men and [only] 3 Most Powerful Women in Corporate America" (*Forbes,* June 15, 1987).

2. A growing number of women have come to feel that the corporate skills route is painfully slow. Owning one's own business has been emerging as an increasingly lucrative fast-track alternative. Evidence of this trend is the fact that according to a recent study by *Savvy* magazine, "more than half of all companies owned by women are less than 15 years old." This may explain why "of the 59,000 women-run corporations [those in which women own 50 percent or more of the shares] only eight tenths of 1 percent have sales of $1 million or more."

3. Women own 25 percent of all the small businesses in the United States and are the fastest-growing segment of the small business community. According to the Small Business Administration, the number of female sole proprietorships alone quadrupled to 2.8 million in only five years. However, most of these businesses have sales revenues of under $25,000.

4. The American Medical Association recently reported that in 1970, there were only 25,401 female physicians in the United States, or approximately 7.6 percent of the total; whereas in 1985, female physicians numbered 80,725, or approximately 14.6 percent of all the physicians in this country! More than 72 percent of these physicians are under 45 years of age. However, only about one-half of the female physicians are self-employed; whereas almost 8 in 10 male physicians are in this category. The AMA also reported in 1986 that the average annual net income of female physicians was significantly lower than that of male physicians ($75,100 versus $118,000).

5. The number of women graduating from law school in-

creased from 801, or 5.4 percent of the total, in 1970 to 13,630, or 36.8 percent of the total, in 1984.

6. While among producers of six-figure incomes there are 10 men for every woman, the discrepancy between male and female wealth holders is much less pronounced. Estate data on individuals with gross assets in excess of $500,000 provides some evidence of the economic importance of the affluent women's market. Women account for one out of every three persons whose gross assets exceed $500,000 (see Table 5–1) and 44 percent of all estates in the over $5 million category (see Table 5–2).

7. The investment holdings of women with gross assets of over $500,000 differ significantly from those of men with comparable gross assets. Women account for over 37 percent of the total assets held by those in the over-$500,000 gross asset category. However, they account for a greater percentage of the total cash holdings (46.4 percent) of state and local bonds (57.1 percent), and of other assets (46.9 percent), which include tangible assets. Women also account for a significantly smaller percentage of total debts (20 percent), life insurance equity (7.7 percent), notes and mortgages (26 percent), and noncorporate business (29.9 percent).

Women account for 41.2 percent of the total gross assets held by those in the over-$5 million category. They do account for a significantly larger percentage in the following categories: cash, 49.3 percent; corporate and foreign bonds, 64.7 percent; and state and local bonds, 46.5 percent. Conversely, women account for a significantly smaller percentage of total debts (22.6 percent), federal savings (16.7 percent), life insurance equity (11.4 percent), notes and mortgages (30.6 percent), and noncorporate business (31.6 percent).

Caution should be exercised in utilizing the dollar amounts given in Tables 5–1 and 5–2. These were estimated by assuming that estate data could be projected to the affluent population in general. This assumption has several basic faults. Its most significant fault in the context of the women's market is that the estate multiplier method greatly overestimates the number of affluent women who

TABLE 5–1
Individual Wealth Holders with Gross Assets Greater than $500,000

Item	Total		Men			Women		
	Number of Top Wealth Holders (000s)	Average Amount	Number of Top Wealth Holders (000s)	Average Amount	Percent of Total	Number of Top Wealth Holders (000s)	Average Amount	Percent of Total
Total assets	1,838.6	$1,954.5	1,237.7	$1,216.9	62.3%	600.9	$737.6	37.7%
Debts	1,770.2	293.9	1,211.6	235.2	80.0	558.7	58.7	20.0
Net worth	1,838.6	1,660.6	1,237.7	981.7	59.1	600.9	678.9	40.9
Types of assets:								
Cash	1,776.6	167.4	1,217.4	89.7	53.6	559.2	77.7	46.4
Corporate stock	1,477.2	483.7	1,022.0	309.4	64.0	445.2	174.3	36.0
Bonds, total	736.5	117.7	444.3	60.1	51.1	292.3	57.6	48.9
Corporate and foreign	294.3	9.0	180.6	4.6	51.1	113.7	4.5	49.9
Federal savings	218.7	2.2	136.0	1.6	72.7	82.6	0.6	27.3
Other federal	278.0	33.6	183.6	22.6	67.3	94.4	11.0	32.7
State and local	461.6	72.9	244.8	31.3	42.9	216.7	41.6	57.1
Life insurance equity	1,412.6	23.4	1,131.5	21.6	92.3	281.1	1.8	7.7
Notes and mortgages	876.9	74.5	638.7	55.1	74.0	238.2	19.4	26.0
Real estate	1,643.1	592.7	1,166.6	397.4	67.1	476.5	195.3	32.9
Noncorporate business	827.6	122.1	611.4	85.6	70.1	216.2	36.5	29.9
Other assets	1,780.7	372.9	1,205.7	198.0	53.1	575.0	174.9	46.9

Source: Marvin Schwarts, "Preliminary Estimates of Personal Wealth, 1982: Composition of Assets," *Internal Revenue Service Statistics*, 1985.

TABLE 5–2
Individual Wealth Holders with Gross Assets Greater than $5,000,000

Item	Total — Number of Top Wealth Holders (000s)	Total — Average Amount	Men — Number of Top Wealth Holders (000s)	Men — Average Amount	Men — Percent of Total	Women — Number of Top Wealth Holders (000s)	Women — Average Amount	Women — Percent of Total
Total assets	38.2	$11,669.0	21.4	$12,243.9	58.8%	16.8	$10,936.7	41.2%
Debts	36.6	890.4	20.3	1,242.1	77.4	16.3	452.4	22.6
Net worth	38.2	10,778.6	21.4	11,001.8	57.3	16.8	10,484.3	42.7
Types of assets:								
Cash	37.9	537.7	21.1	489.6	50.7	16.8	598.2	49.3
Corporate stock	37.3	5,606.7	21.0	5,617.2	56.4	16.2	5,627.5	43.6
Bonds, total	27.1	1,568.7	14.0	1,628.9	53.6	13.1	1,504.4	46.4
Corporate and foreign	12.0	261.9	5.7	194.9	35.3	6.3	322.5	64.7
Federal savings	2.6	255.4	1.7	325.3	83.3	0.9	123.3	16.7
Other federal	11.8	1,084.8	5.9	1,234.2	56.9	5.9	935.4	43.1
state and local	20.9	1,239.4	11.0	1,259.8	53.5	9.9	1,216.8	46.5
Life insurance equity	24.0	45.8	18.0	54.1	88.6	6.0	21.0	11.4
Notes and mortgages	25.7	626.5	14.8	754.9	69.4	10.9	452.1	30.6
Real estate	36.4	1,999.2	20.5	2,236.8	63.0	15.9	1,692.9	37.0
Noncorporate business	27.7	1,500.3	16.3	1,744.8	68.4	11.4	1,150.6	31.6
Other assets	37.8	1,116.5	21.1	1,160.2	58.0	16.8	1,054.9	42.0

Source: Marvin Schwarts, "Preliminary Estimates of Personal Wealth, 1982: Composition of Assets," *Internal Revenue Service Statistics*, 1985.

are still living. Much of the wealth of affluent women originates from the estates of their husbands. Most of the affluent women in the over-$500,000 gross asset category are over 55 years of age. However, the estate multiplier method does appear to provide a logical base for estimating the ratio of affluent males to females at the time of their deaths.

The fact that more people are going into the above-mentioned professions makes it easier to understand the increases in the number of women in these professions. However, due to the "glut" of professionals entering the marketplace, these professions are becoming extremely competitive. An increasing number of the young professionals who become millionaires will do so because of their marketing and entrepreneurial ability and their investment/financial lifestyles, not because of their professional training.

Fewer women (and men) will become affluent working for a large organization or in a highly competitive profession. However, women will gain wealth by pursuing other alternatives. Those alternatives include entrepreneurship, sole-proprietor businesses, and basic business ventures. The big monetary winners in the professional ranks will be specialists in growth segments and venture types who will own and operate chains of dental offices and medical clinics, employing other professionals to work for them.

After weighing the pros and cons of the affluent women's market, Dorothy still wanted to focus on this market segment. She asked me, "If you are interested in the women's market, what should your strategy be?" First, understand that this market contains prospects who are widely distributed along an active/passive investor continuum. At one extreme, there are completely self-made and independent women. These women are likely to make up their own minds about investment alternatives. This market is a growing one, and it does provide opportunities for security brokers. However, one must be very intelligent about how to approach it and how to target segments.

At the other extreme are women who are totally passive about investment decisions. These women are prime targets for asset management accounts with full discretion. Affluent women who inherited the bulk of their wealth differ significantly from the general affluent male population. These women are prone to invest in low-risk, high-liquidity categories and to buy tangible items. Many of these women never had a career of their own. They are often widows of dominating, hard-driving, wealthy entrepreneurs. For many, they followed the dictates of their late husbands: "Don't work," "Don't worry about finances," and so on. These women, often well educated, gave up a possible career and the development of financial intelligence for a very traditional family lifestyle. The passive segment of the affluent women's market still presents marketers of investments with greater opportunities than those presented by the active segment.

Both the active and passive segments of the affluent women's market provide opportunities, but each of these segments requires a different orientation. The passive or traditional segment will be discussed first. This segment is created by situations in which the affluent husband dies before his affluent wife and by divorces of affluent couples.

How can one capitalize on the opportunities that exist among the passive segment? Simply stated, endorsements must be gained from attorneys who specialize in estate law, and divorce specialists should be a target for referral support. Brokers who wish to penetrate the passive segment should also volunteer to speak at selected meetings of women's organizations on the investment needs of affluent widows and divorcees. The details about strategies and tactics that several ESPs employ in this regard are discussed in several sections that follow.

The active segment of the affluent women's market is not as easy to define as the passive segment. There are significant geographic variations in the distribution of self-made affluent women. For example, according to the Small Business Administration, 37 percent of the female-operated nonfarm sole proprietorships are located in just five states: California, Texas, New York, Illinois, and Florida. Also, nearly 15 percent of all women physicians are located in New York State, and 56 percent are located in just eight states: New York, California, Illinois, Pennsylvania, Texas, Massachusetts, New Jersey, and Ohio.

Businesses and Professions

What about the specific areas in which women are likely to operate businesses? The growth rates of female-operated businesses in

America provide excellent clues about where the opportunities lie for marketers of securities. According to the Small Business Administration, the female growth businesses include business management and public relations services, nursing and personal care facilities, legal services, accounting services, security brokerage, commodity contract brokerage, insurance brokerage, apparel and textile production, and general building contracting.

Women account for at least 20 percent of the workers in the following affluent occupational areas: accountants, computer specialists, life and physical scientists, personal and labor relations workers, pharmacists, college and university professors, writers, artists and entertainers, bank officers and financial managers, buyers, health administrators, purchasing agents, sales managers, school administrators, insurance agents, brokers and underwriters, real estate agents and brokers, stock and bond sales agents, manufacturing industries sales representatives, and printing craft workers.

What advantage does Dorothy have over her male counterparts in marketing to and servicing the active affluent women's market? Remember that the number one criterion an affluent prospect uses to evaluate financial advisers is empathy for goals. Whether brokers are male or female, those with more empathy will get more of the active affluent's dollars. Many successful female brokers share some common experiences with their affluent female prospects, but this in itself is not enough to secure business from this market. The last thing the self-made affluent woman wants is to be patronized. She does, however, want to be respected for her intellect and her significant achievements. Dorothy should find out who the self-made affluent women are and what their accomplishments are before she ever discusses investment opportunities with them. I advised her to join and be active in local business organizations patronized by successful women. It seems that every city of any size in this country has a Women's Business League, an Executive Women's Club, a chapter of Executive and Professional Women, Inc., and so on. I suggested to Dorothy that she read the literature of these groups, head up committees, volunteer for speeches, and perhaps more important, write articles for their publications. Remember, an expert is someone whom others perceive as an expert. This perception is greatly enhanced by speaking and writing on the topic of women and investing. Focus on the long run in terms of both investment advice and relationship development.

ESTHER M. BERGER BECOMES A RECOGNIZED AUTHORITY ON WOMEN AND MONEY

Designing an Affiliation Group for Affluent Women

Dear Marketer:

Do not be discouraged about the poor turnout at your investment seminar for widows. In terms of the female affluent market, you are correct in assuming that the widow segment is the most significant. Since the only speaker listed sells only a very narrow line of investments, I have to say that I am surprised that anyone showed up at all. Widows and soon-to-be widows need a much wider variety of information and support than just investment information.

Also it is likely that many of your prospects were frightened because of their perception of many types of financial advisors. In fact, most widows and their formal, as well as informal advisors have a negative image of people who sell investments.

Let me recommend that you reformulate your package. But do not lose sight of your target. Instead of having one seminar, you should consider starting your own affiliation group for affluent women. This affiliation group or organization should become a permanent part of your effort to provide important advice and support to affluent women in need. Too often people in your business attempt to master many, many targets. But the best people in your business typically pick a specific target and stick with it.

If you are interested in targeting affluent widows, do so, but be willing to make it the focus of your career for life. Several people in your industry have been successful in establishing themselves as experts in the context of this market. One former top-producing stock broker employed by Prescott, Ball and Turben developed an interesting affiliation group.

He called his ongoing seminar for women, "Women, Are You Prepared to Become Widows?" This fellow told me that the program consistently sold out. There were several reasons for his success. First, the title is most provocative. It reflects exactly the concerns many affluent women have in regard to their financial and emotional future. This is especially true of the majority of women who are married to hard-charging, domineering, first-generation millionaires.

Second, the program was not limited to investments. On the contrary, many speakers were not financial people at all. Some were spiritual leaders. Others were affluent widows. In essence, these professionals provided a fabric of support to women who pondered their economic future.

Third, the focus was on interaction among audience members, as opposed to a one-way dialogue from a marketer of investments to the audience.

Fourth, the husbands of many of the attendees did not object to the program. Husbands viewed this affiliation group as something other than a hard-sell investment seminar. In fact, they viewed it as an opportunity for their wives to share some of their ideas and concerns about their future. Interestingly, the broker who started this program apparently did so well in terms of production that his firm promoted him to a senior executive position. Because of this, the program ceased to exist. I am sure that there are many women throughout the country who would like to see programs of this type in their own backyards. But just like the weather, everybody seems to be talking about marketing investment services to the women who control significant portions of wealth in this country. But few, if any, do more than talk about how to capture this significant portion of wealth.

So, it is up to you. Step up to the plate with the bases loaded. Make a significant contribution to your field. Or sit in the bleachers with the hundreds of thousands of people you compete with who are smiling and dialing their way into oblivion.

Developing a program of this type will not take a great deal of money. It will, however, take considerable time and intellect. Let me suggest, first, that you need a provocative title. Why not borrow from our top producer as previously mentioned? Use the headline title, "Women, Are You Prepared to Become Widows?" Underneath this heading in your news release, in your brochures and flyers, it should state, "Find out how to deal with the trauma of being on your own." And then mention the real substance of what you deliver. Speakers will include several prominent women who will help you prepare for this stage of your life. These prominent women are not only affluent, but they are, in fact, widows. And they, in turn, will be the centerpiece of your seminar.

You should also include a prominent psychiatrist or psychologist who will make a presentation about the psychological problems related to grief. Also included in your program should be a spiritual adviser, that is, someone from the clergy who can talk about the spiritual needs of widows. In addition to these professionals, I would suggest that you add an estate attorney. The estate attorney can sensitize members of the audience to the legal, as well as clerical, issues related to estate planning.

Finally, let me suggest that you ask a distinguished asset manager to make a brief presentation about various forms of investments in which women may consider placing their financial assets.

The provocative nature of the proposed program will certainly allow you to network with prominent psychiatrists and psychologists in the community and various clergymen and estate attorneys as well as asset managers. They, of course, can also be very important clients as well as spheres of influence.

Obviously, your target for your promotional material will not only be affluent women. It will include some of their advisers as well as members of the local, regional, and national press. Members of the press should be particularly interested in attending a program of this type since the topic is not only provocative but growing in importance in terms of their readership.

I would also suggest that you develop a mailing list of top-grade professionals in the speaker categories as previously mentioned. You may also benefit from the wisdom of Ms. Esther M. Berger in developing an affiliation group for affluent women. I first met Esther at a seminar that I conducted on marketing to the affluent last summer. During the seminar, she told me of her strong commitment to helping women in America with their investments and other related problems. In terms of targeting women, Esther has developed one of the best affluent marketing programs that I have yet encountered. What is amazing about this is that Esther has developed this program in such a short period of time. But it was not easy for Esther to accomplish this. She is a very well disciplined young woman, hard working, very ambitious, and totally committed to her mission of helping women deal with financial issues. This is not a 9:00 to 5:00 job. Nor will you likely receive immediate compensation for every effort that you make. But in the long run, Esther Berger will be a major player with an international reputation for helping women achieve their financial, if not spiritual goals. Her accomplishments are many. She has already appeared on the Financial News Network discussing the topic of women and money. Esther is currently writing a book on this same topic. Esther also had a full-page article about women and money published in *Newsweek*. She is also an account vice president with a major Wall Street−based investment firm. Since she specializes in women and money, she has a special understanding of the anxiety and uncertainty that keep women from achieving financial independence. This is her strong suit. This is essentially why women seek her out to help them solve these types of problems.

Her professional expertise is specifically directed towards women in terms of overcoming their fears and gaining confidence to accept the responsibility for their financial future. Esther recently helped co-found the Westside Organization for Women, also known as WOW, a nonprofit Los Angeles organization that provides a forum for women to receive and exchange ideas on matters of finance and investment, taxation and business.

How successful was the WOW concept in attracting women? During the very second workshop sponsored by WOW, 200 affluent women paid $15 to attend. Esther anticipates that this number will significantly increase during the next few years.

Esther Berger is one of the new breed of financial advisers in this country. She is not only committed to disseminating information to a group that desperately needs counseling. Esther also has demonstrated significant strength and stamina and organizational skills in terms of developing her very own affiliation group.

I have enclosed several pieces of communication that I received from Esther over the past few months. I hope that this information will help you develop your own style of addressing the needs of affluent women. I wish you the best of luck in your endeavors. Please keep me posted about your progress in this regard.

Sincerely,

Thomas J. Stanley, Ph.D.
Chairman, Affluent Market Institute

Steps in Becoming an Expert

September 13

Dear Tom:

Last week, I attended the Southern California Conference on Women. Right there under one roof in Anaheim were 5,000 qualified prospects. That is my idea of heaven on earth! I also picked up the premiere issue of *Entrepreneurial Woman* at one of the exhibit booths. There, in living color, were the stories of successful women business owners. With your words echoing in my head, I picked up the phone and dialed the president of a firm ($100 million in 1988 sales). She not only returned my call within 10 minutes but agreed to meet with me next week after her return from a business trip. I'm a happy camper!

I find women increasingly attracted to the idea of working with women professionals. My clients are wonderful referral sources and are just terrific in terms of being supportive of other successful business women.

If you'd like me to fill in the blanks regarding my personal and professional background, please give me a call.

Tom, thanks again for your words of wisdom.

Best regards,

Esther M. Berger
Account Vice President

February 18

Dear Tom:

I am enclosing my press kit as well as an advance copy of my submission to *Newsweek*'s "My Turn" column. I am also enclosing information about the Westside Organization for Women, an organization which I co-founded to educate women about financial matters. My affiliations also include Women in Business, the Southern California Women's Law Center, both the Beverly Hills and Century City Chamber of Commerce Women's Division, as well as the business and professional group of the United Jewish Foundation.

Esther M. Berger
Account Vice President

February 26

Dear Tom,

I enjoyed talking with you this morning and appreciate your wonderful support. As you can imagine, I am thrilled beyond words at the prospect of being published in *Newsweek*.

Briefly, let me retrace for you the chronology of events that led me to market myself as a women's financial consultant. My first month of production was October 1987 (good timing, huh?!). Needless to say, in a post-crash environment with most investors completely shell-shocked, I found myself floundering around for business like most other rookie brokers. I had no marketing plan whatsoever and talked to whomever would talk to me. This became increasingly frustrating as my efforts were totally directionless and unfocused. I decided early on what I would not do was cold call from a telephone directory.

One of my strengths has always been public speaking and generally getting out and "schmoozing" with people.

In March and April of 1988, I teamed with a colleague in my office and spoke to a number of real estate brokers on the subject of retirement planning. As a result of those speeches, several brokers became my clients. One in particular mentioned repeatedly that she preferred to do business with other women. This was in the latter part of 1988. At this point, this particular client had introduced me to many other affluent women of like mind. This started me thinking seriously about marketing my professional services primarily to women. In January 1989 I began focusing my efforts full-out in that direction. I have done a great deal of public speaking to Chamber of Commerce women's groups and other women's business and professional groups as well as philanthropic organizations. I have also joined many women's organizations offering many excellent networking opportunities. In addition, I co-founded the Westside Organization for Women along with a CPA, estate attorney, and a clinical psychologist to educate women on financial matters. Over 175 women attended our first seminar entitled "Women and Money: A Partnership of Wealth and Identity."

Then, in mid-1989, I attended your workshop on "Marketing to the Affluent." You really helped validate my marketing approach and shared excellent ideas about attaining public visibility. I began exploring the idea of retaining a communications consultant to help get the word out to the media as well as prospective clients. I positioned myself as a women's financial consultant. My objective is to establish my reputation as an expert on the subject of women and money on both the local and national levels.

As I mentioned during our telephone conversation this morning, I just received word that my essay on women and money will be published in the "My Turn" column of *Newsweek*. I have also submitted to a literary agent an outline for a book I propose to write on the subject of women and money.

Tom, I should note that my gross production last year more than doubled my gross production from the year before. I believe this is a direct cause and effect of focusing my marketing direction on women and following through on my plan.

Esther M. Berger
Account Vice President

February 28

YOU AND A GUEST
ARE CORDIALLY INVITED
TO
AN EVENING WITH
KATHLEEN BROWN
CANDIDATE FOR TREASURER, STATE OF CALIFORNIA

AND

EMILY CARD
AUTHOR OF *MS. MONEY BOOK: STRATEGIES FOR
PROSPERING IN THE COMING DECADE*

THE WESTSIDE ORGANIZATION FOR WOMEN BOARD
OF DIRECTORS

Esther M. Berger
Women's Financial
   Consultant
Account Vice President,

Pamela A. Garvin
Attorney at Law

Selwyn Gerber
Managing Partner
Gerber, Rosenfield &
   Co., C.P.A.

Clara Zilberstein,
   Ph.D.
Clinical Psychologist
   and Corporate
   Consultant

MISSION STATEMENT

The Westside Organization for Women is a nonprofit group created for the purpose of providing a forum for women to receive and exchange ideas and information on a variety of topics concerning finance, investment, taxation, and business. The organization's intent is to educate, inform, and empower women in areas of finance as it relates to their business and personal lives and encourage women to set and attain financial goals.

A SEMINAR SPONSORED BY
THE WESTSIDE ORGANIZATION FOR WOMEN

WEDNESDAY, FEBRUARY 28, 1990
7:00 P.M.

OPUS BALLROOM
MA MAISON SOFITEL
8555 BEVERLY BOULEVARD
LOS ANGELES, CALIFORNIA

March 12, 1990

Tom:

FYI: (One full page) Esther M. Berger, "Why Women Fear Money," *Newsweek*, March 12, 1990, p. 10.

Esther

March 16, 1990

Dear Esther:

I'm so proud of you. You're a role model for this industry. Thank you for your interview and contribution.

All the best,

Tom

P.S. I understand that one full page of advertising space in *Newsweek* costs almost $60,000. So you really received quite a deep discount. Hope every one of their 3 million plus readers read your article.

An Interview with Esther M. Berger

DR. STANLEY:

Esther, why did you become a financial consultant?

MS. BERGER:

I became a financial consultant because I always had an affinity for money. I had a very stereotypical view of women and their roles and views of money. I didn't think it was appropriate for me. For years I resisted doing what I really wanted to do. It was truly at the suggestion of my broker.

DR. STANLEY:

All right.

MS. BERGER:

I was in marketing and advertising copywriting. I said to him, "I'm getting a little burned out." He goes, "You really ought to be in my business." I found it uproariously funny because women just didn't do this.

DR. STANLEY:

All right.

MS. BERGER:

I talked to some of the women that he referred me to that were in the business. And they were not terribly positive. They were not terribly convincing in terms of getting me to do it. But I just decided that it was something that I would try. It was appealing to me, and I gave it a shot.

DR. STANLEY:

You went from advertising to the financial consulting business?

MS. BERGER:

I came in and I applied for the job. I just kept plugging and plugging for two months. I kept calling repeatedly, like trying to get a new client. And when she hired me, she said, "Esther, you wore me down."

DR. STANLEY:

So, Esther, in your first weeks on the job, what did you do for prospects?

MS. BERGER:

I didn't want to build a business based on friends or relatives or anything because I was concerned that if things didn't work out, they were my friends and family. So I started doing some speaking engagements. There were some realtors' offices here in Beverly Hills. It is a very wealthy community. And I went and I started talking to them about retirement planning and about IRAs, which are very appropriate for real estate professionals who are self-employed. It was very brief. They have these Tuesday morning meetings. That is traditional. I knew that I had a captive audience. I called the managers, and I said, "May I get 10 minutes of your morning meeting?" And I went into a dual constituency that was largely female. A few of them actually called me up, and they said, "I like what you had to say." And we started doing business. And one of them in particular was very typical. She is a very wonderful and valuable client to me today. She said to me, "I like dealing with women." They say you are very persistent, but you are not pushy.

DR. STANLEY:

So, your first clients were sales people?

MS. BERGER:

My first clients were sales people. They really helped me a lot.

DR. STANLEY:

Female sales people?

MS. BERGER:

Female sales people. They like doing business with women. And there were very few women brokers. And this gave me the idea. I'm missing the boat if I don't start talking to women because there were a lot of women out there who deal with their own finances, and if they are not, they ought to be. I met women who were very successful in their careers and very unsuccessful in their personal money management. And I felt like, well gee, this is a need that is not being addressed and no one else is doing it.

DR. STANLEY:

Well, give me some examples of the places you spoke.

MS. BERGER:

One of the most successful has been the Century City Chamber of Commerce. They have a women's group. About a month ago, they asked me to sit on a committee to select the Woman of Achievement for the Century City Chamber of Commerce. So I became involved in that. And this morning, they called me and said we are nominating you as the Woman of Achievement. I am going to be speaking for them in mid-May. The title is "Money Secrets for Women." They are doing all this wonderful publicity, so that has been very successful.

DR. STANLEY:

Esther, in terms of WOW, what is it?

MS. BERGER:

Westside Organization for Women.

DR. STANLEY:

Yes. Maybe you could tell me how that started.

MS. BERGER:

That started because a client of mine who is a clinical psychologist introduced me to her CPA. We were talking over lunch, and I told him what I am doing. He said what we would really like to do is put together a seminar where we invite enough speakers so we are really covering the complete woman, if you will. So he and I and our mutual client who is a psychologist and an estate attorney put together a seminar. No one else is doing it, and there is clearly a need now. So, we thought maybe we would get 20 or 30 people showing up. We did our first get-together in November, and 175 women came. And we hardly publicized it—a one paragraph little piece in the *Los Angeles Times*. We had an amazing turnout. I didn't have to go chasing. The organization has credibility of its own now. And our name is out there. We are known.

DR. STANLEY:

How many did you have for the second one?

MS. BERGER:

We had 200. A good turnout.

DR. STANLEY:

That's amazing.

MS. BERGER:

And we started charging for them. The first one we did free. And now we have membership dues. And we are going to publish a newsletter as well.

DR. STANLEY:

Esther, how did you get your article published in *Newsweek*?

MS. BERGER:

I think the way I do everything is listening. I listen to everybody around me. And when people tell me it can't be done, I think it is a great challenge. And I find it very exciting.

DR. STANLEY:

All right.

MS. BERGER:

After I took your class, I came back and I thought to myself what I probably ought to do is start really getting published. I started interviewing some communications people. One said to me, "What you ought to do is write in the "My Turn" column for *Newsweek*. So about a month ago, I decided that I would just take a weekend and sit down and do this. And I did it, and I sent it in.

DR. STANLEY:

You just sent it to *Newsweek?*

MS. BERGER:

I just called their recording. They have a little recording, and they tell you how many words and what the format is, and they tell you how many submissions that they get. They called me two weeks ago Monday, and they said, "Can we send a photographer?" They let me do all the editing.

DR. STANLEY:

So you got a full-page article published in *Newsweek?*

MS. BERGER:

Yes.

DR. STANLEY:

Did they ever tell you, Esther, how many people do submit and how many get rejected?

MS. BERGER:

They say on the machine they get 500 submissions a month.

DR. STANLEY:

Esther, what has happened since the time that your article was published?

MS. BERGER:

Tomorrow morning I have a talk show for KABC, the premier talk radio station in Los Angeles. A place up in Portland called me to be on their radio talk show. Time Warner Television Syndicate called me today. I had a call from *USA Today* earlier; they want to have someone interview me. I have talked with Gannett, and they are interested as well. The response has been amazing.

DR. STANLEY:

Where is this going to go in the future for you? Where would you like it to go?

MS. BERGER:

I really want to be known nationally as an expert on women and money. I want to write a book. I want to do talk shows. I want to be quoted, and I want my name to be associated with women's issues, with financial issues. More than that, I want to make a difference. I would like to start making money on speaking engagements. I want to make a major-league impact. Without overstating it, I want to affect women's lives.

DR. STANLEY:

Esther, what do you think the top one or two problems for women really are in terms of money?

MS. BERGER:

I think the top problem is that women feel that they cannot understand money. It is really a holdover from a lot of very sexist beliefs. None of us, particularly in my generation, was brought up to believe that she had the capacity for understanding money. It is an issue of self-esteem. There is nothing more devastating than seeing an inordinately bright woman sitting there telling me how abjectly stupid she is and believing it. And that's an awful issue as women divorce more and receive large divorce settlements. And as women become more successful in the workplace, they don't translate that into their personal money power.

DR. STANLEY:

Esther, what about your organization in terms of dealing with very affluent women who essentially have not had a career of their own—who were dominated by Type A (male) personalities and who are on their own for the first time?

MS. BERGER:

Women have a natural resistance to money. I'll relate a story. I just had lunch with a woman who is exactly what you are talking about. She said, "I never open my brokerage statements." I said, "Why is that?" She goes, "Because I am not going to understand them anyway, so why bother?" That was a very telling comment. She is extremely wealthy. And she had inherited it through her husband's death. Unfortunately, she was a woman who had only signed checks, who was on a budget literally every month, and who is completely lost. She is a walking prey to less-than-ethical advisors. Women call me and say, "Where do I start? I'm really scared." So when I talk to women, I start them out really slowly and I just tell them the basic differences between stocks and bonds. I explain what a CD is because most of the time they don't understand. I give them some very introductory reading material.

DR. STANLEY:

Are you actually giving them intellect and confidence?

MS. BERGER:

I think the most important thing I give apart from education is when women come in here and kind of push all their paperwork to my side of the desk. I push it back to the middle physically. And I say to them, "I don't want you to give your responsibility over to me and feel like I am taking care of you because that is not what this is about. I will not put you out on a ledge and leave you there. I am here for you. You may ask any question you want to ask and understand I am not judgmental. Ask the questions you feel too foolish to ask anyone else. By the same token, it is your money, and I want you to remember that and to be responsible for it." Because what I don't want to do is say, "Terrific, trust me, I'm handling it, honey." Because that is what they have heard all their lives.

DR. STANLEY:

Esther, do you say that in programs and speeches?

MS. BERGER:

Absolutely.

DR. STANLEY:

Esther, what advice do you have for young aspiring people who might want to follow in your footsteps?

MS. BERGER:

You have to do what feels right to you. It is just what I tell my investors. If somebody tells you that you must cold call and it is not who you are, then you better not do it because you are not going to do it with conviction. You will think that there is no place for you in this business. I said it may take you longer to get where you are going, and people may not approve of it. They may think that you are out of your mind, nuts. But if your way is a different way, that's what you need to do. They all told me, "I've been to women in business. Forget it, it is a waste of your time." So my biggest advice to people is don't listen to your colleagues who tell you it can't be done. People don't buy what I am selling; they buy me. Our society is moving more and more toward relationship business—whether it is retail clothiers or stock brokers.

DR. STANLEY:

Esther, were most of your relationships started with face-to-face meetings?

MS. BERGER:

You got it. The woman I had lunch with, the same woman, said, "You know I dealt with a fellow for four years, and he never invited me to his office." A $3 million account, Tom. This is not small potatoes. Never invited her to the office. A $3 million account! I say to myself, how does a fellow like this stay in business? How do they make a living like this? When they don't pay attention to their clients? My people know me. You miss the boat if you don't develop these relationships.

DR. STANLEY:

Esther, in terms of young women out there who are contemplating finishing undergraduate or graduate school, why should they get into your business?

MS. BERGER:

I'm not sure that most people should. It is a very tough business. There aren't many women in the business, and the ones that are making it in this business are few and far between.

DR. STANLEY:

What is the toughest thing about it, Esther?

MS. BERGER:

The toughest thing is dealing with the resistance that you get from your colleagues. And if you are not a real strong personality who believes real strongly in yourself, people will naysay you to death. Until you finally pick up and quit and say, yeah, they are right.

DR. STANLEY:

But, Esther, you have been able to develop your own affinity group, though, of other supporters, right?

MS. BERGER:

Sales people, professional colleagues, attorneys, CPAs. There is one thing about women. They are the most amazingly wonderful support system if you look for the right people. If I just sat and listened to everybody telling me what couldn't be done, I'd be out of the business.

AN ENCORE PERFORMANCE BY
ROGER THOMAS

Dear Tom:

Early in my sales career I seized upon the idea of holding seminars for groups that already met regularly. I arrived at this strategy one day when, without any conscious effort on my part, I was invited to speak to the local Rotary Club. Gazing down from the podium, I realized that my audience was composed of 60 to 70 of the very people I had been trying to see for six months. Moreover, I was struck by how much larger and more prosperous this audience looked than the 8 to 10 people who showed up for free cookies and punch at my regularly scheduled seminars.

A quick trip to the chamber of commerce yielded a list of 48 clubs in town and the names and addresses of all their current presidents. I went to see them all to offer my service as a guest speaker on topics of money, investing, saving, anything they wanted me to talk about. Success!

I learned that while I thought of clubs in terms of the Rotary, Kiwanis, Lions, and so forth, there actually were hosts of special-interest clubs hungry for speakers. For example, there was the Henry County Motorcycle Club (no, not with black leather and Harleys—rather a group of affluent, retirees with huge ElectroGlides they rode to state parks on weekends), the Ladies VFW Auxiliary, literally a dozen local Grange associations and—EUREKA— the Garden Club.

I want to explain at this point that the following material regarding my sales strategy to club members should in no way sound as if I victimized widows. In fact, I am proud of the portfolios we put together for these ladies—portfolios that included government and tax-free bonds of different maturities, well-managed mutual funds, and annuities. Widows often are portrayed as hapless victims in the media, and I recognize that charlatans prey on the weak and vulnerable. However, I found these women to be so cautious, strong, and appreciative as clients that when treated with respect, they revealed larger and larger percentages of their investable assets.

I did my best for each and every one of them and mean to imply no disrespect in anything I have said about them.

PRO FORMA ROGER

Personal Call, Usually at the Front Door

MR. THOMAS:

Mrs. Widow, my name is R.T. with XYZ Investment Firm here in town. I'm sorry to barge up to your front door like this, but I got your name and address from the chamber of commerce and wanted to come by and meet the president of the Garden Club in person.

MRS. WIDOW:

[Easing the door closed an inch or so.] Well, that's nice. But why would the chamber of commerce give you my name? I don't have any money.

MR. THOMAS:

Oh, I stopped by the chamber office to learn the names of all the clubs in town and their presidents because I have found the club presidents are important and influential people to meet when you are new in town as I am. In fact, I call people like you centers-of-influence. I hope that doesn't offend you.

MRS. WIDOW:

Why, no, I'm not offended, but I don't think of myself as an "influencer" either.

MR. THOMAS:

I'm sure some of your club members would disagree with you there. By the way, how many members are in your club?

MRS. WIDOW:

Well, we have about three dozen; but not all of them are active, and—you know—it's been nice talking to you, but I have some cookies in the oven I need to attend to. Thank you for stopping by. Good-bye.

MR. THOMAS:

Good-bye, Mrs. Widow. It's really been a pleasure to meet you. Say hello to your club members for me and let me leave this calling card with you. Thanks.

A Thank-You Note

That night Mrs. Widow received a handwritten thank you note from me saying: "Thank you for letting me stop by today and introduce myself. I am afraid I did too much talking and not enough listening because I find myself now wanting to know more about you and your club. Next time I am in the area I will stop by and see if you would allow me to ask a few more questions. In the meantime, if I can be of any service to you or your friends on matters of conservative investing, please let me know. Thanks again. I look forward to seeing you again. I would love for you to meet my wife, Pat, and our daughter, Amy, someday. Best Regards, R.T."

A Handwritten Letter

These handwritten notes were closely followed by a handwritten letter that went like this:

Mrs. Widow
President, Garden Club
1122 Main Street

Dear Mrs. Widow,

How is this for a formal-looking letter? Well, I guess if it was a real business letter it wouldn't be handwritten, but I like it better this way, don't you?

Anyway, the reason I wanted this to look more formal is because I think I have a service to offer that may be of interest to your club. I have found clubs like yours frequently entertain the idea of guest speakers. I imagine conservative investments like government bonds, corporate bonds, and insured tax-free bonds aren't standard topics of conversation at Garden Club meetings, but it could be an interesting change of pace.

I hope you won't think I am being forward to suggest such a thing, but many clubs have found one of these types of talks a welcome addition to their normal discussions. Besides, I would love to attend one of your meetings and learn what you and your members do discuss. I have a terminally brown thumb. Maybe you could even teach me how to be a gardener.

I will call on you soon to see if I can be of service. As Club president, your advice on how to provide service to your club members is especially valuable.

Thank you again for your time.

Best Regards,

R.T.

A Personal Visit

My next visit took place in person on Mrs. Widow's doorstep about a week to 10 days after the letter was mailed.

MR. THOMAS:

Mrs. Widow, hello. It's me, R.T., again. How are you today?

MRS. WIDOW:

Fine, but busy. How are you?

MR. THOMAS:

Just great. My wife and daughter and I are getting settled in our new home, and we love it. You know, this is a very friendly town. We were worried when we moved about how difficult it would be to make friends, but we shouldn't have worried at all.

MRS. WIDOW:

That's nice. We like it here, too.

MR. THOMAS:

I'm sure you do. By the way, how long have you lived here?

MRS. WIDOW:

Well, Frank and I moved here 38 years ago this spring when our kids were just little things, and except for moving across town once to this house, we have never thought about living anywhere else.

MR. THOMAS:

I can see why. Your home is lovely from the outside, and the gardens are beautiful. I have always loved big, old homes. They give you so many opportunities for adding your individual style instead of all looking the same as the homes do in the new subdivision where I live.

MRS. WIDOW:

Why don't you come in and let me show you around. Things are kind of a mess, but I guess it will be okay.

MR. THOMAS:

[As we step inside the house.] By the way, how old are your children?

MRS. WIDOW:

They're 28 and 24 now with kids of their own.

MR. THOMAS:

[Gesturing to fireplace mantel.] Are these your kids and grandkids?

MRS. WIDOW:

Yes, that picture was taken last year in the backyard.

MR. THOMAS:

[After a tour of the house and numerous pleasantries about the decor, photos, and mementos.] You know, Mrs. Widow, you said you were busy, and I respect your time. But I don't want to leave without offering my services as a speaker for your club members. Do you think they would be more interested in a discussion of tax-free bonds or government guaranteed bonds?

MRS. WIDOW:

I don't know.

MR. THOMAS:

Then why don't we schedule an opportunity for me to drop by during a club meeting and, without wasting much of your time, take a quick poll of what topics they would like to hear about? Then I can get back with you for a date to talk about the topics in which they seem most interested and answer any questions they might have.

MRS. WIDOW:

That would be fine. We have a meeting at Mrs. Widow II's home next week. I'm sure she wouldn't mind if you dropped by for a few minutes.

An Affluent Convoy Called the Garden Club

The Garden Club was the jackpot for me. My once murky marketing strategy became sparkingly clear after my first invitation to talk to the ladies of the Garden Club, which came on about my fourth or fifth visit with Mrs. Widow-President.

Regular semimonthly meetings of the Garden Club were attended by 15 to 30 members who came for tea, cookies, and talks about what to plant and when, followed by bridge and more conversation. I became a regular, every-other-month speaker, opening accounts with virtually every member of the club. My original idea of getting next to the people who already had big money began to pay off. These women were cautious, conservative, intelligent about matters that interested them, and affluent. Plus they wanted an advisor they knew and trusted.

I gathered lots of information from the women including their birthdates and began my campaign of winning their trust. In fact, as an aside, I made arrangements with a local baker to bake cakes for me. On short notice, the baker would decorate a cake to my specifications, and I began delivering birthday cakes to members of the Garden Club. Never have I encountered such happy elderly ladies as when I showed up at their doors with birthday cakes, often with several of their Garden Club friends in tow. It was not unusual for my cake and mobile birthday party crew to be the only special activity of the day for these women. Often their own children had forgotten the date.

These affluent wives and widows weren't ready to entrust their savings to me because of birthday cakes and every-other-month discussions about conservative investing, however. They were tough clients who knew what they wanted in terms of income and risk levels. Once their friendship was gained, the job of selling began. These women already knew me and my wife, so my cold calls were actually warm calls by this time.

The Sales Call

MR. THOMAS:

Mrs. Widow, this is Roger Thomas again. How are you today?

MRS. WIDOW:

Fine, Roger. How are you?

MR. THOMAS:

Well, I know this is going to be a surprise, but I'm not calling today to see if you can go with me to a birthday party. What I would like to do today is stop by and visit with you about your savings. You know, those talks I've been giving at the club meetings may have some very special importance for you. When would be a good time to stop by?

MRS. WIDOW:

Roger, I don't know. I have most of my money in the bank except for some of the stocks and bonds Frank owned when he died, and I haven't done anything at all with them.

MR. THOMAS:

Mrs. Widow, I was sure you hadn't done anything with the savings already established. However, I think a review of the situation could give you the opportunity to earn more income on the same dollars without increasing the risk. What would you do with an extra $1,000 or $2,000 a year in income?

MRS. WIDOW:

I suppose I would visit the grandkids more often. It's such a long trip to Texas for me alone.

MR. THOMAS:

That's exactly what I had in mind, although I also think you should set aside some of it to spend just on yourself. What have you always wanted to do, or what have you held off on doing just because you were apprehensive about spending the money?

MRS. WIDOW:

Well, I shouldn't be telling you this, but I've always wanted to go to New York, take in a Broadway show, shop in some of those stores you hear so much about, and stay in a luxury hotel. But I could never do anything like that by myself. It's just a fling I've thought about.

MR. THOMAS:

Why don't we bring it up at the next Garden Club meeting and see if anybody else has the same fling in mind? You may be surprised at the group we could put together if we just asked. Now, Mrs. Widow, how would you feel about getting together to see if we can increase your income and make an extra trip to see the grandkids and a "wild" week in New York both possible?

MRS. WIDOW:

That would be fun. When can you stop by?

MR. THOMAS:

I can be there this afternoon at 2:00 P.M. But before I forget about it, tell me, how are Tom and Diane and Tom, Jr., and Frank [son, daughter-in-law and kids] doing?

The Investment Interview

The actual investment interview would proceed in a very standard fashion, probing cautiously for securities held that had special significance (i.e., "Frank loved that stock in Pepsi so much; I couldn't think of selling it." Or "My banker told me once never to put any money in a mutual fund.") Often the objections like the banker's mutual fund advice had to be overcome. But I would never, ever recommend the sale of Frank's favorite Pepsi stock.

Closing was easy with these ladies if the proper groundwork had been laid. These weren't quick, one-time sales. These were relationship-building experiences that had to be sincere or they didn't work. Frequently, it would take several of these selling meetings before the women would reveal a significant portion of their investable assets. Even though they trusted me, liked me, and had done some small business with me, it generally took four to five sales calls before they revealed more than 50 percent of their net worth (and even then much of it, like Frank's Pepsi stock, was untouchable). Caution was habit to these ladies. However, portfolios of more than $500,000 in CDs and various stocks and bonds were common. In fact, the individual most accurately depicted in the pro forma remembrances above had a portfolio of well over $5 million. And that didn't include the $1 million inheritances of each of her three children! Of course, she insisted that I visit with all three of them about their conservative investment plans also.

Through referrals I ended up with most of the affluent widows in town as clients, even the nongardeners! The same strategy worked for other special clubs in the county.

Regards,

Roger

CHAPTER 6

PROSPECTING ASIAN AMERICANS: BECOMING AN ADVOCATE FOR AFFLUENT AFFILIATION GROUPS

INTRODUCTION

Paula Keyes Kun, a communications manager for Metropolitan Life Insurance Company, recently issued a statement about her firm's marketing strategy. Metropolitan Life is very sensitive to changes in the marketplace. Kun revealed that it had responded aggressively to the growth of the Hispanic population in America and was now, in overall market share and consumer awareness, the number one insurance company in the Hispanic American market segment.

In what other growing market segment is Metropolitan interested? Apparently, it is interested in the segment that several recent reports and a recent article by Pauline Yoshihashi ("Why More Ads Aren't Targeting Asians," *The Wall Street Journal,* July 20, 1989, B1) have called the fastest-growing minority in America, the Asian Americans.

When the 1980 census was taken, there were nearly 4 million Asian Americans. This segment, according to Kun, is growing 14 times as fast as the entire American population, and Bouvier and Agresta stated that the Asian American population grew by 142 percent between 1970 and 1980 and would double in size by the turn of the century. Moreover, the Asian American segment is ideal for marketers of insurance not only because it is growing rapidly but also because it is highly concentrated geographically. Nearly 70 percent of all Asian Americans live in five states: California, Hawaii, New York, Illinois, and Washington.

But the geodemographics of this segment are not the only factors that make it attractive to Metropolitan. Kun stated that her firm's research had revealed that many Asian Americans have a strong desire to provide an economic foundation for their survivors and to educate their children. Also, the Asian American population has a significantly higher income than the general U.S. population. Yet, many Asian Americans, especially the numerous first-generation Asian Americans, have no insurance and have little or no knowledge of insurance products. Only 4 in 10 Asian Americans were born in the United States.

Of critical importance to marketers is not only the growth and orientation of the Asian American segment but also the character of that segment's current and future affluent subsegment. A significant subsegment of the Asian American segment is affluent today. However, I forecast that into the next century the Asian American subsegment of the affluent market will grow more rapidly than any other racial subsegment of that market.

What evidence is there to support this contention? The proportion of racial groups that attend top-rated colleges and universities has always been a bellwether for predicting affluent trends along these lines.

Fox Butterfield recently asked, "Why Are Asians Going to the Head of the Class?" (*The New York Times,* August 3, 1986). According to Butterfield, although Asian Americans made up only about 2.1 percent of the U.S. population, they accounted for 8 percent of all undergraduates at Harvard and for 11 percent of its freshman class. At the Massachusetts Institute of Technology, Asian Americans made up 19 percent of the undergraduate body and 21 percent of the freshman class, and at one of the finest state universities, the University of California at Berkeley, one in four undergraduates was an Asian American. According to the American Bar Association, the number of Asian Americans enrolled in accredited law schools nearly doubled from 1975 to 1985, and similar trends have been noted in the enrollment figures of medical schools and graduate schools.

In this same article, Murry Kahn, the assistant principal of New York City's elite Stuyvesant High School, stated: "The Asian-

Americans are very similar to the Jewish immigrants of the 1930s and 1940s . . . with their emphasis on learning and the family and the sheer energy they get from their new opportunity in America."

Despite their lust for learning and their high educational achievement, not many Asian Americans are selected for top corporate positions. In "Asian-Americans Charge Prejudice Slows Climb to Management Rank" (*The Wall Street Journal,* September 11, 1986), Winifred Yu contends that Asian Americans are often viewed as "the model minority" (i.e., diligent and dependable workers) and that employers seem more interested in hiring them for technical positions than for executive positions. Yu cites statistical evidence to support these contentions. In 1985, Asian Americans accounted for about 8 percent of all private-sector professionals and technicians but for only 1.3 percent of private-sector managers.

The difficulties that Asian Americans encounter in obtaining corporate executive positions probably translate into their choice of alternative fields. These fields often require high levels of education but not necessarily the pesonality and political orientation required by the corporate executive handbook. As a proportion of their respective populations, Asian Americans are several times more likely than whites to be medical doctors, engineers, architects, and scientific researchers.

Despite the barriers that prevent many Asian Americans from obtaining senior management positions as well as other forms of discrimination, many Asian Americans have reached the affluent income category. Jonathan E. Robbin, the founder of the Claritas Corporation, estimates that at the $100,000 (and higher) annual household income category, several Asian American subsegments are outperforming the white population in this country by a wide margin.

In terms of income, who are the most affluent Asian Americans? Only 14 of every 1,000 American households and only about 16 of every 1,000 white American households have annual incomes of $100,000 or more.[1] However, about 47 of every 1,000 Korean

---

[1] These 1988 estimates were based on the 1980 Decennial Census Study updated by the Census Bureau's 1984 Current Population Survey and adjusted to reflect the impact of inflation and changes in real income.

American households are in the affluent income category. Thus, Korean American households are almost three times as likely as white American households to be in the affluent income category and more than three times as likely as all U.S. households to be in this category.

The Asian-Indian subsegment also has a high proportion of affluent households, 47 per 1,000 households or about the same proportion as that of the Korean American subsegment. Several other Asian American segments also have a proportion of affluent households that is higher than the national norm. These subsegments include the Japanese Americans, the Chinese Americans, and the Filipino Americans. However, the proportion of affluent households is not nearly as high in these subsegments of the Asian American population as in either the Asian-Indian American or Korean American subsegments. Approximately 23 out of 1,000 households in these three subsegments are in the affluent income category. In many areas of the country, however, the Japanese American, Chinese American, and Filipino American populations are much larger than either the Asian-Indian American or Korean American populations. Moreover, the Japanese American population has almost double the average proportion of upper-middle-income ($50,000 to $100,000) households: 177 in 1,000 Japanese American households are in this income category, whereas in the population at large, only 94 in 1,000 households are in this category.

Given the high level of affluence within the Asian American segment as a whole, the relative lack of focused competitive threats in this segment, and the heavy concentration of the segment in only a few geographic areas, the Asian American segment holds great opportunities for the enlightened marketer.

UNDERSTANDING THE AFFLUENT ASIAN AMERICAN MARKET

The Asian American population has a significantly higher level of educational achievement than the American population in general. Only about 7 percent of the heads of households in the entire U.S. population have had two or more years of graduate school; however, more than 40 percent of Asian-Indian American household heads and about 17 percent of Korean American household heads have attained this level of education.

The high educational attainment of these two Asian American subsegments relates directly to their occupational status. Asian-Indian Americans are much more heavily concentrated than white Americans in the engineering and scientific professions and in the medical profession. Korean Americans are heavily concentrated in the medical profession and entrepreneurial ventures. Most of the other Asian American subsegments account for a disproportionate share of medical, technical, and entrepreneurial positions. The heavy concentration of Asian Americans in several key occupational categories is an important attribute for the marketer. This feature of the Asian American market segment coupled with other traits of this segment provides a foundation for a rifle marketing approach.

The Asian American Population

Although it might be argued that a market segment constituting about 2 percent of the U.S. population is a difficult one on which to focus, a counterargument, namely, the high geographic concentration of Asian Americans, is much more compelling. As mentioned, about 70 percent of Asian Americans live in just five states. In addition, about 90 percent of Asian Americans live in metropolitan areas. More Asian-Indian Americans live in New York than in any other state. However, California contains more of the other categories of Asian Americans than any other state.

Also, the Asian American population is growing rapidly. In "Why More Ads Aren't Targeting Asians," Yoshihashi cited statistics compiled by Leon F. Bouvier and Anthony Agresta, who made the following estimates of the size of the various Asian American subsegments in 1990 and of their respective percentage growth by the year 2000: Chinese Americans, 1,259,038 (33.7 percent); Asian-Indian Americans, 684,339 (47.0 percent); Japanese Americans, 804,535 (6.5 percent); Korean Americans, 814,495 (62.2 percent); Filipino Americans, 1,405,146 (47.4 percent); and Vietnamese Americans, 859,638 (83.0 percent). These growth rates are dramatically greater than the predicted 18 percent increase in the total U.S. population projected for the same time period by the most recent Census Bureau estimates.

The growth of the two most affluent Asian American sub-segments in two states is an important consideration for market strategists. It is estimated that by the year 2000, the Asian-Indian American population in California will number 133,000, an increase of 122 percent over the 1980 figure, and California's Korean American population will number 286,000, an increase of 178 percent. "By 1990 . . . estimated in the [San Francisco] Bay Area . . . [there will be] 400,000 Filipinos, 350,000 Chinese, 100,000 Vietnamese, 80,000 Japanese, 80,000 Koreans, and 50,000 Pacific Islanders (Eleanor Yu, "Asian-American Market Often Misunderstood," *Marketing News,* December 4, 1989, p. 11).

The Asian-Indian population of New York State is expected to reach 145,000 by the year 2000, a 113 percent increase, and the Korean American population of New York State is expected to reach 97,000, an increase of almost 200 percent.

> New York [City] has 950 Korean green-grocers. But Koreans in New York also run 1,100 delicatessens, liquor stores and grocery stores, 1,300 dry cleaners, 100 importers, 250 garment manufacturers, 700 general-merchandise stores, 600 to 700 fish markets and more than 400 nail salons. (Anne Newman, "Korean-Americans succeed in Business by Really Trying," *The Wall Street Journal,* December 13, 1989, p. B2)

Marketers of big-ticket consumer items, such as luxury automobiles, household furnishings, and financial services in the direct investment, whole life insurance, and asset management categories, are always interested in virgin affluent market segments. These are market segments in which a significant portion of the population is not being prospected at all or is being only lightly prospected. Members of such segments would be receptive to information about trends in products and services. The Asian American affluent market segment is a market segment of this kind.

Why are so many affluent Asian Americans ignored by marketers of big-ticket consumer durables and services? One reason is that some sales professionals give much weight to the argument that affluent Asian Americans prefer to deal only with other Asian Americans. It is believed, for example, that in the securities industry, a disproportionate share of affluent Asian American brokerage clients deal only with registered representatives who are also Asian Americans. However, such relationships were often established because Asian American registered representatives had a superior awareness of the Asian American market segment. Marketers should not allow themselves to operate under the often erroneous assumption that race is of overwhelming importance in explaining patronage habits. One very affluent Asian-Indian American physician recently suggested why he was so lightly prospected by security brokers: "I don't think they feel confident in the ability to pronounce my name correctly so they just move on down the list of wealthy physicians until they reach Jones or Smith."

Some marketers have ignored the Asian American segment because they believe that the affluent Asian American market has been fully accounted for by "other" providers. However, even within a narrowly defined product class, no rapidly growing affluent segment is likely to be deeply penetrated by one marketer.

An increasing number of Asian Americans, especially the younger Asian Americans, have been reaching the affluent income level in this country. The affluent Asian American market may be compared to a fast-moving stream. Ice cannot cover a fast-moving stream even during the coldest winter, and likewise, no marketer can monopolize the affluent Asian American market, which is perhaps the fastest-moving affluent stream in America. Thus, this market will continue to provide opportunities for those marketers who may have overlooked it.

What qualities of the affluent Asian American market account for these opportunities? Among the American population in general, the largest number of affluent households, those with incomes of $100,000 or more), are headed by individuals in the 45- to 55-year age bracket, since it typically takes a considerable number of years to achieve affluent status. Among Asian Americans, however, the largest number of affluent households are headed by individuals in the 35- to 44-year age bracket.

Highly trained Asian Americans often reach a six-figure income before their 40th birthday. This is especially true among top-grade physicians in well-paying specialties such as neurosurgery and orthopedic surgery. Many top-grade Asian American scientific researchers and scholars achieve affluent status before many Asian Americans in the medical profession. In addition, certain Asian American subsegments, such as the Korean Americans, are likely to achieve affluent status via the entrepreneurial route at a relatively young age.

Characteristics of Asian Americans

Despite having achieved affluent status at a much younger age than is typical, many foreign-born affluent Asian Americans have not yet solidified strong patronage habits. About 6 out of 10 Asian Americans were born outside the United States, and many of them were not commercially socialized in the same manner as most Americans. These Asian Americans often arrived in this country already well trained and well able to generate high income but without ever having encountered a single commercial message from an American marketer. The work ethic of Asian Americans and their aggressive pursuit of demanding careers often translate into a poverty of time for such activities as financial planning and shopping. This affluent segment can justly be called virgin territory.

There is a characteristic of many affluent Asian Americans that makes this segment particularly attractive to marketers of investments and related offerings: They are much less likely to be conspicuous consumers than are many of the other affluent segments in this country. Many affluent Asian Americans feel that an ostentatious lifestyle is in bad taste. Often, their marginal propensity to save and to invest is higher than that of other Americans in the same income/age category. For example, the 1980 population census showed that the proportion of households receiving between $500 and $5,000 in interest and dividend income per year was almost double among Japanese American households than among households in general (31.6 percent versus 17.9 percent). In addition, fully 61.5 percent of Japanese American households realized some interest income as opposed to 40 percent of all households in America. Many first- and second-generation affluent Asian Americans regard understatement of wealth as the proper perspective. My research suggests that the purchase of an expensive home or automobile by an Asian American may be undertaken because these artifacts are perceived as part of an occupational uniform and not as a symbolic way of communicating socioeconomic superiority. Thus, promotional themes directed to Asian Americans should emphasize normative occupational/reference group consumption patterns.

The affluent Asian American tends to borrow less money for the purchase of a home or business than do other affluent Americans. He is more likely to accumulate personal income and business income in anticipation of a major purchase. It is not unusual for members of this segment to invest a significantly greater proportion of their own (nonleveraged) dollars in a business or home than do other affluent Americans. This behavior provides an opportunity for financial service marketers.

Accumulating a considerable number of dollars in anticipation of a major purchase creates a problem for many Asian Americans. They seek advice about what to do with this short-term transition money, which sometimes exceeds six figures.

In a simple analysis, three segments of the affluent Asian American population can be conceptualized: (1) self-employed professionals, (2) entrepreneurs, and (3) highly paid scientific and technical employees. All three segments typically have a long-term planning horizon for investment goals. Planning for the distant future, especially for retirement, is a critical dimension even for affluent Asian Americans who are under 40 years of age. This may result from the fact that social security and pension systems are either nonexistent or unstable in their countries of origin. Despite the strength and stability of our own social security and corporate pension systems, many affluent Asian Americans prefer to invest more heavily for their retirement than other affluent Americans in the same age group.

Offerings of pension and profit-sharing services are of special interest to Asian American entrepreneurs and self-employed professionals. Tax-advantaged investments, including related insurance products, are especially interesting to the very highly paid Asian American scientists. The dollars that accumulate in pension plans, profit-sharing programs, and universal life insurance products may be considerable. As previously stated, many affluent Asian Americans reach the affluent income standard at a relatively early stage in their life cycle.

These future-oriented affluent prospects also attach considerable importance to business-related insurance. The family and the business are regarded as one and the same by many Asian Americans. Any threat to the business, such as the unexpected death or disability of a key contributor, is also viewed as a threat to family goals. Seven-figure face value insurance supported by the business and designed to compensate the family will assure continuity of the family's traditional lifestyle and high-quality college education for its children. Proposals for big-league key man insurance as well as buy-out plans are well received by many Asian American entrepreneurs and their families.

Most affluent Asian Americans (especially Asian-Indian Americans, Korean Americans, Chinese Americans, Japanese Americans, and Filipino Americans) will tell you that they attribute much of their success to their educational achievement. Thus, they regard high-quality education for their children as an absolute prerequisite to their families' continued success in this economy. Typically, the Asian American household sees the minimum educational requirement for its children as graduation from a top-grade undergraduate school plus advanced training. This type of education will probably cost between $100,000 and $300,000 by the turn of the century. The Asian American household with such educational goals seeks information and investment products that will help it achieve those goals.

The financial service needs of the affluent Asian American household can be viewed as a jacket with many pockets, each pocket representing a distinct financial goal and need. Among the pockets are transition into a new home, transition in anticipation of starting a business or a professional practice or of purchasing an existing business or an additional business, educational funding, and insurance funding.

Marketing Methods

The marketing methods used to find, approach, and penetrate the affluent Asian American segment are not radically different from the tactics used with other segments of affluent Americans.

Through geodemographic targeting, high concentrations of upscale Asian Americans can be identified. Updated small-area census data can provide valuable estimates about the productivity of alternative branch sites or direct-mail campaigns designed to capture a larger share of the affluent Asian American population. System-linked neighborhood typologies via the Claritas Corporation's Prizm System and syndicated advertising research studies can be used to evaluate media.

Identifying Asian-Americans who are self-employed professionals is not difficult. The professional categories that have the highest concentration of affluent Asian Americans are medicine and related health areas. Even the yellow pages can be scanned for Asian American surnames. However, identification is not the key issue in marketing to these affluent Americans.

Gaining the endorsement of key patronage opinion leaders is critical in penetrating this market, especially for marketers of investment management services, pension and profit-sharing programs, and large face value life insurance policies. Who are those opinion leaders? They include other successful Asian American professionals as well as the accountants and attorneys they patronize.

Affluent Asian American prospects in the medical profession are often most influenced by their so-called mentors. These mentors are often other successful Asian Americans who helped the prospects with their educational or professional development. However, it is not unusual for the mentors to be white Americans.

Mentors are very often found in high concentrations among the faculty of medical schools and teaching hospitals. Thus, one of the most important lists that the marketer should obtain is that of medical school faculty. The endorsement of a single mentor can generate dozens of affluent Asian American clients.

A growing number of Asian American physicians have been emerging as leading authorities within various medical specialties. Ask the typical Asian American physician whom he most admires. More often than not, he is likely to mention the leading authorities within his specialty. Thus, the marketer should concentrate on capturing the business of those who are considered authorities. Having such individuals as clients assures the marketer that some of their esteem and credibility will rub off on him.

How does one go about finding these authorities? Visit a medical school library and examine the current literature. People who write articles in prestigious journals and certain kinds of books are typically perceived as being authorities. If you gain the endorsements of such authorities, you can leverage those endorsements in marketing to affluent Asian American physicians all over the country. Too often, marketers fail to capitalize on such endorsements outside the metropolitan area in which they live. Endorsements from mentors/authorities are often so powerful among Asian

American professionals that by means of such endorsements, the business of these professionals can be captured by long-distance telephone.

Affluent Asian American entrepreneurs can also be identified and marketed successfully. Almost every metropolitan area of any size has some affluent Asian American business owners. Often, information about their success and stature is not published in the local "for general consumption" newspaper. In that case, the marketer must turn to the Asian American newspapers for information about these affluent prospects. Almost every ethnic group in America has its own newspaper, and many ethnic groups have several. Some of these newspapers are more business oriented than others. A marketer who wants to identify affluent Korean American business owners should subscribe to newspapers and related periodicals that publish articles about them.

Asian American business owners whose endeavors are publicized are often patronage opinion leaders. Thus, the marketer should concentrate his initial efforts on obtaining the business and the endorsement of such opinion leaders. These opinion leaders are often held in very high esteem both by other affluent Asian American entrepreneurs and by Asian American entrepreneurs who aspire to be affluent.

There are also other sources that can be used to identify affluent Asian American business owners. Like other affluent American segments, affluent Asian Americans tend to regard their accountants and attorneys as credible sources of patronage information. Other excellent sources of such information are local business organizations such as the Korean American business owners' association or the Asian-Indian American business owners' association. The enlightened marketer will focus on the leaders of such groups. These leaders have a significant influence on the choice of speakers for monthly meetings. Speaking at such a meeting is an endorsement by the group's leadership of the presenter and his offerings. Yet, business organizations of this kind often have to expend considerable effort in order to obtain speakers for their meetings.

The marketer should always position himself as an expert who is willing and able to speak to Asian American business owners' groups. His image as an expert will also be enhanced if he is quoted in the Asian American press and more widely distributed business periodicals. Many affluent Asian Americans are extremely receptive to marketing approaches from those who have been endorsed by credible media sources. For example, a well-placed article about how a financial consultant helped selected Asian American business owners with their pension and personal investing problems will generate inquiries from other Asian American business owners with similar needs. The marketer who wishes to penetrate the affluent Asian American segment should therefore place a high priority on public relations. In this context, it is important for the marketer to cultivate good relations with the Asian American press as well as the more general business media.

Without personal endorsements from patronage opinion leaders and/or media support, it is difficult for a marketer to penetrate the Asian American entrepreneur market. It is often advisable to gain media support before seeking endorsements from opinion leaders. A simple rule should govern relationships with the press: Share your knowledge with the press, and it will give you coverage. The marketer should scan Asian American print media, and anytime an article relating to his area of expertise appears, he should inform the reporter of his interest and provide additional insights. Most important, he should tell the reporter of his willingness to provide information in the future, especially in interview format. The marketer's communication objective must be to become an important information resource for business writers and reporters. This applies both to the Asian American press and to more widely distributed communication vehicles, such as *Time, Business Week, The Wall Street Journal,* and *Fortune.*

High-income Asian American employees in the scientific and technological areas are also an important market. A high proportion of the top scientific, technological, and medical researchers in this country are Asian Americans. These affluent individuals are often overlooked by marketers, but not because they are Asian Americans. Such individuals tend to be neglected, whether or not they are Asian Americans, because most marketers—even many seasoned marketers—believe that university faculty are not affluent. In fact, many university faculty members are very well paid, the highest-paid faculty members often being members of medical school teaching staffs. It is not at all unusual for even a junior member of a medical school faculty to have a salary in excess of $100,000. A growing number of medical school faculty are Asian Americans. In addition to their base salary, many supplement their incomes by writing books, providing consulting services, inventing technological innovations, and so on.

Other fields with a disproportionate number of high-income Asian Americans include advanced engineering, architecture, and scientific research. It is surprising how little prospecting is directed at affluent Asian Americans in these fields. Some telephone or mail prospecting does take place in cases where the potential client has a "Dr." in front of his or her name. However, cold calling such individuals is not very productive.

As with the groups discussed above, personal influence and credibility are important issues for these affluent Asian Americans, and the persons whom they are most likely to hold in high esteem are, once again, the persons whose achievements they admire. The opinion leaders of these well-educated prospects include their major professors/mentors and their most productive colleagues. Here, productivity refers to publishing significant research, receiving awards/recognitions of achievement by peer groups, and developing important innovations. Gaining endorsements from such opinion leaders can be leveraged throughout the related professional community almost independent of geographic location.

To gain the endorsement of such opinion leaders, the marketer must be perceived by them as a credible source of product and/or service and related intelligence. Enlightened marketers will attempt to gain credibility in three ways: (1) obtaining endorsements from the prospects' employers, (2) publishing articles and letters to the editor in trade journals and periodicals, and (3) becoming active in the trade associations that the prospects patronize.

Many employers of these affluent prospects and the prospects themselves recognize the need for quality financial planning. Such employers are often willing to provide complete funding for periodic financial planning for their employees.

Few marketers of financial services have ever published an article about the financial problems of high-income scientists. Certainly, some of the trade journals read by scientists would be receptive to such material. Also, many of the trade organizations that such prospects join would be delighted to have financial experts address their membership. In addition to speaking engagements of this type, there are trade show/conference opportunities. Such activities would create a favorable image for the marketer in the eyes of both employers and patronage opinion leaders within various scientific fields.

The enlightened marketer will use his endorsements from credible publications and trade/scientific associations to penetrate the core of patronage opinion leaders. Once this has been done, he can use these opinion leaders as sources of influence and prospect information. Affluent Asian American scientists as well as other affluent scientists often perceive the leaders in their fields as being more than experts in science, so that even the consumption patterns of such scientists are often influenced by the opinions of these leaders.

ON BECOMING AN ADVOCATE OF AFFLUENT AFFINITY GROUPS

David Monday, a marketing executive, once related to me his favorite case study on how to capitalize upon the advocacy concept. How did a young financial consultant successfully prospect the chief executive officer of a major oil company?

The young financial consultant apparently read an article in a major newspaper that condemned this oil company for being insensitive to environmental issues. The half-page article never said one positive thing about the company. It only mentioned its oil spills, which were actually minor compared to most. It also expressed outrage over the insensitivity of the firm exemplified in its history of drilling in environmentally sensitive areas. Moreover, it criticized the firm for not using double-hulled ships that would reduce the possibility of oil spills from punctures in tankers. And the article finally pointed out that the firm did not support research and development on alternative fuel systems. Not one good word was written in the article. The article was, in fact, one-sided.

The company actually had one of the better track records in reducing the probability of oil spills, as well as cleaning up those for which it was responsible. It also gave up many options to drill in some environmentally sensitive areas. Moreover, the firm donated millions to support minority courses and education. And it was voted as one of the best companies for which to work. It had an outstanding minority hiring program and a program that supported women's rights, and it even contributed heavily to environmental causes.

So, what did this bright, articulate financial consultant do after reading the criticisms in the newspaper article? The financial consultant wrote a long letter to the editor of the newspaper. His letter was titled "The Other Side of the Argument." He pointed out that the reporter who wrote the article had a bias in reporting the news.

The young financial consultant also specified in the article all the positive things that the firm had done in relationship to environmental, as well as other important issues. In essence, he talked about the good side of the firm.

He sent a copy of the letter to the editor of the newspaper, but he also sent a copy to the chairman and chief executive officer of the oil company. He addressed the envelope and placed the words *Personal* and *Confidential* on it. He included a note with the letter. It stated, "I appreciate all the good work you and your firm have done for this nation and our energy problems. Our firm and many of our clients frequently suffer from the bias, self-serving mentality, the selective perception and shallow research and reporting of the popular press. Therefore, we have some common ground. I hope we will have a chance to talk over these issues in more detail in the future."

Shortly after receiving the letter from the financial consultant, the chief executive officer called him and not long after that opened a sizable account with the young man.

I am sure that the CEO of the oil company received hundreds of nasty letters as a result of the negative press that it received in the newspaper article. But it is more than likely that only the one empathetic financial consultant wrote a letter to the editor of the newspaper and sent a copy along with a personalized note to the CEO.

I am also reasonably certain that buying any product or service on the personal side was way down on the list of priorities of the CEO in light of the recent bad press and letters he received. So, how smart was this financial consultant to focus on the number one need of this CEO? More than any product or service at this particular moment in time, the CEO needed an advocate, a supporter. Probably the only advocate and supporter who sent a letter, as an advocate should do, to a newspaper was the financial consultant.

The CEO couldn't help but appreciate this clever marketing, this reciprocal relationship and, in fact, was sensitized to buying something from someone who offered more than the mundane core product.

One can read each and every day newspaper articles that criticize affluent targets. Correspondingly, each day a sales professional could write a letter to the editor supporting those criticized by the press. But this policy can quickly become very stale. In essence, it is a tactic to become a temporary or part-time advocate.

Part-time advocates may, in fact, be viewed as manipulators, and the entire concept may be seen as a subterfuge on the part of the sales professional to gain a business relationship. In the long run, it is much more productive to be a permanent advocate for the cause of affluent affinity and affiliation groups.

A fast-track young professional once approached me and said, "I am black but most of my clients are not. Should I spend more time relating to my own racial affinity group?" What I said to this young man relates to the broad spectrum of marketing to the affluent. Affiliation in regard to the problems and opportunities within your prospects' and clients' careers, that is, relating to industry and business, is much more important than one's race, sex, age, geographic location, language, or anything else. Target those with specific and common problems relating to career, well-being, revenue, politics, and so forth.

Along these lines, think about the enormous opportunities that sales professionals have in this country to become advocates of affluent affinity groups. There are countless affluent affinity groups in this nation that are desperately in need of strong advocates and supporters. These groups range from affluent women to high-income-producing fishing fleet owners. Women often face bias in competing with men for high-paying positions. They frequently have to contend with the bureaucracy and red tape of government regulations, while fishing fleet owners must endure their own form of bureaucracy and archaic legislation and mandates about fishing.

It is not possible to reflect upon the needs of various affluent affinity groups. However, the suggestions given below provide a pro forma analysis of how one might develop oneself into an advocacy position for one of the important affiliation groups in this country.

One afternoon a young financial consultant telephoned me. He had heard me speak about the enormous potential of affluent Asians in the United States. I also discussed the concept of geographic anatomy of affluent Asians. One of the issues addressed was affluent Vietnamese business owners in the United States.

This young man told me that he had little success in prospecting Vietnamese Americans. He claimed that a language and ethnic barrier made it difficult for him to explain his offering. He said, "It's hard to get them on the phone, and once on the phone, it's difficult to communicate with them."

My reply in truncated form was, "Your focus is your product, not their problem. First be an advocate; then be a financial consultant."

A LETTER TO A FRUSTRATED FINANCIAL CONSULTANT

Dear Marketer:

I regret that you have failed to penetrate the affluent Vietnamese American segment within your trade area. It is more than likely that your lack of success with this particular segment relates more to approach than to the opportunity available. Telephoning these people can be a difficult way to sell. Yes, there is a language barrier; still, many of these people would prefer to deal with someone in person. In addition, from what you have told me, you have essentially discussed your product and your problem and not really related to the problem that many of these people face.

Their problems are more than investments. In fact, they want to deal with not only an investment expert but someone who has a demonstrated interest in the unique needs of this affinity group. These needs very often transcend financial services and, particularly, investments.

It may be useful for you to hire a sales assistant as a young superstar in the insurance industry recently has done. This young man hired a Vietnamese American sales assistant to help him prospect among the affluent American Vietnamese business owners in the community. In less than six months, this young sales professional and his assistant sold enough life insurance in this segment of the population for him to become the number one agent in a large agency.

With your unique background, it may be useful for you to become more than just someone who sells financial services to this segment. In fact, you may wish to become an advocate for Vietnamese Americans. But to do so you must have a sincere liking and affinity for these people and their specialized problems. You must be willing to make a long-term commitment to these people and the issues which are most significant for them. Becoming an advocate will take a considerable amount of time, but it will greatly enhance your ability to penetrate into this market.

You can continue to telephone affluent Vietnamese Americans and continually find that they are not interested in investing with you. This directly relates to the message as well as the method of communication.

I would suggest that you try an alternative strategy. Walk into a business owned by an affluent Vietnamese American. Speak to the owner directly. Ask about the owner's concern for his brothers and sisters and fellow countrymen that would very much like to become naturalized American citizens also. This is one of the most compelling emotional issues among this segment. If, in fact, you can develop an advocacy position to help these people improve the plight of the Vietnamese who seek citizenship, you will go a long way in developing a strong affiliation with your target.

I have enclosed some information along these lines. This information may be helpful in the context of you developing an advocacy position. Enclosed you will find a pro forma post card that will provide evidence of your being an advocate to this group. The post card, you will note, is addressed to George Bush, the president of the United States. The message on the back, as you can see, asks the president to put pressure on the British and Hong Kong governments regarding the Vietnamese refugees that are now in camps in Hong Kong. Both of these governments have a policy that these 50,000 refugees be forcibly repatriated and returned to Vietnam. This is a burning issue among many Vietnamese Americans. Also enclosed is a suggested news release indicating and promoting you as an advocate along the lines of helping these Vietnamese refugees.

You will find by approaching and asking affluent Vietnamese American business owners to sign one or more of these post cards that they will want to talk to you about your products, your services, and your problems.

I hope that this information will be useful. Please keep in touch and advise me of your continued success.

Sincerely,

Thomas J. Stanley, Ph.D.
Chairman, The Affluent Market Institute

PRO FORMA POSTCARD PROVIDING
EVIDENCE OF BEING AN ADVOCATE

	STAMP
Mr. George Bush	
The President	
The White House	
Washington, D.C. 20500	

Date: _____

Dear Mr. President:

We urge you to use your influence in changing the inhuman policies adopted by both the British and Hong Kong governments regarding the future of thousands of Vietnamese refugees. Encourage them to grant political asylum to those Vietnamese boat people who are now living in the squalor of camps in Hong Kong. Forced repatriation of these people will greatly tarnish the image that Americans have of the British and Hong Kong colony's leaders. How can these governments, which claim to be democratic, turn their backs on these thousands of men, women and children who have risked their lives to reach freedom? To ignore this problem, Mr. President, is to endorse these inhuman policies and to support the wishes of the barbarians in Hanoi. We also ask you to urge all of the other countries in the free world to offer a home for these freedom loving refugees.

NAME (Print) _____ Signature _____

STREET _____

CITY _____ STATE _____ ZIP _____

TELEPHONE (___) _____

PRO FORMA NEWS RELEASE PROVIDING
EVIDENCE OF BEING AN ADVOCATE

ACME SECURITY COMPANY

FOR IMMEDIATE RELEASE
APRIL 22
CONTACT: AMY McCLUNG
111/197-9999

WAR VETERAN PETITIONS THE PRESIDENT
TO SUPPORT VIETNAMESE REFUGEES

Are we turning our backs on the Vietnamese refugees who want to live in a free country? According to Larry John-Doe, that is exactly what our government is doing. Mr. John-Doe, a locally based financial consultant, is trying to change our president's policy concerning the 50,000 Vietnamese refugees who are now living in wretched conditions in camps in Hong Kong.

According to Mr. John-Doe, "Our president, by doing nothing about this problem, in fact has endorsed the policy of forced repatriation adopted by both the British and Hong Kong governments. Forcing freedom-loving people to return to Vietnam violates the principles upon which a democracy is built. It is inhuman to support these policies and to play into the hands of the barbarians in Hanoi."

Mr. John-Doe is taking matters into his own hands. He is once again helping Vietnamese. In 1968, as an Airborne Ranger, he was credited with saving the entire population of a village near the Ashau Valley. The village was scheduled for attack by nearly 200 North Vietnamese army troops.

Today, Mr. John-Doe has an even tougher battle. He is trying to persuade Washington to pressure the Hong Kong and British governments into reversing their policy of forced repatriation. He is also an advocate of having all democratic nations offer political asylum to those freedom-loving refugees.

Mr. John-Doe stated that he first became aware of the problems of these refugees when "several of my Vietnamese American clients told me that they wanted to help these refugees in

(concluded)

some way, but they felt powerless." But Mr. John-Doe told them that they had political power and grass-roots support. He then initiated a campaign to send thousands of "protest post cards" to the president of the United States and selected members of the Senate and House of Representatives (see enclosure).

Mr. John-Doe asked each of his current clients to sign a protest post card and send it to Washington. He has also requested that several thousand other concerned Americans in our area send protest cards to our government leaders. His goal is to generate at least 10,000 protest messages and deliver them to Washington. In addition, Mr. John-Doe is networking with four other financial consultants in four other cities that contain high concentrations of Vietnamese Americans. He stated, "We plan to initiate our protest card campaign throughout the United States.

Mr. John-Doe has spoken to several local civil and trade associations on the topic of the plight of the Vietnamese refugees who face forced repatriation. He has been successful in gaining the support of many members of these groups. Mr. John-Doe is scheduled to speak on May 2 to the Vietnamese American Business Owners Association from 1:00 P.M. to 1:45 P.M. at the Great South Hall.

CHAPTER 7

PROSPECTING SUCCESSFUL AUTHORS

INTRODUCTION

An ever-increasing number of affluent prospects refuse to even speak with you. Even those who will initially listen to your introduction cut you off and end the conversation abruptly. How can you win if your prospect is so skittish? The same time-tested methods of prospecting, approaching, and capturing important targets are becoming less and less productive. You are not alone. Many sales professionals in America are finding out that traditional prospecting methods often result in merely frightening the quarry.

Some extraordinary sales professionals in this country are extremely productive in soliciting business by unconventional means. Their methods are different and often successful even under some of the harshest conditions. Their solution to the problem of relating to timid targets can be classified as "prospecting by defense." Actually, prospecting by defense, like many other marketing concepts, is deeply rooted in military practice. Take, for example, the events that took place on November 19, 1941. On that day, the heavily armed Australian cruiser HMAS *Sydney* was sunk in the Indian Ocean off the western coast of Australia. It is not unusual for capital ships to be sunk during wartime. What is unusual are the circumstances under which the sinking took place.

Was the *Sydney* sunk by a vastly superior foe? Was it devastated by a large group of heavily armed capital ships or a squadron of dive bombers? No! The *Sydney* was destroyed by an adversary less than one-third its size and one that had only about one-half its speed. The *Sydney* was lost without a single known survivor. It was dispatched so quickly that it was unable to even radio a distress call. The *Sydney* was sunk by what its crew thought was a small (7,000 ton) friendly freighter. Why else would *Sydney*'s captain venture so close to the *Kormoran?* Why else would *Sydney* come to almost a complete stop within 2,000 yards of an unidentified vessel? Yes, *Sydney* was a major-league ship with heavy armor plate and large cannons. But it was targeted and destroyed because *Sydney*'s captain assumed that the small, innocent-appearing freighter must be on defense—could only be on defense. Correspondingly, *Sydney*'s crew, sitting behind its armor plate and large metal-piercing projectiles, could only believe that they were on offense.

> *Sydney* . . . rashly approached . . . *Kormoran* suddenly . . . torpedoed her. . . . a terrible example of the dangers of approaching an unidentified merchant ship too closely . . . without proper precautions. [Patrick Beesley, *Very Special Intelligence,* (London: Hamish Hamilton, 1977), p. 92]

The HMAS *Sydney* was a capital ship that was defeated because it let down its defenses. The *Kormoran* was one of the several

> . . . ghost cruisers . . . converted merchant ships of some 7,000 tons . . . fitted out with dummy funnels, telescopic masts, false derricks, and deck guns, all of which conjure the appearance of a peaceful merchantman, but concealed behind hydraulically operated flaps were batteries of guns and torpedo tubes. [Terry Hughes and John Costello, *The Battle of The Atlantic* (New York: The Dial Press, 1977), p. 75]

Sales professionals who target the affluent can learn a great deal from the exploits of the *Kormoran.* This is not to say that you should ever deceive clients into thinking that you are not in the business of selling. However, it is important to focus on the needs of the prospect. Often, the needs of the targets relate to their desire to be on offense. Most affluent people in this country have a product or service that they must market. Some extraordinary sales professionals approach their targets by first focusing on this need—the need of the target. This is especially important during the initial stages of your first contact with an affluent prospect. Targets will find it difficult to cut your conversations short if you demonstrate something other than a purely offensive posture. Some targets need to be told that they are winners and that their company and products are outstanding. I know of several ESPs who actually purchased their targets' products during their initial contact. Allowing the prospects to think that they are on the offense and you are at least partially on defense is a technique that works well for some top-producing sales professionals.

ROBERT READ

Robert Read's method of prospecting by defense is the best version of this game that I have witnessed to date. All of us can benefit from the marketing genius of Robert Read. In the telephone dialogue that follows, Read demonstrates why he is considered to be an ace among aces in capturing business by playing defense. Follow the steps that he employs in successfully persuading the affluent.

Step One.   Identify suspected affluent target that is likely to be euphoric because of favorable changes in economic and/or career situations.

Robert Read has something in common with many very successful marketers. He reads a great deal. But while some only read for enjoyment, Read also exploits his passion for reading in terms of finding prospects that are worthwhile contacting. His initial contact is made when he senses that the target is in the proper mood or can be readily placed in the mood to be sold. Those prospects most likely to say yes to his offers are euphoric. Euphoric in this context refers to a prospect's feeling of excitement over positive changes in financial situations and/or recognition of significant career achievements.

Where does Mr. Read find his targets? As the head of British Naval Intelligence during World War I once stated, 95 percent of intelligence comes from public sources. Mr. Read exploits public information sources that others ignore. He prospects those who write or are written about in newspapers, magazines, and even trade journals. He also prospects a selected group of those who advertise their products and services. Most people view advertisements as offers to buy; Mr. Read views them as opportunities to sell to those whom he suspects are generating significant revenues.

Step Two.   *Contact, qualify, and initiate the conditioning process of a prospect suspected to be euphoric. Encourage prospect to play offensive and boast of his achievements. Control by listening, not by talking. Encourage prospect to convince himself that his new station in life warrants adopting you and your offerings.*

First contact: Late morning, middle of the week.

DR. STANLEY:

Hello, this is Tom Stanley.

ROBERT READ:

Good morning, Dr. Stanley. My name is Robert Read. I noticed that your book was advertised in *The Wall Street Journal* today. Your publisher must feel that they have a winner in *Marketing to the Affluent* to give it its own quarter of a page.

DR. STANLEY:

Well, we all have high expectations.

ROBERT READ:

Was the advertisement for the book just in the eastern edition of the *Journal?*

DR. STANLEY:

No, the ad appeared in all regions—national exposure.

ROBERT READ:

Your publisher is one of the best in the business . . . very, very serious about selecting manuscripts. They must think your book will be a major success if they are spending dollars for national coverage in the *Journal.*

DR. STANLEY:

You know, all the reviewers like the material. I can send you their comments if you would be interested.

ROBERT READ:

Dr. Stanley, I'm already sold—just from the three statements that were made by the reviewers in the *Journal.*

DR. STANLEY:

Well, I hope you're not disappointed. There is a money-back guarantee.

ROBERT READ:

I'm convinced that I won't ask for my money back. But let me tell you why I called. First, I want to be among the first to congratulate you on your achievement. I'm sure your family is proud of you.

DR. STANLEY:

They, especially the children, view it as a major factor in negotiating an increase in their weekly allowance. My wife is just as glad it's over. I estimate that Janet made more than 1.5 million key strokes in word processing the first and second drafts of the manuscript.

ROBERT READ:

Well, speaking of family, I want to purchase three copies of your book. My son will graduate from college this coming spring. He would really enjoy reading a copy of *Marketing to the Affluent*—he can find out how his dad makes a living, and I want a copy of my own.

DR. STANLEY:

I'm not sure that the book stores in your area have the book on the shelf. Let me suggest that you call the 800 number listed in the *Journal*.

ROBERT READ:

I can't wait a couple of weeks. I want the book this week.

DR. STANLEY:

Well, you can call the special-order person at the publisher. That should cut the delivery time in half—a week to 10 days.

ROBERT READ:

No, that won't do. I'm wondering—do you have any copies of the book that you could sell to me?

DR. STANLEY:

Yes, I do have some.

ROBERT READ:

Could you send me three copies today by Federal Express?

DR. STANLEY:

I would be delighted. They are expensive you know—$49.95 each, not including air express charges.

ROBERT READ:

Not a problem. Send it Federal Express today.

DR. STANLEY:

You will have them tomorrow morning. Give me your full name and address.

ROBERT READ:

Dr. Stanley, let me ask you for a favor. Would you mind autographing the books. I love quality books and very much admire authors. In fact, I have a collection of first editions—autographed books by some of America's best writers. I want to add yours to my collection. Your book will be in excellent company. My collection includes . . . [Read names five best-selling authors as "just for example."]

DR. STANLEY:

I would be delighted to autograph your books.

ROBERT READ:

Now for my son's copy. I would like it to say the following: "Bob, Jr., with the compliments of your father, Robert Read. Regards, Tom Stanley."

DR. STANLEY:

And what about the third copy?

ROBERT READ:

It's for the young salesman in the office who thinks of me as his mentor. I get a great deal of satisfaction helping youngsters move ahead. I want him to have it as a gift from his mentor.

DR. STANLEY:

Bob, you're very kind to share your ideas with those young sales professionals who show potential. I find the biggest producers in the sales force are those most willing to act as mentors. Thanks for your order.

ROBERT READ:

Tom, have you ever considered becoming a dean of a school of business? The reason that I ask is that there is an opening at the business school up here. You are ideally suited for the task. You have a practical view of business. They need someone who can relate to the businessman—somebody with a worldly view of what a business program should be all about.

DR. STANLEY:

Well, it's nice of you to ask, Bob, but I never enjoyed the bureaucratic red tape with which administrators have to deal. The best things about a university are contact with students and being paid for reading and researching—for constantly improving your knowledge. Administrators lose out in both cases.

ROBERT READ:

I understand, but I would still think about it if I were you. I'll put a check in the mail today. Good talking with you.

DR. STANLEY:

It was good talking with you, Bob. I hope you enjoy the material. Bye.

Step Three.   *Condition, condition, and continue to condition the prospect. Encourage the prospect to place himself in your debt and continue to stimulate target offensive posture. Position yourself as a defensive player. Continue to stimulate the prospect's need to boast. Raise the prospect's sensitivity to balance his new status position with his adoption of your service offerings.*

Second contact: Late morning, middle of the week.

DR. STANLEY:

Tom Stanley.

ROBERT READ:

Tom, this is Bob Read. I have just read a portion of your book.

DR. STANLEY:

What do you think of the book?

ROBERT READ:

You have captured the essence of how to market to wealthy people.

DR. STANLEY:

Does this mean you like it? Will it enhance your productivity?

ROBERT READ:

It would take someone a lifetime to learn to sell like this. It took me 30 years to figure it out, and you have it all right here in one place. It's amazing!

DR. STANLEY:

Well, I spent many long days and nights in the effort. I hope it will help a lot of sales people out there who are trying to succeed.

ROBERT READ:

Tom, I already learned some things that I know will work in increasing my production, and I'm in the top fraction of the investment industry already. I started marketing independent asset managers before this concept became a product.

DR. STANLEY:

Well, I appreciate your comments, especially since you're a major-league producer. This tells me that less productive people will also benefit from these ideas.

ROBERT READ:

It's going to change my marketing style. I now know that I have been doing some things incorrectly—not fully exploiting opportunities in targeting—the Big-League Orientation.

DR. STANLEY:

Bob, have you ever published some of your ideas?

ROBERT READ:

I have good ideas, but I never published—thought it would be a waste. My neighbors don't know who I am . . . how successful I am. Tell me, where do you get all these great ideas?

DR. STANLEY:

Bob, if you want to catch a cold, associate with sick people. If you want to learn a great deal about marketing, talk to the top markɜters, like yourself. I interview top-producing sales and marketing professionals on a regular basis. And naturally, when I speak to a group of ESPs as I often do, the opportunity is always there to gain some intelligence about how the cream of the crop markets to the affluent.

ROBERT READ:

So, you give speeches on the topic of selling to the affluent? The reason I ask—our firm could benefit from your program. Would you be interested in something like this. Now that I think about it, a few of our top producers in the region have heard your speech.

DR. STANLEY:

I would be delighted.

ROBERT READ:

Could you send me any materials on your programs? I'll pass them along and see if we can get you up here for a day or two. I'm sure that our managers would be interested in sponsoring you. You certainly have my endorsement. I'll even pick you up at the airport.

DR. STANLEY:

I have spoken at many meetings of top producers. In fact, I was the top-rated speaker at the Wharton Institute. Also, I was the main platform speaker at the Million Dollar Roundtable's international convention.

ROBERT READ:

Tom, have you ever thought about doing consulting with individuals? I pay a fellow each year to help me plan my time better. We talk by phone from time to time. It really does not take much of his time or mine. It seems that your material would be a natural for some kind of an arrangement like that.

DR. STANLEY:

It's very difficult to service hundreds of individual producers.

ROBERT READ:

Okay, well, I understand. Let me find out about having you speak up here and I will get back to you. So long.

DR. STANLEY:

Goodbye, Bob. Thanks for your support. I really appreciate your comments about the book.

Step Four. *Continue to condition your prospect. Deploy the added conditioning dimension of fulfillment of affiliation need. Most affluent targets need to affiliate with those in their profession/ industry. Test speculation of prospect's upswing in current cash flow, feelings of indebtedness, and consistency needs by making a trial close.*

A week passed before Robert Read called again.

Third contact: Late morning, middle of the week.

DR. STANLEY:

Tom Stanley.

ROBERT READ:

Hello, Tom. Bob Read. I wanted to get back to you about coming up and speaking to our group. Our management has agreed. We just need to work out the details.

DR. STANLEY:

Bob, that is terrific. I appreciate the opportunity.

ROBERT READ:

Listen, Tom, while I have you on the phone, I want to ask you if you would be interested in doing appearances at book stores and autographing your book. I know several people in the business; they are friends and clients.

DR. STANLEY:

Bob, I really appreciate your suggestion, but *Marketing to the*

Affluent is not an impulse item. I think that only those that are presold before they walk into the store will buy. And it's an expensive book designed for a targeted audience.

ROBERT READ:

Well, Tom, I will still talk to some of my contacts in the book business to see if they have some suggestions for promoting your product.

DR. STANLEY:

I would like to hear what they have to suggest.

ROBERT READ:

Say, have you ever considered joining a literary club? I'm a member of one of the most prestigious literary clubs in America. Everybody in writing and publishing are members. You should join as a nonresident member. It's not expensive, and you can meet the who's who in your field. I have some information about the organization. Are you interested?

DR. STANLEY:

Yes, Bob. Please send it to me. It sounds like the type of people I should get to know. Maybe I can sell them all a copy of my book!

ROBERT READ:

How is your book selling, by the way?

DR. STANLEY:

Quite well, I understand. In fact, one firm just bought copies for all of their top producers. The biggest wholesaler in the West just reordered. That's a major indicator of high future sales.

ROBERT READ:

I know your book will be a success. And it's your ideas that are selling. You are going to have to figure out what to do with the royalties. Is anyone helping you? Who is your stockbroker?

DR. STANLEY:

He is Mr. O.

ROBERT READ:

Is he any good?

DR. STANLEY:

Well, he is an important generator of revenue for my firm. He and his firm are clients, very important clients. In fact, all of our investment business goes to our clients.

ROBERT READ:

Well, investment performance is most important, isn't it?

DR. STANLEY:

Yes, of course, but other factors such as reciprocal relationships also play a major part. Mr. O. and his firm helped pay for my house. Anyway, Bob, I have not yet received even my first royalty check.

ROBERT READ:

Oh, I agree with reciprocity. Well, let's talk soon. We will need to firm up a date for your program up here.

DR. STANLEY:

I look forward to talking with you. So long.

Step Five. *Recontact prospect when he is expected to be euphoric because of forecasted changes in his cash flow.*

Robert Read called just 22 hours after the target received his first royalty check.

DR. STANLEY:

Tom Stanley.

ROBERT READ:

Hello, Tom. Bob Read calling.

DR. STANLEY:

Hello, Bob.

ROBERT READ:

I just called to see if anything new was going on at your house!

[To be continued]

Five Dimensions of Robert Read

Robert Read's marketing methods are superior to traditional selling methods employed by most of those who target the affluent. Bob is a major producer in terms of revenue. He is a giant in regard to his innovative marketing skills. He is a member of a group I call the aces in persuading the affluent.

The telephone conversation that I had with Mr. Read does not give the full story of his marketing genius. Thus, it is appropriate to reflect upon the major components that explain Bob's success.

(1) Courage
All great extraordinary sales professionals (ESPs) have courage. Bob is no exception. He never gives the impression of being uncomfortable while conversing with major-league affluent targets. Nor is he intimidated by the status/success symbols that are often associated with some of his prospects/clients.

While Bob has achieved ESP status, he is constantly in search of new business. He is a master of telephone contact. But part of his success is the warmth of his calls. He knows what people want to hear. He understands and communicates in the language of the target. Remember, ice cold calls make cowards of many of us, while warm calls produce ESPs.

Courage is a direct function of practice in asking the question of patronage relationships. But the way in which the question is asked and the quality of the foundation that has been laid down by the sales professionals directly relate to their level of courage.

Let us compare Bob's method of asking the P (patronage) question with a fellow who called me the day after he attended one of my recent seminars. Mark is a 33-year-old registered representative with a CPA background. He recently accepted his first "sales" position with a major securities firm.

DR. STANLEY:

Tom Stanley.

MARK O.:

Ah . . . ah, Dr. Stanley, I did not expect you to answer the phone.

DR. STANLEY:

Do you want to speak with someone else?

MARK O.:

Ah . . . ah, no. I heard you speak yesterday. I'm just getting into the business. I was an accountant. But I think I can make more money in the investment business.

DR. STANLEY:

You may be right. How can I help you, young man?

MARK O.:

Well, I'm calling people today to see if they have an interest in mutual funds. You would not be interested in investing your money in a mutual fund, would you?

DR. STANLEY:

Are you telling me not to buy mutual funds from you? Are you asking me for my business?

MARK O.:

I'm just getting started in the business, and I'm not very good at this yet. I guess you don't want to listen to some of my suggestions.

DR. STANLEY:

Not if you don't feel comfortable about telling me! Courage, as I told you yesterday, is the fundamental characteristic of all ESPs.

MARK O.:

Well, Dr. Stanley, would you mind if I called you some time in the future?

DR. STANLEY:

Not at all, Mark. Call me anytime. Bye-bye.

How do Robert Read and Mark O. differ? Clearly, Robert Read has more experience in the business. But he has something else. He conquers fear and apprehension by understanding the needs of the target. In other words, he has an excellent idea of what the people in his targeted cluster want to hear before he calls someone. He has considerable knowledge of the needs of several important segments of the affluent market. And Bob has the battle-proven technique for charming the target. In turn, the sources of information that he uses in identifying prospects also provide Bob with intelligence about the needs of the target and the words the client wants to hear. All these factors contribute to Bob's special brand of courage—the courage to cold call big targets on a regular basis.

(2) Knowledge
In *Marketing to the Affluent,* I stated, "ESPs are more likely to have superior knowledge of the market segment that they target." Bob Read is a master of target marketing. He possesses significant knowledge of several affluent segments. Of course, one of these is the publishing industry. This segment includes affluent writers, editors, educators, publishers, and marketers of publications.

Why does Bob target the publishing industry? Perhaps because he always enjoyed reading. His avocation provided a base for exploiting a segment of the affluent population. Others fail to capitalize upon their experiences, backgrounds, and interests. In sharp contrast, Mark O. is targeting hundreds of segments including at least one author in the publishing segment. But does Mark O. have knowledge of the needs of the individuals that make up hundreds of targets? Unless he develops a much deeper understanding of the needs of his targets, he will always be just scratching the surface of significant opportunities. He will never be able to compete with the Robert Read types who are very deep in their understanding of their targets.

The first thing that the Mark O.s of the world should do is to ask themselves the K (knowledge) question: About which affluent segment in America do I know the most? Perhaps Mark O. should consider initially focusing on accountants. CPAs are in my top-10 list of occupations that have the highest concentrations of $100,000 income generators. Accountants want to talk about themselves, their accounting practices, and their problems. Authors want to talk about their books, their achievements. Mark O.'s contacting an author is as logical as him seeking accounting advice from a writer and publishing advice from an accountant.

But Mark O. is not alone. Many sales professionals, even some

ESPs, violate the rules of marketing to the affluent, that is, first consider focusing on the affluent target that you know best. Consider this case.

A fellow approached me just after I had given a speech to a group of ESPs.

> "Dr. Stanley, you would not believe this, but I never, ever called on anyone in the affluent industry you just mentioned. It is the industry I know best—the heating and air conditioning contracting industry. I graduated from engineering school with a major in heating and air conditioning (mechanical engineering). Then I worked for several years in the industry. I know more about the industry than anybody I compete with. But I guess it's so logical to focus on what we know best that I just overlooked it."

I asked the young man where his office was located. "Florida," he responded. I then asked if he thought there were any air conditioning contractors in Florida. The ESP just smiled and nodded his head. According to my data, the largest concentration of air conditioning contractors is in the state of Florida. Air conditioning contractors want people that solicit their business to demonstrate *knowledge of needs*. Their needs often are not primarily financial but industry-centric, product-centric, and ego-centric.

Why should anyone waste their potential strengths, their marketing foundations, and the distinct qualities/background advantages that they possess? Almost everyone who targets the affluent has some background, some area of experience upon which they can capitalize. However, it is my experience that only a minority of sales professionals closely examine their own qualities and leverage these traits in the marketing arena.

Robert Read is part of this minority. He loves to read and is always on the lookout for new offerings, that is, potential best sellers. He is also sensitive to the comments made about books by literary critics as well as industry-specific opinion leaders.

Superior knowledge of the character of a specific affluent segment and the corresponding needs of individual targets within the industry is a hallmark of most ESPs. Robert Read's superior knowledge of the publishing industry demonstrates this long-term commitment to the deep and narrow posture.

(3) Technique

Robert Read's technique of conditioning prospects to like, admire, and respect him is perhaps his greatest attribute in the sales equation. It is difficult for an author to dislike anyone who tells him that his writing is superior. Sincere compliments turn cold calls into very warm calls.

Admiration and respect go to those sales professionals who are associated with the leaders in the author's field. Of course, the basic components of indebtedness and consistency are used by Robert Read with textbook precision. If someone buys your product, aren't you indebted/obligated to return the favor? The best ESPs realize that to receive business you must often first give business. And it would be inconsistent in the target's mind not to feel a need for asset management services after he just boasted of the success of his book and speaking programs.

Would you prefer to be contacted by Robert Read or Mark O.? Mark focuses on his needs; Read focuses his conversations almost exclusively on the need of the prospect. Most affluent prospects are achievement-oriented. They have a strong need for their achievements to be recognized. Why else would achievers in virtually every field of endeavor go through the ordeal of giving away hours of their valuable time to media and sitting for hours while a press photographer takes 400 pictures "just to get a good one?" They reason that it is very worthwhile as long as someone publicizes good things about them.

A young attorney who struggled for years to move up to partner needs and wants to be told that he is a winner. Those people who praise him, recognize him, and compliment him will be liked by him. The same concept holds true for authors. Recall from the previous discussions how Robert Read handled yours truly.

> Your publisher must feel that they have a winner.

> Your publisher is one of the best . . . very serious about selecting manuscripts.

> . . . to congratulate you.

> Reviewers comments are excellent.

> I want to add yours to my collection . . . autographed books by some of America's best writers.

It would take someone a lifetime to learn how to sell like this . . .you have it here in one place.

It's going to change my marketing style.

Recognition also comes in the form of proposing that I act as a consultant and speaker and even as a dean of a major business school.

Focusing on the needs of the target is also demonstrated by Robert Read's role as the buyer of products and services. A large majority of the affluent market is composed of owners of businesses and/or high-performance professionals. How many sellers will be rude to a potential buyer? Would an author hang up on someone who calls to purchase several autographed copies of his book at full price? An affluent prospect will likely be responsive to a purchaser who calls. Also, most people feel indebted/obligated to reciprocate. Even if the initial purchase from the affluent target (author of a book selling for $49.95) is small, he will likely feel obligated to reciprocate in much larger dollar volumes.

What a wonderful variety of offerings were made by Robert Read (i.e., book purchases, consulting time, speaking engagements, a deanship, literary club membership, and a book promotion via key retailers). It was and is still clear to me that Robert Read could have a significant influence on my cash flow as well as my publishing career. He is an important person for an author to know. Also important is the speed with which he convinced the target of this fact. Read is much like another ESP who attended one of my seminars. During the program, I showed the audience of top producers a picture of the top-ranked entrepreneur in the American candy industry. "What would you talk about if I give you the phone number of this owner of a private candy company?" I asked. Only one person among 60 in the room volunteered to play the role of the sales professional in front of the audience. This ESP simply stated that, first, he would "flatter the target with comments and accolades about being top in his field. Then, I would tell him that I admire his product so much that I want to buy some for each of my best clients." The ESP's presentation was given the top score by the audience and seminar leader. What would you expect from someone who had a net annual income of just over $1 million?

(4) Sources of Information

Robert Read's high propensity toward reading is not limited to books. He is also an aggressive consumer of information that appears in newspapers and other types of periodicals. To date, *Marketing to the Affluent* had been promoted in six advertisements that appeared in *The Wall Street Journal*. All of these ads were in the national edition. I understand that *The Wall Street Journal* has a primary circulation of about 2 million "readers."

Based on this heavy advertising in the "trade journal of investments," I expected at least a modest level of prospecting from marketers of investment products and services. Only Robert Read called me. Not one sales professional from the insurance industry or the auto industry called. In fact, I did not receive one single call from any other sales professional from any industry. I have spoken to dozens of successful authors in the past few years, and their observations are the same as mine. Most have not been called, not even by Robert Read. Most marketers never identify targets and, correspondingly, never contact an affluent prospect whose success is being promoted in even some of the most popular categories of national press. Some argue that this type of calling is useless because large numbers of solicitations are being made to the prospect. Nothing could be further from the truth. Yes, this is analogous to your high school reflections. The prettiest girl in your high school class sat home on Saturday night because all the male students assumed she had a very heavy schedule.

If affluent targets, whose success is being promoted prominently in the national press, are underprospected, what about those targets who are in the local, regional, and trade press? They are even less likely to be contacted.

The reluctance of some sales professionals to call targets because of the so-called prettiest girl in high school hypothesis is only part of the explanation. I firmly believe that most underachieving sales professionals are either nonreaders or readers of materials that have little market intelligence value. More than one in two sales professionals who call my office to inquire about printed materials on the affluent market claim they never heard of *Marketing to the Affluent*. This is an interesting clue to their level of readership. Most are marketers to the affluent. But they don't read one of the top affluent publications (e.g., *The Wall Street Journal*).

Robert Read and other ESPs in his league not only read the national press, they often are consumers of affiliation press. What is affiliation press? This is best explained via an example. Like many other organizations that satisfy the affiliation needs of the affluent, the literary club that Robert Read suggested I join publishes a newsletter. The newsletter that Robert Read reads contains high-quality market intelligence information about the careers and achievements of current members, as well as new members. It provides one with the insights about the who, how, what and when of the affluent equation. The newsletter reads like recognition incorporated, that is, who's who in the publishing and related industries.

There are hundreds of thousands of affiliation publications. I would wager that the vast majority are completely ignored by those who target the affluent. Even if you are not inclined to become part of an affiliation group, consider those print sources that you encounter almost every day. Dozens of "affiliations," a.k.a. newspaper classified sections, provide clues about who the affluent prospects may be, how many dollars will be transferred in the forthcoming transaction, where and when those dollars will probably be transferred, and how the affluent prospect can be approached. The marketer to the affluent must look at advertisements, not for opportunities to buy but for opportunities to sell. These advertisements are significant artifacts of the lifestyle of the affluent. Examine the more significant classified advertisements such as this one: "For sale, liquor store, annual sales in excess of $6 million. Heavy check-cashing clientele, near major factories, auto assembly plants, and offices. Price $1.3 million. Owner will consider financing."

Reading the current classifieds is very important for two basic reasons. First, it enables the marketer to discover and identify affluent prospects. Second, it helps to identify such prospects when significant cash flow changes will take place. Yet, I find from my research that only the more sophisticated and enlightened marketers "sell via the classifieds." Most marketers see them as a source of information on something to buy, not something to sell. This gives a strategic advantage to those marketers who would like to take advantage of the classifieds.

All great marketers who target the affluent feel it necessary to have a variety of sources of information with which to identify affluent targets. Developing one's own source material is as important in this field as having a product to sell. Remember, you cannot sell if you cannot identify those who are ready, willing, and able to say yes.

(5) *Big-League Orientation*

Most who target the affluent never develop a big-league orientation. Even many ESPs concern themselves too much with finding individual targets than with more significant opportunities. These opportunities can be uncovered in high concentrations of affluent targets. These concentrations are often found in selected affiliation groups. Robert Read is a master of affiliation marketing. Less-productive sales professionals focus on individual targets. In sharp contrast, Robert Read fully exploits the character of the affluent market. Bob has a strategy for identifying high concentrations of wealth, the affluent convoy. His self-taught, big-league orientation places him squarely inside the affluent convoy.

One of the single most profitable industries in America is publishing and related communications media. My own data and discussions with key informants point this out. Also, in 1988, *Forbes* found that 73 of the Forbes 400 generated their wealth from media enterprises. In 1989, *Forbes* also reported that the communication media industry ranked second in terms of profitability (return on equity) among 15 major industrial classifications. But most of the affluent targets in the communications industry operate businesses that are not public corporations. Sales professionals will find that these targets are not easily identified without being inside the affiliation convoy.

The big-league orientation is a philosophy of marketing. It is a strategy based upon the military theory that one should direct his greatest energy toward targets that will provide the greatest return. Most sales professionals, however, do not follow this axiom. They either fail to attack any members of an affluent convoy/affiliation group, or they may capture one or two random ships in the affluent convoy but fail to exploit the opportunity that resides within the affluent affiliation group.

Almost every working day a different sales professional calls me to ask how he can become more productive. He always asks about new affluent opportunities outside his current client base. What he fails to realize is that some of his current clients are members of affluent affiliation groups. Robert Read realized this fact early in his career. In the current fiscal year, the typical sales professional will seek new business from individual targets that may represent new business among literally hundreds of independent affiliation groups. But he will never fully exploit the wealth inside any of these clusters.

Along these lines, let me give an example of what I call the little-league orientation that sharply contrasts with the big-league strategies employed by Robert Read.

SUGGESTIONS FOR MR. YOUNG

MR. YOUNG:

Dr. Stanley, I want to know what are the best affluent opportunities I have in the state of Maryland.

DR. STANLEY:

How many clients do you currently have?

MR. YOUNG:

Over 600.

DR. STANLEY:

Describe your best client. How does he make his money?

MR. YOUNG:

He is a printer.

DR. STANLEY:

How many other printers do you have as clients?

MR. YOUNG:

None.

DR. STANLEY:

Who is your second most profitable client? How does he make his money?

MR. YOUNG:

Among other things, he owns several dry cleaning stores.

DR. STANLEY:

How many other dry cleaners do you have on your books?

MR. YOUNG:

Ah . . . none.

After reaching the sixth-ranked client description and getting the same response, I proposed the following:

DR. STANLEY:

Mr. Young, if these folks are your six best clients, why is it that you have only one printer, one dry cleaner, one owner of a headhunting firm? You are using the "one from each category" form of selling.

MR. YOUNG:

Well, I just never thought about calling on others in these businesses.

DR. STANLEY:

From what you are telling me, there is a strong possibility that none of your clients has anything in common except that they are your clients.

MR. YOUNG:

Is that a problem? Should I look at some new opportunities?

DR. STANLEY:

What are the basic dimensions that underlie the affluent market in America?

MR. YOUNG:

I'm not sure.

DR. STANLEY:

First, most people who have significant amounts of money own and manage their own businesses. Second, most affluent business owners have a strong need to affiliate themselves with others in their industry; and third, most are active members of one or more trade associations. Have you ever attended a trade conference?

MR. YOUNG:

Yes, several in fact.

DR. STANLEY:

What groups sponsored them?

MR. YOUNG:

I believe it was an association of financial planners—another was for people . . . salesmen, ah . . . people with a license to sell securities.

DR. STANLEY:

Do you think you could rank the top 10 producers at this meeting?

MR. YOUNG:

I could come pretty close.

DR. STANLEY:

Okay, now tell me who are the top 10 most productive printing companies in your state? Which one will cash in their chips this year?

MR. YOUNG:

I don't know. I guess I should.

DR. STANLEY:

Don't be depressed. Most people in your industry are more interested in conducting competitor intelligence than target market intelligence. Have you ever attended a conference or trade show for printers or dry cleaners?

MR. YOUNG:

No, is this important?

DR. STANLEY:

Often, the highest concentrations of affluent prospects can be found at a trade conference. I'll bet that your best clients are typically part of these events.

MR. YOUNG:

What should I do?

DR. STANLEY:

First, focus on your top six clients. Ask each one about their respective trade associations. Ask each to recommend you as a speaker at the next month's luncheon meeting. The fellow that helps me with my pension plan followed my advice last year. He was invited by a client, a printer, to speak about pensions and investments to a group of local printers. In the 20 years that this trade association has been in business, no one had ever given a speech before. One year and seven months after the speech, he now has several pension accounts in the low-seven figures. This success was directly related to getting inside the affluent convoy of printers.

MR. YOUNG:

Should I just focus on printers?

DR. STANLEY:

Initially, I would suggest that you take a close look at the opportunities within five of the six trade groups. Begin with those of your five or six best clients. Ask your best clients about their trade associations. Focus on becoming an associate member of the group. Then prospect within the group—inside the affluent convoy as part of the group. And not as an outsider. Become a known, admired, and respected part of these associations. When you do, you will find that cold calling will become warm calling. There is absolutely no sense in prospecting randomly in hundreds of groups. Be choosy. Focus on the most affluent and most accessible groups. Target those in which you already have a beachhead, an ally you can count on to get you inside the association, endorse you to fellow members, introduce you to program chairmen, and assure you that your articles about what you do will be printed in the "trade journals of the affluent." Begin by approaching your top clients—the printer, the dry cleaner, and so forth. That is all the time I have. I'm backing into a 3:30 P.M. meeting. So long.

MR. YOUNG:

Thank you for your help. Goodbye.

Chances are good that Mr. Young is on his way to becoming the next generation of Robert Read. Robert Read's intuition was correct in marketing via the affiliation groups. I am absolutely amazed at the number of trade association meetings (local, regional, national) that contain hundreds, even thousands, of affluent targets. Even more amazing is the fact that most often sales professionals who target the affluent are not present at these meetings. Few, if any, ever join an affiliation group other than the one that their competitors join! This is analogous to duck hunters looking for ducks in a field with several hundred other hunters. What Robert Read has figured out is that some of this nation's most affluent affiliation groups contain little or no competition. Read, in this context, is akin to a young soldier who is smart enough to find and board a transport ship filled with 6,000 pretty nurses who have been at sea for many months. The sailor's problem is an enviable one, but he must use great care in allocating his resources. Do such things really happen in the business of marketing to the affluent?

Last year Pizza Expo was attended by nearly 7,000 people. More than 6,000 were pizza retailers. More than 600 were suppliers to the pizza industry. For several days, thousands of affluent prospects were in one room. How many sales professionals in Robert Read's business, the business of marketing to the affluent, were at the meeting? According to the list of commercial attendees that I received, *not one!* At the same time that this meeting was taking place, I am sure there were thousands of sales professionals making ice cold calls on random targets. It is time to move inside to the warmth of the affiliation groups that bind the affluent market together. Follow the path to affluent affiliation blazed by Robert Read. He is truly an ace of aces among even the most extraordinary sales professionals.

KEITH CALLED WHILE YOU WERE OUT OF TOWN

Keith is a young financial consultant based in Houston, Texas. He attended my seminar entitled, "Marketing to the Affluent when They Are Euphoric," in mid-November. By the first week in December, his participation in the seminar already bore fruit.

The message that he left at my office was as follows:

> Took your advice about prospecting authors. I saw a first-time author on C-Span. I understand that the author received a

significant number of dollars up front from a major publisher. Just wanted you to know that the advice and help you gave me worked out perfectly. When I called the author, he was not in, but he did return my phone call. This morning, I followed your directions to the letter, and the author will open an account with me.

This was not the first time that Keith called my office. The previous day, I spoke to him on the telephone. He indicated his interest in prospecting authors, especially the one that we just reflected upon. However, he was not sure how he could contact this future best-selling author. I told Keith that he should call the publisher and ask to speak to the editor of this particular book. Of course, when Keith did call, the editor was reluctant to give the author's telephone number to Keith. I told Keith that this would be the case and not to be discouraged by this reaction. I instructed this young man to indicate to the editor that he would like to purchase five copies of the book, personally autographed to his clients. And also to make it very clear to the editor that the purchaser was, in fact, a security broker.

With this information, the editor not only gave Keith the business phone number of the author but also gave him his personal home telephone number. Why would an editor give out this information? Why would an author be very positive in his response to Keith's telephone call? Why? Because both of these individuals are looking for some indication of the future success of the book to which they both have contributed. Both of these individuals are euphoric because of the C-Span publicity about the book and the response from people like Keith. They are, in fact, both vulnerable to solicitation because of their euphoria. Keith has essentially capitalized in terms of timing his solicitation with this feeling of euphoria.

After Keith had completed his discussion with the author concerning the purchase of five personally autographed copies of the book, he asked the author if he had ever had a brokerage account. The author indicated that he had not and that he was very interested in opening one with Keith. Now Keith is euphoric. I could tell from his telephone conversation that the adrenaline was really building inside of this young man. His excitement about being able to capture a major account using the euphoria concept had made his day.

However, euphoria does not last forever. I hope, and of course I am betting, that Keith will further exploit his newfound knowledge about how to target the affluent. If Keith has one future best-selling author today, I would hope and I would suggest to him that he prospect within this affluent convoy. Otherwise, he will just be starting a new business every single day in a new industry.

A Letter to Keith

Dear Keith,

Thank you for sharing your experiences with me, and congratulations on your latest triumph. I am sure that you are proud of yourself in terms of your ability to capture big publishing dollars. But let me urge you to go beyond having just one client in one industry and to consider seriously deeply penetrating the publishing industry, not only having one client but having many clients within the context of writers, editors, publishers, and executives in the publishing industry. I am sending you the most recent copy of what I consider to be the number one publication that will help you understand and identify opportunities in the publishing industry. *Publishers Weekly* is the international news magazine for book publishing. You can subscribe to *Publishers Weekly* by sending a check for $97 to: Publishers Weekly, P.O. Box 1997, Marion, Ohio 43306-2079. You will receive 51 issues for the year's subscription; that is for domestic mailing.

The reason that I suggest you read *Publishers Weekly* is reflected in one of its most recent issues. It is chock-full of advertisements that indicate future best-selling books. It is not unusual for a single issue of *Publishers Weekly* to contain dozens of names of future best-selling authors. How can one predict that someone's book will be a best-selling item? Very simply. An advertisement such as the one that might appear in *Publishers Weekly* indicates how much money is being put into national and regional advertising, the number of cities that will be covered by the author on a national tour, the prepublication reading copies, the posters, the election by a book-of-the-month club, floor displays, and other types and pieces of information. These are the foundations of future success.

Also indicative of future success is the confidence that a publisher has in an author. This confidence is best expressed in the number of books that are run off the first printing. When you see a first printing in the 50,000, 100,000, even 200,000 range, you can bet that the publishing company is wagering that this book will be a megasuccess.

In the January 5, 1990, *Publishers Weekly,* the first eight pages of advertisements were purchased by Harper & Row. They contained advertisements for 24 books that will be or are currently available. They also indicate the amount of support that they are giving these books. In essence, these advertisements are not for consumers; they are for people in the wholesale and retail trade. They are, in fact, influenced by these advertisements, and of course, they stock and support those books which they think will be winners. And in many respects, they predict that the winning book will be one that has been given significant support by the publisher. Significant support in this context is indicated, of course, in these advertisements in *Publishers Weekly.*

In addition to advertisements which indicate future and current best-selling authors, there are also numerous articles which talk about different executives who are moving in and out of affluent circles—who has been appointed president and chairman of publishing companies, who has been taking the reins of this company from this person, and so on.

In the "People" section of *Publishers Weekly,* one will find much information about the movers and shakers in the publishing industry—who has been appointed publisher for law books, who has been made editor for cookbooks, children's books, who has been made chairman of this company, president of that company, and so on.

In the same issue (January 5, 1990) of *Publishers Weekly* is an interesting article called "A Decade of Mega

Sellers." This article discusses in some detail the top 25 fiction best sellers in the 1980s as well as the top 25 nonfiction best sellers of the 1980s. And of course, it reflects upon the authors. The top fiction best seller of the 1980s is *Clear and Present Danger* by Tom Clancy. At the top of the 25 best selling nonfiction books is *Iacocca, An Autobiography* by, of course, Lee Iacocca with William Nowack.

Another interesting article in the same issue, and it certainly is an opportunity, is entitled "Learning the Lessons of 1989," in which 14 industry leaders discuss the problems of the 1990s in the publishing industry. This is a great opportunity to identify and understand the views of 14 movers and shakers and possibly very affluent prospects in the United States.

In the very same issue is an interesting article called "The Passing Parade," which basically presents the comings and goings of prominent people in the publishing industry. There are several dozen major players in the industry who are on the move, who are typically being promoted and going to areas of greater opportunity. Several dozen euphoric individuals are identified by one single article.

Another enlightening section of *Publishers Weekly* which is absolutely essential for someone who wants to prospect affluent authors is the section entitled "Forecasts." The "Forecast" section gives brief but significant reviews of books that will be offered in the future. These reviews are of critical importance because they are used as proxies in terms of sales success by people in the trade. Wholesalers and retailers reflect on these reviews in terms of estimating the demand for the books. In essence, their evaluation of the book by these reviews tells them how many books to order in the future.

It is not unusual for a single issue of *Publishers Weekly* to contain several dozen reviews about future offerings in the publishing arena. It covers areas all the way from poetry to paperbacks to science fiction to mysteries to fiction and nonfiction.

Also, an important part of *Publishers Weekly* is its weekly statistics on the best-selling books in America. The sections covered include the top 15 fiction, the top 15 nonfiction, the top 15 mass-market paperback best sellers, and the top 10 trade paperback best sellers. All of this information is contained in *Publishers Weekly* including the title of the book, the author of the book, the publisher, and the price of the book, where it ranked this week, last week, and the number of weeks it has been on the best-seller list.

It is very important to realize that most authors are not affluent. Most authors will never be affluent. According to *Publishers Weekly*, there will be more than 53,000 books published in the United States in one year. The serious prospector of affluent authors would be interested in fewer than 1 percent of the authors in these 53,000 events. How could I identify these aces of aces within the publishing industry? I would read and thoroughly digest the information contained in *Publishers Weekly*, and I would also pay strict attention to the issue of timing. Authors are euphoric when nice things are written about them in their industry's trade publications.

According to the recent Audit Bureau of Circulation's estimates, *Publishers Weekly* has a paid circulation of 36,517, and 7,400 paid subscriptions are from book sellers. In essence, *Publishers Weekly* is the most significant and influential publication of its type among those who influence the sales of books in America.

Beyond reading *Publishers Weekly*, it may be useful for you to join a local literary club. In this way, you have an opportunity to interact with other people who are interested in books and authors. It may be very useful for you to establish yourself as a leader within the local literary club. It would be appropriate for you in your leadership role to correspond with best-selling authors as well as future best-selling authors.

You will find that these prospects will be much more likely to respond to your letters, as well as telephone inquiries when, in fact, you can provide them something other than your core product. Authors and publishers are extremely sensitive to the views and opinions that officers of literary clubs have about them. It may also be useful to try your hand as a critic. Why not propose to some of the local, as well as neighborhood, publications in your community that you write book reviews from time to time? You will be amazed at how many people will send you free books if, in fact, you take up your avocation as a book reviewer. In addition, you will be amazed at how nice authors will be to you when you tell them that you are reviewing their books!

I hope this information will be useful to you. Please keep me posted about your continued success, and remember, once you have one ship in the affluent convoy, it will become progressively easier to obtain additional ones.

Very best of luck.

Sincerely,

Thomas J. Stanley, Ph.D.
Chairman, Affluent Market Institute

PROSPECTING FOR A SPECIAL FORM OF TUITION REFUND

The publishing industry does produce a large number of affluent individuals. Like many other segments, publishing is composed of several subsegments which include: high-performance authors, publishers, agents, attorneys, publicists, booking agents/speakers bureaus, specialty printers, book wholesalers, and retailers. For a closer study of the affluent in this field, we shall examine the components of the author subsegment.

There are a variety of authors. Some write children's books;

others focus on science fiction. Most authors are specialists in that they concentrate most or all of their efforts in one narrow area. In this regard, they are successful marketers who target the affluent population. Their success, in part, is explained by targeting via the "deep and narrow." Thus, those who target these specialists should be sensitive to the character of these specialty areas.

Few people are experienced enough to immediately launch a successful sales campaign across a broad spectrum of affluent targets within the "generic" publishing segment. Only a small fraction of sales professionals are as well read as Robert Read. Even a smaller portion have his knowledge of the affluent players in the publishing industry. But one must remember that it took many years for Robert Read to develop his understanding of his targets and his unique prospecting techniques.

Should an inexperienced sales professional even give consideration to targeting the affluent within the publishing industry? The novice can succeed if he follows the basic principles of targeting the affluent. The publishing industry not only contains thousands of affluent prospects, but the size of this segment is growing. It is, in fact, the heart of the information economy. But there is an equally compelling reason why one should consider addressing affluent prospects within the publishing industry. Many of the most important subsegments are either not prospected or prospected ineffectively. Take the college textbook author segment as an example. Most people perceive college professors as something other than affluent in terms of either high incomes or net worth. Some who write books are quite wealthy. Are all authors of college textbooks affluent? Most will never become affluent from their book royalties. Most college textbooks never go beyond the first edition. They make little or no money for either the publisher or the author. Thus, the key issue in addressing authors of textbooks is to identify those who receive significant royalty checks. This is not as difficult to do as it may seem because this type of information is free. It will take a modest investment in time and in the development of some intelligence-gathering skills.

During a recent affluent marketing sales seminar that our institute put on for an insurance company's sales force, I mentioned the concept of prospecting authors. A few days after the seminar, one of the attendees telephoned my office seeking advice about how to distinguish affluent authors from the rest. I first asked the young man if he had attended college. His alma mater has over 1,600 full-time faculty members and places a major priority on having its faculty publish. The first category I refer to is the "not-for-profit scholar" segment. These faculty are most interested in adding to the growing base of scientific knowledge. They publish articles in top-ranked reference journals. Also, they write books which often provide significant academic insight but are not widely adopted by "rank-and-file" undergraduate classes. Their works are often adopted by small groups of upper-level graduate classes. In essence, these types of faculty are more interested in gaining the respect and admiration of their colleagues than generating large royalty checks.

In sharp contrast with the not-for-profit scholar segment, the "academic entrepreneur" segment often generates sizable royalty checks. This segment is composed of university and college faculty who have a strong interest in selling large numbers of books. How does the academic entrepreneur increase the probability of selling large numbers of books? The answer to this question provides a clue to identifying affluent textbook authors. As I suggested to the young insurance sales professional, "Look for key words in the title of the book and/or note the designated college course." What are some of these key words? They include, but are not limited to, the following: (1) *Basic . . .*; (2) *Fundamentals . . .*; (3) *Introduction to . . .*; (4) *Elementary. . . .* Correspondingly, the best-selling college textbooks are used in undergraduate courses that are required for all students or all business majors, and so forth. One merely needs to examine a college's course catalog to determine what basic/elementary courses are required by the largest number of students.

Often, other parties will compile lists with this type of information and provide it to you free. Such a list was obtained free of charge by the life insurance sales professional. The university he attended was only a few blocks from his office. I suggested that his first step in targeting affluent authors should begin with a trip to the university's book store. Many book stores display the books that have been written by the university's faculty. But the university book store that the sales professional visited went beyond displays. When he told the manager of the book store about his interest in the books written by the university's authors, she gave him a complete computer printout of the names of the books, edition, names of authors, and the department of each author. How many authors of currently published books were on the list? More than 200 authors were listed. Many professors on the list were the authors of several current books.

Should this sales professional prospect all of those on the list? Perhaps, but a more important question needs to be addressed. Who on the list is most likely to receive the biggest royalty checks? Once again, I referred the sales professional to my previous suggestions about the important clues in the affluent equation (e.g., are the books for basic/required courses?). There are several other important proxies for identifying the successful authors. Be sure to note the edition of the book. Most books fail to reach the second edition. Other books succeed for 10, 20, or more years and may go into the fifth edition, seventh edition, and so on.

Some are even revised long after the original author has passed away. Many successful books are revised every third or fourth year, thus defeating the best intentions of sellers of used textbooks. It is not unusual for authors of the top five textbooks in any basic/required course to receive annual net royalty checks in excess of $200,000. How much does this translate into when one considers 5, 7, even 10 successful editions over a 25-year period of time?

Beyond the affluent prospecting clues that relate to book and course designation and edition, there is one other dimension that I mentioned to the sales professional. Many of the most affluent textbook authors write more than one book. Some have several books in print at any one time! Thus, the most affluent prospects on a list of college faculty are likely to be authors of books that:

1. Bear the title of basic, fundamental, elementary and/or introductory on their covers.
2. Are used in introductory courses which are required for all/most undergraduate students.
3. Are in at least their second edition.
4. Have multiple titles.

In my 20-year career as a university professor, I have found that few affluent groups are more underprospected than the "academic entrepreneurs." I have spoken to dozens of highly productive authors who invariably say the same thing. They are either completely ignored or else infrequently cold called by random-dialing sales professionals who have no idea of their importance as a target.

The response to my most recent interview is prototypical of the previous information obtained from successful authors. John has published several textbooks in his university career. But one of his texts did exceptionally well in terms of adoptions. It is a course requirement at many business schools at both the undergraduate and graduate levels. John's best-selling textbook is now in its fifth edition and is published by a top-five firm. Surely John would be a target for those who prospect the affluent. Since business students, as well as many seasoned marketing professionals throughout North America have purchased his book, one would speculate that John is heavily prospected. Not so, according to John. He told me without hesitation, "I have never, never, ever been prospected by one salesman who knew that I was an author." This is just another example of one more textbook author being ignored in spite of his having a winning product for more than 20 years. However, one will not find the titles of textbooks on *The New York Times* best seller list. It will take a bit more research to find authors of the "latent" best sellers such as textbooks, children's books, and so forth.

Are all the best-selling authors mentioned in *The New York Times* heavily prospected? I have not surveyed this affluent market category. Thus, my response to this question is based on conversations and observations and not on a representative sample. But the following case scenario provides some interesting food for thought.

Recently, I was asked to give a one-hour speech to over 400 sales professionals who target the affluent. These individuals were all in the top 5 percent of their firm's entire sales force. During the opening dinner for the conference, I was seated at a table for 12 with the keynote speaker for the next day's program.

The gentleman had written a book which had sold over 8 million copies. However, as he told me, "I make a lot more money giving speeches." This revelation about the financial benefits of public speaking confirmed some of my previous speculations about the writing versus speaking trade-offs.

We discussed the publishing and lecturing opportunities in both domestic and foreign markets for more than two hours! He mentioned that his latest manuscript was recently accepted for publication by a "house that paid the biggest up-front royalty in the history of nonfiction literature." Given these affluent indicators and the fact that his presence at the meeting was well publicized, how many of the 400 sales professionals present took the initiative of introducing themselves to this most famous author and lecturer? How many asked him to autograph his very best seller?

In spite of the informal and casual atmosphere before, during, and after dinner, only one of the 400 top-producing sales professionals said hello to one of the largest affluent targets in the publishing segment!

Once the affluent textbook authors have been identified, several other issues in the personal selling equation must be addressed. The key questions to be answered include the following:

1. Where should these targets initially be contacted?
2. When is the best time to make contact?
3. What themes and messages are likely to be productive in prospecting/conditioning the target?
4. What are some of the themes that should be avoided in an attempt to favorably impress the target?

Before approaching any major-league-caliber textbook author, it may be useful to sharpen one's skills on smaller targets. There is no substitute for learning by doing. Even out of a list of 200 authors, it is likely that fewer than 1 in 10 are producers of best sellers. Thus, it may be productive initially to prospect those targets that "one can afford to lose." Making mistakes is part of the maturing process. This is likely to be the case even for those seasoned professionals who begin targeting unfamiliar segments of the affluent population. The loss of a dozen "first-edition" authors can be more than compensated for by gaining one prolific author. While real life experience is the best teacher, there are some basic concepts that relate to both small and large targets in this arena. Most of the targeted authors can be reached successfully in their college or university offices during regular designated office hours. This time period has specifically been set up for scheduled and unscheduled meetings with visitors. The authors' department telephone numbers can be found by calling the university's information operator. The departmental secretary or receptionist should be able to provide information about the regularly scheduled office hours of the targeted author. Also, it is useful to inquire about the specific times within the given office hours parameters when the prospect is most likely to have the fewest visitors. Key informants such as secretaries and receptionists can also provide advice about when the target would be least receptive to walk-in visitors. Remember, these targets often have extremely demanding schedules. Thus, it may not be productive initially to contact them when they are facing writing deadlines and at the same time grading 70 mid-term exams.

Beyond the question of visiting hours, there is another critically important issue that relates to timing solicitations. One of the most important rules in marketing to the affluent is to time one's solicitations with the target's change in cash flow. Textbook authors usually receive royalty checks twice a year. Generally, the size of the royalty payment is significantly larger from book sales that take place during the fall quarter or semester. The number of books sold during the spring semester is usually not as great because more used copies of the text are available along with books still remaining in inventory and thus not credited as a sale.

Many publishers tally book sales for the six-month periods ending June 30 and on December 31. Some publishers provide a clause in their contracts with authors "to render statements thereof and make settlement therefore within sixty (60) days thereafter." Affluent targets are more likely to say yes to offers to buy when they are euphoric. Euphoric in this context refers to the prospect's feeling of economic elation. Obviously, the ideal time to visit the affluent target is when he is contemplating how to allocate his dollars. Prospect authors who are about to receive their royalty checks. Try to avoid one of the fundamental sins committed by most of those who attempt to sell to the affluent (e.g., soliciting with complete ignorance of changes in cash flow).

The choice of proper conversational themes in soliciting business is a subject with which most sales professionals have a lot of difficulty. First, it is important to reflect upon the themes that will not be well received by the targeted author. These include such salutations and greetings as follows:

> Good morning, Dr. Smythe. I understand you make a great deal of money from your textbooks.

Never suggest to someone who positions himself as a scholar and writer that money is the major motivating factor in his endeavors. Also, many successful authors are constantly being kidded by their colleagues about the big royalty dollars they generate. This is often a very sour issue with authors. Therefore, the money theme in an initial conversation should be avoided to ensure future contact with the target.

A better approach is illustrated by the pro forma case example given by a young insurance sales professional.

Time:	9:45 A.M., Thursday.
Target:	Dr. Walter D. Smythe, professor and author.
Place:	Dr. Smythe's office at a major university.
Posted office hours:	Tuesday, 9:00 A.M.–10:30 A.M.; Thursday, 9:00 A.M.–10:30 A.M.
Sales professional:	Lewis Wood.
Date:	January 16.

MR. WOOD:

Good morning, Dr. Smythe. Is this a good time to ask for a few moments of your time?

DR. SMYTHE:

That's what my office hours are for. But you don't look like a student.

MR. WOOD:

You're right. I'm not a student, but I am trying to learn. I'm interested in determining what your industry is all about. I have to make a decision about whether I should focus my energy in this direction.

DR. SMYTHE:

What do you mean by focusing your energy?

MR. WOOD:

I'm thinking of offering my services to authors—especially those who write books which are well respected in the industry.

DR. SMYTHE:

What business are you in?

MR. WOOD:

I provide deferred compensation plans and tax-advantaged annuities. I also design pension plans and fringe benefit programs.

DR. SMYTHE:

How did you get my name?

MR. WOOD:

Well, Dr. Smythe, I visited with the manager of the university book store last week. I asked for the names of the top published scholars on this campus. Your name was at the top of the list.

DR. SMYTHE:

It was?

MR. WOOD:

Yes, sir. In fact, she told me that your *Principles* book was a megalevel success in terms of adoptions. You must feel proud of the fact that most of the best colleges and universities are using it.

DR. SMYTHE:

It's done very well. But are you here to sell me something?

MR. WOOD:

Not today. I have been told that the most successful people in my field focus on just a few types of industries. I am seriously considering focusing on the publishing industry. That's why I'm here. I thought you might be able to tell me about the industry and where it is going.

DR. SMYTHE:

What do you want to know?

MR. WOOD:

If your son or daughter were going into academia, would you encourage them to write books?

DR. SMYTHE:

Book writing is not what it used to be. It is more difficult from my vantage point to produce a winner.

MR. WOOD:

Why do you feel this way?

DR. SMYTHE:

There are so many knockoffs. Do you realize that within three years after I published my first edition of *Principles,* there were four other books that copied the style, structure, even direct context from my literature revisions. Not only that, but there are over 100 books that have been written to fit into the same course slot as mine. Some of these things come in cheap paperbacks. But only five books are really big sellers, and mine is still number one.

But there is another issue that is discouraging. Book sellers are placing increasing emphasis on selling used books. They buy low from students, add a good margin and then sell it back to the next class. I don't get a dime on those sales. My own university actually imports used copies of the book from resellers at other colleges. It's incredible. These people are eating my lunch.

MR. WOOD:

Allow me to change gears for a moment. Does your publisher give its authors a lot of support?

DR. SMYTHE:

My publisher is way above most of the others. But it could be smarter and more aggressive in doing promotions and managing its sales force. I would be delighted if it would just deliver the books on time. But they are still light-years ahead of some of the other publishing houses.

MR. WOOD:

Would you think that it would be valuable for me to ignore authors who sign on with lesser known publishing houses?

DR. SMYTHE:

Well, there are some notable exceptions. However, "all things being equal," there are only six publishing houses in my general area that consistently produce good results. [Dr. Smythe lists all six.] Take the basic accounting book that's in its . . . I don't know . . . seventh edition. Every business student in the western hemisphere must take basic accounting. That author must be doing seven figures easily. It's probably a good book, but more than that, the publishing house has the best sales force and promotional support in the business. The best publishers won't sign up with just anybody. And if its name goes on the book, every decision maker and every business school will give its adoption some serious consideration. Yes, most of the folks that publish with these houses have a current or future winner.

MR. WOOD:

So, you would not recommend that your son or daughter become an author.

DR. SMYTHE:

If that's what they want, I would not discourage them. But it is very hard work. I'm just not sure the rewards are there. It's not like it used to be.

MR. WOOD:

What about student enrollments?

DR. SMYTHE:

The handwriting is on the wall. The baby boom has moved on. I project that there will be a steady decline in the number of students enrolled in colleges. And of course, the state legislature has never showed us a great deal of financial support anyway. Now they think they have some legitimate reason for re-designing our school's budget.

MR. WOOD:

But you still have some support in typing and graduate research assistance don't you?

DR. SMYTHE:

I can't get a chapter correctly typed even if I wait two or three weeks. Low priority is given to manuscript typing anyway. I'm really considering paying to have my work typed outside. I hate to do that . . . it's so expensive . . . a dollar or two a page. And graduate research assistance? We keep getting cutbacks, and the students we do have often have a real problem with the English language. You know, most of them are just off the plane from Korea and India—very bright but not fast starters in terms of the English language or library research.

MR. WOOD:

How much longer are you planning to stay in this profession?

DR. SMYTHE:

I don't know. I was planning to retire at 70. But I may want to bail out earlier. Of course, I have been saying this now for the past decade. I'm really thinking about adding a co-author to all the revisions in the future. Then I can focus on new material.

MR. WOOD:

Are you referring to your *Principles* book?

DR. SMYTHE:

Yes, but you know, I have two other books. Plus I'm working on another one right now. It's for the junior college market. A lot of authors overlook the two-year schools. It's a big market, and in my area, the prospects are looking better each year.

MR. WOOD:

Dr. Smythe, do you think that most of your fellow authors incorporate?

DR. SMYTHE:

I can't speak for the others. But I never incorporated. My accountant keeps telling me to incorporate, but we never have moved in that direction.

MR. WOOD:

Do you think that your colleagues have pension plans independent of the university?

DR. SMYTHE:

I have my pension here plus a 403 plan. But that is it. And you know, you can't put one-half as much into a 403 plan as you used to. It's a real tax bite. But Mr. Wood, I have a few students outside my door that need to speak with me. I hope that you appreciate where the business is today. Publishing is not what it used to be.

MR. WOOD:

Dr. Smythe, I really appreciate your advice. Your time is very valuable. I would like to meet with you sometime in the future. I have some ideas about tax-advantaged programs that we offer.

DR. SMYTHE:

That would be fine.

MR. WOOD:

What would be a good time?

DR. SMYTHE:

How about two weeks from today.

MR. WOOD:

I look forward to our meeting. Thanks.

Dr. Smythe, like so many high-performing textbook authors, has yet to be discovered by any major-level supplier of financial advice. He will not retire early. He will continue to author best-seller textbooks. And without some major changes in his financial patronage behavior, he will continue to pay large sums of his royalty dollars to the tax man. Most Dr. Smythe types are not spenders. They are very hard workers with a high propensity to generate income. However, many are not well versed in how to minimize their tax liability.

In spite of his youth, Mr. Wood has established the foundation for a successful client relationship with Dr. Smythe. Why will Mr. Wood succeed in capturing the business of the Dr. Smythe's of the world? Because he contacts the right target at the right time with the proper message. The message is that Mr. Wood appreciates the position and achievements of a top-producing textbook author. Dr. Smythe cannot help but be favorably impressed with a young sales professional who takes the time to recognize all of his great achievements. Mr. Wood controlled the situation by allowing Dr. Smythe to tell "his story." All self-made affluent individuals have a strong need to be recognized as winners. But interestingly, most of these prospects feel that few, if any, people, especially sales people, ever pay them homage. Most people who fail in their attempts to penetrate the affluent market are guilty of too often telling only their own stories. How is this perceived by the prospects? They feel that the sales professional has little interest in their real needs.

Mr. Wood was also successful in encouraging Dr. Smythe to like him by associating his questions with Dr. Smythe's achievements and needs for recognition and respect. This is in very sharp contrast to the students who are waiting outside Dr. Smythe's office. They are interested in telling Dr. Smythe that they do not agree with the grades they received on their mid-term exams. Few, if any, will preface their challenge of authority with a few statements along the lines of, "This is an outstanding course, and your textbook is extremely well written. I just wanted to stop by and ask you for your suggestions on how I might improve my grade on your next exam. *I respect your suggestions.*"

I WILL MISS HIM, AND SALES PROFESSIONALS, YOU OVERLOOKED HIM

On December 9, 1989, Lou Holtz, head football coach at Notre Dame University, was a guest on NBC's television program "Today." The night before he was part of the Heisman Awards Dinner program. During both appearances, Mr. Holtz reflected upon his successes. It is likely that he surprised more than a few viewers with his comments. He was most candid about the fact that he was not always successful. In fact, Mr. Holtz pointed out that at one point in his adult life, he was very far from being referred to as a success. He was unemployed and far behind in his mortgage payments.

How did Lou Holtz move from the down-and-out category and become a winner? During the interview on the "Today" show, he indicated that a book that he read had changed his life. Mr. Holtz reflected upon the key elements of the book that provided the road map to his success. These included the importance of becoming goal-oriented as well as thinking big about what one can achieve. After reading the book, Mr. Holtz listed many goals for himself. One of these was to become the head football coach at Notre Dame University.

I have never had the pleasure of meeting Lou Holtz in person. However, I was a colleague and friend of the author of the book that had such a profound influence on his career. I served on the faculty with Dr. David Schwartz from 1976 until he passed away in 1988. David was a pro forma American success story. Moreover, he was in a category of the affluent in this country that I refer to as balance sheet types. Balance sheet affluent types are prodigious accumulators of wealth. They are not conspicuous consumers. David never bragged about his successes. He dressed well but never extravagantly. He drove a Volkswagen Rabbit and a Chrysler K car. He did not need to demonstrate his high levels of achievements by way of status symbols. He once told me that early in his career, he had several luxury automobiles. But he said, "When you sell a lot of books, you don't need pseudo symbols of success." Most people that attempt to target the so-called affluent choose what I call the pseudo-affluent or vapor prospects. Those targets spend a great deal of their income as well as energy on purchasing luxury goods. I have often stated that the consumption of luxury goods is a substitute to wealth accumulation, not a complement. So it was for David.

David was raised on a farm during the Depression. He attended the University of Nebraska as an undergraduate. He told me that he was a good student with a high grade point average. However, he was a bit embarrassed at the C he received in a speech class. David was an outstanding speaker as well as university lecturer. He was often asked to give more than 200 speeches a year. Also, he won several teaching awards.

Giving a great many speeches each year (more than 3,000 in his career) certainly can do more than merely supplement one's university income. But speaking was not the only way David expressed himself. His book *The Magic of Thinking Big* sold over 3 million copies. Also one of his tapes on the same topic has sold to date over 11 million copies. David was also the author of two successful text books. One was an introduction to business book. Books of this type have perhaps the very largest potential demand of any text book category. His other well-received work was positioned as a basic or introduction to marketing text.

David was a mentor to many of his younger, less experienced faculty. We would spend many hours in his office seeking his insight. Dave, along with a few other faculty members, would always laugh when someone would say, "Well, David, one more day is over, and not one salesman called you to sell you anything." It is quite interesting that in spite of David's great successes as a best-selling author and lecturer, he was all but totally ignored by sales professionals. He would have been an outstanding client for anyone who wanted to sell investments as well as legal and accounting services.

Why was David ignored by so many marketers that seek affluent clients? There are many possible explanations. First, David never flaunted his achievements. Second, most people, especially sales professionals, firmly believe that teachers and professors are not affluent. Third, some people feel uncomfortable about prospecting authors of best sellers. Often, this uncomfortable feeling is rooted in their lack of knowledge about this segment of the population.

A person who wishes to succeed in selling to the affluent must reorient himself. Finding clues to the identities of important prospects is something that a person can be trained to do. Interestingly, David, as a possible prospect, could have been easily located by anyone interested. All they would have needed to do was to look at the back cover of his best seller for his name and address!

Being underprospected could not be explained by David's inaccessibility. He was frequently in his office, and his office hours were posted for public scrutiny. David was a delightful fellow who had an "open door to anyone" policy. I miss David. He was an unusually talented and prolific writer. We can all learn from David. As he stated in *The Magic of Thinking Big,* "Set your goals high . . . then exceed them." Lou Holtz certainly benefited from David's advice. So can most sales professionals who wish to go after big targets.

David was a very creative academic entrepreneur. He was the president and owner of Creative Educational Services, Inc. But few could ever recognize his high level of success by the modest choice of the brand of his clothing, by the make of his car, or by his academic occupation. In harmony with this life style, he was quite adroit at accumulating wealth. Yes, he had a very traditional consumption lifestyle. There is a significant number of David types in our academic communities. In fact, according to the National Science Foundation, more than 3,000 engineering and science professors in this country own companies independent of their respective universities (David Brock, "Faculty Business: Professors' Push for Profit Spurs Growing Concern," *The Wall Street Journal,* August 27, 1988, p. 33). Most are yet to be discovered by those who intend to target the affluent.

CHAPTER 8

ALARM: RETIRED AND OTHER TYPES OF MILLIONAIRES ARE MOVING INTO YOUR MARKET AREA

THE BISMARCK EXAMPLE

I have often stated that the strategies and tactics used in selling resemble those used in war. Military strategists have often capitalized on the success stories that emanated from their targets. The British navy, for example, used the "success story" method in locating the German battleship *Bismarck*.

On May 24, 1941, the *Bismarck* sank the British battle cruiser *Hood*. Realizing that the British navy would mobilize large forces to avenge the *Hood,* Admiral Lutgens, commander of the *Bismarck,* decided to make for the French port of Brest immediately.

Early on the morning of May 25, 1941, the British lost contact with the *Bismarck*. They did not know where it was or where it was headed. The *Bismarck* would probably have made it safely to port except for a fatal mistake. The mistake can be clearly classified in the "success story" category. The Germans actually told the British where the *Bismarck* was and where it was heading.

> The German Admiral . . . decided he would report details of the [successful] engagement with the *Hood*, the successful detachment of *Prinz Eugen*, . . . and his determination to make straight for France. [Patrick Beesley, *Very Special Intelligence* (London: Hamish Hamilton, 1977), p. 79]

Thus, British Naval Intelligence was able to obtain three important pieces of information. First, it was able to determine the location of the *Bismarck* by plotting the coordinates of the point from which the wireless signal originated. Second, by decoding the admiral's message, it learned that the *Bismarck* was headed for France. Third, it learned from a French resistance officer that the German navy was preparing a large reception in Brest, France, apparently for the crew of the *Bismarck*.

BE THERE FIRST AND BE ARMED WITH THE RIGHT MESSAGE

During the course of a focus group interview with five multimillionaires, I asked these gentlemen to provide background information about themselves and their occupations. The fifth and final respondent to this request told me that he "owned a drug store." When he said that, I was concerned that this individual might not have the net worth parameters that we had set in terms of screening respondents. The respondents to this focus group interview had to have a minimum of $10 million in net worth. I asked the respondent if, in fact, he was certain that he met the net worth parameters. He said, "Oh, yes, I easily meet those parameters. I not only own a drug store, I am involved in several other types of businesses." And then this respondent was kind enough to discuss some of his other income-producing adventures.

One of the most interesting types of businesses that this man owned was something that he referred to as business brokerage. Apparently, the respondent was not only a pharmacist, but he was a rather successful business broker. He indicated that a business broker is one who helps owners of small- and medium-sized businesses find buyers. Brokers also assist buyers in finding small- and medium-sized businesses. I then wondered what synergy there was between owning a pharmacy and being a business broker. He got a puzzled look on his face when I made that statement. In reality, who is the first to know when an entrepreneur is really sick? First, the doctor recognizes an irregular heartbeat, heart murmur, or other ailment. He communicates this to the entrepreneur. The entrepreneur communicates this to his wife, and his wife enters the pharmacy with a prescription for nitroglycerin pills. So, maybe he is among the first to know when an entrepreneur is likely to sell his business.

In essence, this respondent was successful in his business brokerage activities because his other profession provided him a marvelous conduit of critical information about when the need for a business broker was precipitated.

Many of the greatest marketers in this country have an uncanny ability to discover information sources that will help them identify affluent people when they are in a critical stage of need. So it is with David Cariseo, president, Fidelity Investments, Fidelity Investor Centers. David demonstrated considerable aptitude in selling the affluent early in his career. At the age of 26, he developed an innovative method of identifying and assuring that he would be first to contact new affluent residents within his south Florida trade area.

The information that he used as a foundation for this method for identifying affluent prospects was not only in the public domain, it was obtained free upon request. Before David ever asked anyone for his business, he personally delivered a gift to the new resident of the Boca Raton, Florida, area. The gift provided David a vehicle with which to condition prospects about his genuine sincere interest in helping people. What gift did David give to prospects? It was a booklet titled, "What to Do about Your Money when You Move to Florida!"

Prospects and his contacts probably felt indebted to David because of his kindness and because of his professional, low-key approach to selling investment products to new residents. In fact, David pointed out that he never really asked for their investment business during the first visit to their homes or offices.

During his first personal visit with a prospect, David played the role of a Florida orientation consultant. This system that David developed was not only brilliant; it, in fact, can be adopted by a wide variety of marketers of products and services. For example, auto dealers who are marketing automobiles and automobile services to the affluent may be able to provide a similar booklet for new residents. However, this booklet would contain information about how to transfer automobile licenses from one state to another.

Also, marketers of such products as life insurance, alarm systems, executive clothing, pools and spas, health clubs, country clubs, travel agencies, private schools, stables, and yachts may find it useful to develop a system as David did to identify and to capture successfully the affluent market within their market territories.

Many managers of security brokers would be skeptical if a young sales professional was not sitting at his or her desk calling affluent prospects hour after hour. David started his career and immediately skyrocketed to the position of top producer within a branch of a successful securities firm. Many of the people that he competed against were cold calling people via the telephone. Very often these prospects were not in need, nor were they in the mood to change patronage habits or even establish new ones.

David points out that people who are moving to an area or who have just moved to an area are often very sensitive to solicitations by people who are providing them information and products and services. His uncanny ability to target the affluent goes beyond merely finding people who are in the mood to buy.

What is the most important thing that a marketer can do for his or her affluent client? Again, David provides a pro forma example in terms of answering this question. He acted in the capacity of a business agent for both prospects and affluent clients. He would always ask new residents whom he contacted if they were in need of a lawyer or CPA or some other type of professional. Those who indicated an interest in establishing such patronage habits with these types of professionals would be given the names of professionals that David had as current clients. What would he do if he did not have a current client in a particular professional capacity? He would ask several of his clients whom they dealt with and correspondingly provide these names to prospects and, of course, current clients.

The single most important thing that a marketer to the affluent can do for the affluent prospect, as well as client, is to provide these individuals with increases in revenue. Consider how many professionals would want to deal with people like David, especially when they fully realized the value of developing patronage habits with such an outstanding professional. They would not only be able to purchase investment advice and products from David. But in reciprocal fashion, David would provide referrals for these professionals and other business owners and thereupon help the career and the revenue status of businesses and professional organizations owned by affluent prospects and clients.

Interview with David Cariseo

DR. STANLEY:

Dave, could you tell me whom you worked for when you developed your system of selling to the affluent?

MR. CARISEO:

This was when I was a stock broker my first year with Hayden Stone.

DR. STANLEY:

All right.

MR. CARISEO:

Because I was in Florida, I knew there would be a lot of people moving down there. And I also knew that as a stock broker, customers always want to be able to deal with someone they can get to. So, I knew that all these people moving to Florida from the north would need a new broker. I also knew that as happens with most people, they don't do something until they are forced to, and so, most of these people would have had investing habits that really were built toward increasing their capital. And taking a little bit more risk because they were at their peak earning years. They were making a lot of money. They were devoting a lot of time to their job. *But the day they are retired, all of a sudden they would take a look at their situation. Wow, I'm retired; I have got to do something about this.*

DR. STANLEY:

I understand.

MR. CARISEO:

They might likely change to sell the stocks they had in their company or change from a growth portfolio that might have been concentrated to a diverse income-oriented safety portfolio. It made me very aware, because I had moved to Florida, that the [welcome service] lady never comes the first day you are there. She comes a month later.

DR. STANLEY:

I understand.

MR. CARISEO:

And I also knew that I needed to be the first to get to these people. I knew that. I started thinking about what you need when you move in. You need a phone, but that's the phone company, and you can't . . . they are not going to tell you when somebody signs up. It's none of your business. And they [new residents] need electricity, but that's a private business, and the electric company isn't going to tell you that. And so I started looking at what I needed. And water came to mind. I knew that you have to get your water turned on. In order to do that, you have to go to the city because the city supplies the water. You have to give them a deposit and have your water turned on. And as a city, everything in a city is public information.

DR. STANLEY:

Go on.

MR. CARISEO:

So, I go over to the water department every morning on my way in [to the office]. I would ask for the receipt book. I would get the receipt book, and I would have everybody's name and address the day after they signed up for new water.

DR. STANLEY:

That is amazing!

MR. CARISEO:

So, I would then be able to call the telephone company and get their number, and I would be the first one who called them.

DR. STANLEY:

Well now, Dave, were these people home owners who had to have their own water turned on? In other words, they were not apartment dwellers?

MR. CARISEO:

That's right.

DR. STANLEY:

So did that filter out people with money?

MR. CARISEO:

It filtered out . . . , That was very good, Tom.

DR. STANLEY:

Well, that's what I meant. I'm taking that out. What I'm saying is that some people that move into communities don't have a lot of money.

MR. CARISEO:

But I didn't want to deal with people who didn't have a lot of money.

DR. STANLEY:

Yes. But I mean did you have to call them and qualify them to some extent, or were they pretty well qualified in terms of where they bought a house?

MR. CARISEO:

I could tell because I had the address of where their house was and how big it was . . . whether it was a little house or a small house. I knew every neighborhood, so the people who moved into 10 South Second Street in the little shanty—I did not call them. I only called those who moved into affluent sections or high-rise condos. I knew exactly by a self-directed process who to sell.

DR. STANLEY:

Well, in terms of you calling them, what did you say to them when you called them?

MR. CARISEO:

I said I am calling to welcome them to Florida. I knew they were new to the neighborhood and that I was sure that they had a stock broker. But I wanted to let them know that I was there, and if they needed anything at all, I would be more than happy to help them. And I gave them an idea of what I could give them. If they needed Standard & Poor's tear sheets, if they needed dividend payment dates, just call me and I would be glad to help them.

DR. STANLEY:

I understand.

MR. CARISEO:

And also I had something for them, a little booklet called "What to Do about Your Money when You Move to Florida."

DR. STANLEY:

Where did that come from?

MR. CARISEO:

I don't remember. I said, "I think you should know about this because it tells you what you need to do to become a resident of Florida, which you want to do because there are no estate taxes. The other thing you need to know is that in Florida, if you don't have your will witnessed by a blood relative or a bank, your will is invalid here. There are some things like that." So then I would ask, "When would it be convenient for me to stop by and bring it out to you?" I would say, "Here is my card. If I can do anything for you, call me."

DR. STANLEY:

In terms of percentages of the people that you contacted, how many said, "Come by and give the booklet to me?"

MR. CARISEO:

Eighty to 90 percent.

DR. STANLEY:

Did you personally deliver the booklet?

MR. CARISEO:

Yes.

DR. STANLEY:

What proportion of these prospects were retired?

MR. CARISEO:

Maybe half. There were a lot of people who were moving to start their own businesses. There were a lot of people who were moving to Florida to develop IBM in Boca and Florida Atlantic University. A lot of businesses for the geriatric types were beginning to grow. And a lot more professionals were moving in.

DR. STANLEY:

Did some of the people sign up for water for their businesses—small businesses? Was business stipulated in the receipt book? What did you do in that case?

MR. CARISEO:

I went to see them at their business. I never minded making those calls. I knew I couldn't sell anything the first go round. So I wanted to bring the booklet and not sell anything on the first go round.

DR. STANLEY:

How many eventually invested with you?

MR. CARISEO:

From the day I started, one year later I was the biggest producer . . . in one year.

DR. STANLEY:

How old were you then?

MR. CARISEO:

It was 1966; I was 26.

DR. STANLEY:

What did the other brokers think about you? I mean, they didn't know what you were doing at the water department?

MR. CARISEO:

No, they had no idea. It was my idea. I would never tell anybody. If I was a broker today, I wouldn't have told you.

DR. STANLEY:

But, Dave, in terms of your progression, where did you go from there? You gave them your book . . . .

MR. CARISEO:

In March of 1969, I was asked to be a branch manager of a community branch. At the time, I was the first one to ever get an exception to the three-year rule, and I was the youngest person ever to be a branch manager.

DR. STANLEY:

Well, did they let you keep your book? Could you produce?

MR. CARISEO:

No, I didn't produce as a manager. I felt that if you are the manager, you ought to manage.

DR. STANLEY:

Dave, let's get back to the booklet. After you visited these prospects and gave them the booklet and everything else, typically, did they call you or did you call them back?

MR. CARISEO:

I would say that I had to call back 90 percent of them. And I would call back and ask them if they had gotten a chance to look at the booklet and if they did, did they have any questions. Did they need any of the forms? Did they need any further information? Since they were moving there, did they need an attorney, did they need an accountant? I would be happy to recommend three or four people in the area that I was dealing with or had customers who dealt with them.

DR. STANLEY:

I understand.

MR. CARISEO:

I would ask them at that point who was handling their investment business. I would ask them if they wanted to let me know what securities they owned. I told them I would be happy to give them stock quotes any time.

DR. STANLEY:

So, then typically after that, was there a transaction made?

MR. CARISEO:

Yes. The best story was when I was a broker, there was one man in Florida in Boca Raton, and I kept hearing all these brokers say, "Boy, I wish I had his account." And it just dawned on me that if all the brokers only wished they had his account, then nobody actually had it. So then I knocked on his door.

DR. STANLEY:

Was this a cold call?

MR. CARISEO:

Yes. But he said he was busy. And I said I was sure he was, but I was sure he would want to talk to me and he said hello. I said, "I just want to ask you one question. Do you deal with any brokerage firm in town?" He said, "No." I didn't think so. "Where are your accounts?" He said, "Well, I deal with people in New York." And I said, "Why don't you deal with anybody in town?" He said, "Because no one ever asked me." And I said, "How would you like to have me as your account representative in town?" And he said, "That would be fine." He opened an account, and he became my biggest customer.

DR. STANLEY:

That's amazing.

MR. CARISEO:

I think it never bothered me to go do those things.

DR. STANLEY:

Was he a multimillionaire?

MR. CARISEO:

Yes.

DR. STANLEY:

That's incredible. Dave, what did you do after your career in that branch as manager? Is there anything you want to share?

MR. CARISEO:

After branch manager, I became regional manager, divisional manager, director of marketing, and president.

DR. STANLEY:

Going back to the information from the water department, let me ask you this. How many people signed up for these services each day?

MR. CARISEO:

If you walked in there at 7:00 o'clock in the morning, or 8 or 9 o'clock, there were 20, 30, maybe 50 names.

DR. STANLEY:

Do you remember how many there were in an average day?

MR. CARISEO:

On an average day, probably 25. It was pretty good stuff. I mean probably 50 percent of them were names I could use. In other words, the people that were qualified by the house and all of that. You have much better odds of doing well than if you are just cold calling.

DR. STANLEY:

I understand.

MR. CARISEO:

So, I knew that with the 10 calls I was going to make, or 15 or 5 or whatever, I was not wasting a lot of energy. I knew where these people lived. What I didn't know was what their investment capital was. That's what I had to find out.

DR. STANLEY:

Well, some of them had some investible capital. But, Dave, were a lot of these people business owners?

MR. CARISEO:

Yes. You know, all kinds of businesses.

DR. STANLEY:

You thought of it intuitively that this would be something you would do?

MR. CARISEO:

It is a matter of saying to yourself, "I am going to be the one that does it." I looked at how everybody else did their prospecting. I wanted to look at how I could do it differently. It didn't strike me that everybody else wasn't doing it so well.

DR. STANLEY:

Dave, you have been a real sport. I appreciate it very much.

MR. CARISEO:

When I come down to Atlanta, I'll give you a call.

DR. STANLEY:

Please do. So how is your business? Good, I hope?

MR. CARISEO:

It's terrific. I can't believe it. It keeps getting better and better and better.

DR. STANLEY:

I think you are dominating with your advertising.

MR. CARISEO:

It works. So long.

DR. STANLEY:

So long, Dave. Thank you.

MR. CARISEO:

My pleasure.

TARGETING AFFLUENT MOVERS EVEN BEFORE THEY MOVE: GREETINGS FROM RANCHO MIRAGE

Helping his father enhance his sales career is a noble form of behavior for a young man. This behavior is often manifested among the young sons of firemen. They wear dad's hat, and they put out imaginary fires with their fire (lawn) hoses. Young offspring of policemen put on make-believe badges and arrest their younger brothers and sisters and incarcerate them in the clubhouse. This form of behavior demonstrates the admiration that a young child often has for his dad and his dad's occupation.

But what can the sons of high-performing sales professionals do to express their respect and admiration for their dads' vocation? After all, selling relates to the intangible aspects of marketing. Sales professionals don't wear badges, nor do they have specific sets of pro forma visual clues that might indicate admiration. One young man that I recently had the pleasure of meeting shows his admiration for his dad in another way. He actually helps his father with increasing his sales revenue.

Those who sell to the affluent must have a constant source of new business. A top-performing real estate sales professional in one of the most affluent areas of California has a special source of new business. His son was interested in following in his footsteps but found selling real estate extremely difficult in the very competitive market where he attempted to establish a business. The young man took up a different vocation. He became a limousine driver. His task typically was to chauffeur affluent individuals from airports in southern California to fashionable retirement and resort areas and, of course, from these areas back to various airports.

Each day he met many different affluent people from all over the United States as well as from foreign countries. While driving these affluent people around these fashionable areas, he often heard them discussing how very much they would like to purchase a vacation and/or retirement home within the area. Upon hearing comments of this type, the young man would indicate that he knew an outstanding sales professional that would be delighted to show these people some of the residential real estate offerings in the community. And who did the young chauffeur recommend? It was none other than his father.

The father genuinely benefited from this source of information about the identities and interests of people that were vacationing within the area. Thus, the real estate sales professional in this case had an inexpensive, accurate, and timely method of discovering the identities of people who expressed an interest in buying real estate within his market area.

Often, the young man would overhear conversations precisely at the time when people first voiced an interest of any type in possibly moving to the resort area. Because of this, the young man was the first person to discover the needs these prospects had and, of course, to transmit this information to his father. Being the first to know when the affluent prospect is in the mood to buy is among the more critical issues in successfully selling to the affluent.

TEMPORARILY IN YOUR NEIGHBORHOOD: MR. D. CHEERS JUST SURFACED INSIDE AN NBA CONVOY

He looked somewhat despondent sitting to the right of my podium. It is sometimes difficult to tell what people in the audience are thinking about. But certainly Mr. Cheers was not in an optimistic mood. My speculation was confirmed during a conversation with his employer several months after the program.

Mr. Cheers attended one of my seminars along with a dozen other marketers of investment-grade gems. During the program, I strongly urged the attendees to concentrate their marketing fire power on a limited number of very affluent targets. During this section of the program, Mr. Cheers had a frown on his face. He subsequently asked about how one should initiate a focused strategy. My response centered on the concept of first "knowing thyself."

Often, sales professionals are caught up in serving their current clients and following every conceivable prospect. Because of this, they never sit back and analyze their strategic opportunities. With this "can't see the forest for the trees" preface, I began to ask some fundamental questions of Mr. Cheers. The first two questions did not generate information that I felt would provide him with a strategic base with which to penetrate specific segments of the market. In other words, neither his major in college nor his previous work experience would provide him with a marketing platform. However, the next set of questions and responses generated several lightning bolts throughout the room.

DR. STANLEY:

Tell me, Mr. Cheers, what college did you attend?

MR. CHEERS:

The University of North Carolina.

DR. STANLEY.

Were you involved with any extracurricular activities?

MR. CHEERS:

Yes. I was a cheerleader for the basketball team.

DR. STANLEY:

The varsity team?

MR. CHEERS:

Yes, the varsity team.

DR. STANLEY:

Were the teams that you cheered for any good?

MR. CHEERS:

Yes. In fact, they were national champions one year and got real close the other years.

DR. STANLEY:

Did you get a chance to interact with any of the varsity players?

MR. CHEERS:

You bet. I spent many an hour on buses.

DR. STANLEY:

Are any of the players that you interacted with playing professional basketball?

MR. CHEERS:

Why, yes. Several are stars.

DR. STANLEY:

Have you ever contacted any of these people since you were in college?

MR. CHEERS:

No, never.

DR. STANLEY:

You never told any of these people that you market investment-grade gems?

MR. CHEERS:

No, never.

DR. STANLEY:

Why do you seek out strangers who often have no money to invest? Why do you turn your back on those quality targets that have the highest probability of doing business with you?

MR. CHEERS:

I don't know. I just never thought about it. But I will now.

This case example illustrates one of the main reasons why most sales professionals' attempts to target the affluent fail. They are so busy looking at other people's resumes that they forget to look at their own. But Mr. Cheers was not about to fail now that he had some insights about how to leverage his background and experiences with prospects with incomes in the "ozone level."

Mr. Cheers's employer was kind enough to share some of the events that had taken place since the seminar which they both had attended. As soon as Mr. Cheers returned to his office from the seminar, he telephoned a star player on one of the better known teams in the National Basketball Association. This same player and Mr. Cheers spent many hours on team buses during college. They reflected upon their college experiences for a while. Then, Mr. Cheers informed the player that he was a supplier of investment-grade gems. The player expressed immediate interest in learning more about Mr. Cheers's offerings. He agreed to set aside some time for them to meet when his team would be in town to play the Atlanta Hawks.

The meeting did take place. The player is now a client. And, yes, Mr. Cheers demonstrated his marketing intellect and courage by asking the player to introduce him to the entire NBA team. Mr. Cheers successfully surfaced in the middle of one of the highest-paid convoys of professional athletes in America. According to his employer, Mr. Cheers's income went from $18,000 the year prior to his surfacing to over $100,000 for the year following the seminar. But Mr. Cheers now realizes that one affluent convoy can lead to the next. Just think of all the agents, attorneys, sponsors, owners, and promoters of sports who are very affluent. Each of these professionals are, in turn, part of another affluent affiliation group. What is the best way to penetrate these convoys? An endorsement as "the approved supplier of investment-grade gems" to a team of players in the NBA will likely pay major dividends. Good hunting, Mr. Cheers! We can all learn something from your experiences. Your successes add support to the growing base of knowledge concerning the power of endorsements from within affluent affiliation groups. Industry-specific endorsements within the context of how affluent people generate their income are extremely powerful in generating new business.

Even Superstar Athletes Pay for These Shoes

Large feet are typical of professional athletes, and most have had problems finding the right fit. Not so in Atlanta. Athletes, especially players in the NBA, have found the perfect store—Friedman's. And at Friedman's (size 10 and above), there's no business like shoe business.

The weathered brick building is nestled among a number of boarded-up shops, just off the corner of Mitchell and Forsyth streets in downtown Atlanta, across from a modern, multitiered parking facility. A first inclination is to keep walking, but that would be a big mistake.

Especially for those with big feet.

Especially for pro basketball players with big feet.

"It's like a candy store," said Phoenix Suns forward Tom Chambers, owner of size-15 feet. "When you're a kid growing up, it's virtually impossible to find shoes in large sizes. But you walk in there and see all different sizes and styles, and you can't make up your mind. So you buy a lot of everything."

Friedman's Men's Shoes, established in 1929, is owned by Bruce Teilhaber and family. It is the shoe store of the rich and famous and the not so rich and famous. But it's definitely the shoe store of choice for the majority of players in the NBA.

Julius Erving parked his limousine in front and strolled in earlier this year. Charles Barkley brought the entire 76ers team with him in February. James Worthy and A.C. Green introduced Yugoslav Vlade Divac to Friedman's in March and literally had to tug the wide-eyed Laker rookie out the door. Benoit Benjamin, as an NBA rookie, bought 23 pairs in one visit.

The typical scenario is this: If a team arrives in Atlanta the evening before a game against the Hawks, Teilhaber lingers in

(continued)

the store, awaiting a phone call from a hotel bellman. He then quickly sends a van to get the players, oversees the very low-key sales process (the players already know most of the employees, and most of the employees know the players' preferences and sizes), then drives the players back to the hotel.

When a visiting team arrives on game day, Teilhaber usually receives the call late in the morning or early afternoon. But he invariably receives a call.

"The only people [in the NBA] I can think of who haven't bought shoes are Pat Riley, and I haven't met the Sixers coach [Jim Lynam] and Larry Bird," said the owner, wrinkling his brow in thought. "But I hear Bird's not into dressing."

True. But his teammate, Robert Parish, 7 feet 1, is one of Teilhaber's "biggest" customers, as is Akeem Olajuwon and Dominique Wilkins.

Olajuwon recently asked Teilhaber to pick him up on a Sunday afternoon, although the store normally is closed. "He called and said he *needed* shoes," said Teilhaber. "Now, Akeem doesn't *need* shoes—I send him shoes all the time—but what he meant was that he *wanted* shoes. So I drove over to the hotel, picked him up, and sold him 30 pairs."

The best customer?

"Dominique, by far," said Teilhaber. "I've been taking care of Dominique for years. He's No. 1. He'll come in, talk with other customers about basketball, then buy something like six pairs a week for 24 weeks. Every shoe in this store, in his size [13], he has. He really knows his way around."

The entry to the store leads into a small reception area, with signs guiding prospective customers up a short flight of stairs and toward rows of dust-covered shoe boxes.

"Up the other stairs," Teilhaber motions, pointing to the left.

The second stairway leads to the real thing—a large room with rows and rows of leather shoes, encircled by walls adorned with autographed pictures of players and teams from various leagues—college and professional. Near the back is a small, semiprivate room that attracts the most fashion conscious.

"That's our skins room," said Teilhaber. "That's the Rolls-Royce. Cows, ostrich, alligator, snake, lizard—we have them all. The only thing we don't carry is fish. To be honest, I saw some of

(concluded)

those once, and it kind of grossed me out. So, I wouldn't buy them. I *couldn't* buy them. But we have everything else.''

Although he was unable to estimate the size of his inventory, Teilhaber says the downtown store—the other one is run by his wife, Davida, in Buckhead—covers 17,000 square feet, with 20 percent of his stock consisting of shoes in sizes 10 and above. The average price of a pair of leather shoes is $100, while a pair of "skins" generally sells for $400.

According to several players, there isn't another store on the NBA circuit that rivals Friedman's in either volume, diversity, or price—factors Teilhaber began to capitalize on shortly after purchasing the business from his father-in-law almost 20 years ago. His first move was to join forces with Stephen Fuchs, a New York-based importer who succeeded in persuading manufacturers in Italy to produce products in larger sizes.

"You have to understand," said Teilhaber. "People in Europe are short, with short, wide feet. At first they didn't believe there was a market for people with 14, 15, or even size 18 feet. But Stephen did a great job."

The word spread quickly, and in the last 20 years, the store has accommodated large athletes from all sports.

"The people are terrific to deal with," said the Milwaukee Bucks's Jay Humphries. "They know your size, the type of shoe you like, and they don't use pressure tactics. A lot of guys just order shoes on the phone and have them shipped to their homes."

Suns diminutive coach Cotton Fitzsimmons, proving that short people can find fulfillment at Friedman's as well, compared the place to a sports bar, minus the booze and the big-screen TVs. "It's a happening," said Fitzsimmons, "not just a shoe store."

Source: Ailene Voisin, "No Business Like Shoe Business," *The Atlanta Journal/The Atlanta Constitution*, April 15, 1990, p. 1F. Published with permission.

PART 3

INFLUENCING PEOPLE WHO INFLUENCE THE AFFLUENT

INTRODUCTION

Ted is a management consultant. His success is directly attributable to his special brand of networking. Ted's primary target for his services are owners/managers of privately held corporations. Better known and bigger consulting firms often approach these same targets, but Ted can hold his own with the so-called best consulting firms in the business. Ted's competitors typically approach prospects with egocentric consultant jargon and shopworn themes of "management by objectives" or "superordinate corporate mission statements." But Ted, in his initial contact with targeted entrepreneurs, always focuses on their needs. Often, his prospects are not initially sensitive to the need for consulting services. To assume that they are is typically an incorrect speculation. It is one of the main reasons that many inexperienced consultants never succeed in selling their services to major-league targets.

What does Ted talk about when he personally visits with a prospect for the first time? Ted only leads the discussion. He believes in the 80/90 rule, that is, 80 percent of the management and consultant revenue goes to those who allow the prospect to provide 90 percent of the conversation. Ted realizes that business leaders need to be recognized for their achievements. One of the greatest forms of recognition is encouraging the target to talk of his successes. Conversely, a shock approach with demeaning comments about the "poor state" of the target's business shows little empathy for the recognition/achievement needs of the prospect.

Ted wins not only because he conditions the prospect by listening to his story and his problems, but he also impresses his targets with the interesting network he has developed. One method of impression buildup is leveraging his relationship with authors of current as well as predicted best-selling books. After listening intently to a prospect tell his story, Ted might leave a small gift with his target.

TED'S PRO FORMA DIALOGUE

Listen in on Ted's comments just prior to his departure from an initial meeting with a CEO.

TED:

> John, I greatly enjoyed our conversation. I really think the story of your successes should be published. Entrepreneurs all over this country would benefit from your experiences. Oh, speaking of publishing, I almost forgot—have you ever read anything by Mr. Best Seller (B.S.)?

JOHN:

> Yes, I have a copy of his book over there in my library.

TED:

> Do you enjoy the B.S. view of our business economy?

JOHN:

> I could not put the book down.

TED:

> Well, John, while I'm writing up our proposal, I thought you would like to read B.S.'s latest book. It's hot off the press—not even in the book stores yet—a prepublication copy.

JOHN:

Ted, where did you get it?

TED:

Read the note in the front of the book. [John reads the following handwritten note: "Dear John, you are a great business leader and an inspiration to our next generation of entrepreneurs. With the compliments of my friend Ted. Regards, B.S."]

JOHN:

Ted, I did not realize that you knew B.S.

TED:

I just spoke to him last week. Great fellow. If you like the book, you may want to give a copy to all your sales professionals that exceed quota this year.

JOHN:

We should send a copy to every one of our top suppliers and customers. It would be a much better gift than one of our famous letter openers. Do you think you could get B.S. to autograph a bunch of copies if we decide to do it?

TED:

He would be delighted, John. By the way, B.S. asked me if you would be interested in writing a paragraph or so about your impressions of the book. He would like to have your comments printed in the four-color brochure his publisher will be mailing out to 100,000 business executives.

JOHN:

I want top billing, and I want my company affiliation mentioned. Of course, it would be great just to be included.

TED:

John, they are also going to include several reviewer comments in the national edition of *The Wall Street Journal.*

JOHN:

How soon would you want my comments?

TED:

Well, I can get a proposal delivered over here the day after tomorrow. And I would like to go over it with you back here about a week after that. I don't know if you will have time to read B.S. in such a short time.

JOHN:

I will finish it this weekend. And I'll have the review for you when you come back to go over this proposal.

TED:

That will be fine John. Let's set up a time.

JOHN:

How about 11 A.M. on the 30th. We can talk things over and then go to lunch.

TED:

That's great, John. See you at 11 on the 30th.

Two hours after Ted left John's office, he called Mr. Best Seller.

TED:

Hello, B.S. This is Ted.

B.S.:

Hi, Ted. Did you ever get that case of books we sent out?

TED:

Not only did I receive them, I just visited with John, the CEO of Exeter Corporation. He was absolutely elated to receive a copy of your latest work. He went into orbit when he read your note. I really appreciate your personalizing all those books. I realize that you are extremely busy.

B.S.:

Not a problem, Ted, I was glad to do it. Did John say he might be interested in writing a paragraph about the book?

TED:

Not only will he write it, I will have it faxed to your publisher on the 30th. And I have some other great news. John is considering adopting your book as an incentive for all of his sales force.

B.S.:

Ted, I really appreciate your support. John has quite an operation. I want to put him in my next book.

TED:

Wait, there are more good things to talk about. John is seriously thinking about sending copies of your new book to all of his top customers and suppliers.

B.S.:

How many customers and suppliers does he have?

TED:

Thousands. But it goes beyond this first level. If each of the folks endorses your work like I know they will, you will sell many, many more from their credibility alone.

B.S.:

That's fabulous. Just great.

TED:

You'd better stock up your supply of black pens.

B.S.:

I'll autograph every one of them. This is great. I really appreciate your going to bat for me. You should be in the public relations business, Ted.

TED:

B.S., I want to ask you about your publishing house. It's privately held, is it not?

B.S.:

I would call it closely held. Sid and his family still control it, and of course, Sid runs it. I mean really runs it. He insists on even signing every check the company writes over $1,000.

TED:

Well, who's idea was it to *get into the video business?*

B.S.:

That was Sid's brother Alan. He is no longer directly working for the firm. They lost their shirt on that part of the business. They know books, but they don't know anything about the video business.

TED:

Well, I agree completely with your assessment. And I have some ideas that I would like to share with Sid. I wonder how I could get hold of him.

B.S.:

I'll give you his phone number. In fact, I can give you the number for Sid's "hot-line," you know, his private line.

TED:

That will be great. Can I mention that we spoke?

B.S.:

Tell him that I suggested you call. He could really benefit from some consulting advice.

TED:

Do you think he would object to me using his private line? Is there any chance that you might be speaking with him in the next day or so?

B.S.:

I'll call him and tell him you will be contacting him.

TED:

That would be outstanding if you would be so kind. Please don't forget to tell him that I sell more books for his house than his PR agent.

B.S.:

It's a done deal. By the way, Ted, did you ever send out your information newsletter this month?

TED:

It's being printed as we speak.

B.S.:

Did you include your comments about my book?

TED:

Yes, your review took up the entire first page. I wrote the entire review myself. I titled it "An Absolutely Positively Must Read."

B.S.:

That's fabulous, Ted. How many people receive your newsletter?

TED:

Well, this fall issue is being sent to an expanded number of prospects. So, we are talking about around 2,100 owner/managers of privately/closely held corporations.

B.S.:

That's fabulous. Let me get off the phone now so that you can do your mailing and I can call Sid.

TED:

It's a deal. How many copies of my newsletter would you like for your own?

B.S.:

Send a couple of dozen.

TED:

It's a deal. Talk to you soon.

B.S.:

Good-bye, Ted.

CONDITIONING FOR THE FUTURE

How did Ted initially develop a relationship with B.S.? They did not meet at a country club or charity fundraiser. No, Ted took the proactive posture. B.S. was first recognized by Ted from a book review that was published about the author's first work. The review was not prominently displayed in the literary section of the newspaper. Most people never read book reviews. Even fewer have an interest in reflecting upon reviews of books by unknown authors. But Ted is not the typical reader. He reads strategically. He realized that often an initial positive review even in a minor-league newspaper can have a dramatic influence on sales. Important published reviews in the future can be predicted by some initial positive comments even by some obscure reviewers from publications with relatively small circulations.

Ted called B.S. immediately after he digested the review of his book. From what source did Ted obtain B.S.'s number? Ted first tried to obtain a copy of the book. However, it was not yet available in Ted's local area book stores. Ted reasoned that the book would contain some biographical information about the author's hometown. Without the book, Ted did the next best thing. He called the book reviewer and told him how much he enjoyed his comments. After several minutes, Ted mentioned that he wanted to contact B.S. to obtain an autographed copy. The reviewer supplied Ted with the name of the city where B.S. resided, as well as with the name of his company. Ted needed only to telephone long distance information to obtain B.S.'s home as well as office telephone numbers.

Ted's next actions should qualify him for the Marketers Professional Services Hall of Fame (if one is ever established). He called B.S.'s office and asked to speak with his secretary.

TED:

Hello, this is Ted. Are you Mr. B.S.'s secretary?

ROSE:

Yes, this is Rose. How can I help you?

TED:

Rose, I just read a great review on the book that was written by your boss. Did you help prepare the manuscript?

ROSE:

Prepare, type, edit, spell—and I was happy to help Mr. B.S. He is a super guy. Would you like to talk with him?

TED:

Well, I am just wondering if I would be intruding on him. He is not in the middle of writing another book, is he?

ROSE:

No. He goes through what you call air cycles. He's in the calming-down stage right now. He would love to talk to you about the book review for sure. Hold on for just a second.

B.S.:

Hello, this is B.S. How can I help you?

TED:

Hi, Mr. B.S., this is Ted. I just read a review of your book, and it's really piqued my interest.

B.S.:

Where was it reviewed? And what did they say?

TED:

The self-designated literary editor of our local paper wrote the review. He must have really liked it. He never usually gets excited about anything.

B.S.:

Could you be more specific?

TED:

Well, let me quote from the review: "B.S.'s contribution to the literature demonstrates an unusually candid, factual, and exceptional grasp of the factors that underlie the success of all entrepreneurial undertakings." And it even gets better: "This work will likely rank among the outstanding contemporary reflections produced within the last several years."

B.S.:

Could you send me a copy of the review?

TED:

I would be happy to. By the way, I just sent a copy of the review and a note to the business editor of *The New York Times.* I strongly recommended that he call your publisher and obtain a copy. Hope you don't mind.

B.S.:

Not at all. I can send him a copy. I have several cases sitting here on the floor.

TED:

I'll send his name and address along with the copies of the review and the note. But, Mr. B.S., I wonder if you would sell me a few copies. None of my book stores have it. How much is the book?

B.S.:

I can send you a copy. It retails for $24.95. What is your address?

TED:

[Gives his address.] Mr. B.S., do you have any fliers or brochures about the book?

B.S.:

Yes, I do.

TED:

Could you send me 300?

B.S.:

300!

TED:

Let me tell you what I would like to do with this information. Of course, with your approval. Every few months I send out some ideas to my clients and other contacts who are CEOs of some important companies in this country and a few located in Canada, the United Kingdom, and West Germany. Some refer to it as Ted's newsletter. But it's really not that sophisticated yet. I just put down some ideas on paper and send them out with copies of a couple of outstanding newsclips or articles. I would like to send the flier about your book as well as its review in my next mailout.

B.S.:

Do you think your clients would be interested in my work?

TED:

If your book is one-half as good as the review suggests, I will do more than recommend that they read it. In my next newsletter, I will place it on my "great Christmas gifts for clients and employees list." The price is right and under the $25 limit.

B.S.:

Well, I'll call my publisher right away. I'm sure that they will be glad to send you as many as you need. This is very nice of you to take this interest in my work. I hope there are others out there that will have the same reaction to the book. You have made my day.

TED:

No problem. I'm happy to assist a future star in the publishing business. Oh, I forgot—I want to send you a check for your book.

B.S.:

Oh, let me send you a copy with my compliments.

TED:

No! No! I would not think of it. In fact, I may as well buy several from you for some of my best clients and contacts.

B.S.:

What kind of business are you in Ted?

TED:

I'm the CEO of a management consulting firm—Ted Hunter and Associates. We design strategies for many of the best private corporations in this country. I enjoy working the entrepreneurial types. You know, like the folks you write about.

B.S.:

Sounds like we have a lot in common.

TED:

Before I let you get back to work, let me ask if it would be possible for the author to autograph my copy of the book.

B.S.:

I would be delighted.

TED:

>   Just say, "To my friend, Ted Hunter. All the best in what you do. Regards, B.S."

B.S.:

>   No problem.

TED:

>   Now, on the others. I would like to buy eight more. Please just say, "With the best wishes and compliments of Ted Hunter. Regards, B.S." I can give your secretary the names of the folks that I want to have the books personalized for.

B.S.:

>   No problem, just give them to me. Is it okay if I send them all to you? [Names given and written down.]

TED:

>   Of course. I want to hand deliver each one.

B.S.:

>   I can get them out of here today.

TED:

>   Please send them by air express. I'll give you my account i.d. number. I'll put the check in the mail today. That's a total of nine books times $24.95. Is that right?

B.S.:

>   You are correct. Also, Ted, would you send me your newsletter and put me on your mailing list?

TED:

>   It's a done deal. Thanks for your kindness. So long.

B.S.:

>   Bye, Ted.

TED IS A MENTOR AND PROMOTER

How long did it take Ted to get to know B.S.? Only a few minutes. But more than being just acquaintances, B.S. feels indebted to Ted for his help. Ted does not view this young author as a target for his consulting services. B.S. is someone that Ted will genuinely enjoy helping with his career. But more importantly, this association with best-selling authors enhances his own confidence and self-image. These factors, in turn, are foundations for establishing credibility with prospects. One of Ted's major weapons in "breaking the ice" with targeted prospects is to reflect upon his associations with authors of best-selling books. Ted's method of persuasion can be summed up in just four words: *Credibility Enhancement by Association.*

Play the role of mentor and informal promoter of soon-to-be best-selling authors. In the future, they will likely return the favor many times over by allowing you to associate yourself with their prestige, their fame, their credibility. Credibility enhancement by association is the basis of most successful commercial conditioning strategies and tactics.

CHAPTER 9

ENDORSED BY THE MEDIA

SO, YOU WANT TO BE A TALK-SHOW HOST

The telephone rings. My secretary tells me, "It's David from a radio station. He would like to know if you would do an interview. Would you like to speak to David?" I'd be delighted. What an interesting young man David Robinson is.

David is a self-employed financial consultant based in the Orlando, Florida, area. He has his own interview show on WBZS, a business radio network program which, in this particular case, originates in Orlando. David asked me if I would do an interview from 6:15–6:45 P.M. on Friday. I agreed to do the interview, especially after he told me some of the people he had recently interviewed were noted celebrities. David also mentioned it would be a good idea for me to be interviewed because their listening audience included many people who were sensitive to business information, as well as people who would be potential candidates to purchase books.

David obviously is a great marketer because he focuses on the need of the target, not only on his own need. In fact, David reflected upon the fact that he would be delighted if I would mention the name of my book and a telephone number people in the listening audience could call to obtain a copy of the book.

Interestingly enough, I asked David how he became involved with having his own talk show on such a prestigious network program. He responded by telling me that about 10 months prior to this telephone conversation, he saw a small news item in the business section of the local newspaper. It indicated that one of the Orlando radio stations was changing its format from music to an all-business format.

David described himself as a talk-show junkie. Obviously, he has been fascinated with this concept. So he wrote a short proposal and sent it to the principals at the radio station, suggesting that they have a program running about 30 minutes once a week to discuss critical issues in the business and investment area. He was shocked when he got a response from the principals of this radio station suggesting that he become the host for this radio show. He had never done a show, but they were so impressed with this outline and perception of the needs of the audience that they would not accept a refusal.

So, David is on the air . What a great way to communicate with the target audience. He is also a financial consultant, and his credibility is obviously enhanced as well as his exposure to target affluent populations. And of course, he is very clever in the sense that he is able to associate himself with those public figures who hopefully have significant credibility and expertise in areas of importance to listeners. This conditions affluent targets to view David as a highly credible source of information because he is, in fact, a local celebrity and associates with people with significant intellect about investments and business-related issues.

David has used a noncommercial avenue, that is, not-paid-for advertising, as a way to communicate with the target audience. This very often is much more important in terms of productivity and image development than paid-for advertising. It is not easy to put on a weekly show. It takes a tremendous amount of effort and diligence on the part of David, but he is a person who is willing to work hard to achieve his goals of exposure and credibility development on his target audience.

FRED, CAN YOU SEND US ONE MORE ARTICLE?

And Now at the End Of Our Seminar—

"Thank you for your support of our seminars on marketing to the affluent. Your continued patronage is greatly appreciated. You now have in your marketing arsenal some of the latest and most innovative weapons with which to penetrate the affluent market.

Acquiring new ideas and methods for improving one's market performance is an interesting and exciting experience. However, the time you spent gaining this knowledge can be wasted. Courage and discipline on your part are needed to capitalize on your newly acquired strengths.

On your journey home today, think about your most important client. Most often, the client who generates the highest commissions/fees for you owns a business. But what kind of business? If you don't know, promise yourself that you will call your client on Monday and ask the critical question about the source of his wealth.

Also, take a vow right this moment that on Monday you will ask your best client the following questions: (1) What trade journal do you read most often? (2) Can I have your old copies? (3) Who is the editor of the trade journal? (4) Would you recommend me to the editor as a possible source of an article?

Remember, your goal is to leverage your newly acquired knowledge as well as your relationships with affluent clients. Are you like most sales professionals who seek the affluent? Most have only one client from upwards of hundreds of distinct industries. Your goal should be to penetrate specific affluent targets deeply. Your first client from within a specific industry is generally the most difficult to capture. Others from within the same industry will be more likely to do business with you if you already deal with one or more of their cohorts.

One highly efficient method of prospecting relates to the use of trade journals. The trade journal that you will pick up Monday at your client's place of work may be a treasure chest of market opportunity. Most trade journals contain articles and news reports about successful business owners who are part of a specific industry. This information can be highly valuable if you take the time to use it. When is the ideal time to contact a prospect? The ideal time is when he is euphoric about being cited in his favorite trade journal such as *Sludge Tomorrow* or *Scrap Metal Diary*. Consider capitalizing on his needs and values. He wants his achievements to be recognized in these trades. You, too, would be proud with an acknowledgment in your own industry's trade journal as a top-performing sales professional. So have some empathy for the same needs of the superachievers in your targeted industries. Identify them from the trade journals. Contact them and congratulate them. Affluent prospects are more likely to deal with sales professionals who have clients from within the same industry and who recognize their achievements. But, *in most cases, these achievements will never be publicized in the local newspaper. So, look beyond the so-called popular press.*

How else can you capitalize on trade journals? This coming Monday, you will identify the editor of your best client's favorite trade journal. Call the editor and ask the critical public relations question. Ask if he would be interested in publishing your article. Even ask your client to call the editor on your behalf. More often than not, editors of trade journals are in need of articles. Why not establish yourself as the industry expert by sharing your wisdom? If you lease automobiles, write about the important features that should be included in a lease agreement. If you sell investment services, you may wish to discuss the alternative types of pension plans. But whatever you discuss, always provide industry-specific case examples from the targeted segment. If you target environmental engineers, then include cases and comments from people in this industry. Remember, successful business owners have strong affiliation needs. They often prefer to read articles by and also deal with sales professionals who relate to the people and problems of their industry. Publishing articles will give you significant exposure and credibility within your targeted industry. It will help make your cold calling within such industries much warmer. Also, publishing will encourage prospects to take the initiative of calling you!

Thank you; have a safe trip home and a great weekend. But don't forget your promise to call your best client on Monday.''

No Grass under Fred's Feet

Fred was one of the members of the seminar audience. He was 30 years old and had been in sales for only three years. But despite his youth and inexperience, his employer saw potential in him. Fred's company picked up all of his tuition and travel for this seminar. How perceptive Fred's employer was in selecting him for advanced sales training.

Early on the Monday following the seminar, Fred telephoned

his best client. This call was the foundation for Fred's commu- nications campaign. He did more than publish in the trade journal recommended by this client. Within one year following the seminar, Fred has had his articles published in five different trade journals!

Fred's strategy for having his ideas published can be readily adopted by others who target the affluent business owner. Follow Fred's path to gain exposure and credibility.

Fred Wins with Bingo Cards

Few trade journals will pay cash to those who supply them with manuscripts. But cash payment is not the reason that Fred pub- lishes his ideas. Obviously, writing enhances his credibility with specific target markets. The degree to which publishing facilitates Fred's selling greatly outweighs the stipend issue.

Often editors of trade journals will actually apologize to au- thors because, as they state, "We can't pay you for your manu- script." What is the proper reply to such a statement? There are many services that an editor can provide an author like Fred. And they frequently do not entail cash outlays. Yes, bartering is big business in the publishing arena. First and foremost, Fred and others wise enough to see the value of writing want their articles published. The first reply to the "no money" statement should be along the lines of a guarantee to publish within a specific period of time. Promising to publish one's manuscript within the next two years is not of real benefit to people in Fred's position. Ideally, the editor should make a commitment to publish within one year or even six months. In addition, the editor should be willing to specify a particular issue in which the article will appear. This is a real commitment. Also, it will be beneficial to advise clients and pros- pects who read the targeted journal precisely when the article will appear.

Fred has also discovered other elements of value in supplying his manuscripts to editors who cannot pay cash for them. The Bingo Card Service, as Fred refers to it, is provided to him free of charge. The following statement is strategically positioned at the end of each of Fred's monthly articles in *SNIPS:*

> Note: For additional details on investment in the area dis- cussed . . . circle 342 on postcard.

The very day that I interviewed Fred by telephone, he had just received four requests from readers who wanted further information from him.

Bingo cards/reader service information cards are often used by trade journals to help their advertisers develop prospect lists. Prospects self-designate themselves by circling numbers that correspond to the products or services about which they wish to learn more. In Fred's situation, the use of this tactic in conjunction with his articles is quite innovative and productive. These reader service information cards are mailed (postpaid) by prospects directly to *SNIPS Magazine* in Bellwood, Illinois. Periodically, *SNIPS* sends Fred a complete computer printout of the names of those who circled "his number" on the bingo card. Also contained on the printout are several other important pieces of information about the respondent and his business, including occupation/title, job function, number of employees, type of business, company name, company address, company telephone number, and date the card was filled out.

The advantage of using bingo cards over traditional methods of prospecting is quite evident. By "playing bingo," interested prospects self-designate themselves. They ask the sales professional to contact them. Conventional prospecting is much less efficient. In such cases, the sales professional often has to contact thousands of people just to uncover that small number of prospects who are "interested in receiving additional details." Winners in the game of marketing understand the importance of concentrating their fire power. Fred is in the winner's circle because he targets those whom he already knows are interested in his offerings.

Beyond Bingo

Fred's involvement with trade journals has generated business for him from unexpected sources. In fact, Fred's system of marketing works so well that often affluent prospects take the initiative of asking for his service. An editor of one of the trade journals to which Fred submitted an article is in this proactive category. He was so impressed with the investment ideas contained in Fred's manuscript that he opened an investment account with him! With the addition of this client, Fred is now only steps removed from the really affluent occupational group in the trade journal industry—the publishers. But his close affiliation within this industry should enable him to penetrate this subsegment. Certainly, the publishers of the journals to which Fred contributes feel that his ideas are valuable to their readers. Fred's services should correspondingly be of significant value to the publishers. After all, since they cannot afford to pay him in cash for his articles, they should be willing to pay for his investment products and services. Fred should ask his favorite publishers about those who handle their companies' pension plans and cash management accounts. One way or another, Fred will be compensated for his labor.

One must remember that editors and publishers admire writers. And what if a writer just so happens to also be a marketer of investment services? In such cases, the marketer has an inside tract in gaining new clients from their occupational categories. Fred is finding a growing number of his new clients who share his common interest in literary pursuits.

Fred now receives complimentary copies of six different trade journals. These publications are the ones to which he contributes articles. He often pages through these journals to gain insights about the various industries that he has targeted. While paging through one of the more "obscure" publications, he came across an especially attractive advertisement. Fred was so impressed with the advertisement that he called the president of the sponsoring firm to compliment him. During their conversation, Fred mentioned the article that he had published in the same issue in which the advertisement appeared. Before this conversation ended, the president became yet another client. Fred took the time to recognize and compliment the president about the achievements of the firm in terms of advertising. He also explained to the president that they were both affiliated with the same industry, same trade journal, and same market segment. Flattering and affiliation translated into patronage.

When Fred called the president to congratulate him, he never intended to sell him anything. But often some of the most remarkable marketing tactics are discovered by accident. Fred now knows that he can greatly expand his business by prospecting those who advertise in the trades as well as those who are featured in the articles of those journals. Paying homage to a prospect's industry-specific achievements often translates into his patronage.

An Endless Chain of Heavy Readers

Can you describe the heaviest readers of trade literature? Answer this question correctly, and you will be able to appreciate how Fred has been able to expand greatly both his exposure and business within selected affluent targets. I estimate that the most ardent readers of Fred's articles are editors and writers of competitive and complementary trade journals. Yes, Fred is being read by the writers in the same industry that he is targeting. But why do they wish to read Fred's material? They seek ideas and suggestions. But more importantly, they are in constant search of people who can help them with their number one problem. There are over 6,000 trade journals. Assume that every one of them needs at least five articles for each monthly issue or 60 per year. A conservative estimate is that 360,000 manuscripts are needed each year by the trade journal industry. Just think of 360,000 deadlines which have to be met. Often, editors are in dire need of the manuscripts that the Freds of the world can contribute. Also, in-house writers often seek publishable information from Fred and his cohorts.

Given the great need in this country for articles that can be published in trade journals, it is no wonder that an increasing number of editors are asking Fred to supply them with manuscripts. But of course, they "can't pay for his contributions!"

Many publishing companies own several trade journals. Impress the management of these types of publishing companies with your writing ability and what can you expect to happen? Fred published one article and was then asked not only to publish more in the same journal but to contribute to sister periodicals that targeted different audiences/industries. Exposure and increased business are certainly correlates of Fred's writing habits. However, as he told me, there is one problem: "More and more editors are calling me requesting articles. That's the problem. I'm running out of articles!"

FOLLOW FRED'S FOOTSTEPS

Successful marketing programs begin with good ideas. But ideas have little value if they are never implemented. Fred, however, is the type of sales professional who actually capitalizes upon new ideas. The process that Fred followed in establishing his position with several affluent industries can be of great value to those who take the initiative to act. Often sales professionals complain that they are not given innovative weapons with which to penetrate the affluent market. This speculation should have little validity for those who reflect upon strategies such as Fred's. Every sales professional can benefit from reviewing these simple yet effective approaches to the affluent market.

The steps are as follows:

1. Contact your best client who owns a business.   What if none of your current clients own a business or you feel a bit uncomfortable about asking a business client for a favor? Then refer to Pro Forma Letter 1–A which follows these steps.

2. Ask this key contact for the names of the trade journals that he feels are most important in his industry.

3. Request that he keep his old copies for you.   Don't be shy about asking for current copies if he agrees to share his old copies with you.

4. Review each trade journal and determine the name, address, and telephone number of the editor(s).

5. Write or telephone the editor.   Explain to him that you are interested in having your manuscript published in his trade journal. Be sure to explain that one or more of his subscribers/industry members recommended that you call him. Prior to this, be certain to gain such endorsements from your key contact(s). (See Pro Forma Letters 1–B and 1–C.)

6. Emphasize to the editor that your area of interest is compatible with the needs of his readers and sponsors. Remember, you do not necessarily have to write about your specific product offering. In fact, some articles have a higher probability of being published if they are not product-specific. Some who sell investment products write about the changing demographics of our population, while others who wish to market luxury automobiles to affluent readers/ business owners may wish to write about the pros and cons of auto leasing in light of recent tax legislation. (See Table 9–1.)

7. Once your article is published in a particular trade journal, explore the opportunity of republishing it in other noncompeting outlets.   But be sure to ask for the approval of the editor of the journal where your material first appeared.

8. Ask each editor who has accepted your article if his pub-

TABLE 9–1
Focusing and Capitalizing on the Needs of Editors of Trade Journals

Editor's Needs	Typical Comments Which Reflect Editor's Needs	Sales Professional's Needs	Response to Editor's Needs
Hold all costs to absolute minimum.	"I'm sorry, but I can't pay you for your article"	Significant exposure to specific segments. Condition editor to feel indebted to writer/sales professional.	"Being published is more important than cash payments for an article."
Demonstrate to publisher ability to barter for manuscripts.	"But perhaps we could assist you in some other way."	Help editor fulfill his need to minimize cash outlays.	"Instead of cash payment, would it be possible to have my name, address, and phone number printed at the end of my article?"
Publish articles that will be of considerable interest to subscribers and prospective subscribers.	"I just wonder if your topic will be of real interest to our readers."	Provide written material which is of enough interest to generate inquiries from readers/prospects.	"I have already shared my ideas with several of your subscribers. Every one of them felt that this article is of critical importance to *your* target audience."
Demonstrate empathy for the achievement/recognition needs of subscribers.	"But what we are really looking for are articles which focus on the people in our industry."	Meet/affiliate with affluent/ successful business owners from targeted industries.	"I plan to interview several of this industry's leaders. Their comments will be incorporated in my manuscript. I have already received commitments from five of this industry's most respected businessmen."

Meet all publishing deadlines.	"A lot of nonprofessional writers don't understand the importance of delivering their work on time." "Our subscribers and advertisers don't like to be kept waiting. We must deliver when we promise to deliver."	Demonstrate ability to meet all schedule parameters stipulated by editors. Condition editor to feel that the writer/sales professional is an important and dependable resource to be exploited. Encourage editor to think of writer/sales professional as a *regular* (monthly) contributor.	"I know just how you feel. One late manuscript can hold up your entire issue. I have never failed to meet a deadline. In fact, I can deliver my work at least two weeks before your deadline. I can fill in for others who drop the ball (fail to deliver their article to you). I always have several manuscripts in various stages of development."
Demonstrate that the publisher made the right choice in hiring a new editor.	"My publisher just hired me as the new editor because he has great expectations for this journal." "Publishers often believe that editors can perform miracles without resources."	Help the newly appointed editor solidify his position and enhance his reputation. Convert editor from the category of business acquaintance to a *friend* for life.	"All eyes are upon you right now. Everyone expects great things from you. I know you will do well. Please let me know how I can be of assistance to you. Think of me as a resource for articles, advice, whatever. Let me give you my office and home phone numbers. Call me anytime."
Publish material that will not appear in competing journals. Make exclusive agreements attractive by offering services on barter basis.	"You will have to give us an exclusive on your material. There is nothing worse than seeing the same material in competing publications." "We can offer writers a great deal even beyond exposure."	Provide evidence of strong allegiance and commitment to editor and his journal. This will enable the writer/sales professional to leverage/barter for services.	"I would be delighted to give you an exclusive within this industry. But I would also expect that you will consider me as your key contributor in terms of my own product area."

TABLE 9–1 (concluded)

Editor's Needs	Typical Comments Which Reflect Editor's Needs	Sales Professional's Needs	Response to Editor's Needs
Offer reciprocal agreements on exclusivity.			"I notice that you provide reader service information card (bingo card) services. Can I get a number? It's a lot easier for your subscribers to request additional information from me."
Increase advertising revenues by expanding sponsor base.	"I'm not sure that our sponsors will see much value in having your article next to their advertisements."	Focus on the editor's need to increase revenues by attracting new sponsors.	"Financial service firms will want to place advertisements in the issue that contains the pension-planning article; automobile manufacturers will wish to sponsor advertisements in a journal which discusses the pros and cons of auto leasing; and so on."

lisher owns any other trade journals. If so, offer to contribute similar articles within the publisher's family of trade journals.

9. Ask all editors who seem to be impressed with your work if they would consider you as a regular contributor to their respective publications.   Contributing material in this manner will assure you of gaining exposure with your target audience. It may also preclude any of your competitors from publishing their ideas in the same journal. (Also, see Step 11).

10. Always write to the prospects/clients who assisted you in having your article published.   (See Pro Forma Letter 1–D.)

11. Be sure to write a letter thanking the editor for publishing your article. This is also an excellent time to recommend that he consider publishing a special issue related to your area of expertise. (See Pro Forma Letter 1–E.)

12. Order reprints of all your articles. Send these reprints to selected prospects within the targeted industry. What if a prospect subscribes to the trade journal that publishes your material? Send the reprint to him anyway. Your reprint should be accompanied by a note suggesting, "You might be interested in reading my latest article which appeared in *our* industry's trade journal. Since you are considered to be a leader in this industry, I would appreciate your reviewing my work and critiquing it for me. I'll call in a week or two to get your thoughts."

13. Be sure to send copies of your article to those people who are written about in the journals that publish your material. Also enclose a copy of the article that mentions them. Be sure to write, "Congratulations on being selected as entrepreneur of the year (or being selected to the board of directors). Enclosed is a copy of the article in which your achievements are recognized. I am sure it will come in handy." Follow up on these mailings with telephone discussions.

14. Send reprints of your article to the heads of those companies that place advertisements in the same journals that publish your articles. Congratulate them on the quality of their advertising. Follow up your mailing with a telephone call to their executives. Always ask them about their business and their opinions about your work. Ask if they would be interested in receiving information about your product offerings.

15. Facilitate unsolicited inquiries by having your name, address, telephone number, and affiliation printed at the end of each of your articles. Also, include an offer to provide additional information; this should stimulate more inquiries. This offer is even more effective when used in conjunction with a reader service information card (the bingo card).

16. In anticipation of receiving unsolicited calls and letters from prospects who have read your published material, prepare an information dossier. This dossier should include reprints of all your articles, your biographical sketch, promotional material about your product, and an audio or video tape which features you and your philosophy about your product or service offering.

17. Ask these industry-specific prospects to do business with you. Time your actual telephone or in-person solicitations so that they are in harmony with the prospect's need and cash flow horizons. This can be determined during your first contact with the prospect. Always inquire about his or her purchase intentions and cash flow patterns.

LETTER 1–A

Pro Forma Letter Asking Prospects/Clients for Copies of Their Industries' Trade Journals

Mr. Richard F. Fisk
President
Clean and Neat, Inc.
4420 Wells Avenue
Long Beach, CA 90801

Dear Dick:

After having all of my dry cleaning done for the past six years at your Irvine store, it was nice to finally meet the owner. Clean and Neat has yet to break a button on my shirts or to lose any of my clothing. Even more importantly, you folks always make me look like I am concerned about my personal appear-

LETTER 1–A (*concluded*)

ance. This is especially significant since my profession calls for a great deal of interaction with clients and prospects.

My goal for this year is to write at least one article for *The Dry Cleaner Today*. Since our visit, I had a chance to read over the issue you were so kind to give me. Your concerns about what the future holds for the industry are certainly reflected in the journal. Several writers mentioned the problems that the industry faces such as the rapid growth in competition, legislation banning some of the industry's most productive cleaning solutions, and the increasing number of law suits initiated by people who claim damage done to their "new and expensive" clothing.

In spite of these problems, this industry provides some wonderful economic opportunities both for owner/operators and for those who choose to supply products and services to the more productive firms.

I have made a decision to focus on your industry. This is why I am writing an article about pension planning for dry cleaners. Your suggestions about pension needs would really improve the quality of the manuscript. I hope you will not mind if I ask for some of your ideas and comments sometime in the near future.

As I mentioned to you this morning, your industry's trade journals provide me with important resource material. Are you still willing to pass your old issues along to me? Assuming your response is still yes, I have enclosed one box labeled "Dry Cleaning Journals: Please Deposit Old Issues and Hold for Bruce D. Representative. Before making any deposits, please remove and consume one custom apple crumb cake from the kitchen of Bruce and Wanda." I will stop by your office periodically to pick up the journals you deposit. Thank you for your assistance.

Sincerely,

Bruce D. Representative
Vice President

LETTER 1–B

Pro Forma Letter Asking Editor of Trade Journal to Publish Your Article

Date: Today

Mr. John D. Ross, Editor
Pizza World
1960 Trade Lane
Boston, MA 02100

Dear Mr. Ross:

I enjoyed speaking with you yesterday. As I mentioned, Charles R. Major, a distinguished member of your industry and trade association, suggested that you may be interested in publishing some of my ideas. Contributing to *Pizza World* is important to me. Several important industry leaders, including Mr. Major, are very interested in enhancing the productivity of members of the pizza industry. Mr. Jeno E. Sifone of Jeno's Big East Pizza and Mr. John C. Stella of West Hartford Pizza also assisted me in better understanding the investment needs of your readers.

Enclosed are three copies of a draft entitled "What You Should Know before Choosing a Money Manager" that I would like to have considered for publication in *Pizza World*. Also enclosed are my biographical profile and an abstract of the draft. You will note from the abstract that my firm monitors the performance of hundreds of some of the nation's best independent investment managers. My role is to match my clients with managers that best fit their investment needs and objectives.

If you would also be interested in considering publishing a series of my articles on various investment topics, please let me know. I have always enjoyed writing and appreciate your need to receive manuscripts in a timely fashion. I have never failed to

LETTER 1–B (*concluded*)

meet a writing deadline. Other topics that I write about include pension planning, tax-advantaged investments, investment products and objectives of the business owner, and investing the proceeds from the sale of a business.

Please note that I would be more than happy to make any modifications to the draft that you might recommend. Also, feel free to "cut and paste" if your layout parameters warrant such changes. I will call you next week to see if you have any questions about my manuscript. Also, I would appreciate it if you would help me identify two or three other industry leaders who operate in the New England area. I would like to interview several of these operators in order to enhance the quality of the article.

Thank you for your consideration. I look forward to speaking with you.

Sincerely,

Bruce D. Representative
Vice President

Enclosures

cc: Charles R. Major
      Jeno E. Sifone
      John C. Stella

LETTER 1–C

Pro Forma Letter to Industry Leader Requesting an Interview in Concert with an Article You Are Writing

Mr. Robert S. Russo
Boston's Best Pizza
One Big Wharf
Boston, MA 02111

Dear Mr. Russo:

The editor of *Pizza World*, Mr. John D. Ross, suggested that I seek your advice. I am in the process of writing an article that is targeted for publication in *Pizza World*, your industry's leading trade journal. The manuscript would benefit very much from the insights and suggestions of acknowledged industry leaders like yourself.

The topics which will be presented include discussions about the needs that retail pizza operators have for pension planning, tax-advantaged investments, cash management, estimating the value of the business, and investing the proceeds from the sale of the retail pizza operation.

If possible, I would like to interview you next week. The interview will only take about 20 minutes. I will call your office later this week to determine if we can set up a suitable time for an interview.

Thank you for your consideration.

Sincerely,

Bruce D. Representative
Vice President

LETTER 1-D

Pro Forma Letter Thanking Prospect/Client for His Assistance in Having an Article Published in His Industry's Trade Journal

Mr. Richard F. Fisk
President
Clean and Neat, Inc.
4420 Wells Avenue
Long Beach, CA 90801

Dear Dick:

Be sure to look at the June issue of *The Dry Cleaner Today* (pp. 31–36) when it arrives. Yes, they have accepted my article, "Pension Planning for the Owner/Operator." Several of your insightful comments are included along with your name and the name of Clean and Neat.

Thank you for all your help.

Sincerely,

Bruce D. Representative
Vice President

LETTER 1-E

Pro Forma Letter Thanking Editor for Publishing Your Article and Suggesting a Special Financial Service Issue and a Regular Column on This Topic

Mr. John D. Ross, Editor
Pizza World
1960 Trade Lane
Boston, MA 02100

Dear John:

What a delight to see my article published in the March issue of *Pizza World*. Thank you for the extra copies. My manager showed a copy to each one of my colleagues. He also praised me for taking the initiative of sharing my ideas with an important segment of industry. I learned a great deal from the industry leaders that I interviewed for the article. During these interviews, it occurred to me that a special annual issue of *Pizza World* may be well received by your readers. This special issue would be devoted almost entirely to the financial service needs of pizza operators. Topics of great interest might include: (1) sources of business credit; (2) 10 things to consider before selling the business; (3) pension-planning alternatives for the business owner; (4) several ways to earn high interest on your business's cash balances; (5) the profitability of retail pizza operations—industry norms; (6) the impact of tax law changes on business owners; (7) insurance packages for property and casualty coverage; (8) special variations of key man life insurance; (9) estate planning for the business owner; and (10) funding the college education for your children and grandchildren.

Please let me know what your thoughts are relating to the special-issue concept. I am interested in contributing in any way that you would suggest. I am certain that many major-league advertisers from the financial service industry will be interested in buying up space.

As an alternative to the special issue, a regular column about financial topics should stimulate readership as well as

---

LETTER 1–E (*concluded*)

sponsorship. If you feel a need to have a regular columnist, I know the perfect candidate, AKA "yours truly."
    Hope to talk to you soon.

Regards,

Bruce D. Representative
Vice President

ADDENDUM TO CHAPTER 9

Three Extraordinary Cases of Credibility Enhancement

ASK PAUL, THE EXPERT IN ADVISING LOTTERY WINNERS

LOTTERY WINNER:

    I've just won the Florida Lottery. What should I do with the money?

BANK TELLER:

    Oh! You should ask Paul. He has advised many lottery winners. He's assembled a checklist of more than 20 do's and don'ts for lottery winners to follow.

Paul W. Fleming is an investment consultant working on a daily basis with the clients of a major bank. In this capacity, Paul has been involved with a large number of lottery winners. He developed what is now Chapter 1 of his book, *When You Win,* as a checklist of suggestions to be used in initial meetings with these winners. His checklist includes recommendations regarding: the

---

Addendum to Chapter 9 (*continued*)

press and publicity, security, guilt feelings, consumption habits, and lifestyle changes as well as 15 other suggestions.

Paul is a certified financial planner and holds a master of business administration degree. He speaks to groups in the fields of mutual funds, asset allocation, and retirement planning. He is an active member of the International Association for Financial Planning.

Dear Tom,

It was a pleasure meeting and talking to you in Acapulco. Your talk, like your book, *Marketing to the Affluent,* was great.

I have enclosed two items of relevance to targeting the affluent: First, this discussion of the newly affluent such as lottery winners; second, a copy of the manuscript of my book, *When You Win.* My manuscript is addressed to the lottery winner, but the advice it contains applies to any recipient of a windfall. It covers financial, as well as general, advice for the newly affluent. I am just starting the process of sending this manuscript to publishers. Any advice you have for me in this area would be appreciated.

As an investment consultant for a bank, I often am involved with people who have "new money." For example, about 30 million people play the lottery. In Florida alone, over 100 families became millionaires in the past two years through winnings from the lottery. In addition, we are known as a "sue-happy" civilization, and lawsuits put a lot of money into people's hands. Moreover, pension plans have grown in recent years, and as people move jobs and companies change ownership, more people have large pension payouts to handle. It is estimated that over $8 trillion will be passed to heirs in the next 20 years.

While not all of this new money will put people in the multimillionaire class, there is a considerable amount of windfall money available every year. There

Addendum to Chapter 9 (*continued*)

are several categories of the newly affluent, and these categories may be divided into recepients of:

1. Lottery winnings.
2. Insurance settlements (accident and malpractice).
3. Life insurance payouts.
4. Pension plan payouts and rollovers.
5. Divorce settlements.
6. Inheritance.
7. Business and property sales.

For lottery winners, receiving this money is a complete surprise. People in all the other categories have at least some time to think and plan before the money is actually in their hands.

The common feature of lottery winners is fright. Typically, the winnings represent more money than the winner has ever seen, and he is afraid of making the wrong decision. Quite often, therefore, lottery winners make no decisions—at least for a while. I have seen hundreds of thousands of dollars sit in savings accounts for over a year. The lottery winner, for some reason, is also often arrogant and exhibits a "know-it-all" attitude which impedes professional advisors.

It seems that people in all the categories have the proverbial "brother-in-law who knows all about investing." This relative or acquaintance is frequently the first contact of the newly affluent individual. With a vaunting ego, the relative gives advice even if he or she is totally unqualified to do so. Since this advice is the first information the newly affluent individual hears, it tends to stick in mind. All other advice is measured against it.

The second contact is usually a bank employee. The newly acquired check must be cashed, and most people perceive banks as trustworthy institutions. If the relationship with bank personnel is good, the banker gets a chance to give advice and suggest other advisors.

Personal referral is the best, indeed, almost the only,

Addendum to Chapter 9 (*continued*)

way to meet the newly affluent. It is not necessary to be the first person in the financial industry to meet this individual. Often the subject will shop around for advice and information. By about the fifth such session, the newly affluent person is so full of conflicting advice and ideas, a professional who can organize thoughts and clarify concepts will end up doing business with him. Third-party endorsements work well here.

Although a less common occurrence, it is sometimes possible to seek out the newly affluent. I am reminded of the movie in which Paul Newman, playing a lawyer, distributes his business cards at funerals.

While funds from the sale of businesses are not exactly windfalls, the people who receive money from such sales have some of the same characteristics as other newly affluent. They worked hard to build their businesses and are afraid to risk financial mistakes. They may know all about their businesses but little or nothing about investing. If anything, they err too far on the side of safety and neglect the future ravages of inflation.

Indeed, inflation must be high on the agenda in any discussion with the newly affluent. If you are advising a new lottery millionaire who will receive, for instance, $50,000 before taxes for the next 20 years, you will have to talk him back to reality and explain what $50,000 will buy in the year 2010.

In short, all newly affluent must be educated as well as reassured. Unfortunately, the process of education sometimes alienates the newly affluent individual; he thinks he is automatically rich.

I look forward to meeting you again and to reading your new book.

Sincerely,

Paul W. Fleming

Addendum to Chapter 9 (*continued*)

THE ULTIMATE FORM OF CREDIBILITY: ENDORSED BY THE MOST SENIOR PARTNER

Dear Tom:

I'll admit to having second thoughts after our conversation about having my experiences related to marketing. But after some "meditation" last night, I concluded that life's endeavors—be they business or ministry—ARE marketing. And in the deepest sense, my book, *The Thoughtful Christian's Guide to Investing*, is a definite attempt to market a balanced concept of true wealth or "affluence" to investors. So I would simply ask your sensitivity when relating my experiences.

If I might relate my most important lesson in this experience, it is to help people first and the rest will take care of itself (Christians express it as "seek first the kingdom and all this will be added unto you."). As a broker, I used to start my months with production quotas and then worry about how to reach them. I'm afraid I would not have made interesting material for your book.

But my simple efforts to help others have prompted letters from the White House, Mr. Templeton, Dr. Schuller, and others. Heady stuff for a simple investment broker. It's been a humbling lesson and one I hope I never forget.

Hope to see your newest work soon.

Sincerely,

Gary Moore
Senior Vice President
Investments

Addendum to Chapter 9 (*continued*)

Gary Moore is a senior vice president of investments in the Tampa, Florida, office of a major Wall Street investment firm. He is a member of the Social Investment Forum, the Council on Economic Priorities, and the Christian Stewardship Association. With his wife, he has founded the Institute for Thoughtful Investing which studies, lectures, and writes about those professionals and organizations which apply the Judeo-Christian ethic to the modern management of wealth. (He is studying for ordination in his spare moments.)

CHUMMING FOR LARGE FISH VIA THE TRADES

March 19 (At the End of a Seminar)

MR. JEFF M.:

Dr. Stanley, my office is in Washington state. Could you suggest an affluent industry that I should target?

DR.STANLEY:

There are several important ones in your area. Why not first consider targeting commercial fishermen and apple growers? Start by writing an article for one of their trade journals. Then the "big fish will chase your boat."

MR. JEFF M.:

I'll give it a try. Thanks.

DR STANLEY:

My pleasure. Keep me posted and don't forget to send me a copy of your article.

May 11 (A Note from Jeff M.)

Addendum to Chapter 9 (*concluded*)

Tom:

    This [my] column is sent to 17,000 fishermen every two weeks. My first lead was a fisherman with $400,000 in cash and $600,000 in other accounts. I should land him in July. I'll let you know.

    By the way, the column cost me zero dollars.

Jeff M.

Alaska Commercial Fisherman

(May 11, 1990, p. 4)

Q's and A's about Money

Q Retiring . . . like to sell my boat and invest . . . to get highest return with least . . . risk. What should I do?
A Market risk . . . the stock market . . . applied to fishing . . . a pound of salmon . . . next year $2 or 50 cents.

July 20 (A Phone Call from Jeff M.)

DR. STANLEY:

  Hello, Tom Stanley.

MR. JEFF M.:

  Hello, Tom. This is Jeff M. Remember that lead I mentioned in the note I sent you?

DR. STANLEY:

  Yes, I certainly do.

MR. JEFF M.:

  The fellow I mentioned came to see me. He opened an account with me. He also promised to introduce me to all his colleagues in Alaska. He is a pillar of the fishing community up there!

CHAPTER 10

LEVERAGE YOUR AFFLUENT TARGETS' NEED FOR SEMINARS AND SPEAKERS

NO, YOU'RE NOT TOO YOUNG TO PERSUADE THE AFFLUENT

Only six weeks had passed since Larry had attended one of my seminars. But in six weeks, this young man demonstrated more initiative than the vast majority of his fellow sales professionals. My presentation included a brief discussion of proactive marketing tactics in regard to targeting business owners. I asked the following question of my audience:

> If you cannot predict when an affluent business owner will sell his company, why not precipitate this event? If you are wise enough to precipitate the sale, then you will be the first to know when the target will encounter a major upswing in cash flow. The affluent are most susceptible to solicitations when they are euphoric because of positive changes in liquid wealth. Why not develop seminars on valuing the small/medium-sized company? You will be able to attract business owners that are contemplating the cashing in of their chips. . . . Other professionals would be delighted to participate in your seminar. Ask a CPA from a prestige firm to discuss various ways of valuing a business. Allow him to illustrate real-life examples. Invite an attorney from a well-established firm to discuss the significant legal elements that should be included in the sales contract. This is especially important because sellers often transfer ownership before they receive full payment. Then you can discuss various investments that would be most productive for all those transition dollars."

I expected some of the seasoned, top-producing sales professionals in attendance to act upon my suggestion. But I never anticipated that a fellow with just two months' sales experience would capitalize upon the tactics that were presented. But Larry, age 26, of Chicago, wasted little time in showing his resourcefulness.

DR. STANLEY:

Hello, this is Tom Stanley.

LARRY:

Dr. Stanley, I'm calling to seek your advice. I was part of the audience in Chicago when you told us how to target groups of affluent business owners who are interested in cashing in their chips.

DR. STANLEY:

Oh, yes, I remember. You don't want your money back?

LARRY:

No, no. Just the opposite. Anyway, some partnership companies paid my admission fee.

DR. STANLEY:

Well, I hope you will be nice to those folks. I certainly appreciate their support. How can I help you, young man?

LARRY:

I have had my proposal for business valuation seminars endorsed by several chambers of commerce. They will do all the promoting and administering . . . the business valuation seminar. It fits into their existing seminar programs.

DR. STANLEY:

Do you mean that they already have on-going seminars and lists of previous attendees?

LARRY:

Yes! They offer programs to [owners of small/medium-sized business] members and get members to attend.

DR. STANLEY:

Larry, what you have done is absolutely brilliant. I have seen so many sales professionals get completely turned off from doing seminars. They get so involved with the administrative details that they lose sight of the objective. The objective is to get exposure and also to condition groups of prospects to want to do business with them.

LARRY:

I don't want to deal with hotels.

DR. STANLEY:

It looks like you will not have to become a reservationist. It can really stifle your production. Your co-op with the chambers of commerce is their implicit endorsement of you and your ideas. You will not find many stronger sources of credibility. Add this to your co-op with a quality CPA and attorney, and you are on your way.

LARRY:

Well, not quite yet. I have a problem. I've only been in the investment business for two months. What can I tell these people about investing? I'm not an investment expert . . . only 26 years old.

DR. STANLEY:

Well, don't let your lack of experience discourage you from going ahead with the programs.

LARRY:

But I'm not an expert.

DR. STANLEY:

You are the leader, the coordinator of the program. There are at least 100 top-grade independent portfolio managers who would be in your debt for a long time if you placed them in front of a group of affluent business owners. You introduce the panel to the audience. You ask the questions. You're in control—the master of these ceremonies.

LARRY:

Why do they need me?

DR. STANLEY:

Larry, this is your show. You're in control of the talent that will appear on the platform. Just tell those managers that you select that they can manage the investments of those prospects in the audience who become clients. But insist that all security transactions will be brokered by you. Most should be delighted to *work for you.*

LARRY:

I feel better about this now.

DR. STANLEY:

You can call any good law firm, CPA group, or even business brokers and ask them to send you a proposal about what they "can bring to the table." You're in control like a talent scout. And of course, this is a great way to meet affluent prospects from the legal, accounting, and business broker industries. Your panel members may feel that they would like to reciprocate . . . return your kindness . . . by having you invest their money. Just go ahead and get started.

LARRY:

I'll do it.

DR. STANLEY:

Do your very best in making these programs successful. Make sure that all those professionals whom you invite are not only well versed in their disciplines but also high-quality communicators. And always ask the audience to rate (via written evaluation form) all aspects of the program. They will tell you what they liked as well as what they didn't like. Always seek to improve your programs. Make your program indispensable to the chamber of commerce, your audience of business owners, and your panel members. If you don't, you may lose a great opportunity to address a large number of groups with high concentrations of wealth.

LARRY:

I'm going to do it. By the way, I just showed up last week (emerged in the middle of an affluent convoy) at the national convention of the National Association of Women in Construction. When I called their association, a woman warned me that I would be the only man . . . only broker in the convention center. She was right. I can learn to deal with this!

DR. STANLEY:

I'm sure you will be able to handle it, Larry. So long.

LARRY:

Good-bye, Dr. Stanley. Thanks for your suggestions and support.

DR. STANLEY:

My pleasure, young man. Keep me posted on your successes. So long.

Why will Larry be successful in targeting the affluent? There are many factors that explain some portion of the variation in performance. However, Larry possesses one of the most important traits. He has empathy for the needs of very influential people. Think of the problems faced by those individuals who are in charge of programs for their respective chambers of commerce. Oftentimes, they have to satisfy hundreds, even thousands, of members. These members expect that the programs offered by the chamber will be informative, innovative, and even provocative. They often expect dozens of programs to be offered each year. Yes, the membership expects high-quality programming. However, it is not unusual for the individuals who develop programs to feel constrained. They may lack significant funds for outside lecturers. Also, some have too few human resources for recruiting outside speakers and lecturers.

How will a director of programs likely react to a proposal from individuals such as Larry? Most would welcome the assistance that he offers. For Larry offers a practical solution to the number one problem faced by program directors, that is, satisfying the incessant demands of members for quality programs within narrowly defined cost and staff parameters.

Larry will succeed for another reason. He is determined not to wait 10 or 20 years to target high concentrations of the affluent. Often, sales professionals build psychological barriers that isolate them from the affluent. Some tell me that they are "not old enough to target the affluent." Others argue that they came from humble beginnings and, therefore, don't know any millionaires. People give me thousands of excuses why they cannot relate to the affluent. But for every one that they voice, I will give back 10 compelling reasons why they can succeed in marketing to the affluent.

Most people who target the affluent were not born into wealth. Along these lines, more than 80 percent of the millionaires in America are first-generation affluent. The vast majority are business owners. They need and seek advice on how to make their businesses more productive. The chamber of commerce plays an important role in satisfying this need.

Other young sales professionals without Larry's insight shy away from "doing programs" for affluent business owners. After all, how could a sales professional in his mid-20s hope to impress such a mature audience? Larry does not pretend to be an expert except in one area. He is an expert in selecting an outstanding group of professionals who can provide important information to the business owner. In so doing, he will gain exposure and credibility with the target audience. He will, in turn, generate business from both the primary target and from the professionals with whom he collaborates on this venture. The number one favor that a sales professional can do for accountants/attorneys as well as business brokers is to help them increase their revenue and corresponding client base. Larry is one of those young sales professionals who understands that you must first give favors before you start to receive them from important people.

For those who still doubt that they can impress an affluent audience, I have yet another case history to substantiate my argument. Not long after I first spoke with Larry, a fellow from a radio station asked me for an interview. There was nothing unusual about such a request. But several other factors were indeed unique about the circumstances associated with this interview.

The interviewer that called did approximately 50 shows for a top-grade PBS affiliate. The time of day that the show was broadcast as well as the demographics of the audience were factors that explained my enthusiastic response in the affirmative. The interviews were broadcast in the middle of prime time—drive time. More than 100,000 upscale individuals listened to these shows. I estimated that these people had a very high propensity to purchase books. A great many listeners were affluent business owners and professionals. Thus, I speculated that they were a perfect target for books that dealt with the topics on the affluent in America. I told myself what a great opportunity. I hoped that the shelves in the local bookstores were filled with my latest offering. Better call my publisher to make sure that he advises the bookstores of the impending surge in sales. Without optimism why would someone invest thousands of hours into any project?

But I caught myself before completely leaving reality. "Enough of your needs, Tom. What about the poor fellow that has to do all those interviews?" I thought to myself. "He probably gets a very small salary, perhaps not one at all." I was now determined to assist the interviewer in every way possible. Along these lines, I immediately agreed to his request to be interviewed at a specific time and date. The date agreed upon was several weeks away. I assumed that this time would be needed for the interviewer to bone up on all the books and other materials generated by future interviewees. If an interviewer has 50 authors per year on his show, how many books must he have to read to develop a set of intelligent questions? Reading a book a week and doing all that interviewing would be more than a full-time experience. Could anybody in this business even have an hour to do moonlighting? But what a great way to meet people. Who could turn down a request for an interview on such an important station? Successful people/affluent people are typically flattered and delighted to tell their story. Who would be foolish enough to hang up on someone of this interviewer's status? What a wonderful job. An interviewer could get up close to the most successful people around.

Shortly after I made a commitment to be a guest on the radio show, a form letter from the interviewer arrived. The information it contained completely refuted all my a priori hypotheses. No, the interviewer did not have to spend even a modest amount of time reading books or any other detailed material about the backgrounds of invited guests and their products. How could this be possible? The information contained in the form letter made a specific request of the interviewee.

Please send a prompter sheet to the above address seven days prior to your interview. This should be *one* page—three or four sentences of "news copy" to interest the audience in the relevance of the topic followed by three or four biographical phrases.

Thus, the interviewer could do hundreds of interviews each year without having to generate his own deep understanding of the backgrounds of his guests.

No, the interviewer did not have to take an Evelyn Woods reading dynamics course each month to maintain his high-speed reading skill. He used an uncanny method of generating a list of intelligent questions to ask his guests. This is an especially innovative method that did not require even a shallow knowledge of the interviewee's product. Who may be the best person to generate questions for guests to answer? Once again, his approach was revealed in the form letter:

> To mentally prepare: imagine yourself riding to work with an upper-middle-class [resident] who is asking you 10 practical questions about your area of expertise. The style will be conversational. The questions should be *practical* and answerable in nontechnical terms in about 30 seconds.

Yes, the interviewer does have time to moonlight. In fact, his job as an interviewer was his moonlighting position. His "career" position was given in the form letter: Registered Investment Advisor. Why else would he ask me, prior to the interview, if I needed any help managing the income generated from my product and seminar offerings!

No, the interviewer did not have to be an expert in a wide variety of fields. Nor did he pretend to be an expert in such areas. The interviewer did demonstrate his wisdom in a different context. He was very wise to provide a service that the radio station and its listeners needed. The interviewer focused/had empathy for the needs and desires of those who control programming. Certainly he has demonstrated his expertise in recognizing and taking action when an excellent opportunity presented itself. How many other registered investment advisors speak to more than 100,000 upscale prospects each week? In essence, the person who asks the questions of experts controls the interview. And the person who controls such interviews is perceived as an information expert with high credibility.

Sales professionals should be advised that they do not have to wait for their next birthday to be old enough to be a controller of experts. Inspirational "programming" ideas such as those conjured up by the genius of Larry, who helps numerous chambers of commerce with their seminars as well as those of the interviewer just discussed, are not limited to only those with grey hair.

SUSAN'S SPECIAL BRAND OF TELEPHONE CONDITIONING

MS. PEGGY SMYTHE:

Program development. Peggy Smythe speaking.

MS. SUSAN ROGERS:

Good morning, Ms. Smythe. My name is Susan Rogers. One of my clients suggested I call you. Bill Winters tells me you put together the best programs for business owners in the state.

MS. SMYTHE:

Well, Bill is so easily impressed! Actually, he has a lot to do with it and of course, the other members of our advisory board.

MS. ROGERS:

I guess birds of a feather do flock together. Bill is one of the best street-paving contractors you will ever find.

MS. SMYTHE:

I fully agree. In fact, that is why I urged him to become part of our advisory board.

MS. ROGERS:

Bill is not easily impressed. However, he told me that your programs are the very best that he has ever attended. In fact, he can't wait to attend your upcoming programs next year.

MS. SMYTHE:

Well, we don't have all of our programs finalized yet. We did by this time last year. But this year we promised to add six new programs plus all those that were offered last year.

MS. ROGERS:

I hope you're getting a lot of support. Seems to me you could use a few extra hands.

MS. SMYTHE:

We don't have the budget to add any staff personnel. We have to rely on volunteers. And they have given us a great deal of help in the past. But this next year is a problem because of our commitment to add new courses. We have the same budget as last year but have a commitment to add all these new programs.

MS. ROGERS:

That's why Bill suggested that I contact you. We were discussing the needs of business owners. One of the real problems they face is not knowing how to sell their businesses.

MS. SMYTHE:

Don't most business owners pass the business to their children?

MS. ROGERS:

Well, only about 1 in 3 family businesses are passed on to the next generation. And only 1 in 10 are run by the third generation.

MS. SMYTHE:

That is amazing. I had no idea that the ratio was so low.

MS. ROGERS:

I have several new articles that I clipped out of the papers and a few business journals. I can send them over. But I also wanted to tell you about my ideas for a program. Have you ever offered a program about how the business owners should deal with the problems of sell-out?

MS. SMYTHE:

No, we have not. In all honesty, we have never even touched upon it.

MS. ROGERS:

Would you be interested in hearing about my ideas for a program of this type? If I can have just a few more minutes now . . . I can send some of my thoughts in writing over tomorrow.

MS. SMYTHE:

Fire away. I'm all ears, and my eyes are wide open.

MS. ROGERS:

I have already contacted several local area experts. Richard Reese works for a big-eight accounting firm. He is a seasoned professional who specializes in valuing small-and medium-sized family businesses. Everybody who owns a business wants to know how much it will bring on the market. Mr. Reese told me he would be delighted to lecture.

MS. SMYTHE:

We can fill up a room or two with that discussion. My husband will be in the front row. He has been talking about selling his business since he started it 23 years ago.

MS. ROGERS:

Well, that's not all. Bruce Johnson of the law firm of Johnson, Johnson, and Brown expressed a whole lot of interest in telling business owners the do's and don'ts of putting together a solid sales contract. You know a lot of people have sold their businesses but never received full compensation, even though the title was transferred.

MS. SMYTHE:

I know Bruce is a very competent attorney and a great speaker, I understand. He can certainly draw a crowd, especially if he will share his ideas about protecting the seller. This is wonderful.

MS. ROGERS:

That's not all. Dr. Martin Bluestone, the well-known psychiatrist, has already agreed to be one of the lecturers.

MS. SMYTHE:

A psychiatrist! What would he talk about?

MS. ROGERS:

Dr. Bluestone has treated many business owners who encountered depression and withdrawal symptoms after selling their businesses. For some, it is a very traumatic experience. So, Dr. Bluestone proposes to talk about how to deal with "post-sell-out depression." He has published several written articles on the topic. He would be happy to make copies of them available at no charge to all of your attendees.

MS. SMYTHE:

That's very interesting. I'm convinced that a lot of business folks feel a real loss when they no longer can control something that they spent a lifetime building. I hope Dr. Bluestone will not be too technical, you know too Freudian, at the podium.

MS. ROGERS:

No, not at all. He can really relate to business owners. Most of his clients are business owners and professionals, especially the high achievers.

MS. SMYTHE:

I would love to hear what he has to say. So would my husband. He would probably have a rough time dealing with the sale of his business. This segment would be a real sell-out.

MS. ROGERS:

And that's not all. Mr. Harry Parnes of the United Business Brokers Ltd. told me just yesterday that he could lecture for hours on how to package or market one's business to enhance the probability that it will sell for a good price. He has all kinds of case examples; most are already on slides. He has pictures of businesses and advertisements and dollar figures.

MS. SMYTHE:

This is terrific! We can make this a full-day program. I'm sure our members will be interested. We can even attract new members.

MS. ROGERS:

Well, I'm not quite finished yet. As part of my own career in the investment business, I come into contact with some of the very best independent investment managers. In fact, my firm monitors the performance of more than 1,000 of these people. I have already contacted two managers who live in our area. They are both top-notch. Each one has already agreed to lecture. They can discuss various ways that owners might invest some of the proceeds from the sale of their businesses. Their current client list ranges from some of the country's best-run family businesses to important pension funds and nonprofit trusts. I have all the documentation in writing, on my desk.

MS. SMYTHE:

Do you really feel that this part of the program is essential?

MS. ROGERS:

I believe so. Most people who sell their businesses don't know how to invest the proceeds. I have a copy of a research paper that a professor down at State published on the topic. The author states that more often than not, the business owner grossly underestimates the value of his business. Also, the article goes on to say that most business owners are not at all experienced in the investment area. They have been too busy all their lives nurturing their businesses. But they can't keep all their wealth in the businesses forever.

MS. SMYTHE:

My husband knows nothing about investments. So, I can see your point. But, Ms. Rogers, aren't you going to participate in the program yourself? Sounds like you're really up on this topic. Your enthusiasm could be infectious.

MS. ROGERS:

Well, I'm not really in the league with these experts. I'm only 25 and have only been in the investment business for six weeks. But I think I'm a good coordinator, and I have a good eye for judging the expertise of others.

MS. SMYTHE:

Well, you have done more than your share of civic duty. I certainly appreciate your help. I would still like for you to participate in some way.

MS. ROGERS:

Well, I would be delighted to be sort of the master of ceremonies, the orchestrator, if you would agree. I could use the experience and exposure. Right now I feel very wet behind the ears.

MS. SMYTHE:

I can't think of anyone better suited to introduce the lecturers and orchestrate the question-and-answer sessions. But it may eat up a lot of your Saturdays, especially if this program takes off the way I think it will.

MS. ROGERS:

I will be delighted to assist you in any way I can. I owe a lot of favors to Bill Winters, and he loves this entire concept of programs for the business owner. I'm interested in meeting new people. This will give me a great opportunity.

MS. SMYTHE:

I can assure you that you will meet some very interesting characters.

MS. ROGERS:

Can we set up an appointment to get together? I can bring a draft of the proposed topics and lecturers.

MS. SMYTHE:

If you can supply us with the draft, we will do everything else—the promotion, facility arranging, printing, invitations, everything. Can we meet for lunch this Friday?

MS. ROGERS:

I can do it.

MS. SMYTHE:

Can you come by my office at 140 West Elm at 11:30 A.M.? I can give you a brief orientation of our organization; then we can have lunch across the street.

MS. ROGERS:

I will be at your office with a written draft of the program at 11:30 A.M. Friday. Let me give you my telephone number, just in case you need to reach me before then. It is 638-2750. See you Friday.

MS. SMYTHE:

It will be my pleasure to see you then. Good-bye.

MORE THAN JUST SPEAKING ABOUT SELLING EXCLUSIVE TRAVEL SERVICES

Dear Marketer:

Your sales plateau in the exclusive for-pleasure travel category is not directly a result of the quality of your service offerings. Few travel consultants have reached the level of professionalism that your contact personnel have attained. Nor can your revenue performance be explained by the wide variety of exotic travel packages that your firm is able to provide.

Your level of client satisfaction is consistently in the grade A category. Why then, have your sales of exclusive travel offerings lagged behind the growth of your business travel revenues? This variation in performance is directly related to your marketing focus. Almost all your marketing and selling is devoted to business as opposed to pleasure travel. Certainly demand for your travel packages has been directly enhanced by your client relations with the business travel market. However, the very frequent business traveler is not the prime target for expensive, long-term pleasure vacation offerings.

Most frequent travelers have a poverty of time when it comes to vacations. For most, a month or two "on tour" would be totally out of character. Many very frequent business travelers are "price sensitive" regarding traveling for pleasure. Many of these people build up so many frequent flyer miles that they are able to vacation almost free.

Along these lines, a particularly interesting episode relates to an experience that I recently had in talking to one of our clients. This middle-aged sales manager received bonus points, not only for flying but from the hotels in which he stayed. Often he would hold sales meetings attended by several dozen of his sales professionals. His choice of hotel was actually influenced by the amount of bonus points that he would receive. More often than not, he would pick up all the expenses for room and lodging for

25 or more of his sales professionals. He rapidly accumulated points. And he recently told me, "After this meeting, the family will go to Maui for a week; travel and room will be free."

Moreover, some very frequent flyers don't like to travel far from home when they spend more than 100,000 air miles per year working in their own vocations. Understandably, they do not want to go to another hotel or to another airport. They would prefer, perhaps, a more local form of vacation that can be associated with automobile transportation.

How can you enhance the sale of your exclusive pleasure programs? You will have to reach out to those affluent "for-pleasure" travel-prone prospects in your area. As you are aware, this is a competitive market in terms of advertising dollars spent by major firms. It would be difficult and counterproductive to enter into an advertising slug fest with these organizations. Your firm is in the category of high-quality service boutiques. You cannot, you should not, attempt to become anything else. In essence, you need to target carefully your message to segments that have the interest and dollars to adopt expensive pleasure programs. Given your firm's limited promotional budget and overall goals, you should consider an alternative communication strategy.

You should view the market for expensive pleasure travel as composed of hundreds of affluent affiliation groups. These groups range from trade associations to civic, religious, and even social groups that contain high concentrations of affluent prospects within your designated trade area. There are many ways that such groups can be approached. However, a low-key approach will be especially useful to you. Most of these affiliation groups have regular meetings. Many are interested in having guest speakers at such get-togethers. Also, officials of these groups find that providing interesting speakers is a way to retain/attract members. On the other hand, many of these local, state, and national groups have very limited budgets or no budgets at all for paying professional speakers. Thus, this problem provides you with an opportunity. You can help these officials solve their problem. You can provide them with important benefits.

I understand that you are an excellent speaker and hold a master's degree in speech. Why not capitalize on your speaking as well as travel expertise? Why not start your own speakers bureau? You will be the captain of this team. The speakers bureau will find speakers for affluent affiliation groups that are located in your trade area. You can maintain a stable of qualified speakers/experts. Of course, you will be the speaker, the only speaker, who will discuss exotic vacations (for example, from Antarctica to Tibet, paths seldom taken). This, in itself, will give you good exposure to targeted affluent affiliation groups.

There are three major benefits that you will gain from developing a speakers bureau. First, you will come into contact with dozens of potential speakers. These speakers are selected, not only on the basis of their ability to speak but also in terms of their interest in providing certain services to affluent clients and prospects. These speakers are not only speakers, not only providers of services, but are also affluent, and potentially, they can become clients for your pleasure travel offerings.

The second benefit relates to a network concept. Many of the speakers that you will contact will feel in your debt by your allowing them the exposure to affiliation groups. Many of these speakers, in turn, are senior and middle managers who are affiliated with dozens, even hundreds, of other affluent people within their firms and within their industries. For example, one of the speakers should be from the legal industry. It is not unusual for an affluent attorney to be a member of a law firm that contains several dozen, even 100, affluent attorneys.

The third benefit to you in terms of establishing a speakers bureau relates to your exposure to affiliation groups. There are literally hundreds of affluent affiliation groups within your trade area. Because you are in charge of the speakers bureau, you will come into contact with hundreds of officials of these affiliation groups. And even if you do not speak to all of these groups yourself, you will be able to interact with important people in terms of these targeted audiences.

I am sure you are wondering who these affiliation groups may be and how they may be identified. Let me first suggest that you be very careful in targeting the affiliation groups that you would like to contact. Not all groups are by definition affluent. In fact, it is only a minority of affiliation groups that contain high concentrations of wealthy prospects. One of the best sources of affiliation groups is Gale Research Company's *Regional, State, and Local Organizations Encyclopedia of Associations.* This encyclopedia is typically available at major libraries throughout the country. This particular publication includes regional, state, and local organizations by states. In fact, recently in examining this publication for your region, I have discovered there are over 1,000 affiliation groups listed just in your city alone. But again, you do not need to contact all of these affiliation groups. Let me give you some idea of the groups that I would recommend that you contact about your speakers bureau.

Under the heading of Healthcare, I would suggest that you send information about your speakers bureau and the speakers that you represent to your state medical association. In addition, you may find it advantageous to send individual solicitations to subcategories under the medical profession. These would include affiliation groups containing anesthesiologists, radiologists, cardiologists, and neurosurgeons as members. Under the heading of Doctors of Dental Surgery, specifically target groups of orthodontists. And you may be interested in sending some of this information to veterinarian medical associations.

In terms of other professionals, let me strongly recommend that you send information to your local and state bar associations, your associations both local and state for certified public accountants, as well as associations for mechanical engineers, electrical engineers, and architects.

Under the heading of Sales and Marketing, I would

suggest to you that you send information about your speakers bureau to the independent insurance agents association of your state, your sales and marketing executives organizations, your state's sales clubs, your state and local boards of realtors, and your advertising and public relations organizations.

Also, it would be valuable to include the trade associations that represent groups such as scrap metal recycling entrepreneurs; general contractors; developers; highway, street, and paving construction entrepreneurs; plumbing, heating, and air conditioning contractors; real estate management organizations; beer wholesalers; wine and distilled alcoholic beverage wholesalers; manufacturers associations; your state automobile dealers association; your state builders council; your state's investment dealers association; building material supply associations; retail trade associations; consulting engineers council; associations of personnel consultants; trade associations that represent funeral directors in your state and local community; trade associations that represent printers, restaurant associations, manufacturers agents, and sales agents; roofing contractors; associations that represent the executives of associations; and the associations that represent meeting planners. These are just a few of the important affiliation groups that would like to hear about your speakers bureau.

In addition, it would be important to contact various houses of worship. These are listed in the telephone directory in your city. But again, you don't want to contact all of these organizations. Send your promotional information to those religious groups that are located in what you would consider to be affluent zip codes.

Remember that neighborhood quality is closely related to the propensity of residents to purchase exclusive pleasure-travel vacation packages. Affiliation groups that will find your speakers bureau concept to be of interest to them include: Rotary Club, Kiwanis Club, the Junior League, and the chambers of commerce within the various locales in your designated trade area. In addition to the groups that I have recommended, you will find that new groups are popping up from time to time in your local area. Any time you read about a new affiliation group establishing itself in your community, you should contact these people. You will find information in your local newspaper and your local business periodicals as well as information from radio news programs about such affiliation groups. New groups are particularly sensitive to the issue of having speakers at their programs for they are in the process of attempting to grow and to establish themselves within a particular affiliation category.

While it is not uncommon for officials of affluent affiliation groups to be contacted from time to time by sellers of exclusive travel programs, you will contact them with another proposal—a proposal to help them and their members and, of course, to help yourself.

But let me address the issue of recruiting potential speakers for your bureau. Why would anyone want to speak to an affiliation group? Well, some people just like to speak. Other people not only like to speak but have a desire to communicate with high concentrations of affluent prospects. Therefore, you will find it relatively easy to recruit outstanding speakers from your community that will, in fact, wish to gain exposure among target audiences. Who are some of these types of individuals who would like to join your speaking program? Let me give you some examples.

As previously mentioned, you will be the speaker within the context of the bureau that will make presentations about exotic vacation travel. But in addition, I would recommend that you ask Sally Dana to speak on the psychology of an auction. Sally is the foremost expert, not only in antiques and porcelains and related collectibles, but she is also an expert in addressing large groups of affluent prospects and clients.

The next selection will be Leonard Linehart, who will speak on the mystique of managed money. Mr. Linehart is an outstanding speaker and is a manager of several hundred of the best marketers of money managers in the

United States. The topic of money management may be especially intriguing to those individuals who are affluent business owners as well as very affluent retirees. Your next representative will be John E. Jones. Dr. Jones is professor emeritus at the University and an expert of the early history of your city. Dr. Jones is also affiliated with several social and religious "affluent organizations" and is the author of a forthcoming book for which I am sure he would like to get some publicity.

In the next category, I recommend you speak to John C. Peterson, who is the president of Peterson Yacht Company. He can speak on the topic of exceptional yachts in the world and how they are built. Next, I would recommend that you speak to Mr. Bernie Tulley, who is the president of an award-winning landscape architectural firm. He can discuss the landscape architect's design of affluent households in prestige neighborhoods. I am sure he will be able to provide you with color slides and pictures of this information. Ms. Teresa Goodbody, one of the leading fund-raising consultants in the community, could speak about America's great philanthropists.

Also, Dr. Clyde Bosworth, eminent psychologist and author of stress reduction for executive and sales professionals, could speak on the topic of his expertise. In addition to this, you may ask Hartwick J. Estes, president of Estes Executive Clothing, to discuss the clothing needs and habits of men and women in the executive and professional ranks. Mr. Wellington Tadsworth Roots, the golf course architect and designer, would, I am sure, be delighted to speak about the five best golf courses in the United States.

These are just some of the pro forma examples of the types of speakers that would be available through your speakers association. Each one of these speakers should provide you with a detailed biographical sketch and a 30-minute audio tape of a recent presentation that they had made to an audience. In addition to this material, it may be useful to provide a brief video tape with you introducing the concept of the speakers bureau and the topic on which you will speak, as well as introducing each one of the speakers within the context of the bureau. Each of these speakers would then be able to essentially tell their own story by providing you an extraction of a 10- or 15-minute segment of one of their speeches. Written information including a personalized letter from you and a concept statement about the speakers bureau and the experts that are represented by the bureau should be sent to the officials that you have identified in each one of the affiliation groups.

In this letter, you should propose that if the official is interested in further information, he or she can call or write to you for a demonstration tape either audio or video. In addition, you can set up a telephone hot line. This hot line will be hooked up to a 24-hour answering machine that will tell callers how to go about finding additional information about the speakers and the speaking programs. Your message on the recorder should ask interested parties to leave their name, address, name of affiliation group, a short message about interest, and possible meeting dates in the future. In this way, various affiliation groups will be able to contact you. You, in turn, will be able to develop relations with some of the most important people in your community. Also you will gain exposure for your offerings in the context of affiliation groups that contain some of the highest concentrations of affluent people in the community.

Of course, many of these affiliation groups contain high concentrations of people who are, in fact, "travel prone." I don't think it would be too much to ask of officials that have taken advantage of your free speakers bureau service to provide you with a mailing list of their membership which you, of course, will use from time to time in mailing promotional material about the travel programs that your firm offers.

This soft-sell approach will be well received by people who recognize the need to balance their own needs with the needs of speakers and, of course, the needs of the captain of the speakers bureau.

Be certain to send a copy of your printed material along with a news release that announces the creation of your speakers bureau to all business writers and reporters in the local, state, and regional press. These professionals will likely be very interested in writing stories and articles about the unique quality of your speakers bureau. Each and every time one of your speakers has been selected for a program, make sure that each member of the press receives some information about the forthcoming program. This will provide you with a constant source of publicity in terms of the local and regional business press.

I hope that these recommendations about the development of marketing to affiliation groups will be helpful to you and your organization. By following some of these recommendations as outlined above, your firm will be able to enhance greatly its exposure to some of the most affluent individuals and their respective affiliation groups within your designated trade area.

Continued best wishes and much success in your forthcoming endeavors.

Regards,

Thomas J. Stanley, Ph.D.
Chairman, Affluent Market Institute

PART 4

SELLING TANGIBLES TO THE AFFLUENT

INTRODUCTION: A MASTERPIECE OF PERSONAL SELLING

Dear Marketer:

So you're disappointed about not being able to close every prospect that walks in the door. Don't be depressed. For depression will only decrease your sales performance. Sales professionals, including the most gifted, encounter some rejection. You will never close all the prospects that are attracted into your jewelry store.

Remember, a growing number of people in this country are recreational shoppers. Many spend Saturday after Saturday at exclusive malls such as the one in which your store is located. Their purpose is not to buy. Their purpose is to be entertained. One of their favorite forms of entertainment is to "try on" expensive watches and related products like the ones which you sell. However, many have no real ability to purchase your top-of-the-line watches. Often, by day's end, the recreational shopper has purchased only cookies, yogurt, and record albums.

But treat all types of shoppers with respect. It is frequently difficult to distinguish the real prospect from the pseudo prospect. Yes, appearances can be deceiving, especially when some of your best prospects really "dress down" when they go shopping.

You can't always distinguish the recreational shoppers from the serious ones by outward appearances. However, you can debrief "prospects" that ask you to demonstrate your top-of-the-line watches. Ask a few basic questions of your prospect. A simple debriefing can give you good clues regarding those who are only browsing as opposed to those who are really interested in buying.

Expensive watches are not generally purchased on impulse. More often than not, a genuine prospect has done some planning and some shopping before he actually makes a purchase. Ask the following question of those who request a demonstration of your top of the line watches:

SALES PROFESSIONAL:

Are you familiar with this timepiece and its features?

The *real prospect* will often answer yes. Moreover, the *real prospect* will frequently say that he or she has been considering such a purchase for several months, even several years. And of course, those people who walk into your store wearing a well-used model of one of your top-of-the-line timepieces are likely to be genuine prospects. It is typically easier to sell current owners than first-time owners. Of course, some people who have recently purchased a timepiece from your competition will also stop by for a "demonstration." In reality they are trying to determine after the fact if they paid too much for their recent purchase! Others who received a timepiece for a gift wish to determine the price. Always treat even these pseudo shoppers with respect and courtesy. Perhaps they are not really interested in buying from you today. However, make every effort to impress them with your professionalism. They are likely to have need for cleaning and repair services in the future. Moreover, they are likely to tell their friends about the high caliber of professionals who can be found in your store. Remember that word-of-mouth endorsements play a major role in how prospects develop retail patronage habits.

There are several other questions whose answers can be very useful in the selling of expensive timepieces. One of the most important has to do with the occupation of the prospect.

SALES PROFESSIONAL:

Sir, are you self-employed?

This question provides a good opening for a conversation about how the prospect makes his living. Of course, not all people who shop work for a living! But many unemployed shoppers just happen to be married to those who make a very good living.

Many buyers of expensive watches are self-employed individuals with high incomes. High income is a correlate of such purchases. And self-employed business owners and self-employed professionals such as physicians and attorneys account for a significant portion of high-income producers in this country. Two other occupation groups are also important parts of the high-income market. These include high-performance sales professionals and upper-level corporate executives.

For many members of these high-income groups, the purchase of an expensive timepiece symbolizes an important event. These events relate to changes in economic and/or status situations.

Economic windfalls, such as large end-of-the-year bonuses, big sales commissions, as well as promotions to senior ranks and obtaining large contracts from new clients, are some of the factors that may trigger the purchase of your offerings. Thus, the enlightened sales professional should not only inquire about the prospect's occupation but also the purpose/occasion relating to the purchase.

SALES PROFESSIONAL:

Many of our customers tell us that they have a special reason for purchasing this timepiece. For some it is an important symbol of their reaching a major goal in life. A gentleman purchased this same model last week in recognition of becoming a full partner at a prestigious law firm. Do you know the couple who purchased the ladies' model for their daughter who just graduated from medical school?

Buyers of expensive timepieces are often people who think of themselves as being important and/or even superior to others. They have a need to communicate this self-perception. Some reason, "I'm the best at what I do. I should own the artifacts and symbols congruent with my station in life." As a sales professional, you should capitalize on the need that prospects have to balance their self-perception and purchasing behavior.

The role that self-perception plays in the purchasing process can be illustrated by a case history. One of the top sales professionals from the life insurance industry was kind enough to share his experiences with me. Recently, he entered a jewelry store to purchase an "inexpensive" ($30) watch. He was greeted by the store owner. As you will soon determine, the owner, Mr. Jewels, is also an extraordinary sales professional.

MR. JEWELS:

Good day, Sir. May I be . . .

MR. KEN:

I need a watch. Nothing fancy. Just something that tells time.

MR. JEWELS:

We carry a wide assortment of timepieces, as you can see.

MR. KEN:

I just want something that works. I don't need anything fancy. What do you have for $30?

MR. JEWELS:

Well, we do have several items in that price range. But may I ask why you are interested in buying a new timepiece at this time?

MR. KEN:

I wore out my old one. Had it for 10 years. A cheap watch, but it kept good time.

MR. JEWELS:

Are you self-employed?

MR. KEN:

Ah, almost. I sell life insurance.

MR. JEWELS:

Are you a good salesman?

MR. KEN:

Yes. I'm one of the top 20 young salesmen. And we have a lot of salesmen.

MR. JEWELS:

Were you a successful salesman 10 years ago when you bought your last watch?

MR. KEN:

No, I was working in a tire plant.

MR. JEWELS:

Why did you change from tires to selling?

MR. KEN:

More financial opportunities. I make a lot more money in life insurance. Horizons unlimited.

MR. JEWELS:

What is the best quality product that you sell?

MR. KEN:

It is our special brand of universal life. It combines the best features of insurance and an investment account.

MR. JEWELS:

What product is at the bottom of your line?

MR. KEN:

It is our standard term product, $10,000 face value.

MR. JEWELS:

What types of people buy your top-of-the-line universal life policy?

MR. KEN:

They are people that need seven-figure universal life.

MR. JEWELS:

Who needs such a $1 million policy?

MR. KEN:

Smart people who earn high incomes.

MR. JEWELS:

Do you mean successful people?

MR. KEN:

Yes, successful people.

MR. JEWELS:

Are you successful?

MR. KEN:

I consider myself to be successful.

MR. JEWELS:

What kind of insurance policy do you have?

MR. KEN:

I have our best policy, the universal policy.

MR. JEWELS:

Well, that makes sense. You are successful, and you have a policy designed for successful people. It's consistent. You're consistent. You like being consistent, don't you?

MR. KEN:

Of course.

MR. JEWELS:

Put this [timepiece] on.

MR. KEN:

This is not a $30 item. Am I right?

MR. JEWELS:

You're right. Do you know what kind of timepiece you just put on your wrist?

MR. KEN:

I'm not sure.

MR. JEWELS:

It's the timepiece for successful people, people like yourself. It's the top of our best line.

MR. KEN:

I really just want a watch that tells time. Do you have something for under $100?

MR. JEWELS:

The items we sell for under $100 are very much like your term policy product. Do you own a term policy?

MR. KEN:

No. I told you I have our best universal life insurance product.

MR. JEWELS:

That's because you demand the best, and you can afford the best. You are successful. You told me you were successful.

MR. KEN:

I am successful.

MR. JEWELS:

Our under-$100 line is not a favorite among successful people. I'll bet you did not have a universal policy when you worked in the plant. Am I right?

MR. KEN:

You're right. I had a small term policy. How did you know?

MR. JEWELS:

Term insurance is well suited for plant workers; so is our selection of watches in the under-$100 range. But look at the masterpiece you're wearing right now. Who do you think deserves to wear this top-of-the-line timepiece?

MR. KEN:

Successful people. People that have universal life insurance policies.

MR. JEWELS:

What will your clients and prospects think of you if they see that you're wearing the term life watch?

MR. KEN:

Ah. I don't know.

MR. JEWELS:

Well, let me tell you that it suggests to them that you sell term insurance and that you buy term insurance. And perhaps they may think that you are not successful in your profession. Many successful people are very perceptive.

MR. KEN:

Well, you know, I don't want to give my clients the wrong message.

MR. JEWELS:

Of course you don't. But it's your decision. Do you want the universal policy masterpiece or the term policy watch?

MR. KEN:

I want the universal masterpiece. How much is it?

MR. JEWELS:

It's seven. It's really an excellent value when you consider that you will be able to make the right statement with your clients for a lifetime.

MR. KEN:

Seven.

MR. JEWELS:

Yes, seven. It's for very successful people. That translates into less than a dollar a day during the course of a successful career.

MR. KEN:

I'll take the universal masterpiece.

Yes, Mr. Ken did purchase the universal masterpiece. He maintains that he made the right choice. He was a bit unsettled for a day or two after the purchase. After all, it's not everyday that someone trades up from a $30 watch to the universal masterpiece.

Normally Mr. Ken would have been more perceptive about spotting an affluent prospect. However, it was several weeks after the purchase before he realized that Mr. Jewels was a prime prospect for big-league life insurance.

Mr. Ken telephoned Mr. Jewels. He reported his delight with the masterpiece he was now wearing. Mr. Ken also pointed out that he felt indebted to him. After all, Mr. Jewels was kind enough and, of course, perceptive enough to advise Mr. Ken that he was no longer a $30 watch-type person. Mr. Ken made an appointment to visit with Mr. Jewels. During the course of his personal visit with Mr. Jewels, Mr. Ken discovered something about Mr. Jewels that surprised him. His surprise was not a result of learning that Mr. Jewels was successful. Mr. Ken had correctly hypothesized that Mr. Jewels was successful and wealthy. However, his debriefing of Mr. Jewels went beyond success and money. Mr. Ken thought to himself "How could it be possible? Mr. Jewels was not only underinsured with respect to the total combined face values of his life insurance policies but all the policies that Mr. Jewels owned were *term policies*."

MR. KEN:

Mr. Jewels, given your income, you are grossly underinsured.

MR. JEWELS:

You're probably right. I have not bought a new policy since we opened our third store.

MR. KEN:

How long ago was that?

MR. JEWELS:

Ah, eight years and five stores.

MR. KEN:

That's a long time. You should really consider taking a hard look at your current coverage.

MR. JEWELS:

I know. I know.

MR. KEN:

With your current level of income, you need three or four times more coverage.

MR. JEWELS:

You're right. My wife tells me the same thing.

MR. KEN:

Let me give you some information about our best universal policy.

MR. JEWELS:

But I prefer term insurance. Don't you sell term insurance?

MR. KEN:

We do carry a line of term policies. But a term policy in my business is much like that $30 watch that you convinced me about. It is not for successful people.

MR. JEWELS:

Well, I'll have to think it over.

MR. KEN:

Please give serious consideration to consolidating your coverage. You would be much better off with one policy, our masterpiece of the universal variety, than one-half dozen small term policies.

MR. JEWELS:

My wife tells me this all the time. I'll think it over.

MR. KEN:

Mr. Jewels, you're successful. You look successful. You cater to successful people. You wear the masterpiece. But your life insurance habits are not those of a successful person. Everything else you do seems to translate into success. So you will not be comfortable with anything but a masterpiece of an insurance policy.

MR. JEWELS:

Have I heard this somewhere before? I think my own rhetoric is catching up with me. Let me think it over. I will get back in touch with you.

MR. KEN:

Just let me know if you will be comfortable with our masterpiece or the equivalent of your lowest priced line of watches. I know you will make the right choice for yourself.

MR. JEWELS:

I will get in touch.

MR. KEN:

I look forward to hearing from you.

Mr. Jewels called Mr. Ken's office a few days later. Mr. Jewels asked to speak with Mr. Ken. However, Mr. Ken was out of the office. His secretary asked Mr. Jewels if he would like to leave a message.

MR. JEWELS:

Yes. I wish to leave a message. Tell him I want the masterpiece policy—you know, the universal policy. Make sure you get it right. I want the masterpiece policy not the $30 watch term policy.

Mr. Jewels taught Mr. Ken an important lesson. Mr. Jewels always attempts to determine how the prospect views himself. His clever debriefing of Mr. Ken provided valuable information. This intelligence was the foundation for persuading the prospect. He discovered that Mr. Ken perceived himself as a very successful sales professional. Mr. Jewels correctly hypothesized that Mr. Ken placed a great deal of importance on being viewed by himself, as well as by his prospects/clients, as a winner. Mr. Ken's value structure dictated that he be consistent in communicating this "ideal self image." Mr. Jewels communicated to Mr. Ken that an inexpensive watch was not congruent with his image and was inconsistent in terms of a successful career in his profession.

Mr. Ken was conditioned by Mr. Jewels to perceive wide variations in quality and benefits among watches. This was not accomplished by opening up the backs of several timepieces and discussing the differences in their respective technologies. To do so would very likely turn off prospects such as Mr. Ken. No, Mr. Jewels capitalized upon the knowledge that he gathered about how Mr. Ken persuades affluent prospects to purchase his top-of-the-line insurance products. Mr. Ken advocates the best products for his most successful (affluent) prospects. Mr. Jewels' message helped him avoid violating his belief structure. Would Mr. Ken really feel comfortable/confident relating to successful prospects if he were wearing the timepiece that is congruent with someone other than a high-performance sales professional? Of course not. And it was for the same reason that Mr. Jewels was sold on the concept of a masterpiece of a universal life insurance policy.

I hope this case example will help you and your affluent prospects develop a consistent self-image as well as public image of themselves.

Regards,

Thomas J. Stanley, Ph.D.
Chairman, Affluent Market Institute

CHAPTER 11

SELLING LUXURY AUTOMOBILES TO HIGH-INCOME CONSUMERS[1]

INTRODUCTION

When making presentations about marketing to the affluent, I always try to select one slide that will serve as a template for the entire discussion. So, you think that this is an easy task. Not when you have an inventory of over 3,000 slides! But actually, this particular selection was not difficult. For the material in this slide relates very closely to the problems and opportunities that dealers will encounter in the 1990s. You see a picture of a proud young man. He is rightfully proud because he just caught a 23-inch trophy rainbow trout.

The majority of even the most ardent trout fishermen never in a lifetime of fishing land such a large specimen. So you may conclude that Bill, as you see him here, is a well experienced and highly talented fisherman. Isn't it logical to assume that only the seasoned veteran is capable of landing the really big fish? Au contraire. Bill never fished for trout in his entire 33 years of living on this earth until the day that this picture was taken.

How do inexperienced fishermen catch big fish? By the same token, how can even inexperienced sales professionals succeed in selling to the most affluent prospects? You can learn a great deal

---

[1] Some of the material in this chapter was extracted from Dr. Thomas J. Stanley's speech given to the BMW Dealers of North America, November 6 and 20, 1989.

about marketing to very "big fish" by understanding how Bill, my friend and former student, hooked this trophy trout.

To develop a quick understanding of Bill's success, we should examine the contents of the fish's stomach. Let's take a look at the inventory that includes: (A) two minnows, (B) one crayfish, (C) three pebbles, (D) one twig, and (E) one filter from a cigarette. Minnows and crayfish are the traditional staple food for trout at this particular time of the year. But how can the presence of pebbles, a twig, and a cigarette filter be explained? Why would a large, experienced fish swallow such elements? The answer to this question is fundamental to an understanding of how to succeed in marketing to the affluent.

HUNGRY FISH AND EUPHORIC PROSPECTS

To a very hungry fish, many things in the stream look like food. The behavior on the part of large, very hungry fish is directly analogous to that of affluent prospects who are experiencing euphoria. Euphoria, according to Webster, is a feeling of well-being or elation. The affluent are typically euphoric when they are (or will be in the near future) encountering major upswings in their cash flow. Often major positive changes in cash flow are associated with one's occupation and/or socioeconomic position. Euphoria is a critically important concept in understanding the affluent consumer. Those who are encountering it are vulnerable to solicitations by sales professionals. Why? The higher one's income, the more likely that his cash flow will vary significantly from month to month, even year to year. The affluent have a very high propensity to spend when they are euphoric. So, part of the marketing equation proposed for the affluent segment relates to timing. Identifying affluent prospects is important. But the time component is often overlooked. When will the affluent buy? The affluent market is unique. It is composed of many subsegments. And members of these subsegments don't all encounter euphoria at the same time. Determine when the prospect will be euphoric, and you, like Bill, the novice fisherman, will greatly increase your chances of landing the big fish. Bill succeeded in his quest because he possessed strategic information. This information was not limited merely to the latitude and longitude of a particular pool in a river with hundreds of pools. No, Bill possessed the third element, knowledge of the time when the fish would be hungry.

What implication does this third element have for marketers of luxury automobiles? Most affluent Americans are only euphoric (hungry) a few weeks a year. By affluent, I refer to those with a minimum income of $100,000 and/or a net worth of $1 million or more. In both categories, more than 80 percent work for a living. Yes, only a minority of affluent Americans are part of the idle rich. The idle rich live off their income-producing assets. Interest, dividend, annuity, royalty, and retirement income in such cases suggests considerable liquid wealth as well as, in a relative sense, a more stable cash flow. For most of the idle rich, the purchase of a luxury automobile is related much less to euphoria over cash flow than it is for the working affluent.

THE SPENDING FRENZY

But what do the working affluent buy when they are euphoric? Remember the contents of the trophy trout's stomach, and you will appreciate the importance of this question. Often, affluent targets encountering euphoria go into spending frenzies. Yes, the affluent are like trophy fish. Both are a minority in any population. Both sometimes bite at things that are not necessarily their real quarry. Why would a trophy-sized trout swallow a twig, a pebble, and even a filter from a cigarette? Is it only because of hunger (euphoria)? No. The hungry trout positioned itself in such a way as to be able to identify and capture food that was flowing downstream in the current. It just so happened that during this process a filter passed within view and striking distance. If the fish were well fed, it would not have perceived the filter as a minnow. But even if it were very hungry, it would not, could not have swallowed the filter if the filter had not been available at the right time and right place. Think of all the thousands of minnows in the same stream that were not selected by this trout. They, in fact, were a greatly superior product in terms of traditional definitions. Yet they were not selected. Not selected because they were not "offered" to the hungry trout at the right time and place.

My philosophy about how to market to the affluent is deeply rooted in the timing dimension. I believe that firms which target this group can significantly increase their sales if they adopt a proactive strategy. Proactive, in this case, means taking the initiative of identifying "hungry fish" and personally presenting these euphoric creatures with something more than pebbles, twigs, and filters.

As marketers of luxury automobiles, you must contend with more than increased competition from other automobile manufacturers. A growing number of marketers of everything from boats to jewelry and from vacation homes to in-ground swimming pools are also targeting the affluent. However, much of the intra- and inter-industry competition takes place along product, price, dealer network, and mass media lines. But with some minor exceptions, the battle for the affluent customer is not fought with proactive personal selling.

OBSOLETE THEORIES OF MARKETING

Marketers of luxury products place much of their resources into product development and design, advertising, service, and dealer support. But how many overlook the importance of having their sales professionals cold call affluent prospects who are euphoric? While there are a few interesting exceptions, most marketers of luxury products adopt the worn-out marketing theories that relate to specialty goods. What are specialty goods? According to the World War II marketing textbooks, they are supposed to be so unique, so exclusive, and so filled with high-quality features that genuine prospects will seek out the sellers. In essence, the specialty product is supposed to sell itself.

Most marketers of expensive luxury goods are still operating on the obsolete theories of specialty goods. Some may argue that once the prospect enters the showroom, very aggressive selling may then take place. In fact, this is not marketing. Marketing luxury automobiles begins when the sales professional begins searching for prospects. Waiting until the prospect takes the initiative to walk into your playing field is asking much too much from your product quality department, national advertising budget, and dealer location models.

The real winners in the 1990s will be those marketers who have a proactive sales force. A sales professional in this category does not rely on others to generate the bulk of his or her prospects. No, the truly extraordinary sales professional in the luxury automobile arena will seek, find, and close affluent prospects.

Recently, I had the privilege of speaking with three "highly decorated" sales professionals from the luxury automobile market. They discussed their own unique methods of selling. But in spite of their relative success in this field, one noticeable flaw in their marketing plan was evident. Yes, each had some wonderful ideas about how to condition the prospect, how to overcome objections, and how to close. But each defined the selling process as starting in the same manner (i.e., after the prospect walks into the show room). This is reactive or what I call ordinary selling. Extraordinary selling, on the other hand, is based upon taking the initiative of finding, conditioning, and closing affluent prospects who are euphoric.

ESPS ARE PROACTIVE

In studying hundreds of extraordinary sales professionals (those who generate annual incomes from sales commissions of over $100,000), an interesting profile emerged. In essence, this profile explains why some sales professionals are truly extraordinary while most that target the affluent are just ordinary.

Courage is the single most important characteristic that separates these two groups. What is courage? You see four possible answers including:

a. Closing prospects who walk in the door.
b. Closing prospects ready, willing, and able to buy.
c. Selling to currently satisfied customers.
d. Taking the initiative to ask strangers to do business with you.

All of these activities have some element of courage associated with them. However, answer (*d*), "taking the initiative to ask strangers to do business with you," is the single best descriminator that explains sales production in terms of the affluent market.

Courage is so important that some extraordinary sales professionals credit this dimension alone in explaining their success. Their philosophy is if you ask enough people to buy from you, you are bound to consummate some sales.

Courage in selling can be appreciated by one of the top vacuum cleaner salesmen in America. Steve Sklar is the 16th-ranked salesman for Electrolux. (Jeanne Marie Laskas, "So You Think You Have a Tough Sell?" *Sales and Marketing Management,* September 1988, pp. 88–90, 92, 94.) In one year, he sold 407 vacuum cleaners. At an average price ranging between $699 to $1,100, this translates into approximately $360,000 worth of vacuum cleaners. But how did he succeed? Not by viewing his product as a specialty good. And certainly not by waiting in a showroom for affluent prospects to show up. Nor by only hoping that today some happy customer would do a little bit of word-of-mouth advertising in his behalf. No. Mr. Sklar sold nearly $400,000 worth of top-of-the-line units because he has courage. He has the courage to take the initiative thousands upon thousands of times in asking strangers *in their homes* to do business with him. He sells the "Mercedes" of vacuum cleaners. This is precisely why he prospects in "affluent neighborhoods" (i.e., where people drive luxury autos).

Now I'm not suggesting that you send your sales professional out to prospect strangers on a random basis. I am suggesting that a courageous sales force that is trained to target will succeed in marketing expensive automobiles to the affluent.

JACK, YOU'LL NEVER OWN ANOTHER DINOSAUR

Allow me to support this statement by reflecting upon a case study. I recently had the pleasure of dining with the chief executive officer of a major financial institution. During our conversation, Jack told me that he recently purchased a new 7 series BMW. Naturally, I was curious about why he had chosen this model. I quizzed him about the factors which contributed to this decision. Several of the purchase criteria that he mentioned surprised me. Jack is not a car buff. Nor is he by his own admission a technically oriented consumer of luxury automobiles. In addition, Jack never previously owned a foreign-make automobile. Given these facts, how could I explain his responses to my question about his choice of automobile? Why did he purchase a 7 series?

Consider these responses which included: (1) "The *Book of Challengers* convinced me that the 7 is two generations ahead of the competition;" (2) "Its power train reflects the state of the art in automobile technology;" and (3) "It has ellipsoid headlights." *Book of Challengers,* state-of-the-art power train, ellipsoid headlights, I reasoned, were not part of the basic language of the typical car buyer. I considered Jack to be a typical, affluent consumer in terms of automobile preferences. But something or someone transformed him into a much more sophisticated buyer.

The product features that he mentioned were contributing factors to his purchase decision. However, the main reason he bought had more to do with the courage of the dealer who sold him the automobile than with product features. What was the main reason he bought a 7 series? He bought one because someone had the courage to ask him for his business. The situation and circumstances surrounding this decision demonstrate the importance of courage in selling high-priced luxury durables.

One day while Jack was standing beside his traditional, full-sized luxury car that was parked in his driveway, he noticed a stranger coming toward him. Who was this fellow? He was Jack's new neighbor. It seems the man and his family were just moving into the house next to Jack's. According to Jack, this neighbor began his conversation in a rather novel way. (See letter below.)

Mr. Thomas J. Stanley, Ph.D.
Affluent Market Institute

Dear Tom:

Please find enclosed a roll of film which should have four or five pictures on it. The person in the pink sweater with the golf club is Bob Schwab, manager of DeSimone BMW in Evesham, NJ. (also my next door neighbor). The gold BMW is a result of his stopping by when he moved in and saying, "No way are you going to own another dinosaur. I'm a next-door neighbor and a BMW dealer."

It is my understanding that he will be at the seminar you are talking at. I have advised his wife to make sure to be at your seminar, as I felt it was very worthwhile.

Hope the slides turn out all right, as yours truly took them, and the first thing I am not is a gifted photographer.

Sincerely,

Jack

Shortly thereafter, Jack did purchase a 7 series from his neighbor. Three essential ingredients were underlying this pro forma success story in selling to the affluent. These include: (1) a quality product, (2) a dealer/sales professional with the courage to initiate personal contact, and (3) an affluent prospect in the mood to purchase. In regard to the third element, Jack is in the affluent category that I refer to as "permanently euphoric."

EXPLOIT THEIR NEED TO AFFILIATE

I hope you will not interpret my discussion about Jack and his neighbor as an endorsement for dealers of luxury automobiles to move their families next to a millionaire household each week! No, you don't have to live near an affluent prospect to ask him for his patronage. But you can get near such targets in other ways. Near does not only denote physical distance. It also can mean getting closer to affluent prospects in terms of interests and affiliation groups.

Of course, it is easier to ask a neighbor to do business with you than a total stranger. But it is also easier to deal with affluent prospects to whom you have demonstrated experience in dealing in terms of others in their occupation/industry classification. People who reside within the same neighborhood tend to imitate the consumption patterns of their neighbors. But I also believe that the affluent have an even higher propensity to adopt the automobile consumption habits of their occupational cohorts.

Targeting and exploiting the affiliation needs of affluent occupational segments can be extremely productive. Surprisingly, very few marketers of luxury automobiles have ever formally adopted this strategy. One major-league exception is the brilliant strategy developed by Gerhardt Blendstru.

AN INTERVIEW WITH
MR. GERHARDT BLENDSTRU[2]

(At the time of this interview, Mr. Gerhardt Blendstru was vice president of sales and marketing, Porsche Cars of North America.)

DR. STANLEY:

My book. What do you think?

MR. BLENDSTRU:

On the mark. Especially with the point that these people [sales professionals] don't really do any real selling; they are more or less order takers. What we are doing is trying to do a lot of personal selling. We have identified certain [affluent] groups. We are going after professionals and even corporations . . . the young presidents, neurosurgeons, the CEOs, the top 100 companies. That's what we are doing now. We are trying to go into middle and upper economics, direct response, direct mail . . . things like that. Let me tell you a couple of things that we have done or are in the process of doing. In terms of timing, we have maybe two good tools to circumvent timing. One is, in terms of advertising, we are sending a direct video, compared to a direct mail. On the assumption that if you have a direct mailing [the prospect] will throw it away if the timing does not coincide with purchase intentions. But a direct video [he] is much more likely to keep. The other thing that is very successful is leasing to spread the initial investment. The third thing that we did in terms of getting to people was hosting events. I hosted the YPO

---

[2] A special thanks is in order to Mr. Blendstru for sharing his ideas about marketing expensive automobiles to the affluent and for reviewing *Marketing to the Affluent*.

[Young Presidents Organization] conference on the West Coast. You can do it for the neurosurgeon, the Million Dollar Table, the *INC.* 100. The idea really is to make them a deal. Give them something special. It has to be a deal for them, not for us.

DR. STANLEY:

Are you saying "give a deal to affiliation groups?

MR. BLENDSTRU:

We have done a special edition. A special color, a special interior, and a special plaque.

DR. STANLEY:

That's great marketing.

MR. BLENDSTRU:

We have a direct mail out to 900 of one [affiliation group], and 17 bought a car. We sold six or seven 911 slant noses, and they are $110,000 a pop. Peer pressure on display at the conference on opening evening. Lots of people went to the dealership and wanted to order the big one. You probably know of the buyer (a multimillionaire in the real estate field). He had not driven a car for the last 15 years. His chauffeur had been driving him around. He went to the dealership and said, "Well, what is the most expensive Porsche I can buy?" I said, "A red 911 Slant Nose."

DR. STANLEY:

He won't let the chauffeur drive that!

MR. BLENDSTRU:

No. He was like a kid. He shifted at 3,000 RPM. When he let me drive, I took it over the 3,000 RPM. You get a tremendous boost in the rear. He said, "Oh, does this [boost] come with the car, too?"

DR. STANLEY:

That's wonderful.

MR. BLENDSTRU:

With one affiliation group meeting, we had them for three days. Every afternoon we had a driving school on a 17-mile drive. We had 150 people experience our car while we were there. There were a lot of sales.

DR. STANLEY:

You know, there are many people who are just waiting for somebody to call them. They have the money; they just need to be pushed. And if you can take more control of the selling function, you can probably sell twice as many cars. Do you agree?

MR. BLENDSTRU:

There are many companies who have to invite their best business friends to events. And normally you invite them to golf or tennis. Well, I say don't do that; I will offer a Porsche outing. You pay for the luncheon or brunch, or you pay for the nice resort, and we will bring the car.

DR. STANLEY:

Well, I might be able to help you. What about top-ranked sales professionals?

MR. BLENDSTRU:

I'm now talking with a Million Dollar Round Table group.

DR. STANLEY:

I recently spoke to their members. Thousands of them. But I don't recall seeing anyone there who was marketing automobiles.

MR. BLENDSTRU:

They have a convention, and they need special events.

DR. STANLEY:

That's the interesting thing about the affluent market. The affluent have a need to belong to affiliation groups.

MR. BLENDSTRU:

We'll do it [design a] special [model] for you, special color [for your affiliation group].

DR. STANLEY:

Well, someday I might have one. If my book sells a lot of copies. I'll call you.

MR. BLENDSTRU:

I really enjoyed reading your book, and I gave it to my training manager.

DR. STANLEY:

Thanks. Have a nice trip home.

MR. BLENDSTRU:

You, too. Good-bye.

AN INTERVIEW WITH AN ORDINARY SALES PROFESSIONAL

It is interesting to contrast Mr. Blendstru's strategy with that of a fellow who called our office recently. This ordinary sales professional sells luxury automobiles. He opened our conversation with the statement, "I'm having a bad two months."

After a brief discussion about the so-called downturn in the automobile market, I asked this fellow one of the fundamental questions about marketing to the affluent. "Tell me, what does your best customer do for a living? You know, the biggest ticket you ever wrote." He did not know what his biggest client, in terms of dollar sales, did for a living! I suggested that he find out about the occupations of his top clients and then call me back. He did call back. He informed me that his best customer is a neurosurgeon.

DR. STANLEY:

How many neurosurgeons have you ever attempted to sell to?

ORDINARY SALES PROFESSIONAL (OSP):

One. One that I'm aware of.

DR. STANLEY:

Who is your number two client?

OSP:

He owns an insurance agency.

DR. STANLEY:

> How many owners of insurance agencies do you have as customers?

OSP:

> One.

DR. STANLEY:

> And the occupation of your number three customer?

OSP:

> He is a cardiologist.

DR. STANLEY:

> How many cardiologists do you have as customers?

OSP:

> One.

DR. STANLEY:

> Who is your fourth ranked customer in terms of the size of the actual purchase price he paid for your automobile?

OSP:

> He is a stock broker.

DR. STANLEY:

> How many stockbrokers do you have as customers?

OSP:

> One that I'm aware of. I have only been in the business for a year.

DR. STANLEY:

> How about your number five customer?

OSP:

> She owns a chain of hair care centers.

DR. STANLEY:

> How many other owners of hair care businesses do you have as customers?

OSP:

One.

DR. STANLEY:

How about your sixth ranked customer?

OSP:

He is an attorney. Ah, a collection attorney.

DR. STANLEY:

How many collection attorneys have you ever attempted to sell to?

OSP:

One.

DR. STANLEY:

Young man, you are a marathon man. Don't you know that the need for people within the same affluent occupational category to imitate each other is very, very strong? Why haven't you taken the initiative to call affluent prospects from these six occupational groups?

OSP:

I did not know that I was supposed to do that. You can't tell who will walk into the showroom. I can close a lot of them once they get inside.

DR. STANLEY:

Where did you learn your showroom skills?

OSP:

We have an excellent instructional program series. It also includes details about our products and the competitors'.

DR. STANLEY:

What is the best product on the market today?

OSP:

It is our top-of-the-line series. The critics love it. They tell their readers that we are number one. They know it, and I know a lot about this unit.

DR. STANLEY:

Well, sounds like you deserve a grade of A in product knowledge. But tell me, who are the top 10 neurosurgeons in your market area?

OSP:

I don't have any idea.

DR. STANLEY:

Who are the owners of the top-ranked insurance agencies in your trade area?

OSP:

You have me again!

DR. STANLEY:

So, young man, you have a grade of A in product knowledge and an F in market knowledge.

OSP:

Well, I'm trainable.

DR. STANLEY:

Do you think that people who are at the top of their professions should drive top-ranked vehicles?

OSP:

For sure.

DR. STANLEY:

Then, why don't you take the initiative of calling these types of people in your community?

OSP:

I'm sort of new to this area; I don't know any of these people. I would not know how to talk to them even if I knew them.

DR. STANLEY:

Well, you do know one neurosurgeon, one insurance agency owner, one cardiologist. Why not call these "happy" customers and ask them who the top professionals are within their respective fields in this town?

OSP:

But what do I say to these hot-shot people when I call them?

DR. STANLEY:

Tell them that it is only appropriate that professionals who are at the top of their respective fields drive the best luxury car currently available. By all means, do not forget to tell these prospects you call that one or more of their cohorts told you that they were tops in their professions. Also, inform them that you have at least one other client from their professions. The affluent tend to buy what others in their professions/industries purchase.

OSP:

Will it work?

DR. STANLEY:

It will only work if you take the initiative and seek out these prospects. Or you can sit in your office and just hope that people with money will stop by. You already have "one of above" from all the affluent professions you mentioned. Next year why not have five customers from each category? Son, the game just begins not ends when you sink your first ship in the affluent occupational convoy. I have to go now. Best of luck. So long.

OSP:

Thank you. Good-bye.

SHARE THIS LETTER WITH YOUR LUXURY AUTOMOBILE DEALERS

Dear Marketer:

Thank you for the hospitality and privilege of addressing your dealers. I just wanted to take this opportunity to reemphasize and elaborate upon the suggestions that I made during our marketing seminar.

Your dealers can no longer rely solely on your products' quality and advertising to "get prospects" into the showrooms. Your dealers must adopt a proactive marketing philosophy. They must encourage and compensate their sales professionals to take the initiative of finding affluent prospects in the "cash position" to buy. Each of your dealers possesses some significant marketing resources that he or she can capitalize upon. Your dealers are not only marketers, they are also important clients for many affluent business owners and professionals. Dealers patronize many different types of service and product providers.

Product and service providers in the United States make up the bulk of people who are affluent. This is reflected both in terms of high income and/or net worth. Take a look at your typical dealers and what are you likely to find? They are patrons of life insurance agents, casualty insurance agents, temporary service and employment agencies, permanent service employment agencies, advertising agencies, direct-mail and promotional organizations, public relations firms, law firms, accounting firms, security brokers, health care professionals, auctioneers, real estate sales professionals, fuel oil dealers, wholesalers of auto parts and accessories, construction/building contractors, architects, mechanical design and engineering firms, factors of accounts receivable, and marketing and sales consultants.

Many of your dealers patronize these types of service and product providers, and many of these providers are, in fact, affluent. I know that many, if not all, of your dealers encourage reciprocity. It is fundamental to good business to ask that people from whom you purchase also purchase from you. This is not news to your more productive dealers; however, judging from the facial expressions, as well as subsequent discussions with many of your dealers, the concept of *affiliation marketing* was a revelation.

What do I mean by affiliation marketing? Let me give you an example. Every one of your dealers utilizes the services of an advertising agency. I understand that your corporation's vision is to localize advertising; thus, each of your dealers will be spending even more of his own dollars directly on advertising through an advertising agency. Spending and controlling the dollars is an issue that should be capitalized upon. I am sure that your dealers will be even more aggressive in selling automobiles to their designated advertising agency. But that is typically where aggressive/proactive marketing stops.

Your dealers must begin to market to clusters of the affluent, not just individual targets. There are thousands of advertising agencies in this country. Many of your dealers have dozens or even hundreds of agencies in their own defined market areas. Thus, it is counterproductive for your dealers to attempt to solicit business only from the principals of one particular advertising agency, that is, from the agency with which they particularly deal. If a dealer has been successful in encouraging the principals of one advertising agency to purchase a luxury car from him this year, why not 5 or 6 or 10 principals of 5 or 10 advertising agencies by the end of next year?

But who are these advertising agency principals? Where would one find them? When should they be addressed? What do they need? Why do they buy? How should they be approached? Let me reflect upon the answers to several of these questions. It is not difficult to identify advertising agencies and their principals. You can even identify agencies from merely examining the yellow pages, or you can look at any type of agency directory that would be available at the dealer's advertising agency. But there is a better way for your dealers to identify principals, especially those that are encountering significant upswings in their cash flow, for you do not want to prospect the principals of every agency.

Not every agency provides an affluent income for its principals. The yellow pages tell you nothing of the critical time dimension about when people are encountering euphoria because of success in their businesses. All industries, including advertising, have several significantly important trade journals. One of my very favorite trade journals for targeting the high-income advertising agency principal is something called *ADWEEK*. *ADWEEK* is published 51 times a year. It has six regional editions. Why should your dealers read *ADWEEK?* Let me answer that question by asking another question. When are the principals of an advertising agency most likely to purchase a luxury automobile? When are they most likely to be sensitive to solicitations made by some of your more aggressive proactive-oriented sales professionals? You are right. The principals of an advertising agency are in the mood to buy immediately after finding out that their ad campaign has been selected by a major client. This information is published in *ADWEEK* long before it appears in the popular press.

One needs just to examine the regular feature content of *ADWEEK* to appreciate the quality of information it provides. This information details who the winners and, of course, who the losers are in terms of acquiring new accounts and keeping old accounts. Feature articles constantly discuss who has just won an account, how many dollars are involved. Often they detail the principals, not only of the advertising agency but the principals and heads of marketing and advertising for the client's firm. Remember, when it is indicated in a feature article that a client's firm has significantly increased its advertising budget, it is often indicative of significant increases in incentives and bonuses for the client's principals and their marketing representatives. Obviously, people who have just won campaigns are the people to call. Obviously, you may not find it productive to call upon those principals of agencies that just found out that they were not selected to represent an important prospect.

There is another section of *ADWEEK* which is also important. It is called "The News Hotline." It might say, for example, as a pro forma picture: "Adam Smyth Named Executive Creative Director." Also, "Acme and Acme Names President." Also, Advertising Club of Atlanta Selects New President."

One of the most valuable sections that recurs in all issues of *ADWEEK* is a section called "Accounts in Review." In one issue of *ADWEEK*, 13 accounts, totaling over

$45 million in just one regional edition, were specified. This section listed the client, location of the client, the incumbent advertising agency, the contenders in this race, and the decision dates.

Also, another potentially valuable section is called "Adweek Critique." It provides a detailed analysis of the good and bad points of particular advertising campaigns, listing the advertising agency, the client, the creative director, the director, and the art director. Remember, when affluent prospects are praised by their peers, they are euphoric. And euphoric prospects are often vulnerable to solicitations by your proactive dealers.

Another section is called "Newsmakers." Very important people are featured in *ADWEEK*'s newsmakers, such as the presidents/owners of the top-ranked advertising agencies, the real movers and shakers in the world of advertising.

There is also a section called "People on the Move." Once, 42 people were selected to be noted in "People on the Move," including John Smyth, as a pro forma example, being promoted to creative director. In addition, there is a section called "Calendar." "Calendar" is very important because it specifies where high clusters of important people in the advertising industry can be found. One of the most important clusters, in terms of the movers and shakers in the advertising industry, is an organization called the Ad Club. Most major and even middle-level cities in the United States have an Ad Club or an advertising club that meets at least once a month for a luncheon program. Why not have your advertising agency's principal take one of your top sales people to one of these luncheon meetings? In this way he or she will have an opportunity to meet important affluent people in the advertising industry who are potential prospects for your luxury cars.

I recommend that your dealers subscribe to *ADWEEK* for $69 a year. It is a very good marketing investment. Of course, each of these dealerships should subscribe to the particular regional edition that encompasses the area where their dealership is located. If, in fact, they do not want to spend the $69, of course, they can ask their current advertising agency for its back issues. However, I would like to reemphasize the importance of having one's own subscription. Generally, time is of the essence in prospecting affluent people who are euphoric.

How does one go about actually approaching a euphoric principal of an advertising agency? There are various ways that this can be done. These methods range from simply calling the principal and congratulating him about his victory as noted in *ADWEEK*, to inviting one or more principals of the winning agency to lunch. Or call the offices of the designated advertising agency and ask to speak to the principal's assistant or secretary. Then ask if it would be possible to deliver a laminated copy, either on just a plastic backing or on walnut, of the page from *ADWEEK* that designates the agency and the principal as the winner of their solicitation for a new client. Some of your more innovative sales professionals may even ask a euphoric prospect if it would be possible to take him home from the airport after he arrives from an out-of-town trip. Of course, he will be picked up in one of the top-of-the-line luxury cars with which you are trying to match him.

If you have any doubt about the propensity of principals of successful advertising agencies to purchase luxury automobiles, let me make a suggestion. Drive into the parking lot of an advertising agency and look at the automobiles in the "executive slots." Or even take a look at the parking lots at hotels that are hosting Ad Club and advertising award types of programs. I find that most marketing people, including advertising principals, public relations executives, and top sales and marketing professionals have a high propensity to consume. They look for luxury as a way to denote success, as a reward for their victory, as a way to extend the euphoria, and sometimes to remind themselves of their successes when things get tough. But like most people who are successful, these people buy when they are euphoric, not when they are depressed. That's why it is very important to not only identify people who are successful in advertising but to contact them during this temporary feeling of euphoria.

Some sales professionals are reluctant to place a telephone call to a principal of a successful advertising agency. They may want to reduce their fear of rejection by sending laminated copies of the "success" articles from *ADWEEK* by mail and then following up with either a telephone call or a note. However, I firmly believe that the best way to approach is the most direct approach. First telephone the offices of successful people and then attempt to visit them personally. I particularly prefer the method of calling the target's assistant and enlisting his or her cooperation in having one of your sales people come by to deliver a laminated copy of the "success" article.

Allow me to give a pro forma example of how conversation may be initiated in terms of soliciting business in the context of the principals of advertising agencies. Bill Smart, an aggressive sales professional of luxury automobiles, initiates a telephone call to the Adams and Adams Advertising Agency. "Hello, Adams and Adams Advertising. This is Rhonda. Can I help you?" "Yes, this is Bill Smart with Europena Luxury Automobiles. I just noticed in *ADWEEK* the story of your advertising agency's success, and of course, the success of its principals. I have a laminated copy of the article which highlights your recent victory in gaining the Super Quickie Oil Change contract. I wonder if there is sometime this afternoon that I might be able to come by and present it to Ms. Adams?" "I'm sorry, Mr. Smart, but Ms. Adams will be out of town until Friday. However, on Friday afternoon from 2:00 to 4:00 she does have several moments where you might come by." "Fine, Rhonda. Let me suggest that I could come by at 3:00. I hope she won't mind." "Oh, I don't think she would mind at all." "Obviously, I would like to give her the laminate, but I would also like to talk to her about luxury automobiles. Is she in a good mood?" "She is in a very good mood, Mr. Smart. It might be appropriate for you to come

by. I'll put it on her calendar. I think that she could probably only give you 10 to 15 minutes." "That's all I would
really need, Rhonda. No problem. See you on Friday at
three o'clock. Oh, but before I sign off, Rhonda, let me ask
you this question. How many other people have called to
congratulate Ms. Adams and to offer a laminate of the
article in *ADWEEK?*" "You are the first caller; you are the
only caller. I think that's why Ms. Adams would greatly
appreciate your kindness."

What does Bill Smart say when he arrives at the offices of Adams and Adams Advertising? He has already
developed an ally in terms of Rhonda, the assistant to Ms.
Adams. She has specified a particular time that he can
come by to give the laminated copy of the article that
highlights the victory for Adams and Adams Advertising.
"Good afternoon, Ms. Adams. I'm Bill Smart with European Luxury Automobiles. I just noticed the success
that you recently had in gaining your latest client. It was
mentioned in *ADWEEK*. I always read *ADWEEK*. I thought
that you would be interested in having a laminated copy of
the article highlighting the good news. I hope this walnut
backing matches your office decor. It seems like it would."
"Mr. Smart, you are very kind. I certainly appreciate this.
I must apologize, however, for being so busy right now. I
don't have much of an opportunity to speak with you this
afternoon." "Well, Ms. Adams, I was also hoping that I
could interest you in perhaps taking a demonstration ride
in our new top-of-the-line 7 series. The European critics
indicate it is the finest automobile produced in the world
today." "Sorry, but I don't have time right now." "Then, Ms.
Adams, I am wondering if I might be able to give you a ride
home in the 7 series I have outside?" "I don't think that
would be possible, Mr. Smart. I have my own car here, and
I would like to take it home." "Well, Ms. Adams, how about
if I meet you back here at closing time. I'll drive your car
home and you can drive our series 7 home; we can swap
cars once we get to your destination. Would that be appropriate?" "It would be very appropriate, Mr. Smart. I have
been thinking about buying a new car. Can you meet me at

5:30 in the parking lot?" "Five-thirty it is. I am driving the black-on-black 7 series. Where is your car located?" "My car is located in number one spot indicating Ms. Adams, Sr. vice president. See you there at 5:30." "Thank you, Ms. Adams. I will see you at 5:30, and I think you are really going to enjoy driving one of our new top-of-the-line models."

Successful advertising executives are only one of dozens of affluent targets that the dealers come into contact with. But let me give you some other examples of how to take advantage of what we would call affluent situations. I find in my own research that security brokers and the managers of security brokers are in the top 10 occupational classifications in terms of producing $100,000 annual incomes. Recently, I discussed this fact with the owner of several automobile dealerships. This dealer does business with four different security brokers, from four different major firms. One security broker is responsible for this dealer's corporate cash. Another deals and provides services for asset management. A third services his personal investment portfolio. The fourth handles his pension plan.

What is interesting in this case is that while the owner has attempted to solicit business in terms of luxury car sales with all four of these brokers, the same dealer has never asked for a referral from these different brokers in the context of the industry called investment services. Has this dealer ever asked any of the brokers that he deals with for the names and telephone numbers of other top-ranked security brokers, branch managers, district managers, or regional directors? No. Many of the people in the brokerage industry have affluent incomes in the $100,000, $200,000, and even $300,000 and $400,000 annual range. All major national as well as regional brokerage firms have formal programs with which they recognize the achievements of their extraordinary sales professionals. Sales professionals in this industry may be designated as members of such groups as President's Club, Chairman's Council, and so forth. These are the people that are in the top 15, the top 10, the top 5, the top 1 percent in terms of great achievement in sales. Of course, great achievement in sales means that someone is well compensated for his work.

What this dealer needs to do is to ask his four different brokers for a list of the extraordinary sales professionals that are within the market area. The brokers in this case all have access to the names of the other successful brokers who are employed by the same firm in the region. In addition to this, why not have these brokers introduce the dealer to branch and regional managers of their respective brokerage firms? Ask these managers if they would be willing to have one or more cars displayed and/or demonstrated at monthly and annual meetings where great sales people are being recognized. To sweeten such proposals, a dealer may offer to pick up the lunch or bar tab for some of these meetings.

Many of these meetings need to have added excitement. Certainly, it would be added excitement to have some of your top-of-the-line high-performance luxury cars on display in an arena where there is the highest concentration of high-income sales professionals for a two- to three-hour period, or even a two- to three-day period. This is essentially marketing to the affluent via the big-league orientation, that is, providing a message and product and, of course, solicitation to a high concentration of prospects that have what we would call affiliation need.

Affiliation need, in this context, suggests that people within a particular industry tend to imitate other successful people within the same industry. Why not designate your top-of-the-line product as the vehicle to purchase and enjoy if, in fact, you are a top producing security broker? But the security brokerage industry is not the only opportunity for dealers in the luxury automobile area.

Also ranked high in terms of $100,000 incomes in the United States are people involved in the life insurance industry. The life insurance industry also designated people who are extraordinary by their performances. Such designations as Member of the Million Dollar Roundtable or the Top of the Table or more specific designations in terms of a particular firm recognizing greatness are also valuable clues in identifying successful insurance agents. But any dealer that patronizes an insurance agent should always ask the agent about the identities of the other winners in a community. Successful agents typically know who the other successful agents are and very often interact with these people, even if they work for different firms. In addition to the agent, dealers would be wise to attempt to solicit business from general agents within regions that essentially share much of the success of their own sales force in the context of high income.

Beyond insurance, there are many other affiliation groups that should be of interest to people who attempt to market luxury automobiles to the affluent. Think of all the health care professionals within each of your dealers' respective trade areas. But tell your dealers to be selective. Not all physicians are affluent. Most will never reach the $100,000 income category. However, many of the specialty groups, such as neurosurgeons, radiologists, cardiologists, and orthopedic surgeons, typically generate very high incomes. They also associate with other winners within their respective areas. Once a dealer has been able to solicit the business of one well-known and respected radiologist, why not 5 next year and 10 the following year? Progression this way is highly probable because of the referrals within a specific industry of affluent professionals.

Top performers in industrial real estate are also highly prone to adopt luxury automobiles. Often, the successful people within the industrial real estate arena are identified annually in the local newspapers and business periodicals within a community. They are flattered to be recognized, and they are flattered to be recognized particularly by other people in marketing. That is why a laminated plague suggesting a "salute to your success" at the bottom would be well received by many of these people.

Moreover, you will also find that many people who are in the construction contracting field and mechanical design industry have high incomes and are susceptible not only to flattery but also to information about the physical characteristics of superior automobiles.

Of course, don't forget those marketing sales consultants who are typically euphoric after landing a major consulting contract and/or providing a series of important and, of course, valuable seminars!

In essence, the successful dealer who attempts to market luxury automobiles must stimulate his sales force in terms of seeing the big picture and of focusing on the affluent within designated industry targets such as life insurance, security brokerage, advertising, head-hunting services, and direct-mail services. Of course, don't overlook the legal industry which is a top-five market for generating $100,000 income prospects. Why not ask one's current law firm to provide information about who the most successful lawyers are in a particular community? Why not read what lawyers read? Ask your lawyer what he reads.

In every major market area in the United States, there is a trade publication called, in a generic sense, the publication of record. This publication is essentially the trade journal for attorneys within designated market areas. Each goes under a different heading. In Atlanta, the publication of record is the *Fulton Daily Record*. It has legal information, but it also specifies who the movers and shakers are; who the winners are in terms of different law firms; who won the lawsuit, who lost the lawsuit; what firms represented the different clients; and who is incorporating in terms of business. This is a very important publication for dealers to read, consume, and capitalize on when finding law firms and, of course, clients and other business owners that are euphoric.

In soliciting business from successful people, some very basic elements come into the sales equation. People who are the tops in their profession typically attempt to have consistency in their behavior. Isn't it logical to ask a successful person the following question: "If you are the top in your field, why aren't you driving one of the top automobiles produced in the world?" In addition to this, a small gift such as a laminated copy of an article from the publication of record designating someone as a winner can be important in developing some reciprocity in the context of having these people do you a favor by driving and possibly buying one of your top-of-the-line luxury products.

Another element in the sales equation is what we would call imitation. People who are successful, people who are ambitious, people planning to be successful attempt to imitate the winners within their particular profession and/or trade association. That is why it is so valuable once you have one successful person as a client that you capitalize on this relationship by encouraging others within this affiliation group also to adopt a similar product. I once asked several hundred top-performing sales professionals, all of whom had earned annual incomes in the over-$100,000 category, a simple question. If during this meeting the very top sales professional within this group of several hundred walked into this room wearing a three-piece polka dot suit of sky blue and white with a matching beenie with a propeller on top, how would you folks dress at the next meeting? Everyone laughed, but they all agreed that they would seriously consider adopting a new form of dress—a three-piece polka dot suit and matching beenie with a propeller on top.

Many marketers think that the role models for the general population include J.R. Ewing and people from the "Dynasty" programs and other situational types of programs on television. But more often than not, affluent people tend to imitate those who are the most successful within their professional associations and trade groups. This affiliation need is probably the most overlooked opportunity in terms of marketing to the affluent. This is surprising since I find it one of the most valuable tools that can be used to exploit the opportunities among the affluent population in this country.

As you have requested, I have profiled the five types of sales professionals that represent automobile dealers.

Grade F—Sales professionals in this category attempt to sell their offerings only to prospects that have entered their showrooms. Prospects in such situations visit the showroom for reasons totally independent of the marketing activities in which the Grade F sales professional may engage. These Grade F sales professionals rarely recontact even prospects that take the initiative of walking into these particular showrooms on their own. In addition, the Grade F sales professional never seems to join any affiliation groups that have any type of concentration of potential affluent prospects.

Grade D—These professionals usually take the initiative of recontacting prospects but, again, only after the prospect has walked into the showroom on his own. As in the case of the Grade F sales professional, prospects visit showrooms because of factors other than those related to the activities of the sales professional. The Grade D sales professional occasionally takes the initiative of calling people whom he may suspect are interested in purchasing a luxury automobile.

Grade C—These sales professionals are what I consider to be diamonds in the rough. They aggressively recontact all qualified prospects that they meet. They also take the initiative of mailing information to targets that may be interested in buying a product from them. However, the problem with the Grade C professionals is they do not have a clear focus in trying to identify and solicit business from "suspected affluent targets." But they can learn, and they want to learn.

Grade B—Sales professionals in this category aggressively take the initiative of contacting prospects. This aggression is also demonstrated in their direct mailing of letters and other materials to suspected affluent targets. This, in itself, is typically done in terms of automobile registrations, that is, where prospects currently own earlier models of the same automobile or competing models in the luxury field. The Grade B sales professional also looks within the service records of his own dealership to determine or to identify people that may be susceptible to solicitations about buying new models of the automobiles that they currently own. In addition, the Grade B sales professional telephones those individuals who have been recognized by the local press as being successful. However, much of what the Grade B sales professional does does not relate to what I would call the euphoria issue, meaning that most of the people that he contacts are not necessarily in the mood to buy. Moreover, much of the source information used by the Grade B professional in identifying the people that he considers prospects is used by others who are above-average sales performers.

Grade A—These sales professionals not only contact people whom they suspect are affluent, but the Grade A sales professionals make a significant effort to identify people who are euphoric because of positive socioeconomic changes in their lives. Not only do they contact people that are suspected as being euphoric in the popular press, they go much further. The Grade A sales professionals identify affluent prospects by reading the trade journals consumed by the affluent population. In essence, they read what prospects read, not what other sales professionals read. These professionals read *ADWEEK* to identify on a weekly basis those 50 people who are euphoric about changes in their socioeconomic lifestyles. Great sales professionals in the Grade A category also read the publication of record to identify affluent lawyers. They also associate with people and read trade publications of people in affluent occupational categories, such as security brokers, life insurance agents, construction contractors, architects, and other types of professionals. The reason that a Grade A sales professional outperforms multiples of the other sales professionals in the F, D, C, and even B categories is that he focuses his energy on industry-specific, euphoric prospects. The Grade A sales professionals are successful because they are able to deliver promotional information at the right time, at the right place. In addition, they consume information that very few other sales professionals consume. They read what is most important to affluent prospects. They are not frightened to take the initiative of asking people who are euphoric to trade up to the best luxury cars in the world.

They are successful because they do what other people do not. They read more. They focus their energy. They target their energy. Most successful sales professionals in the United States who target the affluent are not only knowledgeable about product, but they are extraordinarily knowledgeable about target segments. It is not unusual to find Grade A sales professionals that target the affluent focus much of their energy in regard to three or four or five industries that produce high concentrations of wealthy people. Developing an intimate knowledge of industries that produce affluence and an intimate knowledge of the trade journals and trade associations of an affluent industry are the hallmarks of great selling in terms of the affluent population. But the majority of people who address the affluent population in the United States focus much more on product knowledge than they do on the market function.

While product knowledge is very important in the sales equation, market knowledge is equally or more important. For it is more important to understand the needs and the symbols of success that are industry-specific to the affluent population than it is to reflect upon paragraphs and paragraphs and paragraphs of the quality components of one's product. The sales professional should always remember that his problem is to sell luxury cars and that the client's problem is to successfully be recognized as a winner, to be appreciated, and to adopt symbols of success. That's why it is so important in speaking to an affluent prospect to be able to reflect intelligently upon the client's successes, the client's industries, the client's opportunities, and the client's problems. More and more one will find that successful sales professionals who target the affluent will become experts within a narrowly defined segment or segments of the affluent population.

Please don't forget to save one of your high-performance models for the Institute. All the best wishes for your continued success.

Regards,

Thomas J. Stanley, Ph.D.
Chairman, Affluent Market Institute

PROACTIVE VERSUS REACTIVE SELLING

People in the fishing industry who end a season with several hundred thousand dollars in net income are euphoric. And this euphoria can be capitalized upon without a major expenditure of marketing resources. Who at your dealership is responsible for rubbing shoulders with affluent fishermen? Who is in the medical school library rubbing shoulders with those soon-to-be high-income prospects? Is there anyone in this room who has marketed luxury automobiles at trade shows where the affluent cluster? That's what I thought. Isn't it time to take such actions? Why wait for the affluent to seek you out? But that is exactly what most sales professionals do with their time. They wait. And while they wait, they talk to each other. Why not ask them to stop waiting and start communicating with affluent prospects?

Courage, knowledge, and technique are important attributes in the sales equation. However, the ace of aces in selling to the affluent possesses other traits in addition to these. Beyond these basic three attributes are three other components of extraordinary selling. The first is what I refer to as information. What is strategic information in relationship to marketing to the affluent? Let me give you four possible answers on our multiple-choice affluent market test. These include: (*a*) the names and addresses of current patrons, (*b*) lists of prospects who live in "Blue Blood Estates," (*c*) a list of prospects who are euphoric, and (*d*) a list of the competition's patrons.

All of these categories of information are important. However, I believe that (*c*) is the most crucial piece of information. The others are valuable. But (*a*), (*b*), and (*d*) are commercially available in one form or another. Finding prospects who are encountering major upswings in their cash flow is grass-roots affluent marketing at its finest. This type of information can be and should be gathered and exploited by your sales professionals. And most of this information, perhaps as much as 90 percent or more, is in the public domain. It will, however, take some time to train your sales professionals on how to identify and capitalize on that identification of euphoric prospects.

Affluent people buy when they have the right kind of cash position to purchase. Let me reflect on the prototypical response that one receives when interviewing high-income consumers.

QUESTION ONE:

When did you buy your BMW?

RESPONSE:

Oh, when I received the proceeds from my trust fund that my grandparents set up for me.

QUESTION TWO:

When did you buy your vacation home?

RESPONSE:

Shortly after being promoted to executive vice president.

QUESTION THREE:

When did you buy your boat?

RESPONSE:

September. Two thirds of my annual income is realized in August.

QUESTION FOUR:

When did you join this country club?

RESPONSE:

As soon as I was informed that I would be made a partner [in a top law firm].

QUESTION FIVE:

When did you decide to purchase your first European luxury sports car?

RESPONSE:

When General Electric purchased our firm.

Yes, the time issue is valuable to those with the courage and discipline to exploit it. But from where does this intelligence come? Let me answer this question by reflecting upon several case studies of marketing to the affluent.

NO CALLS FOR HUNGRY FISH

Several years ago the firm owned by one of our clients was purchased by a *Fortune* 50 corporation. The buy-out was well publicized in both the business press as well as in the popular press. Newspaper reports began to surface several months before actual hard dollars changed hands. One hundred and ten share holders in our client's firm received $1 million or more from the buy-out. At the time of the sale, each of these share holders received one-half of his proceeds in cash. The second half was paid several months later. Many of these partners received more than $1 million as part of the first payment.

How many of these euphoric partners received solicitations from sales professionals that market luxury automobiles? Ninety percent? Eight percent? Fifty percent? Twenty percent? I have yet to find one partner who was *ever, ever* contacted by any sales professional from this industry. Never contacted in spite of countless news stories that detailed the buyout. Never contacted in spite of their realized incomes increasing by 3, 4, 5, and even 10 times in some cases. Sales professionals must capitalize on euphoria of this type. Your sales professionals can no longer afford to sit back and just hope that these euphoric partners will show up at their showrooms. This is not marketing; it is outdated reactive selling.

How difficult would it have been to capitalize on the euphoria of these 110 partners? Let me share with you the comments of one of them—a board member and national sales manager. Listen closely to his comments so that you will not miss the next affluent convoy of euphoric prospects.

> It would have been so easy for anybody to find us. The buy-out was put on the front page of *The Wall Street Journal* many times. Everyone of our partners is listed in our telephone directory with a big asterisk next to his name. This signifies share holder. But nobody ever called any of us. More than two-thirds of us all live in the same metro area. Four guys down stairs that work together did something interesting. The four of them walked into a Jaguar dealer and just paid cash on the spot for seven top-of-the-line models. But they did this on their own. They were never called.

Every single day in this country there are affluent prospects that are or will be euphoric in the near future. Much of this euphoria can be exploited. But too often, marketers invest in lists of affluent targets which do not contain the timing or euphoria dimension. My suggestion to you is to develop your own list of new prospects. The ace of aces in this profession of marketing to the affluent develops his own lists. These lists do, in fact, contain the time dimension. Most of the information that is needed to identify euphoric prospects is within the public domain.

PUBLIC INFORMATION

At the age of 38, Mr. N.D. generated an annual income from his career in sales of $1.5 million. How did we discover Mr. N.D.? From the same place we discovered the identity and income ($525,000) of Ms. C.B. What source? Naval intelligence? KGB agents? No. Both of these extraordinary sales and marketing professionals and their incomes were published in *Sales and Marketing Management*. What a secret source! The number one best-selling sales trade journal in America! And by the way, nine other super sales people and their incomes were also listed in the same issue that recognized Mr. N.D.'s achievements.

I just wonder how many people called on the principals at

Campbell Shipyard in San Diego. The October 1989 issue of the *National Fisherman* mentioned that they just signed contracts to build six 257-foot tuna boats.

How many of your sales professionals called the senior partners of the two dozen advertising agencies that were given the good news this week? What good news? All had their campaign proposals selected. And you can read all about the who, what, how much, and so on in *ADWEEK*. But many of your sales professionals only read *Motor Week, Motor Trend,* and *Auto Executive*. It is important to stay current within your industry. But how many euphoric prospects are listed in your industry's trade journals? Many people that target the affluent are in love with their own product and industry. They are guilty of the cardinal sin of marketing. They focus on their own situations, products, and industry. But they ignore the events in the industries from which the bulk of the affluent prospects come.

Owners of businesses that are awarded major contracts are in the mood for a top-of-the-line BMW. But tell your sales professionals that before they mention their need to sell automobiles, they must first focus on the needs of the euphoric prospect. Superachievers, whether they are in sales, shipbuilding, or even advertising, need to have their achievements recognized. Congratulate them and pay homage. And of course, tell them that the BMW 750:L is the ideal symbol with which to reward their extraordinary achievements. Very few high achievers, even those recognized in the press, receive congratulations from even their closest friends and associates. They need and they welcome your praise. Consider positioning your product as the badge or symbol of achievement for achievers.

An extraordinary sales professional who is an associate of mine targets affluent business owners. Two weeks ago I sent him a list of 100 entrepreneurs who were recently designated "the top 100" by their industries' most prestigious trade journal. Often, affluent prospects become euphoric because of such industry recognition. He called every one of them to ask that very big question, that is, did any other sales professional call you about your top 100 selection? Not one other sales professional called any of these 100 euphoric prospects.

There are many other targets of opportunity of this type. But every day thousands and thousands of sales professionals in this industry fail to capitalize upon euphoria.

DEVELOP YOUR OWN LIST

Many people call us to request that so-called list of America's millionaires. We are not in the list business. Our pro forma response to these requests is always the same: "It is better to learn to fish than to be given fish." In other words, develop your own list. Each and every sales professional who targets the affluent should be capable of identifying prospects who are euphoric. In addition, they should be able to contact these people by telephone, personalized letter, and even, in some cases, by the walk-in/in-person cold call. Sales professionals should be able to discuss more than their products and services. Yes, the best sales professionals who target the affluent have considerable product knowledge. But they also have considerable knowledge of the industries from which the affluent population generates its wealth.

THE BIG LEAGUE ORIENTATION

However, the big-league orientation goes beyond knowledge of industries. An increasing number of sales professionals are positioning themselves with affluent industries as "the supplier to deal with." In essence, the big-league orientation translates as marketing to the highest concentrations of affluent prospects.

I realize that your current customers are more likely than others to make future purchases of your automobiles. Also, your competitors' current customers have a propensity to buy your product. These two groups should be targeted. However, I estimate that the number of high-income households (those with annual incomes of $100,000 or more) in this nation will grow by 29 percent in 1990. That translates into nearly 1 million households (991,498). The large majority of this population are not your current customers; nor are they your competitors' customers. But they have the potential of becoming your customers.

How should these potential customers be targeted? Adopt the big-league orientation. Target by industry cluster first and specific target second. The highest concentrations of high-income prospects are not always found by geodemography or neighborhood quality. I prefer industrial taxonomy over neighborhood taxonomy. Yes, most affluent Americans are either owners/managers of their own businesses, or they are in sales/marketing. But before I discuss the reasons underlying my preference, allow me to reflect on yet another fish story.

Roland Martin is a leading authority of sport fishing. Dr. Greg Bambenek, also known as Dr. Juice, is a physician and also an authority on methods of attracting sport fish. On February 28, 1987, he was a guest on Martin's television program (WTBS, Atlanta, Georgia).

Dr. Bambenek is referred to as Dr. Juice because he developed a liquid fish attractor called Dr. Juice. However, he appeared on Martin's program, not to promote this product but to provide insight into the habits of fish and quality fishermen. Martin and Bambenek discussed the habits of fish found in Lake Superior and of the prehistoric Indians who were proficient in catching them. Bambenek's thoughts about the habits of fish should be interesting to those who market to the affluent.

According to Bambenek, the Indians found that the fish they targeted could be caught only during a short period of time each year—the 7 to 10 days a year that they entered the shallow waters near the shore. At other times, they were beyond reach in the middle of the lake in over 100 feet of water. The Indians placed a series of stakes in the ground in order to line up the position of the sun on the horizon during the 7 to 10 days of good fishing. Without this source of information, they could not be sure when the fish would be catchable.

The affluent are much like game fish. Each species clusters for a few days each year at trade conferences. They are likely to respond to promotional information during this time because their receptors are open. They attended these meetings to learn about new offerings. Why not tell them about your new offerings? Conferences last only a few days each year. Thus, marketers to the affluent must seek sources of information that will enable them to determine when the targets are in the shallow water. Current clients who are active in trade associations can act as a series of stakes in the ground that serve as a calendar of significant clustering situations. Or you can refer to Gale Research's *Directory of Associations*. This publication lists all major trade association meetings as well as when and where they will be held. Certainly, every dealer of luxury products should be aware of the affluent trade conferences that will be held during the next year or two in their respective trade areas. Your local area convention bureaus should be able to supply you with a list of names and dates.

THE LOW COST OF HIGH PRODUCTIVITY

You don't necessarily have to spend even a modest amount of money to take advantage of trade conference opportunities. The following example is a case in point. One extraordinary sales professional based in New England attended a recent trade conference at which 6,000 industry members were present along with over 700 suppliers. This young sales professional paid five dollars for admission into one of the highest concentrations of high-income prospects in America. He spent three days at the meeting and left with the names and addresses of over 600 qualified prospects. He was the only sales professional selling an affluent product. Every other marketer at the conference offered only industry-specific products and services.

It seems to me that many affluent attendees at the California Bar Association conference or Georgia Association of Radiologists, for example, would be interested in test driving your latest offerings. Target affluent industries. Accordingly, you will have the opportunity of learning about the identities of the most successful members as well as when members are euphoric. What do attendees talk about? At trade conferences they discuss "who is really doing well." Your sales professionals should become part of these discussions.

A fellow from whom we purchased our latest automobile was selected as a top-10 sales professional on a national basis. He was honored and acknowledged at a top-producer's banquet. But in spite of being in the top 10, he never attended a trade conference that acknowledged and identified affluent prospects. No, for most sales professionals selling begins after the image and promotional information generated by the manufacturers and dealer "gets the prospect to walk into the showroom." Conversely, proactive marketing dictates that one focus his resources upon the highest concentrations of prospects. This means selling at the targets' arena and not always in the comfort of your own environment.

TARGET BY INDUSTRY

The opportunity to target by industry and by affluent affiliation groups cannot be overstated. In doing so, you will likely increase your sales dramatically and not only because "that's where the money is." Equally compelling is the fact that your competitors have overlooked this opportunity. While there are a few minor exceptions—for example, most marketers of luxury goods target clusters of golfers and tennis players, I also wish to support the strategy of targeting other affluent affiliation groups. Since *Marketing to the Affluent* was published just over a year ago, I have given over 70 speeches and seminars on this topic. Two-thirds of these programs were for top-producing sales professionals from three industries including investments, real estate, and life insurance. Almost all of these attendees are in the affluent income category. Several of these groups had to have incomes of more than $250,000 to qualify. Oh, by the way, the three sales groups that I mentioned are, according to our estimates, in the top 10 high-income categories of over 400 that we studied. In fact, sales/marketing occupations account for 5 of the top 10 high-income groups in America.

I always ask members of the audience (captured respondents), "How many of you have ever been prospected by sales professionals that market luxury automobiles?" What portion of these very high-income respondents indicated that they recalled ever being personally contacted? Certainly, it must be a very high portion since these people are euphoric because their superior performance is being recognized both financially and symbolically. So much for initiative marketing logic. Not one of these thousands of high-income sales professionals indicated that they had ever been personally contacted! Not one.

It is not difficult to obtain a list of these top-ranked sales professionals. Some firms even publish such lists in local business periodicals. But an even better method relates to the big-league orientation. Each dealer should consider assigning at least one sales professional to the affluent subsegment called the *high-income sales professionals*.

Such specialists will become experts in understanding the high-income sales professional segment within their respective trade areas. They will be responsible for penetrating this segment. In addition, each specialist should act as an intelligence officer who can provide answers to the following questions:

1. Who are the top-ranked sales professionals in my trade area? Who are those in the $100,000 to $200,000 annual income category, and who makes more than $200,000 annually?
2. When are the bulk of their commissions earned? Realized?
3. When and where will clusters of these prospects be attending recognition meetings?

A WINNING PORTFOLIO OF SALES PROFESSIONALS

Dealers should consider developing a strategic portfolio of their own sales professionals. This portfolio strategy is based upon two important affluent market concepts. First, each geographic area in this nation has a unique economic infrastructure. Analyze the areas where there are high concentrations of wealth. What are you likely to find? High-income sales professionals in Atlanta and Los Angeles; affluent wine producers in the Napa Valley of California; affluent cattle ranchers in Colorado, Nebraska, and Florida; affluent coal producers in Kentucky; affluent science professors in and around Boston; affluent timberland owners in Georgia; affluent apparel producers and printers in New York City; and affluent attorneys and lobbyists in Washington, D.C. Of course, there are many high-income physicians, attorneys, accountants, and engineers in all major metropolitan areas. Accordingly, they should be targeted via the specialized route.

Second, most successful sales professionals who market to the affluent are specialists in regard to both product offering and targeted segments. The productivity of this deep and narrow approach has been well documented in our research.

Dealers must resolve two basic issues which relate to the concepts of the anatomy of wealth in terms of geography and the strategy of the deep and narrow. The majority of dealerships are staffed with sales professionals who work independently in terms of both target selection and product selection. It is not unusual for a dealer to discover that his sales professionals are targeting the same prospects or the same industries with identical products. At the same time, some of the industries that produce a disproportionate number of affluent prospects are all but ignored. It is essential that your sales managers become sensitive to the importance of matching the specific strengths of each of their sales professionals with the unique anatomy of the affluent within a given market area.

There are several advantages of organizing and managing a sales force in this prescribed manner. These include:

1. Placing one's greatest effort in the direction of the most lucrative targeted opportunities.
2. Focusing on an analysis of affluent market segments.
3. Placing each ambitious sales force member into areas of opportunities congruent with his background, aptitude, and motives.
4. Helping managers in recruiting sales professionals based upon strategic needs and market opportunities.
5. Increasing the productivity of both experienced top producers as well as younger achievement-oriented types.
6. Reducing competitive threats by dominating key targeted affluent segments.
7. Accessing critical information about major-league concentrations of wealth and changes in wealth.
8. Developing a reputation of superior expertise for the dealership as well as for the sales professionals.
9. Creating an image that will encourage the affluent to initiate contact with the sales professional.

Each of your sales professionals should have a big-league orientation. Each should strive to become the foremost supplier of luxury automobiles for specific segments of the high-income population. This segmentation strategy is based on the origin of the prospects' incomes.

No matter how hard you try, you will never be able to discover all of the high-income prospects that are encountering euphoria. Yes, some of these prospects will take the initiative of walking into your showrooms. Traditionally, walk-in business was stimulated by word-of-mouth communications between current satisfied customers and prospects. Your image and conditioning via mass media also played a role in generating traffic.

BE PERCEIVED AS AN EXPERT

I would also suggest that you consider yet another way of stimulating traffic. This method is based upon, and is a natural extension of, the *sources of information* and *big-league orientation* components.

A growing number of sales professionals are positioning themselves as the product and service expert for a specific segment of the affluent population. They are speaking about their product to groups that contain high concentrations of affluent prospects. They are also publishing articles in trade journals to which affluent entrepreneurs, professionals, and corporate executives subscribe.

Over 10,000 trade and business journals and related periodicals are published in this country. Often, the editors of these publications are in dire need of articles. Consider having your marketing staff prepare articles for publication in the trade journals that are read by high concentrations of affluent prospects. One ghost-written article, about the pros and cons of leasing versus purchasing a luxury automobile, for example, can be published in 100 different journals, in 100 different trade areas, and in quotes, "authorized" by 100 different dealers and/or sales professionals.

In the past 18 months, dozens of sales professionals have been kind enough to share their publishing experiences with us. Let me quote to you some of their comments.

Tom—

First article (enclosed). Calls from all over the country the first week . . . .

Steve

Published in: *DVM*
Circulation: 36,000
Audience: Veterinarians

Dear Tom:

I have redirected much of my (affluent) prospecting efforts towards "chumming" and am enclosing my first two articles to be published in trade magazines (ghost written, of course).

Fred

Published in:	*SNIPS*
Circulation:	28,000
Audience:	Heating contractors

Tom:

. . . now the editors are calling me for articles. The fish do chase the boat.

Larry

Published in:	*OUTLOOK*
Circulation:	35,000
Audience:	Fruit and vegetable producers, nationwide

Many trade journals, as well as trade associations, are parochial in terms of geographic orientation. They are thus ideal targets for providing publishing as well as local speaking opportunities for your sales professionals.

About what should your sales professionals write/talk? Those who target high-income sales professionals may wish to discuss alternative purchase/lease arrangements as they specifically relate to these affluent targets. Tax implications and payment schedules that match income patterns are of interest to the members of this group.

Writing and speaking are two methods that attract prospects. Also the intraindustry endorsements that one can generate are extremely important in establishing credibility for the sales professional and the dealer. The affluent have a strong affiliation need. This need can be leveraged. Your product, your dealership, and your sales professionals can be endorsed by industry-specific opinion leaders. If they are, you will significantly increase your penetration of the affluent market.

In addition, consider affiliating with organizations that represent retired executives. Most cities in this country have at least one organization of this type. These organizations provide the sales professional with an excellent opportunity to capitalize on an important demographic trend. Retirees with annual incomes of $100,000 or more increased from approximately 10 percent to nearly 20 percent within the past 10 years.

Often these high-income prospects radically change their consumption habits after they retire. Many move from a wealth-accumulation lifestyle to one of "spending their children's inheritance." Why not help them enjoy their golden years from behind the wheel of one of your top-of-the-line units?

THEY MAKE HOUSE CALLS!

Frank Hilson BMW is one of the more aggressive automobile dealers that target the affluent, especially the high-income affluent. I first asked Ken Rogers, the general manager of the dealership, about the sales professionals who worked at Frank Hilson BMW. He told me:

> We never hire former auto sales people. We look first and foremost for people with good people skills. Personable people. They must be friendly, show emotion, excitement and enthusiasm. They must have empathy for customers' needs. Among our top sales professionals today are people from several different and interesting vocations. These include a former sales professional from the shoe industry. A former bartender. A former clinical psychologist and a former stock broker. . . . You can

teach people about cars, but you cannot teach them about people. Each person that we select to represent us as a sales professional must pass through three separate personal interviews
before being hired. All the sales professionals must have what
we would call a fresh, neat, and clean appearance. . . . We try to
be different because we believe that most prospects feel that
going to an auto dealer and shopping for a luxury automobile is
second only to the ill feeling conjured up from going to a den-
tist's office.

That is one of the reasons why Ken's unique advertising has
proven to be so successful. He is especially effective on high-
income medical doctors who reside within the Frank Hilson BMW
trade area. One of the more intriguing ads that Ken put together
states:

BMW buyers: We make house calls! Our customers claim we
are the easiest place in South Florida to buy a new BMW and
maybe the nicest too. Let us prove it to you. If you are too busy to
come to us, we will come to you. Call free. Frank Hilson BMW,
1812 South Andrews Avenue, Fort Lauderdale, Florida.

Doctors call and say, you mean you really do make house calls?
You really do mean that we do not have to come into the showroom? And correspondingly, the sales professionals at Frank
Hilson respond that they would be delighted to deliver a BMW to
test drive. They will deliver it to the home or office, and at the
prospect's convenience. The medical doctors are among Frank
Hilson's very best customers.

Ken pointed out that he finds physicians are extremely sensitive to variations in quality in both product and service. And much
less sensitive to price. According to Scott, the business manager of
the firm:

We sell a lot of BMWs to medical doctors. The very best customer that this organization enjoys having is a medical doctor.
He is a neurosurgeon with an income in the mid-$3 million
range. He found us via a price advertisement that indicated that
we provide exceptional service. In the course of just three
months, the neurosurgeon has purchased three automobiles
from Hilson BMW, totaling $130,000. But even more impor-
tantly, the neurosurgeon has physically delivered eight differ-

ent physicians to the showroom. Six of the eight have already purchased new BMWs. All of these physicians that the neurosurgeon recommended have at least mid-six-figure incomes on an annual basis. He really enjoys coming to the dealership apparently, for when one of his buddies is discussing the possible purchase of a new BMW, the neurosurgeon is discussing different new products while he is in the service and parts department.. . . The neurosurgeon has expressed an interest in starting something called the 750 Club where all his buddies who, in fact, have purchased 750 model BMWs would be given hats, softball uniforms, and other paraphernalia to designate their affiliation with the product and the dealer.

When the neurosurgeon goes into the showroom to contemplate a new purchase, he deals with one of the top sales people at the dealership—someone who has significant product knowledge. Then he discusses the financial aspects with the business manager.

Very often high-income physicians have a high propensity to purchase expensive automobiles as well as expensive homes. In fact, one way to identify people who have a high propensity to spend is to examine the mortgage records in one's trade area. This public information available at the courthouse would indicate, as in the case of the neurosurgeon, the monthly mortgage payments due are $8,600 or slightly more than $100,000 per year. Actually the amount of interest on personal loans that the typical American who makes over a million dollars spends is just about $100,000. And of course, many people will point out that the credit service that is provided the affluent automobile purchaser often provides greater profit than the actual profit made from the automobile. People who spend a considerable amount of money on interest on loans have a high propensity to consume durable products.

Ken Rogers was kind enough to share some other ideas that he has come up with in terms of marketing to the affluent. One of his other creative advertisements starts out with:

Your BMW is so old, it's insured against zeppelin raids. How much will Frank Hilson give you for it? Probably more than you think! It's our 22nd annual model clearance sale at Frank Hilson BMW.

Or another one:

> Our sales manager is a pushover. We call him our rock of jelly.

And then they indicate the price that it would cost per month to lease a 535I BMW.

Ken also shared another rather innovative approach to doing direct mail. Ken believes that targeting people who currently own luxury automobiles can be productive. One especially interesting approach he used was to mail advertisements to all those owners of another brand of luxury imported car. Ken maintains that the brand in this context was slightly less prestigious than BMW and correspondingly priced slightly less. The advertisement states:

> For $17.00 a month you could be driving a BMW. Would you like to move way up in prestige to the BMW for only $17.00 more a month on your lease?

Ken also does mailings to those 25,000 people in the area with a two- or three-year-old lease about to expire on a BMW. Moreover, each of his sales professionals at a particular point of time is assigned to greet service customers and ask if they are in the market for a new model. In fact, in many instances, they will approach people having their cars serviced and ask them if they would be interested in selling their models and, of course, pointing out that this model is particularly in demand and they could probably give them a good price because they could sell it for a good price.

In some instances, sales professionals are assigned to make actual house calls. People call and ask for a car to be delivered and demonstrated at their home or office or somewhere else. At a particular point each salesman must do this. But following the demonstration of the automobile, the sales professional must, as part of his or her job description, ask each prospect for three referrals of people who may be interested in buying BMWs. This, in fact, must be recorded on something they call their referral card.

SELLING LUXURY CARS BY THE PARADE METHOD

Larry Chambers, the top-ranked sales professional from California, shared an interesting case history with me. According to Larry, one of the best targets for luxury motor cars are top-performing commodity brokers. It is not unusual for these world-class brokers to earn incomes in excess of $300,000, $400,000, or $500,000 annually. However, most prospects in this category suffer from an acute shortage of time. Thus, they are sometimes difficult to reach and even more difficult to talk to in some depth about your product offerings.

One of the more enlightened sales professionals in America devised a plan on how to counter the typical objection given to him by commodity brokers. This typical objection is "no time to visit the showroom." The sales professional in this situation attempted to contact a world-class commodity broker dozens and dozens of times. Finally, he was able to make telephone contact with his target. The commodity broker was invited to visit the showroom and to take a test drive in one of the sales professional's top-of-the-line offerings. However, his solicitation was countered by the response, "I'm on the phone all day, all the time. I eat my lunch on the phone, my breakfast on the phone, my dinner on the phone. I even have a telephone in the men's room." The commodity broker did indicate that he was interested in buying a top-of-the-line luxury car but had no time to visit, no time to shop, no time to test drive. The sales professional then asked the location of the commodity broker's office. He also inquired about the floor that the broker was located on and if he had a good view of the street and traffic from his telephone positioning post. The commodity broker indicated that his office and phone were situated in such a manner that they provided an excellent view of the vehicular traffic in the community. The sales professional then made the commodity broker an interesting offer. He proposed to drive a parade of his latest offerings by the commodity broker's window. He indicated, "I'll put together a procession of colors and models if you are really serious about buying." The commodity broker stated several times that he was very serious about making a new car purchase. While the commodity broker was on his telephone talking to clients from all over the world, he was also reviewing several dozen luxury automobiles that passed by his perch on the second floor. After reviewing many models and color combinations, the commodity broker finally signaled with a wave of his hand to indicate that's the one. He liked the color and model very much. He still was interested in taking a test drive but indicated again that he had no time. The sales professional then countered with, "I will leave it with you and I will take your automobile back to our dealership and look it over if, in fact, you would like to trade. Take it home with you. Keep it as long as you would like. Show it to your family and your friends. Take them for a ride. We can swap tomorrow or the next day, right before the market opens. Or we can sign the papers in your office tomorrow morning or the next morning before the market opens. You don't even have to come to our showroom." Because this sales professional of luxury automobiles was able to provide more than a product in terms of understanding the time constraints of the commodity broker, he was successful in selling the commodity broker a top-of-the-line luxury automobile. The papers were signed in the commodity broker's office at the time that he wanted to consummate the agreement.

The commodity broker is no different than many other high-achievement-oriented affluent people. To the commodity broker time is money. Time is the one commodity of which the broker has very little. There are literally thousands upon thousands of affluent people who have the ability to write a check instantly for any type of luxury automobile, and who also, in many respects, have a perceived need to buy one. However, there must be something to precipitate the sale. Many of these people will never shop dealerships or automobiles. They do not have the time.

Aggressive selling, that is, proactive marketing, calling people who are affluent but have a poverty of time, dealing with their time requirements, responding to their time needs, often results in a sale of some of the most expensive types of automobiles produced in the world today. Success in terms of selling luxury automobiles is reflected among those who aggressively pursue new prospects every day. Of course, it also helps to understand the cash flow situation of the target audience. For example, in the case of this sales professional who converted a commodity broker to a customer, he understood that there was a high probability that the commodity broker would be incurring significant changes in his cash flow because of the dramatic shift in the prices of various types of commodities. Commodity price changes, of course, are public information and widely circulated in the *The Wall Street Journal* and other publications, but interestingly, many sales professionals never take the time to review various types of signals that indicate dramatic changes in wealth and income of market segments.

Reading is one of the key underlying factors that discriminates mediocre sales professionals and great sales professionals. Great sales professionals, like many of their affluent counterparts, are heavy readers of information that indicates change and opportunity in the market.

JOHN SELLS MORE THAN LUXURY AUTOMOBILES

Dear Marketer:

During the last few years, I have noticed the increasing number of prospects walking into your showrooms. As you stated yourself, on many occasions, most of the visitors were presold before they entered. But the trend now in the luxury automobile market reflects growing competition. Several major players have noticed your success. They are attempting to penetrate your targeted segment with products that imitate yours. These look-alike imitations are being bolstered by heavy advertising and price incentives. Also, some of these competitors have many more dealers than your organization. It is unclear, at best, if they can match your service record. However, location is still a central dimension that explains market share.

I am aware that your sales force is unusual in its proactive posture in seeking new business. But it is likely that some of your contact people have become complacent because of your product's unparalleled quality image. But complacency must be replaced with aggressive, intelligence-based proactive marketing. Your sales professionals must be trained and encouraged to constantly take the initiative in identifying likely buyers, that is, those who are ready, willing, and well able to purchase your top-of-the-line units. Your marketing strategy will have to be more creative as well as productive. You are competing against those with much deeper pockets in terms of both budgets and troops. I propose that you develop a grass-roots strategy for selected dealerships as well as for their contact personnel.

It is interesting that your current owners have a significantly higher propensity to purchase and read best-selling books than the average car buyer. I believe that you will be able to leverage this relationship to stimulate business. Your organization, at a national level, would be able to purchase large quantities of the latest best sellers at considerable discounts. These selected books could then be resold to your dealers at your cost. Dealers could use these books in several possible ways.

First, dealers may prefer to offer the books as incentives for those prospects who stop in for test rides in one or more of your units. This would be useful not only in stimulating showroom traffic but also in providing your selected dealers with a tie-in. By associating with best sellers and their respective authors, the dealership will be able to enhance its visibility and credibility. Also, your national advertising agency should be able to design news releases and articles on this promotion for each of the participating dealers.

Certainly, your dealers will be interested in gaining publicity in the local media. Often, they complain that national is not giving them support in terms of local public relations ideas. The tie-in with best sellers will change their opinion. Also, the business editors of local newspapers across this country will be very interested, unless they have a large supply of news items as interesting as this tie-in. Most will likely tell you they are starving for items that have this potential interest.

A second possible use of the best-seller concept relates to "bird dog" activities. Your dealers may find it useful to give best-selling books to those individuals who refer prospects to the dealership. Contact personnel may be required to pay for part of this incentive in situations where sales are actually consummated.

The best-seller concept could also be used in making contact with prospects. Your dealers and their designated contact personnel can be trained to identify people who are likely to have interest in purchasing one of your upper-level units. They could be sensitized to the value of prospecting targets that are likely to be euphoric. People usually become euphoric when they encounter or anticipate significant and positive changes in their cash flow and/or occupational status.

Your contact personnel should be encouraged to become proactive in their solicitations. They must begin to initiate sales rather than let them merely take place. Contact personnel should be required to solicit business from prospects that are likely to be euphoric. Every day in every trade area where you have dealerships, prospects are identified in news stories published in the local business press. People who are about to be promoted from manager to vice president or from vice president to senior vice president often feel that their current model auto no longer is congruent with the prestige associated with their new title. Some will be susceptible to making an auto purchase because they are about to receive large sums of money from the sale of the publication businesses (rights to their book), real estate, airplanes, yachts, and so forth. Others are ready to buy a top-of-the-line unit because the firm they own just landed a major contract. Much of the information about changes in money and the corresponding suspected euphoria is published in the local press.

Greater commissions should be given in cases where the sale was consummated via these proactive methods. As an added incentive, add a complimentary best seller for these euphoric prospects who test drive one of our upper-end units.

Your contact personnel will be more willing to cold call prospects if they have a gift as well as a sales pitch to deliver. Please help to support your local authors.

Regards,

Thomas J. Stanley, Chairman
The Affluent Market Institute

John Becomes a Best Seller

It's Monday morning just before 10 o'clock. John has been pacing outside his favorite book store for the past 20 minutes. He has been a customer since he moved here just over five years ago. But John is not interested in purchasing today. Nor will he merely browse the offerings when he gets inside. Today there is something more important for him than buying or browsing. Why else would John miss the "mandatory" Monday morning sales meeting with his manager? John is about to collect important intelligence information about affluent prospects.

Step One. Pick your key informant wisely.
John enters the bookstore. Only two other customers are present. John identifies Cheryl, his key contact. Cheryl is the young assistant manager of the number one ranked book store in, as she suggests, "a city of book stores." John found, over the years, that Cheryl knows more about books and authors than anyone else with whom he had come into contact.

JOHN:

> Good morning, Cheryl. Did you have a nice weekend? Read any good books lately?

CHERYL:

> Great weekend. No reading this weekend. I went to a folk music festival. What are you doing here so early in the morning? Aren't you supposed to be at work?

JOHN:

> I am at work. I need your help. Do you have a section or collection on something designated solely for local authors?

CHERYL:

> No, their books are all over the place.

JOHN:

> Well, how do you folks have all the autograph events you put on? You know, where the local authors come in for a few hours and autograph their books.

CHERYL:

> That's not limited to local authors. But we do have more locals than the others. We like to support the locals.

JOHN:

> But you don't have a list or anything?

CHERYL:

> I can give you the fliers for the past programs and those coming up that list all the authors—I can check off the locals.

JOHN:

> Are most of the locals listed on the fliers?

CHERYL:

> Those on the list are only a small number compared to the total number of locally based authors. We have several authors of children's books who are not on this autograph list, but they do live in town.

JOHN:

> Oh well, I guess I am not going to be able to identify all the local authors. My sales manager is not going to be pleased with me.

CHERYL:

> Why do you want the list of local authors?

Step Two.   Always focus on the needs of your key informant as well as your ultimate target.

JOHN:

> Well, Cheryl, you know I'm in the automobile business. It's a tough business, and I'm always looking for new ideas. That's why I'm here today, playing hooky from my sales manager's mandatory sales meeting. I thought I could walk out of here today with a list of local authors.

CHERYL:

> But what do you want with the list?

JOHN:

The first thing I would do is purchase *from your store* the better selling books written by local authors. Then I would call these folks for an appointment to stop by and have them personally autograph my copy. Of course, I would also ask them if they would like to take a short test drive in one of our top-of-the-line cars.

CHERYL:

John, you must realize that some of these authors do children's books.

JOHN:

I'll bring my kids along for the ride and autograph.

CHERYL:

How about the locals who write only books in the religious category?

JOHN:

I need more religion. My wife tells me this all the time. I'm also thinking of adding even more support to the local author community. Our dealership could give an autographed copy of a local author's book to each person that stops by to test drive one of our units. Of course, you know the store we would patronize in terms of bulk unit purchases. We could even have a few top-of-the-line units parked outside your store. We would invite prospective buyers to visit your store for a fine book, autograph, and test drive. Of course, we would buy the books from you folks.

CHERYL:

Well, John, I can help you put a list together. I'll check off the locals from our autograph schedule. But then we'll have to walk through the store. I'll bet that there are more than 100 local authors represented. Look at this one. We sold 109 copies last month. That does not include special orders. A sales manager came in here last week and bought 25 for his sales force. There must be two dozen other local authors represented in our business and career sections. I hope you brought your lunch, John.

JOHN:

I will buy lunch.

Step Three.   Gather and refine your list.

CHERYL:

You know, John, that most of these books are not on *The New York Times* best-seller list. Of course, some categories are not covered by the *Times* anyway. Some of the best authors of children's books live here in town.

JOHN:

How can I tell if a book is selling well but not in the best-seller category?

CHERYL:

Well, I can tell you about some of them. But we will have to speak with Amy about the children's books. She's our children's selection expert. But you can also tell by looking inside the book. You see, right here on the page after the title page . . . this book was first published last year. It has last year's copyright date. Now look at the bottom of the page.

JOHN:

It says, "Printed in the United States of America."

CHERYL:

Just below that . . . notice the list of numbers . . . 6, 7, 8, 9, 10. Six is the first number. This indicates sixth printing. This book is hot—in its sixth printing, and it was just published last year. Of course, some bookstores still have in inventory early printings. So the numbers at the bottom are not perfect indicators of the book's success. But look at this one. It was first published four years ago, and it's in its 11th printing. It is one of the best-selling "how-to books." You will want to put this author on the top of your list. There are 9 or 10 extremely successful authors here in town. Do you have a pad? Some of these folks are in my rolodex.

JOHN:

I want to take copies of the top three or four books written by the authors. Put them on my account.

CHERYL:

We will even give you our trade discount.

JOHN:

Are all these from the same publisher?

CHERYL:

Yes. That house has done very well in the last few years.

JOHN:

Well, what does this mean when it says "Ajax Press?"

CHERYL:

That's the company that prints the books for the publisher.

JOHN:

Gee, all these books are printed by the same printer. He must make the paper salesmen happy. Maybe I should drive up to see if this fellow is in the market for a new experience in transportation.

CHERYL:

John, you should call the literary agent for these authors. The fellow that represents the author whose book you're holding gets 15 percent of all the authors' royalties. He represents more than two dozen well-known authors.

JOHN:

I will have to ask the authors about their agents when I visit with them.

CHERYL:

Don't overlook their booking agents, publicists, and attorneys. Big authors associate with some really creative and high-priced professional types. But of course, John, you're in sales, so you already know that.

JOHN:

Ah, ah, yes, I was just going to mention other folks.

Step Four. Make contact with the target and begin conditioning process. Focus on the needs of the prospect before addressing your need to sell your product and to gain the endorsement of the target.

EXPLOITING HIS LIST OF TARGETS

John's intelligence-gathering mission and debriefing of Cheryl resulted in a list of several dozen local authors. At least 10 authors on the list were, in Cheryl's terms, "very big" writers. In one evening, John telephoned the homes of four of these authors. The first two were not at home, according to their answering machines. A spokesperson for the third told John that the author was on tour. The fourth author answered his own phone on the first ring.

LOCAL AUTHOR (L.A.):

Hello, this is L.A.

JOHN:

Mr. L.A., my name is John. I just finished reading your latest book. I could not put it down.

L.A.:

I hope the critics get that excited.

JOHN:

I live here in town. I was wondering if I could stop by your office some time next week and get you to autograph my book.

L.A.:

My agent tells me grass-roots support must be served. I finish writing each day at 11:30 A.M. I have a "clean-up hour" between 11:30 and 12:30. Come by any time Tuesday, Wednesday, Thursday, or Friday.

JOHN:

I will come by on Wednesday just before noon. How are sales going so far?

L.A.:

It's really too early to tell, but since the publisher put down some nice up-front money, I'm going to let them worry about getting their investment back. But I do a lot of selling of my own product.

JOHN:

Well, Mr. L.A., I wonder if I could talk to you for a few minutes about having our firm promote your book.

L.A.:

I already have a publicist and a publisher. They are good at what they do.

JOHN:

We are not in the public relations business. We are a dealership that sells luxury European motor cars.

L.A.:

You want to sell me a car? I have five cars, and only three people in my family have driver's licenses.

JOHN:

I would love to put you behind the wheel of one of our top-of-the-line units someday in the future. But I want to talk about supporting your book and helping our dealership at the same time. I find that a lot of authors in this city are not getting any promotional support. I bet that most people, even people that read your books, don't know that you're their neighbor.

L.A.:

Amen! What's the deal?

JOHN:

What would our firm like to do for you? Give an autographed copy of your latest work to each person that accepts our invitation to test drive our new top-of-the-line unit.

L.A.:

How many people are on your list?

JOHN:

Well, more important than even the list, we know that the press would give this idea a great deal of coverage. I really don't know how many books we would purchase up front. At least a case, just to see how well it works.

L.A.:

I don't mind signing a case.

JOHN:

You know, if this thing takes off, I'm going to tell a national sales manager at the office to endorse you to other dealers.

L.A.:

That would be nice. When did you say you were coming over?

JOHN:

Just before noon Wednesday. Is that a problem?

L.A.:

No, but why don't you show up at 12:30 so that we can go to lunch and discuss this in more detail?

JOHN:

Is it okay if I drive over in one of our-top-of-the-line units?

L.A.:

Fine. But if you leave it with me, you have to promise to take two of mine with you.

JOHN:

What are you currently driving?

L.A.:

We have a 560, a 300E, a Land Rover, a Silverado Suburban, and a 20-year-old Cadillac convertible. Don't get your hopes up, we're up to our ears in vehicles.

JOHN:

I understand—no problem. I will see you at 12:30 P.M. on Wednesday.

L.A.:

Wednesday, 12:30 P.M., my office [address given].

JOHN:

Thank you. See you Wednesday.

Step Five. Gain the target's endorsement by offering to enhance his royalty statement. Time solicitation in harmony with positive changes in target's cash flow. Encourage the target to boast of his economic achievements and to recognize the importance of balancing his success with the adoption of products that indicate significant levels of achievement.

FOCUS ON THE NEEDS OF THE TARGET

John visited with Mr. L.A. at the prescribed time. Instead of carrying one copy of Mr. L.A.'s latest book, he had a case in the trunk of the top-of-the-line demonstrator. Mr. L.A. was more than delighted to sign every copy. John paid for all the books out of his own pocket. Even at a 25 percent discount, he had to pay Cheryl's book store several hundred dollars for the case. But one must spend money to sell high-ticket items to the affluent effectively.

John was fortunate in the timing of his visit to Mr. L.A. This author's up-front fee was paid to him just a few days before John called him. Thus, the target was euphoric, that is, in the mood and economic position to purchase. But more importantly, John has gained the endorsement of a well-respected personality. The prestige of the author and his books will greatly enhance John's credibility when he calls upon other prospects.

John is not just one of thousands of ordinary automobile sales professionals. He is an associate of an important author. And when John finally places Mr. L.A. "firmly behind the wheel," he will greatly enhance the demand for his top-of-the-line units.

With Mr. L.A. behind the wheel and John riding shotgun, an interesting discourse takes place.

CONDITIONING THE PROSPECT

JOHN:

So, you think your latest book will be bigger than your other works?

L.A.:

I certainly hope so. But you know that my latest book was really an exception. It sold several million and is still selling. It's been translated into eight different languages.

JOHN:

Does that mean that you will have to learn eight different languages if you're going to give speeches overseas?

L.A.:

With the money the folks in Japan, Hong Kong, and even Germany pay me, I would learn to speak their languages. But I don't have to. English is the number one international language. Besides, John, they translate. But speaking is where the money is—did nearly 100 last year. Publishers are in the business of making money. A lot of authors think that they can outwit the publishers, but few can do it. That is unless they have a great track record.

JOHN:

Well, you have a great track record. And I hope that our promotion here in town will help your sales.

L.A.:

But it took some time for them to respond to that fact. But when I hired an agent, things worked out much better. He played one against the other—had several of them bidding on my current work. I received a bigger up-front fee for this one than all my royalties from the first book I wrote. You should try to sell my agent one of these models. He represents more than two dozen current stars in this business. But he is on the East Coast.

JOHN:

I'll call him anyway. I have some friends at dealerships back east. But I wanted to ask you—besides the fame and the money, what keeps you so highly motivated?

L.A.:

At the end of each annual tour, I take my family to our place in Vermont. That is what keeps me going.

JOHN:

Don't you even reward yourself in other ways? Doesn't your publisher give you something when your book hits it big?

L.A.:

My publisher sends me a royalty statement and a check. I have never received one personalized thank-you piece of mail from them in all my career.

JOHN:

Well, then—you need to reward yourself.

L.A.:

I did that two years ago. I bought myself a 38-foot boat. But we have not used it in more than a year. It did not turn out to be a great idea. It is more trouble than I ever imagined.

JOHN:

You would never have those kind of problems with this unit. What do you think of it?

L.A.:

This is the best-driving car I have been in. It's a fine looking product besides.

JOHN:

What do you drive now, Mr. L.A.?

L.A.:

We have five vehicles, but most often, I drive the Land Rover.

JOHN:

Great vehicle . . . especially for getting in and out of the woods. I'm sure you will want to keep at least one four wheel drive around. But I'm also wondering . . . in light of your latest book's success, if you should be rewarded by moving up to one of these top-of-the-line units?

L.A.:

Well, when you get me to talk at my office, you can look at my current top-of-the-line unit—it's two years old. You can tell me what it's worth.

JOHN:

I'll do better than that. I'll leave you our unit for you to drive for a few days, and I will take yours back to our place for a full appraisal.

L.A.:

All right, but when can we hook up again?

JOHN:

I can exchange with you tomorrow or the next day?

L.A.:

We can figure it out later.

JOHN:

I have a case of your latest books in the trunk. Don't let me forget to have you autograph each one.

L.A.:

I have my pens ready. What are you doing to make sure this promotion works?

JOHN:

I'll be honest with you. We have never done a promotion like this before. But the people at the best book store in town told me that you're the biggest author in this city. Also, I figured that a lot of folks would be willing to test drive one of our products if we gave them a complimentary copy of your book. But anybody can give away books. Your book is special because it's auto-graphed by you.

L.A.:

Well, maybe I should be on retainer.

JOHN:

Our budget would not let us do that. Of course, there are nine other authors on our list, but you're our first choice.

L.A.:

Just kidding, John.

JOHN:

> I'm also searching for the right business periodical to tell your story. I'm amazed that so few people in this city realize that you're a native son—born, raised, and currently residing here.

L.A.:

> You're right about that. Even some of my neighbors don't know who I am or what I do for a living.

JOHN:

> We're going to change that. I want one of the top local or state periodicals to do a feature story on how a locally based author produces a string of winners. I think it would be a nice twist to mention that you're helping promote the book by autographing copies for our prospects.

L.A.:

> I'll autograph every one of them.

JOHN:

> Well, here's the restaurant up ahead. Are you hungry?

L.A.:

> I'm always hungry. Talking always gives me an appetite.

John eventually put Mr. L.A. in a top-of-the-line unit. He was wise to push a lease arrangement. John recalls after debriefing the author that Mr. L.A. was in the Income Statement Affluent category. "Income Statement Affluent" refers to those individuals with very high incomes, relatively low net worth, and correspondingly very high marginal propensities to consume. Yes, Mr. L.A. is a big spender and an ideal target for those who market luxury goods. Often income statement affluent consumers are cash poor. They spend significant amounts of money when they receive major cash disbursements. But the majority of time during the year, they are often living on borrowed funds. Thus, it was lucky for John to approach Mr. L.A. when his cash flow was moving in the positive direction.

Step Six.   Market your ideas to the press. Leverage relationship with highly credible personalities by publishing in targeted periodicals. Gain support of management.

The day that John finally closed the leasing agreement with Mr. L.A., the young sales professional became euphoric. But it did not take long for him to regain his composure. Closing on Mr. L.A. was just the foundation to the overall marketing plan that John developed. With the endorsement of Mr. L.A. and one case of autographed books, he had established a beachhead.

John's next course of action was to gain publicity for himself, his product, dealership, and Mr. L.A. John called five editors/reporters from the local business press. Three of those contacted expressed more interest in Mr. L.A. than in John's creative genius for selling automobiles. John was determined not to allow his story to become someone else's. John, in one such encounter, demonstrates his maturity in avoiding possible loss of a key element in his promotional campaign.

MR. BOB BARRETTE:

Hello, Barrette here. Business desk.

JOHN:

Mr. Barrette, I read your story on the problems of local firms raising venture capital. Outstanding.

B.B.:

Thanks, I got a lot of calls on that one.

JOHN:

I'll bet some of the big regionals would love to carry it.

B.B.:

They are always in need of some original ideas.

JOHN:

Well, I know you have an instinct for putting a lot of creative ideas down on paper, and I thought you may be interested in something our firm is doing. We sell top-of-the-line European motor cars. We have come up with an interesting theme for marketing our products.

B.B.:

With the prices you guys get, you better have some great ideas.

JOHN:

We give a complimentary copy of a best-selling book to each person that takes a test drive.

B.B.:

That's it? You should give them five best sellers.

JOHN:

Well, that is not the point. The books are autographed by our city's top-selling author. In fact, I just sold, actually leased, him one of our units. He is local.

B.B.:

Who is this guy? I would love to interview him. You know, "Local author makes it big." Hey, I appreciate the lead.

JOHN:

Well, I think a more interesting slant for your readers would be how an auto dealer capitalizes upon and also supports local authors.

B.B.:

I'd love to speak with him.

JOHN:

He is a very busy fellow and a private type. I will ask him if he would like to speak with you.

B.B.:

We may have a story here. How many of these local authors do you know?

JOHN:

I think all your business-type readers would be interested in learning how we use innovative concepts in targeting customers.

B.B.:

The real story is the local best seller. Have him call me.

JOHN:

I'll get back with you. So long.

B.B.:

Bye.

John was determined to have *his* story told. But after several Mr. Barrette-type encounters, he was becoming less optimistic. This changed soon after he placed a call to the editor of a recently launched weekly business periodical. This local paper was exclusively devoted to local business news. John "sold" his story to the editor of this periodical. What was the primary reason for his success? John focused on the needs of the editor. Often, new periodicals are desperate for news stories. Also many are understaffed. John did not just offer ideas for a story. He promised to write it as well.

Following is a conversation between John and Mr. Oscar Black:

OSCAR:

Hello, *Business in Our Town,* Oscar Black speaking. How may I help you?

JOHN:

Oh, Mr. Black, I was surprised that you answered your own phone.

OSCAR:

I do phones, write, set type, do coffee, and dust. We are lean right now and are trying to hire a bunch of folks.

JOHN:

I would never have guessed that you were so lean. That feature piece you did on local business leaders was outstanding. In fact, I told all my colleagues at our company to start reading *Business in Our Town.*

OSCAR:

I appreciate your comments.

JOHN:

How are sales coming along?

OSCAR:

Well, if you mean subscriptions, we are a bit behind our original estimates. But that may be due to all the complimentary copies we put out.

JOHN:

If you will send me several dozen order blanks and some back copies, I will distribute them to our customers.

OSCAR:

I'll send you 100. Our advertising revenue seems to be fairly good. Of course, we have the best rates in town.

JOHN:

How big is your editorial staff?

OSCAR:

That's the problem. We need to have two or three writers. I wrote half of the last issue. We are interviewing a bunch of writers now. But we can't find just the right talent overnight.

JOHN:

Well, perhaps I can help. I work for an automobile dealership that specializes in top-of-the-line European luxury automobiles. We have been doing some interesting promotions. We work with this city's number one best-selling author.

OSCAR:

That's interesting. Tell me how it works.

JOHN:

Well, we thought it would be a good idea to give some support to locally based authors. It's amazing how few people in this city realize that their neighbors are authors of the first magnitude.

OSCAR:

You're probably right.

JOHN:

As part of our program we give a complimentary, autographed copy of a best seller to people who test drive one of our top-of-the-line units. Our first offering was written by one of our city's biggest authors.

OSCAR:

I'm from D.C., and I'm just getting my feet wet when it comes to the local environment. How is the promotion going so far?

JOHN:

It has just started. But I'm sure it will work. I have already sold two top-of-the-line units—ah, ah, by the book method.

OSCAR:

Well, we would be interested in probably doing something on this. But we will not be able to put something out for at least a month. We are so shorthanded that it would be at least that long before someone can come out to interview you. But we certainly want to do the story. A lot of our readers are hopefully in the market for luxury automobiles.

JOHN:

Oscar, if the problem is on the writing side, I can help. I'm an excellent writer. I would be more than happy to put my ideas down on paper. I can include some of the comments of the local authors as well as our sales manager and customers.

OSCAR:

You can deliver a story?

JOHN:

Yes, sir. No problem. How soon would you like it?

OSCAR:

Well, today is Wednesday. Could you have it on my desk by next Wednesday?

JOHN:

No problem. But can you tell me if you would publish it?

OSCAR:

Unless it's way off base, you're 99 percent published. Can I send a photographer to your place on Friday? I also want to get some photos of your author friend.

JOHN:

> Friday will be fine. I already have some professional photos of the author and his complete bio.

OSCAR:

> Do you have any photos of the dealership? And of the top-of-the-line model?

JOHN:

> Have it covered. I'll enclose all of this with the article.

OSCAR:

> Send all of the materials as soon as possible.

JOHN:

> No problem.

OSCAR:

> Looking forward to seeing it. I will call you after I read your article. So long.

JOHN:

> So long, Oscar.

ASK FOR HELP FROM A GHOST

John is now closer to his goal of publicizing his ideas, but he really is not a professional writer. He did some writing for his high school yearbook and does write an occasional letter to the editor of the local paper. But now he needs a professionally prepared article. John first gathered all his thoughts about how he developed his relationship with Mr. L.A. He then wrote down in outline form everything that transpired since he first conveyed the ideas of marketing autos and best sellers. Then he took out his tape recorder and dictated a detailed analysis of the who, what, when, where, how, and why of the promotional theme.

John gave some consideration to writing the story himself. But he did not want to chance losing this opportunity because of a poorly prepared manuscript. But who could help John put his ideas into the proper form?

John once again demonstrated his resourcefulness. He called the journalism department at a local college. John discussed his dilemma with the chairman of the department. He told Dr. Jones of his time and tight monetary constraints. The chairman indicated that no faculty member would likely be interested. But he made another suggestion. Several senior-level journalism students were always interested in gaining real world experience. Some even provide their services for free.

Dr. Jones gave John the names and telephone numbers of six top-notch journalism students. John made an appointment to interview four of them on campus the following day. All four were capable of transforming John's ideas into a publishable article. He finally picked Ms. Jane Miller. Jane showed up for the interview with copies of three of her published articles. They fit John's parameters exactly. Also, Jane promised John that she could have a first draft of the story to him in two days and a final draft at least one day before John's promised deadline. Ms. Miller would also deliver more than the hard copy of the paper. She would provide a complete suggested layout with picture positions and the text on a computer disc. With respect to writing, Ms. Miller was wise beyond her years. She told John that to enhance his chances of getting publicity, "John, always make it easy for the editor to say yes. A story that is camera ready or near camera ready is much more likely to be published than something the editor will have to reconstruct." John accepted Ms. Miller's proposal. He felt that the $250 editorial fee she charged was money well spent.

Following his interview with Ms. Miller, John delivered two more autographed copies to prospects who took test drives. Both seemed interested in trading up. Following the test drives, he returned to the dealership to discuss his promotional campaign with Butch Clower, the sales manager.

CONDITION YOUR MANAGER

JOHN:

Butch, is it a good time to talk with you?

BUTCH:

You sell any big units today?

JOHN:

No, but did two demo rides using my best-seller promotion.

BUTCH:

You must have deep pockets.

JOHN:

But I have great news. Remember, I mentioned that the local press would love to do a feature story on our tie-in with the best-selling author?

BUTCH:

Yeh, but don't do anything without my approval.

JOHN:

Well, I spoke with the top guy over at *Business in Our Town*. He wants to do a feature in next week's edition. I want to get some of your quotes so we can include them in the article.

BUTCH:

My quotes?

JOHN:

Yes, Butch—your ideas about how you feel this thing with the author is working.

BUTCH:

My quotes . . . .

JOHN:

Butch, they are going to send a photographer over here to take your picture for the article. They also want to take shots of our showroom and some of the top-of-the-line models. Don't we have some stock pictures of the models and our showroom?

BUTCH:

We have hundreds. The general manager is going to love this. But are you sure that they will say nice things about us?

JOHN:

I'll bet my life on it. No doubt this story will show us as the best dealership in town. And of course, they will tell our prospects and customers that we are the most professional sales group in the industry. Who else has a tie-in with a best-selling author?

BUTCH:

The guy you did that lease on.

JOHN:

That's the one. By the way, Butch, I spent over $200 on a case of books. Do you think I will be able to get reimbursed by the company?

BUTCH:

You pull this story deal off, and I will pay for two cases.

JOHN:

That's great, Butch, because I do have a few other minor expenses.

BUTCH:

I can deal with minor. Just don't go ballistic with expenses before we see how this thing works. We should get Mr. L.A. out here some night for an autograph party and reception for customers and future customers. We could do it at the club when we introduce our new models.

JOHN:

That's a great idea, Butch.

BUTCH:

You bet.

JOHN:

Let's set up a time for the photographer to come out. He said he would need to take 200 to 300 shots to make sure he gets the best possible ones.

BUTCH:

This is going to be big. We will need reprints. Can we get reprints?

JOHN:

No problem on the reprints. We can have them done for 70 cents a copy in quantities of 100 or more.

BUTCH:

Get at least 2,000.

JOHN:

What time can you set for your photo session, Butch?

BUTCH:

You pick the time. I'll be here. It's a top priority. I'll be open all day. This is exciting.

JOHN:

Butch, this would have never materialized without your support and leadership. I'll get back to you with a specific time.

BUTCH:

I'm going to get my hair cut. The next time you see me, I'll be in my new suit.

FOLLOW JOHN'S PROACTIVE METHODS

The scenario played out by John can be adopted by others involved with various types of products or services designed for the affluent. John, like most great sales professionals, abhors reactive selling, or just waiting for the market to play itself out. John is a proactive marketer.

John did not have to spend a great deal of money to become associated with a best-selling author. Nor did he have to expend a great deal of energy persuading the author, the editor, and the sales manager to behave in a way that would be advantageous for all the actors in this play. John clearly has a big-league orientation. He targets affluent clusters and initially focuses upon the biggest targets within these segments. He is also on his way toward becoming a recognized expert on luxury automobiles and the particular motor vehicle needs of the income statement affluent in his trade area.

Much of the information in "John's" article focuses upon his association with the author of a best-selling book. The credibility of the author will rub off on John, his product, and his dealership. All else being equal, affluent prospects prefer to patronize those who are friends and associates of highly credible and trustworthy people. This type of association will make John's cold calls warmer. And he will find that a growing number of prospects will seek his advice about their choice of motor cars. This is especially important since he will never be able to identify all the prospects who are euphoric. Thus, in such situations, euphoric prospects must be conditioned to initially contact John. This method of persuading the affluent is the highest form of the art called marketing.

CHAPTER 12

SELLING REAL ESTATE TO
THE AFFLUENT

JACKIE SPOTA: A MOST EXTRAORDINARY
SALES PROFESSIONAL OF EXTRAORDINARY
REAL ESTATE

Mrs. Jackie Spota is the top-ranked sales professional at one of America's truly outstanding residential developments. The Country Club of the South, a Jack Nicklaus Community, is located in the northern suburbs of Atlanta, Georgia.

Jackie was also the top residential real estate sales person for two years in a row within the Atlanta market area. Most recently she generated annual gross sales of over $20 million.

I first met Jackie when I was invited to meet with several of the managers of the Country Club of the South. It was immediately obvious to me that Jackie was likely to be a top producer. She just exuded confidence and warmth and had an uncanny ability to communicate.

Jackie's success formula has several underlying dimensions. She has a genuine liking of people, a need to satisfy them, and tremendous curiosity and interest in people. She spends inordinate amounts of time researching all the available properties, both new and resale, and of course, lots that are available. She also has an excellent command of investment data and understands exactly how to match the people need with the property availability.

Jackie pointed out that she is sometimes amazed at her own success because she was not formally trained in marketing, nor did she start early in her life selling residential property. In fact, for over 20 years she was a homemaker. It was not until after she reached her 40th birthday that she ventured into sales. But Jackie in short order became one of this nation's most extraordinary sales professionals. The formula of her rapid success provides an important model for those who aspire to achieve greatness in the profession called selling.

Focus, Trade up, and Think Big

Jackie was an agent in Hidden Hills for approximately eight years. Jackie's philosophy in selling has always been one of a focused approach. She originally started working selling for Barton & Ludwick, a small residential real estate company that was eventually sold to Coldwell Banker. While she worked for Barton & Ludwick, she was the agent responsible for Hidden Hills, a modest subdivision in suburban Atlanta. At that time, homes ranged in price from $90,000 to $125,000. Interestingly, one of her brokers from Barton & Ludwick told Jackie that she would never be successful in sales because she was too focused.

Too focused indeed! Jackie had a goal in terms of being the very best agent within one narrowly defined neighborhood, in this case, Hidden Hills. In fact, when she eventually left Hidden Hills, she had 85 listings there, 60 of which were resale listings. As Jackie points out, she knew every house and every family that ever lived in every house in Hidden Hills, and she attributes much of her success to this fact.

DR. STANLEY:

Jackie, why did you sell homes only within one subdivision?

MRS. SPOTA:

I wanted to be a specialist. I wanted to know one area backwards, forwards, upside down. I could tell you every house, who were the five owners, how many kids they had, what they did for a living, and I wanted to specialize in one area. My broker said I was stupid and would never amount to anything. He said any successful person does not specialize in one area. That you had to branch out and go into many areas. And I said, "Well, you may be right, but this is what I choose for my life." And I controlled Hidden Hills subdivision.

DR. STANLEY:

> Did you come here [Country Club of the South] directly from Hidden Hills?

MRS. SPOTA:

> Yes, I have been here now for three and one-half years. Three and one-half years . . . two years as part of the Atlanta Board of Realtors—I won the top sales award.

DR. STANLEY:

> In other words, in less than two years you became number one? And you sell only within one residential development?

MRS. SPOTA:

> Yes. I love it. I love what I do. I love it. The cup doesn't get full. I know you hear it a lot, but it doesn't. But the trouble is, I want more. Like my goals. I set goals for myself. I don't know if all people do in sales. I was looking at some of the goals that other sales people have, and I thought either I'm over-exaggerated or something, because my goals are probably twice as high, or three times as high as anybody else. That's what I want. I couldn't be happy with 3 million in sales a month. I mean if I can get 4 million a month, I'll do four. If I hit 5, or 6, I want everything I can get. But I won't step on anyone either. I won't. I will never burn a bridge. Because it comes back. You know that is true.

Selling from Inside an Affiliation Convoy

DR. STANLEY:

> Jackie, how about these people who walk in and say, "I want to talk to Jackie." Where do they come from?

MRS. SPOTA:

> A lot of people are referrals from other people I've sold houses to and agents I have done a good job for.

DR. STANLEY:

> Jackie, you mentioned that you had sold several doctors that knew each other.

Strongly Suggested Reading

Richard H. O'Kane, retired rear admiral from the U.S. Navy, has written an outstanding book entitled, *Clear the Bridge! The War Patrols of the U.S.S. Tang.* O'Kane, a Congressional Medal of Honor recipient, sunk more ships in less time than any submarine commander in the history of naval warfare. From the time that the button was pushed to release the torpedoes from the U.S.S. Tang, only 70 seconds elapsed before five Japanese freighters went under the waves. How did O'Kane accomplish this? He, in fact, attacked a two-column, 17-ship convoy. Simultaneously, he released torpedoes from front and rear tubes and was able to sink three ships via torpedoes from his forward tubes and two ships from torpedoes that were launched from his rear tubes. This is the equivalent of prospecting affluent targets within an affiliation group.

Richard H. O'Kane. *Clear the Bridge!* (Novato, California: Presidio Press, 1989).

MRS. SPOTA:

It is a group. There are 17 in the partnership. And I have got 5 of them so far. My goal is to get the other 12. In fact, I called one the other day and I said, "Now I have gotten five. You have got to be my sixth one, Babes." He laughed and he said, "All right, all right, come on out."

DR. STANLEY:

Jackie, this is a group of physicians that actually work together? One partnership? Or practice?

MRS. SPOTA:

One partnership. Seventeen physician specialists. And it is a dynamite group. They are all probably very, very wealthy.

DR. STANLEY:

How did you sell the first one, Jackie?

MRS. SPOTA:

The first one was an accident. The first one walked in, and I was in the office. I was on duty. I got him as a walk-in, and I sold him that afternoon. And he told one of his associates.

DR. STANLEY:

All right. And then what happens? Does the phone ring and one of his partners says, "I work with this guy?"

MRS. SPOTA:

Exactly. Exactly. And he says, "My partner is so thrilled with what he bought and how you took care of him, I would like to come and look. Maybe I should look there and buy a lot, too, because I may want to build a house also."

DR. STANLEY:

What about the third, fourth, and fifth physicians in the partnership?

MRS. SPOTA:

They were easy.

Service Is Rewarded and Appreciated

Jackie's business is strong throughout the year except for a two-week period on either side of Christmas. Jackie is busy working during Thanksgiving, the Fourth of July, and many other holidays when many people are having rest and relaxation time. Along these lines, as a testament to Jackie's commitment to provide quality service year round, it is important to reflect upon some of the things that clients have done for Jackie. First, she receives numerous cards and letters that say, "Thank you, Jackie," and of course, these are after the sale. What is particularly noteworthy, a family that Jackie placed in a luxury homesite recently bought Jackie a turkey, dressing, and all the accoutrements for Thanksgiving dinner and had it sent over to Jackie's home, which happens to be in the Country Club of the South. They indicated their strong thanks to Jackie for placing them at the right house and the right development. They also noted that Jackie was so interested in satisfying the needs of clients and prospects during Thanksgiving that she did not have enough time to cook and provide a turkey and the fixings for herself as well as her loved ones. Rarely do you find such gestures in what we would call the impersonal 1990s. However, Jackie is an exception to this rule. Whoever said the affluent do not reward quality service providers?

DR. STANLEY:

Jackie, what about the fellow who called you on the phone and gave you orders? Would you go back over that for me?

MRS. SPOTA:

He arrives on the 8th. He called me up and he said he had heard about me. He was looking for a home up to $5 million. He will not waste time. His company has locations throughout the United States. He does not have the time to fool around. He said, "If you do your homework, I'll never use another agent. But this is what I want. Take notes. You will pick me up at the Ritz Carlton at 8:00 o'clock in the morning."

DR. STANLEY:

You will pick him up?

MRS. SPOTA:

Yes. I will pick him up with a limousine.

DR. STANLEY:

Not your car, a limousine?

MRS. SPOTA:

A limousine. At 8:00 o'clock in the morning. He says, "You will show me five houses. We will stop for lunch. You will show me three more and that's it. But you will show me what I want. I will not take a regular roof; I want six roof lines. I want a French Chalet. I will not look at anything under 1½ million." He said, "Don't you dare waste my time. My time is valuable. And in the meantime until I come there, you will send everything you can with the descriptions of what I want." I said, "Yes, sir." He called me back and he said, "You will Fed Ex it out. It should arrive on the 17th in the morning before 10:30." I said, "Yes, sir." Well, I did it by all the rules. And he arrives on the 8th of next month, and he says if I have done my homework properly he will buy a house from me and his five top people will buy a house from me. Which would open a door for six sales and he goes up to $5 million. That is tough, but he gave me rules. He gave me rules, boom, boom, boom. There was no casual conversation. He doesn't know me. I mean, I couldn't win him personally. You gotta get your personality to correspond with his.

DR. STANLEY:

Well, Jackie, why did he call you?

MRS. SPOTA:

He heard someone say I was good.

DR. STANLEY:

Somebody that bought from you?

MRS. SPOTA:

I asked him how. He said he was on an airplane and he heard about me, and (you will die on this one) he is flying over Europe. Do you believe this?

DR. STANLEY:

Yes, I believe it.

MRS. SPOTA:

And someone said, (they were talking about Country Club of the South) "Ask for Jackie. She is great." Do you believe that?

DR. STANLEY:

Yes, I do. So, Jackie, this is to be continued with him. But he asked you to do your homework and send him information. How much information did you send him, Jackie?

MRS. SPOTA:

Enough until he told me to stop.

DR. STANLEY:

What did you send him?

MRS. SPOTA:

I sent him a video on houses done. We did videos on the houses on the market. I sent him that. I sent him descriptions of chandeliers that were in the houses, rooms, every room, the spec sheets even with the interior decorating. I did colored pictures. You wouldn't believe it. Finally he said, "That's enough, honey, stop sending."

Client Profile

DR. STANLEY:

> In terms of a forecast for the next year, what percent of the homes that you sell will be priced at over $1 million?

MRS. SPOTA:

> Oh, the way we are going right now, probably 50 percent of them. Unbelievable!

DR. STANLEY:

> What are the occupational characteristics of these types of buyers?

MRS. SPOTA:

> Number one, the entrepreneur . . . started like you said . . . all of a sudden he started one little company and it grew. Insurance people . . . they are big here . . . computer people . . . professionals.

Sources of Clients and Influence

DR. STANLEY:

> Do you mean that many successful people from the Atlanta metropolitan area move out here?

MRS. SPOTA:

> And then, of course, a lot of people are transferring in from out of state. Marketing really helps a lot here. The marketing here at the Country Club of the South is wonderful.

DR. STANLEY:

> When a buyer moves in, do they recommend you to a friend?

MRS. SPOTA:

> I get a lot of repeat business. The one thing you have to do, I have to know it better than anybody else. I have to know every little thing about it.

DR. STANLEY:

About the property?

MRS. SPOTA:

Yes. Especially with co-op agents.

DR. STANLEY:

Why do so many top notch agents co-op their clients with you?

MRS. SPOTA:

I tell them not to do any homework. "You don't have to work this, let me do it for you," I said. "Don't waste your afternoon. Let me do it for you. Let me take them around." They love it because they get the afternoon to do something else. I have done their homework. So when I come in I am so prepared, my preparation is unbelievable. If you tell me you want a lot and you want it to slope to the left or to the right and this much frontage, I know exactly where to go. I know this territory backwards and forwards, up and down. I have done my homework. I give them all the figures. When you are dealing with this price range, there is no fudging. Most of the buyers will give compliments. They have never seen anyone like me. But I'll sit there and I'll tell them exactly where the sewer line is and how wide the sewer line is on that lot. Where it is. Every bit about it. So, you gotta do homework.

DR. STANLEY:

Well, Jackie, in terms of why an agent would walk in and say, "I want Jackie to handle this." Is that because you do your homework?

MRS. SPOTA:

I think it is because I—this sounds so conceited—I do a helluva job. I really do. Number one with the people. I handhold the agent. I handhold the people. I know everything about it. It's just preparation.

HOW THE AFFLUENT MAKE DECISIONS

Lunch Could Cost You Dearly

DR. STANLEY:

Jackie, if you would, just reiterate why sometimes it is not a good idea to take people to lunch when they are here on the property.

MRS. SPOTA:

Well, number one, in sales you are pushing all the time and you are selling all the time. All the time. And I am giving a presentation. I am controlling the situation the whole time. I put them in my car. Once I put people in my car, I am controlling them again. I take them. I drive them. I am in control. At that point I am starting to push them into a corner if I take too much control. So I back off; let them relax at lunch without me. Let them have control. Let them order what they want to order. Let them have a drink if they choose. And then let them come back.

DR. STANLEY:

Go on.

MRS. SPOTA:

Especially, you know, the people who want to control. I have to let them be in control and I have to back off and let them have their time to relax. I like them to have power. I can't always be in control. I can't always be in power, otherwise, they will leave and say, "My god, she overwhelmed me. It is too much." You have to know when to withdraw and let them be the star. So I leave them alone during lunch.

DR. STANLEY:

All right.

MRS. SPOTA:

And I think you can push people actually in a corner, and you have lost them. You cannot keep on pushing. Like I said before, you have one shot, one chance to do it, but do it right.

Timing Is Everything

DR. STANLEY:

So, the first-time buyer you can push, but these affluent people you can't? Well, Jackie, do you think that they make decisions during lunch about you and about the property?

MRS. SPOTA:

Oh, yes. Oh, yes. Oh, yes. I think timing is everything. And if I see a certain look in people, I know number one when to withdraw and say, "Well, let's see. It's about lunch time." I'll say to them, "Why don't you go back to the club. Why don't you relax a little bit." You have to watch when to withdraw.

DR. STANLEY:

What are some of the things you look for, Jackie?

MRS. SPOTA:

A man and his watch. God love them, men love watches. I can see it all the time. He will get antsy and keep on looking at his watch on his arm. At that point I start withdrawing. And that's the first sign. And sometimes if you push too much they will start questioning. Like, "How do you know this is the right house, Jackie?" At that point I am the one to withdraw. I'm coming on too strong, so I back off. I believe you win every sale when you back off. I really do. Does that sound stupid to you?

DR. STANLEY:

Not at all.

MRS. SPOTA:

I mean you better be strong. You have to have the courage to sell. But you also have to have the courage to withdraw. Even though you want to close them. You want to close them in tight. It is in you; I want to close them. I want to make this sale.

DR. STANLEY:

All right.

MRS. SPOTA:

Have the courage to withdraw at the same time. I think Mr. B. was probably one of the best examples. I said, "Mr. B., I am your age; I know exactly what you and Mrs. B. are looking for." I said, "Because I love this lot. It is perfect for you." This was three months ago. Three months ago I showed them the perfect lot for them. It took three months for him to come back and say to me, "Jackie, you know what, you are right. It is the perfect lot. Write up the contract." And here is a lot for 300 and some thousand dollars.

DR. STANLEY:

It took three months before he made up his mind?

MRS. SPOTA:

He had to make the decision.

DR. STANLEY:

All right.

MRS. SPOTA:

I made the decision for him to begin with. "I got the perfect thing for you, Mr. B., perfect. Everything. It has got this north-south exposure. It has got the view you want. It has got the status. Your prime street. Investment-wise it is the best location. I have everything down." Then he says, "Well, I don't know, Jackie, I don't know." I withdraw. Then three months later he calls me up and says, "Jackie, I want to come back." He comes back and says, "You know, I really like that lot. Write it up."

DR. STANLEY:

Go on.

MRS. SPOTA:

He should have bought it three months ago.

DR. STANLEY:

Well, Jackie, did you call him a couple of times in the meantime? Or did he call you or anything like that?

MRS. SPOTA:

No.

DR. STANLEY:

How big was the lot?

MRS. SPOTA:

It is 1.03 acres. And it is just beautiful. It has 90 percent hardwood trees on it. Six-foot elevation. And it has got the right north-south exposure. Perfect. I mean it is just perfect for him. But I had to withdraw on him and he came back and bought it. Sometimes with these million-dollar sales you don't get a three-day turnaround. Okay? Sometimes, especially with him, he was not moving here for four years. My job was to sell him a lot four years ahead of the time he needed it. And that is what I did.

Relating to the Husband-Wife Decision Team

DR. STANLEY:

Jackie, in terms of the husband-wife team, do you think it is a joint venture? What are the trends?

MRS. SPOTA:

I know that number one when they come in, I try to relate to both. If I favor the husband, I've lost the wife, and if I favor the wife, I've lost the husband. Often with the wife it's a security blanket—the kids, the home life. With the husband, it's an investment. I can show past history, a 38 percent increase in investment. I am good on numbers. I have a good memory.

DR. STANLEY:

Is it typical that when someone buys here that the husband and wife both have significant influence on it?

MRS. SPOTA:

I think that on a lot, it is both of them. But when it gets down to the house, it is the woman. If it is in his price range, and he can make her happy with moving her from her security blanket from another state, he wants to please her more than anything. And then I think it becomes the woman.

DR. STANLEY:

Jackie, is it two decisions? One is the idea of living here. The next one is a particular house that is in here. Is that right?

MRS. SPOTA:

Yes.

DR. STANLEY:

Who makes the decision to buy something in here?

MRS. SPOTA:

You know, it is funny because you ask that and I lost someone the other day on that. It broke my heart. The husband was coming in three days after the wife. The wife came here first, which is unusual in this situation.

DR. STANLEY:

She wasn't the breadwinner, is that right?

MRS. SPOTA:

Right. She picked the house and the subdivision, and he arrived three days later. And she told me how to treat him. She told me what to do. She said, "Now, I know my husband. Let me tell you how to handle him." I kind of wish I didn't listen to her, but I did listen to her. She said, "Go up and down the street and show him investments." Which I did.

DR. STANLEY:

What did you show him?

MRS. SPOTA:

Investments. Investment purchases. Why it was a good investment. I went to the house she picked out. He opened the door and said, "I feel uncomfortable. I don't want it." And I said, "You didn't even look at the house, Honey." I said, "Picture it with a rug. Picture it with a couch." It made no point. The wife made the decision without him. You see what happened?

DR. STANLEY:

And he knew it, Jackie.

MRS. SPOTA:

He knew it. She wrote a contract with me contingent upon her husband's approval. I had won her, and she said, "I don't want to lose this house, Jackie. What do I do? Let me write a contract contingent upon my husband's approval." I said, "Fine, no problem. We'll do it." He comes in three days later, and it was like she couldn't have control. I don't know how else to put it. He no more than opened the front door. And he said, "I feel uncomfortable." And I said, "Wait 'til you see the kitchen. Wait 'til you see the master bedroom." "No, no, I feel uncomfortable. This is not what we want." I then said to him, "Okay. You are right. You are absolutely right. This house makes you feel uncomfortable. Let me show you what else your wife looked at." He said, "I don't want to see any more." The wife took control; it was bad for him. Do you see it?

DR. STANLEY:

Yes. So in other words, Jackie, he didn't buy?

MRS. SPOTA:

No. So that teaches you a lesson. Number one, I had never met him. I couldn't judge him. She did something she shouldn't do. She made a decision without her husband.

DR. STANLEY:

Do you think that would affect a lot of people?

MRS. SPOTA:

Going back to your question, it is almost like a joint decision between both, and you have got to relate to both in the right way. And the husband probably picks the community, and then the wife will pick the house, but he has got to like the house a little bit. That was a tough person. I never had a chance with that guy. Never had a chance. His wife went out of line.

After Hello, What Do You Say to Prospects?

DR. STANLEY:

What do you say to prospects when they first arrive here?

MRS. SPOTA:

I'll ask probably a hundred questions in the first five minutes. I know everything about them. By the time they leave the office, I'll know everything about them. But you have to.

DR. STANLEY:

What questions are the most important ones?

MRS. SPOTA:

Number one. You know, an average agent will probably say

price range. I ask about their kids, what they do for a living, and how they got started, how did your business get so big, how did he get that large, how long did it take you, and so, I think I just ask the right questions.

DR. STANLEY:

So you ask about their business and how they did it?

MRS. SPOTA:

Yes, and their kids and what their kids like to do. I will tell you that probably, Tom, this sounds so conceited again. But even the little kids like me; they draw pictures of me. And they give me these pictures as presents to paste on my icebox. They do. "Jackie," they say, "put this on your icebox." I love kids. I love kids. That is not phony. I'm a mother . . . I am a perfect Cancer. I really am a perfect Cancer. I care about people, and I adore kids. And I think people see that I am genuine.

Universal Empathy Penetrates Language Barrier

DR. STANLEY:

Jackie, what was your toughest sale?

MRS. SPOTA:

My toughest sale? I don't know what my toughest sale was. I really don't know. I am thinking which one was really a tough sale. Last night, there was a customer who didn't speak English very well.

DR. STANLEY:

Really!

MRS. SPOTA:

And then he said to me, "You turn money [asking price] into yen." I said, "I can't do that, sir, but I'll have it by 9:00 o'clock in the morning." He said, "No understand $760,000 tousand, turn yen, turn yen." I said, "Sir, I'll have it by 9:00 o'clock in the morning. I don't have it right now."

DR. STANLEY:

Is he buying a house or a lot?

MRS. SPOTA:

A house.

DR. STANLEY:

So you turned it to yen for him?

MRS. SPOTA:

Yes. You have to, instead of talking, of course, you have to use your hands and show the house because he understands very little English. He said, "You meet at noon 30. I'll meet you at noon 30." You know that noon 30 means 12:30 P.M.

DR. STANLEY:

But this Japanese fellow? How did he pick Jackie to help him?

MRS. SPOTA:

That was a Japanese agent that I got to know.

DR. STANLEY:

Does he like to play golf?

MRS. SPOTA:

Loves to play golf. They always give you a radio after you show them houses. I got all these little radios.

DR. STANLEY:

You get radios from the Japanese?

MRS. SPOTA:

Oh, they love it. And they love to take pictures. And you have to pose with them. And I offer that because they love cameras.

DR. STANLEY:

Do you take pictures for them while they are standing in the doorway?

MRS. SPOTA:

Yes, they love it. You have got to spend an hour just taking pictures for them.

Avoid Confusion

DR. STANLEY:

> Jackie, do you show the prospect several homes? Do you first show them what you think is best suited for them? What do you do if they want to see many more?

MRS. SPOTA:

> If I show more than seven houses, I'll lose them.

DR. STANLEY:

> Seven?

MRS. SPOTA:

> They can't remember more than that. They can't remember, so even though you want to keep them here all day long, you have to pace them. And like this morning, I showed them two houses; they are at lunch; they are coming back at 2:30, and I'll show them another three or four. All day here. It is my purpose, but I don't confuse them.

The Fastest Sale

What happens when a quality product is supported by outstanding marketing and extraordinary selling? Sales volume is often quite high.

DR. STANLEY:

> What is your best case study?

MRS. SPOTA:

> My best story . . . I sold a lot. Everyone laughs at the office. I sold the lot at the topographical map/model and never went on the property. He actually went into his pocket and pulled out money. He said, "All right, you have sold me." I said to him, "You have not seen the lot or the community yet." He said, "You are so excited about it, it has got to be a good deal." True story.

DR. STANLEY:

> So one day you are working, on duty here, and some guy walks in and he wants to buy a lot or a house?

MRS. SPOTA:

A lot. He wants to buy a lot because he wants to build a house. So I started my presentation at the "topo," and he said, "You have been here this long. You really sound like you know what you are doing." I said, "I do know what I am doing." He said, "Well, what is your favorite lot?" I said, "Let me tell you why I like this lot. This lot is so wonderful." So I went into detail, and I got done talking after about 45 minutes. He said, "I'll take it." I said, "Honey, we haven't seen the lot or the community yet." He said, "It makes no difference; you sold me. I think it is the best investment. I'll buy it." Everyone in the office went hysterical. He absolutely wrote a contract on a lot he never saw and never drove into the community. That was my fastest sale. Forty-five minutes. And he actually pulled dollar bills out of his pocket. Hundred dollar bills out of his pocket. Hundred dollar bills. He was just counting them out.

DR. STANLEY:

Is that right? So how much do you think he gave in a down payment?

MRS. SPOTA:

Well, he only gave me actually $2,000 down, and he had to bring the rest of it. The lot was .8 of an acre, $167,400. Isn't that wonderful? Isn't that good? That was my biggest feather.

DR. STANLEY:

What precipitated him walking in to buy a lot?

MRS. SPOTA:

Number one was he had heard about Country Club of the South. He did not hear about Jackie Spota. He actually walked in cold. He heard that this was the place to buy. Best investment. And he came in. He said he had no intention of buying anything, which I love.

DR. STANLEY:

He had no intentions of buying?

MRS. SPOTA:

No, he just wanted to see the area. And he actually pulled out a wad of hundred-dollar bills and started counting them out. He said, "Okay. You have sold me; write it up."

The Product Jackie Sells: The Nicklaus/Sierra Development Corporations Residential Concept

Jack Nicklaus is recognized as a man whose goals are uncompromisingly high. This insistence on the highest levels of personal achievement has resulted in the partnership with J. Robert Sierra, a developer with a substantial track record of fine residential communities. Their purpose was to create incomparable residential environments, communities whose privacy, beauty, and unsurpassed amenities are recognized as the measure of excellence in golf and country club living. This pursuit of perfection has led Nicklaus/Sierra Development Corporation to prominence as the premier developer of golf course communities in America.

Since January 1983, Nicklaus/Sierra Development Corporation (NSDC) has been carefully analyzing development opportunities across the country. Jack Nicklaus is a working partner, and he shares a financial interest in each Jack Nicklaus Community.

Although Jack Nicklaus–designed golf courses are found in a number of metropolitan markets in the United States and abroad, only communities created by the Nicklaus/Sierra partnership carry all the hallmarks of an environment built to the standards for which this exceptional development team is known. This partnership alone retains the exclusive right to use the registered trademark, "A Jack Nicklaus Community."

The original objective of Jack Nicklaus and Bob Sierra was to introduce approximately one new major Community each year, with the help of a carefully selected and trained staff, in market areas across the United States determined to have a strong potential demand for high-caliber golf and country club living.

Each Community was to be unique in its own way, conceived and created with an emphasis on detail that would ensure communities of highly individual character. These goals have been consistently met, and the team of professionals that has been shaped in the process has made it possible to undertake development in multiple markets while maintaining one constant level of quality: the very finest.

Current Jack Nicklaus Communities include: Country Club of the South, an 870-acre golf course community in North Fulton County, Atlanta, Georgia; The Country Club of Louisiana, an

(continued)

844-acre community in Baton Rouge, Louisiana; Bear Creek, a 644-acre community in Murrieta, California; English Turn, a 1,200-acre community in New Orleans, Louisiana, and home of the USF&G Classic, a PGA tour event; and Wynstone, a 750-acre community in suburban Chicago, Illinois. Future Jack Nicklaus Communities are planned for the Washington, D.C., area; suburban Detroit, Michigan; the East Bay area of San Francisco; and the town of Jupiter, in North Palm Beach County, Florida.

Preparation for a new Jack Nicklaus Community is meticulous, and several years may go into the initial planning stages. Placement of the golf course, which sets the visual and thematic tone of each Community, gets top priority. Jack Nicklaus is involved in every stage of development, along with his staff, planning and overseeing not only the golf course but the aesthetics and standards of the surrounding Community.

Simultaneously, Bob Sierra addresses the crucial development and marketing issues, including homesite size, product mix, and additional facilities and amenities that are needed to set each Community apart and embody excellence in quality of living.

Each Community has certain standard criteria, none of which are negotiable. Each Community features a gatehouse, staffed 24 hours a day to limit access and control the privacy of residents. Each Community has complete perimeter definition to support the gatehouse for limited access. Strict architectural controls are implemented at every Jack Nicklaus Community to ensure design consistency, while allowing for individual tastes. To ensure these policies are clearly communicated,comprehensive but unique design guidelines are developed for each Community. In addition, complete landscape plans must be developed and submitted for approval before home plans are approved for development. Guidelines also guarantee that mailboxes, street lighting, all signage and fencing are designed in keeping with the overall theme of each Community.

A Property Owners Association ensures that each Jack Nicklaus Community will continue to be maintained to the exacting Nicklaus/Sierra Development Corporation standards long after the developer has turned control of the Association over to the property owners. Each Community functions as a quasi munici-

---

(concluded)

pality, and property owners become active participants in setting the policies and maintaining the services that make each Community "the best" in its respective market area.

Jack Nicklaus Communities are well established in a variety of nationwide locations. Because their high level of quality, value, and beauty speak for themselves, these communities have garnered an enviable and a widespread reputation for excellence. They have proven to be successful, with sound and steadily increasing sales levels attesting to their desirability in the national real estate marketplace. In 1989 alone, sales of homesites and homes in active Jack Nicklaus Communities totaled $90 million.

The owners of property, for the most part, are entrepreneur, affluent individuals who own all different types of businesses, top executives of major corporations, and many professional people. The average age is mid to late 40s, and normally two or three children occupy the residence. Most of the homeowners are also members of the private club facilities and a $200,000 plus income affords them the opportunity for the prestigious, exclusive lifestyle of a "Jack Nicklaus Community."

The concept statement was prepared by the Nicklaus/Sierra Development Corporation and is published with its permission.

LUXURY REAL ESTATE FOR YACHTING, GOLFING, OR AS A REWARD FOR SUCCEEDING

Dear Marketer:

Thank you for sharing your ideas and concerns about marketing and promoting the home sites at Doeford Plantation. I propose that you alter your current strategy. The changes would relate both to your overall marketing theme as well as to your media selection.

Currently, Doeford is positioned as an exclusive residential community for yachting and golfing enthusiasts. This message does not clearly reflect the real reasons that members of your target audience will invest $400,000 for a one-half acre of land. Also, placing advertisements in the national media is much too broad an approach. Only a small fraction of the readers of these newspapers have any probability of becoming property owners at Doeford. This relates not only to the income/net worth parameters of the audience. The size of your audience and, correspondingly, the total attractiveness of your product are also lessened because of the yacht and golf theme.

Actually, most of your current as well as potential owners are attracted to the Doeford concept because it represents the fulfillment of a dream. Your ideal target market is composed of those affluent individuals who have spent the majority of their adult lives organizing and managing their own private businesses.

Many of your current owners are people who have never been actively involved in yachting or golfing. Few were previously members of country clubs. Your affluent prospects are individuals who directed their energy at building a business. They ignored the possible distractions of a country club or yacht club affiliation. Also, they lived frugally and returned much of the earnings of the business back into the business.

However, there comes a time in the lives of many of these affluent business owners when they realize a dream. Their dream was to become financially independent. What happens when this goal is finally realized? After many years of hard work and self-denial, the affluent business owner seeks a reward. For your target audience, Doeford should be positioned as the reward for achieving their superordinate economic goal. The reward concept underlies the purchase decision of most of your current clientele.

Examine the backgrounds of your current clients. They have made their money by selling products and services that range from fuel oil to environmental engineering and from wholesaling to dry cleaning. While the industries that they are associated with vary considerably, your clients do have something in common. All were or are currently among the most productive entrepreneurs within their respective industries. Many have recently sold their businesses at a premium. Often, the sale of a business precipitates the adoption of the Doeford concept. In growing numbers, European as well as Asian investors are seeking to purchase profitable, nonpublic businesses in America. This trend bodes well for the demand for your product.

Your target market should include those affluent individuals who recently sold their businesses, are in the process of selling out, and are among the most successful within their respective industries. These sellers are typically euphoric about their substantial change in cash flow.

I have found that the affluent do not purchase major-league real estate when they are depressed. They are most likely to purchase when they are euphoric. Doeford should be positioned as a reward for those who spend a lifetime earning their euphoria. But euphoria is not limited to those selling out (in the game called transition). Entrepreneurs who are industry leaders are also euphoric when their achievements are recognized by their peers. This recognition as "the best in our industry" is often manifested through trade association awards as well as by trade journal designations, such as the "Top of Our Industry Award."

You will find that affluent prospects are most vulnerable to your solicitations when economic/recognition situations generate euphoria. You should focus upon this concept. I have outlined below several suggestions about how to identify those in the "buying mood." Also given are several ideas about how to communicate with these prospects.

Avoid using conventional weapons when marketing your concept. Identifying and communicating with the affluent make up only one-half of the equation. The critical dimension is timing one's communication precisely when the affluent are in the mood to spend. Your best targets may only be ready, willing, and able to buy during a very short period in their adult lives.

Many of your current owners postponed purchasing

the luxury home site for 20, even 30 years. They told themselves each year for the same time period that "next year I'll take up golf . . . next year I'll buy the 57-foot yacht. . . next year, I'll buy my dream home. . . next year . . . next year. . ." Well, next year finally arrived recently for your current clients. And when will your targeted prospects be most sensitive to your solicitations? I understand that your objective is to sell all your remaining inventory within the next 24 months. Thus, your marketing campaign must be designed to uncover affluent business owners who will likely be euphoric sometime during the next two years.

Euphoria is a key factor to consider when marketing your luxury home sites. When the affluent prospect is euphoric, he is very susceptible to solicitations of all types. Some even seek out products and services with which they have little or no experience. Look at the yachts that are currently parked in your basin. Most are owned by people who never owned any type of boat prior to becoming euphoric. Some can't even swim! Also, notice how seldom those boats leave the harbor. For many of your current lot owners, the adoption of a yacht, golf equipment, country club membership, and a luxury home are first-time experiences. Some will not occupy their homes in Doeford for more than a few weeks a year. Seldom will they play golf, and rarely will they use their yacht. Nevertheless, all of these "under-utilized" artifacts are important symbols of achievement. Many feel that they do not have to use these symbols to enjoy owning them.

Your future clientele will come from several sources, including: referrals from current owners, responses to letters and in-person solicitations directed at affluent targets who are euphoric, and inquiries from public relations and paid-for media promotions.

The referral system you already have in operation has generated some new business for Doeford. However, you need to be more focused when asking for referrals. Notice that several of your clients are senior officials of their industry/profession's trade association. They are, in essence, the ace of aces among their respective affiliation groups. They are, by definition, well known and well respected by their colleagues. Also, they have access to considerable information about the identities of the most successful members of their affiliation groups. Right at this moment, your membership group contains several presidents of trade associations. In turn, these associations have high concentrations of very affluent prospects.

It is absolutely essential that you and your sales professionals gather industry affiliation information. Ask each current owner as well as prospects about their industrial classification. Also, ask about their affiliation group activities. Focus your request for referrals among those who have demonstrated a strong need to affiliate with successful people.

Key opinion leaders such as trade association executives can also be valuable providing information about when affluent prospects will cluster in high concentrations. For example, one of your current clients is the president of the professional association that represents the highest-paid specialty group in the dental profession. This organization is scheduled to have both its annual national as well as regional association convention within your designated trade area. You may generate considerable business by promoting the Doeford concept at such meetings. Certainly, prospects will be favorably impressed with your response to their question about "Who are your Doeford owners?" The affiliation needs of most affluent business owners and professionals is very strong. The endorsement of actually having the affiliation group's president as a client is stronger than mere words. Endorsements by the purchase behavior of an opinion leader of an affluent affiliation group speaks for itself.

I also noticed that one of your current Doeford owners is one of the biggest fuel oil dealers in America. Why not ask him for referrals to other top-ranked owners within the same industry?

Beyond referral business, make it a point to ask your

"fuel oil" client about what trade journals he receives. Ask if he would save some of his old copies for you. Examine the content of these journals. I suggest that you subscribe to all of the fuel oil trade and related journals which feature articles and case studies about the top-ranked dealers in America. Each and every article that is published about an industry leader is an opportunity to solicit business. Be especially responsive to those prospects who are in or nearing their golden years.

Send a personalized letter (see pro forma enclosed) to each person who is identified in these journals as an industry winner. Congratulate these people for their achievement and industry recognition. Then, blend in the concepts of achievements and recognition with the Doeford reward. Tell the prospect that Doeford owners are successful business owners "just like you." Mention that one of the owners is a fuel oil industry dealer "just like you." Be sure to ask permission of your current fuel oil client to use his name.

Be sure also to enclose several of your public relations articles about the business owners and their families who adopted the Doeford reward. This is very important because some prospects have apprehensions about whether or not they will fit in with your current owners. Most of your clients as well as your best prospects are first-generation millionaires. Thus, you do not want to communicate an image that will turn these people off. Certainly, affluent legacies are welcomed, but the really big market for your concept is the self-made affluent. Communicate that Doeford is the place for achievers in industry and not snobs. Nor should your product be positioned as something for the "swingers of America." Most of your clients are family people. They view Doeford as a family experience for the children and grandchildren.

Place greater emphasis upon public relations news items in communicating and conditioning your prospects. More than 80 percent of your clientele are from four states. You will find that the statewide, even local, business periodicals will be very receptive to publishing articles about the concept of the "Doeford reward."

Have your public relations professionals contact the editors of selected state and local business periodicals. Ask these editors if they would be interested in publishing articles about the area's successful business owners who happen to adopt the Doeford theme. These articles can be written by your staff. These written materials and your high-quality photos of Doeford's entrepreneurial clients are very publishable. These articles should focus upon the business and professional successes of Doeford's owners. And of course, the story of how these area entrepreneurs rewarded themselves with the Doeford concept should be neatly blended into each article. You must remember that the editors of local and even state business periodicals are always looking for interesting case studies of area entrepreneurs. Correspondingly, they often welcome a manuscript which is camera ready for publication. Many publications of these types have limited economic as well as human resources. Such editors will be in your debt if you can enhance their productivity by doing the conceptualizing, news gathering, and composing for them.

These articles will generate inquiries from readers. Be prepared for some calls from tire kickers. Often luxury products and services like the Doeford concept catch the eye of "fantasy island buffs." These people often require additional information about such items. However, they do not have any probability or ability to buy. They do, however, collect expensive promotional material. They are especially interested in receiving complimentary video tapes and free weekend tours of the property.

How can you distinguish the real prospect from those who are merely fantasizing? There is no fool-proof method. However, before you invite any so-called prospect for a free visit, qualify him. Ask for references and how he first heard about the offering. Most pseudo prospects will indicate that they discovered Doeford via news items in the generic business press and/or advertisements in print media. Don't be reluctant to do a credit search on someone whom you suspect is impersonating an affluent prospect. Always ask about their occupational background and whether or not they own a business. There are not too many used car salesmen who will qualify as a prospect. I understand that at least one fellow in this category (although currently unemployed) requested a free video tape of the concept! This, by itself, argues against continuing to advertise in vehicles that give you shot-gun coverage.

Those prospects who qualify as being ready, willing, and able should be invited for the Doeford tour. There is no substitute for having a face-to-face meeting with a prospect at the point of sale. Before they arrive, be sure to ask about their perceived use of the property. In so doing, you can be sure to emphasize the related key points about Doeford during their visit.

I hope that my suggestions will help you and your staff in marketing the Doeford concept. Always remember that it is better to target one affluent prospect who is euphoric than 10 who are depressed!

Sincerely,

Thomas J. Stanley, Ph.D.
Chairman, Affluent Market Institute

COMMUNICATING WITH AFFLUENT PROSPECTS WHO ARE EUPHORIC BECAUSE OF RECENT RECOGNITION BY THEIR INDUSTRY

Mr. Bruce W. Westnedge
President
Westnedge, Spaulding and
Bowman Environmental Engineering
100 Parkview Plaza
Yonkers, NY 10709

Dear Mr. Westnedge:

Your achievements in solving some of our nation's pollution problems are most commendable. The recent article in *Sludge World* should be required reading for all those young engineers who need an inspirational role model. Your comments about the relationship between hard work and success in America was of special interest to me.

Most of our current owners of residential property here at Doeford Plantation share your philosophy. They are among the most successful business owners and professionals from their respective industries. Why did they choose to build a home in Doeford Plantation? Most of our owners have told me that a home here was the reward which they gave themselves in recognition of their many years of hard work. Often, the Doeford owner, much like yourself, reached the highest levels of achievement and recognition within their chosen field. One of our most-recent buyers mentioned that "each year for 31 years, I told myself that next year I would build my dream home in paradise." This year was finally his year. He sold his business and home on Long Island and took up residence in Doeford.

The article in *Sludge World* mentioned that you would be retiring early next year. I hope that you will give consideration to reviewing the information about Doeford that is enclosed. If you would like to review one of our video presentations, please return the enclosed postcards or call our toll-free number as listed above. Also, if you and your family are interested in personally visiting the Doeford Plantation, please call me at your convenience. We would be delighted to have you spend a weekend at one of our guest homes on the plantation.

Once again, congratulations on your recognition as *Sludge World's* Environmental Engineer of the Year. We at Doeford also wish to acknowledge your success. Enclosed is a laminated copy of the cover that contains your pic-

---

PRO FORMA RECOGNITION/PROSPECTING PLAQUE
[Cover page]

SLUDGE WORLD
[Heading]

SLUDGE WORLD'S ENVIRONMENTAL ENGINEER OF THE YEAR

[Prospect's picture]

[Inserted Inscription, Engraved in Brass]
DOEFORD PLANTATION AND FONSWORTH J. PETERSON SALUTE
YOUR SUCCESS

---

ture. I hope the walnut mounting will blend well with all
the other plaques that you have been awarded.

Sincerely,

Fonsworth J. Peterson
Senior Vice President

FIELDSTON CONFESSIONS

In the preface of *Marketing to the Affluent,* I reflected upon one of
my more memorable childhood experiences.

> The first house we approached was a very large, Spanish
> hacienda-type structure situated on several choice acres. No

lights were on, but I knocked on the door anyway. Nothing happened, but I kept on knocking. Finally, James Mason, the actor, opened the door. He was startled, and I remember distinctly what he said: "No one ever trick-or-treated me, hit on me" during Halloween.

Often, marketers make the assumption that all of the affluent are heavily prospected. My finding on this occasion was just the opposite. James Mason, assuming that no other gremlins would visit, said, "Ladies and gentlemen, I will give you all the silver I have in my home." And he did—every nickel, dime, quarter, and half-dollar he could find.

The next house we visited had a sign posted on the front door: "My husband is ill; please do not ring the doorbell. I have placed coins in different packages for different group sizes in the milkbox outside." I opened the milkbox and found packages for groups of two, groups of three, groups of four, and so on.

This first experience with the affluent market is still vivid in my memory. Those two sales calls generated the same number of dollars that we normally expected from over 100 calls in our own neighborhood.

In reading this information, one may conclude that I am proud of my Fieldston campaign. Does this experience as a youth not demonstrate considerable aptitude in targeting the affluent? No! Actually this is an appropriate time to make an objective evaluation of the Fieldston case. I made the fundamental error that 99 percent of the sales professionals make in targeting the affluent. What did I do after making a major sale from a celebrity? I went home. I celebrated by eating the candy I purchased with the money given me by James Mason. In essence, I withdrew from the campaign too early.

What should I have done in Fieldston? There are more than 100 homes in Fieldston. All but two were ignored. Once James Mason was converted from prospect to a trick-or-treat client, his prestige could have been capitalized upon in prospecting throughout the neighborhood. Why didn't I attempt to solicit business from his neighbors? Why didn't I knock on each door and begin every conversation with, "Excuse me. Good evening. I am a trick-or-treat consultant. I have just been endorsed by one of the most distinguished actors in the world, your neighbor James Mason. Do you want the trick-or-treat option?"

I now recognize that several dozen of Mr. Mason's neighbors could have easily been converted to trick-or-treat customers. Targeting by neighborhood affiliation need is a useful strategy today. But I recommend a different need. The affluent have a strong need to affiliate and imitate the behavior of successful members of their occupational category.

PART 5

CASE STUDIES: THE SELLING OF SERVICES TO THE AFFLUENT

CHAPTER 13

APOSTLES VERSUS
ANTAGONISTS OF
THE AFFLUENT

INTRODUCTION

Barbara is a top-producing sales professional and an apostle to her affluent clients. Webster's defines the word *apostle* as one sent on a mission, an ardent supporter. Barbara's mission is to serve her clients. For her, this mission extends far beyond the core product that she sells. She fully understands that there are many other competitive offerings that her clients could purchase. Moreover, Barbara realizes that many others sell the same exact product that she offers. Why then does she outperform the average person in her industry by nearly 800 percent? As she has stated many times, "First become an apostle to your affluent prospects before focusing on your own need—the need to sell your product."

Why become an apostle to the affluent? How does one become an apostle? It is not an easy task. The case examples given in this chapter, however, will provide some insights into what is required. Most people fail to reach even a modest level of production in regard to selling to the affluent. Much of this relates directly to the issue of empathy for the needs of the affluent. Most sales professionals who never succeed in their task are more antagonists to the affluent than they are apostles.

Barbara provides an excellent role model for others who wish to move from the antagonist to the apostle category. Being an apostle is much more fulfilling both psychologically and financially than being viewed as antagonist. From whom do the affluent really want to buy? An apostle is the correct answer. Barbara understands that most of her affluent clients can live without owning one or more of the products she sells. And in terms of priority, her prospects and clients rank many other issues as being more important than the product she sells. Most of Barbara's affluent targets are high-income-producing professionals, business owners, corporate executives, and salesmen. What could be more important to these prospects and clients than Barbara's core product? Most, if not all, would say that increasing their incomes/revenues/commissions is much more important than any consumer-related product or service. Correspondingly, Barbara has an unparalleled track record for assisting her targets in this endeavor. She constantly networks with affluent prospects and clients. In this regard, she acts as a "for-free" sales agent for hundreds of affluent prospects/clients who have something to sell. She is particularly effective in generating business for many affluent attorneys, accountants, financial consultants, and top-ranked insurance agents. One of the "fringe benefits" of buying from Barbara is to become part of her influence network.

She also has an uncanny ability to find for her client everything from the best loan officer to the finest residential builder in town.

There are no hard and fast rules on how one can become an apostle to the affluent. Barbara's style, however, provides an interesting benchmark to use as a guide in focusing one's behavior.

For every hour Barbara spends talking with her fellow sales professionals, she spends at least eight conversing with clients and prospects. Interestingly, most antagonists to the affluent spend more time interacting with sales professionals from their own industry than they do with affluent prospects.

Barbara relates to affluent prospects as if they will eventually become important lifelong clients. She even gives the young up-and-coming affluent prospect the same respect as she does those who have already achieved significant economic status.

Barbara keeps a record of the times of the year that current clients are most likely to incur a significant upswing in their cash flow. Just prior to these periods of client euphoria, each will be contacted personally by Barbara. The bulk of her business comes from selling to current clients. Before she requests more business from current clients, Barbara makes inquiries about their business, family, and peer recognition. These are the typical questions from an apostle as opposed to an antagonist of the affluent.

CONTRASTS IN ATMOSPHERES

An Antagonist to Air Travelers but an
Apostle to Colleagues

An attendee at one of our seminars once asked how sales professionals who target the affluent spend their time. I believe that most sales professionals, as well as others who service the affluent, spend more time interacting with their colleagues than with affluent clients/prospects! Actually, I find that the top-ranked sales professionals are more often than not somewhat removed from their cohorts. They are not typically part of the bull pen or coffee room crowd. Because of this distance, they are oftentimes viewed as being aloof.

When the mediocre sales professional goes to lunch, he is more inclined to dine with others in his profession from the same office. But when a top sales professional has lunch, he often bypasses offers from his colleagues and breaks bread with an affluent prospect. Great sales people are more concerned about being admired, respected, and liked by the target audience. They understand where their revenue comes from and behave accordingly. Other, less productive sales professionals spend too much time enhancing their relationships with their peers. This behavior, more often than not, also applies to those contact personnel who are not directly involved in selling but do service the affluent.

I recently observed a situation where two flight attendants provided a pro forma example of what I call a peer-orientation problem. During the entire flight, they never stopped talking to one another. They ignored every cue that passengers gave in an effort to get their attention. After the plane reached its cruising altitude, one of the two attendants asked each of the first-class passengers for his or her beverage preference. But even when taking the orders, the two kept their conversation going in spite of the distance between the galley and the seated passengers. The attendant who actually took the orders backed her way toward the passenger audience so that she could keep almost constant eye contact with her colleague. Interestingly, the conversation had nothing to do with topics listed in their job descriptions. Up to this point, their behavior was in the annoying, if not approaching the unprofessional, category. But things deteriorated even further.

One of the attendants distributed all of the beverages with her hand behind her back, still talking to her colleague. Given this conversation and this form of serving, not too much went wrong in the beginning. There were a few mistakes regarding drink orders and a few minor spills. But then the fellow in the aisle seat behind the bulkhead was "serviced." He was the last to be served. But he did not seem to mind waiting a few minutes for a fresh pot of coffee to be brewed. Once again, the attendant backed down the aisle with a hot coffee, "black, no sugar," all the time talking to her fellow attendant. She attempted a right-handed/backhanded/blind serve to the fellow in the white linen suit, still maintaining eye contact with the other attendant. She double faulted! First, the serve missed the passenger's tray. The contents of the cup spilled directly onto the unsuspecting passenger's lap. The passenger attempted to explode out of his seat, but his seat belt prevented much movement. So, for the first few seconds, his arms and legs just flailed wildly in the air while he verbally expressed his discomfort.

ATTENDANT:

Oh, let me help you clean that up, sir.

PASSENGER:

Get away from me.

ATTENDANT:

How about a towel?

PASSENGER:

Keep away from me.

ATTENDANT:

Well, I'll give you the towel and some club soda. Would you like another cup of coffee?

PASSENGER:

[Now screaming] GET AWAY FROM ME. JUST GET AWAY. LEAVE IT ALONE!

The second fault committed by the attendant was her failure to ever say, "I'm sorry, sir. I was not paying attention like I'm supposed to do. This is entirely my fault." Instead, the attendant did announce to her fellow attendant, "He has some coffee on his pants."

After the passenger finished screaming at the attendant, the atmosphere in the cabin changed dramatically. People stopped talking, and most withdrew to a book or magazine. For the remainder of the flight (more than one and one-half hours), there was almost complete silence throughout the cabin. After lunch was over, the two attendants spent the rest of the flight sequestered near the exit of the plane.

No matter how gifted they may be, people who service the affluent will sometimes make mistakes. The best providers, however, understand how to overcome these mistakes. Quickly and candidly admitting one's faults is the hallmark of a superior service provider. Spilled coffee was really never the critical issue in this case. What was most significant was the attendant's focus or orientation. She placed more importance on her interaction with her colleague than on her market audience. In addition, the attendant never really accepted/admitted blame for this incident. Flight attendants are not directly responsible for actually selling airline tickets. However, many times the quality of the service providers such as flight attendants explains a significant portion of the variation in the market performance among competing airlines.

Re: An Apostle Who Really Controls the Atmosphere in the Forward Cabin

Dear Mr. Airline President:

On my recent flight to Boston, the fellow sitting next to me designated himself as a very frequent flyer. He was seated in 3D because someone had positioned himself in my companion's originally assigned seat, 5B. "Can you believe how insensitive some people are today?" he asked. "That guy was sitting in my seat. He told me he wanted to be next to his associate and that I should sit in 3D. He never asked me if I would mind." Later, during our conversation, the same very frequent flyer stated that "traveling by air meant being constantly surrounded by uncaring strangers."

I do not completely agree with this fellow's assessment of air travel. However, there are times when one really does feel the complete absence of warmth and that special personal touch. But the purpose of this letter is not to complain. I am writing to bring to your attention the extraordinary level of service that my fellow first-class passengers and I received on your flight 697 (Boston to Dallas) on September 14.

When I arrived at the gate, the presence of a 727 told me that there would be no movie. I anticipated a long, dull flight—one that would include being in a cold, unfriendly atmosphere. But I now realize that movies and even pilots do not control the atmosphere of your cabins. Your flight attendants can have a significant influence upon the perceptions that passengers have in regard to the cabin environment.

As I boarded the plane, I was greeted by Ms. Y. J. Ms. J., in my estimation, is the ace of aces among superior flight attendants. Like the vast majority of your attendants, her appearance and responsiveness were far above the industry norm. Ms. J., however, also communicated that she had a sincere interest in making the flight entertaining. She encouraged the passengers to become "friends" with each other and with her. She quickly transformed my fear of spending several hours with cold, uncaring strangers into a feeling of camaraderie with my colleagues in the forward cabin.

Ms. J. displayed her humorous nature through several devices which you may want to consider in the future as standard issue for flight attendants. Her weapons for breaking down the lack of interaction among passengers ranged from clever badges to unusual airplane "props."

The badge that she wore stated "Oh-No; Four-Oh." Surrounded by black ribbon, its message gave us the clear impression that Ms. J. wanted her passengers to recognize that they were being attended to by someone with feelings. It was also a device that encouraged all the passengers to say something more sincere than, "Good afternoon; I'll have a light beer." Of course, most of my fellow passengers told Ms. J. that she did not look a day over 36!

My conversation with the fellow seated in 3C lasted almost the entire flight. It began shortly after we reached cruising altitude. Ms J.'s actions once again provided the catalyst for our interaction. She asked me if I had ordered the cold seafood platter. When I said yes, she took out her pen and made a check next to my name. There was nothing unusual about this action. So why did the passenger in 3C break out with a laugh? Ms. J.'s pen was the culprit. The pen was inside the mouth of an eight-inch-long orange-colored rubber fish. Mr. 3C mentioned, "You better have a great set of teeth for that seafood." This began an interesting conversation. And along with the other folks, including Ms. J., the *perceived* flying time seemed more like one hour than four.

The orange fish, however, was not the only artifact of entertainment that Ms. J. employed. In all the years that I have been flying, not once did a flight attendant pass out hot/moist towels before a meal service. But what a wonderful idea. Certainly, most passengers would like to clean their hands before a meal, especially since they just spent an hour before the flight touching nearly every part of a well-used cab and every door opener in a heavily traveled airport. Ms. J., on her own volition, offered each and every passenger in the forward cabin hot/moist towels before as well as after the meal service.

Hot towel service in this context certainly was a very positive break with tradition. Towels are not an inherently interesting topic of conversation. However, the devices that Ms. J. used to distribute them were yet another vehicle which greatly facilitated conversation among an already cohesive group of passengers. The towels were delivered as well as removed by Ms. J. with her special brand of humor. Attached to the end of the tongs she used were a pair of plastic teeth. These lovely dentures included brightly colored coordinated white teeth with flaming red gums. Every single passenger was amused by this clever diversion. And diversion from the rat race is what most business travelers like myself really need. I find that mental as well as physical exhaustion is due more to the sensory deprivation and monotony of traditional travel than it actually is to serving my clients. I do not believe that any passenger in the forward compartment felt deprived or exhausted after reaching his or her destination. The morning following my arrival in Dallas, I had to make an important speech. The program was a major success partly because I felt refreshed. Certainly some of my condition was directly attributable to an unusually friendly and stimulating environment encountered the day before.

During the entire flight, Ms. J. attended to her passengers with the zest and pride of an all-star professional. Not once did she sit down. Nor did she sequester herself behind a bulkhead or curtain. She prepared, served, and conversed with all of her passengers for four solid hours. And during all that time, Ms. J. never gave even the slightest hint of losing her enthusiasm for servicing the passengers.

Ms. J. is an extraordinary provider of service above and beyond even the high standards set by your airline. She should be asked to help train all of your newly minted and seasoned flight attendants. The program could be given the label of "Business Travelers' Needs: Beyond the Norm of Good Service." Why not include in your training kits some of Ms. J.'s "ice-breaking artifacts" (e.g., pen in orange rubber fish, humorous badges, and "serving dentures")? Why not develop a training video of Ms. J. "breaking ice?" Please advise me about how I can obtain a copy.

Much continued success.

Sincerely,

Thomas J. Stanley, Ph.D.
Chairman, Affluent Market Institute
A Very Frequent Flyer

A BANK THAT WINS VERSUS ONE THAT LOSES AN AFFLUENT CLIENT

A Lending Officer Plays the Role of an Apostle to a Young Surgeon

I asked Dr. Joe where he would go for advice concerning estate planning and related trust services.

DR. JOE:

Well, I would go to my bank before I would go anywhere else.

DR. STANLEY:

Why would you seek such advice from your bank?

DR. JOE:

Because I have been working with the bank for 18 years . . . on a personal basis.

DR. STANLEY:

Could you tell us how your relationship started with your bank?

DR. JOE:

They helped me when I was nobody. . . . treated me like someone important. They saw me as someone who eventually would be an important client.

DR. STANLEY:

Who at the bank helped you?

DR. JOE:

My bank's branch manager. I followed my present manager to three different branches.

DR. STANLEY:

How did you first meet this branch manager?

DR. JOE:

I called this man on the phone at a local branch and told him I needed X amount of money because I wanted to buy a piece of equipment for eye surgery. He said that we needed to fill out some forms. I said I hated to fill out forms. Then he said, "What kind of food do you like?" I said, "I am a Frenchman. I love French food." He then said, "How would you like to have lunch with me? I'll fill out the forms for you while we have lunch." I said, "Gee, that's great." He took me to a lovely French restaurant, and nothing came out of my pocket. . . . he said the bank would pay the bill. He was a very nice man, well mannered, and I didn't have to fill out the papers. I was extremely grateful. It was a very nice approach.

The kindness and sensitivity of this branch manger translated into an 18-year client relationship. Even when he was just starting his medical practice, Dr. Joe was shown considerable respect by a bank and its manager. Perhaps they can forecast the future. Today, Dr. Joe is a world renowned eye surgeon and a very important client of the Bank of Perpetual Sensitivity. Banks, as well as other service providers in this category, understand that more than 80 percent of the millionaires in America are self-made. I forecast that this percentage will remain relatively stable. Millionaires have long memories. What is the benefit of being one of those providers that were responsive to their needs well before they became millionaires? You have the inside track for developing them into clients for life!

An Antagonist of Harry G.

During an interview with the president and major shareholder of a corporation that specializes in developing information systems, the topic of banks emerged, and Harry G. became excited. His excitement reflected a need to tell someone about his frustrations from dealing with his bank. Harry G. is typical of many of the affluent business owners I have interviewed. He has an especially negative image in regard to contact personnel at the main bank he patronized.

Harry's business is very profitable. His main product is intellect, that is, strategic information. He has minimal fixed overhead. He is not dependent upon the bank for commercial credit. He uses the bank primarily as a depository and a place to have a commercial checking account.

In all the time that he has patronized the bank (over four years), Harry has never been thanked for his business. He has never received a card or note or letter from the bank. Never has he been recognized as a special customer. The following scenario is just one example of why the Harrys of America are interested in finding quality banks with which to do business.

DR. STANLEY:

Tell me, Harry, where do you do your banking?

HARRY G.:

I bank at the Bank of Abuse!

Harry's nine-year-old daughter wanted a new 10-speed bicycle. Over the course of 15 months, she had filled a large piggy bank with quarters from her weekly allowance. Harry drove his daughter to the Bank of Abuse with her bag of quarters. Harry knew from experience that the Bank of Abuse did not like to count coins unless they were neatly rolled and packaged in popular denominations, but Harry is a cunning devil. He decided to leverage his corporate relationship. He stood in line for several minutes. His turn finally came at the teller's window. He initially gave the teller the number of his corporate checking account. "What is my balance, Helen?" he asked. The reply was "$186,018.36." Harry knew to the penny how much his corporation had in this (noninterest-bearing) checking account before he received the teller's response. He only asked because he wanted to make certain that the teller recognized him as a special/highly profitable customer. Harry felt certain that the teller had become sensitive to whom he was. However, she was not softened up for his next request.

The second question? "Would you be so kind as to take this bag of quarters and count them with your coin counter? I need to purchase a bicycle for my little girl today. She has been saving for it for quite a while, and we would like to know if there is enough to make the purchase. It's her birthday."

"I'm sorry , sir. I don't count coins. But I will give you some paper rolls to place the coins in . . . so that you will not make the same mistake twice. Why don't you go over to that table in the corner and count them right now. We will be open for another 40 minutes."

Harry responded with, "But I'm one of this bank's best customers . . . look at the balance in my company's checking account!" His protest had no effect on the teller. "Rules are rules, sir; besides, we are very busy today." Helen is very democratic; she treats all customers equally.

The Harry drama is playing all across this nation. Many owners of small and medium-sized businesses are banking at a branch of the Bank of Abuse. Harry is now looking for alternative service providers for his company's cash. He views his firm as being too small to warrant a professional corporate money manager. "What can I do with my company's cash? I have to have a corporate checking account at a commercial bank. But I don't have to have it at the Bank of Abuse. I only started banking there because it was convenient in terms of location. But now it's become very inconvenient."

TIMING THE SALES PITCH

The Meat-e-ocrity of Two Antagonists of an Affluent Sales Professional

Mr. Vincent had been on the road all week. It was Friday, and he was finally on his way home. Throughout the week he had encountered an inordinate number of delayed flights, reluctant prospects, cancelled appointments, and insensitive service providers. But as he drove his car out of the airport parking lot and headed for home, Mr. Vincent felt that comfort was only 30 minutes away. The company's top sales executive was now totally exhausted.

He could not contain his enthusiasm for soon he felt he would be back in his favorite chair, enjoying a vodka martini and some of his wife's fine home cooking. His excitement translated into the speed of his vehicle, 20 miles an hour over the speed limit. He just could not wait to get home. For there he would not have to deal with any insensitive people, at least for the next few days. He thought to himself, "I'm safe for the entire weekend."

Mr. Vincent arrived home just wanting to collapse. But there was a surprise waiting for him that altered his plans. As he walked into the front hallway of his home, he heard his wife calling to him. "Welcome home, honey. We are waiting for you in the basement."

He then realized that the "we" his wife referred to must have something to do with the strange van that was parked in the driveway.

Several hours earlier, a young sales trainee, Buddy, and his manager/mentor, Wayne, made a cold call on Mr. Vincent's home. Just prior to the call, the manager had told the trainee that he was disappointed in the rookie's sales performance. But now the master of selling, the ace of cold calling, would show him first hand how to overcome all obstacles to closing the sale. Mrs. Vincent opened her front door in response to the doorbell's ringing and ringing.

WAYNE:

Good evening. I'm Wayne, and this is my trainee, Buddy. I would like to share with you a novel idea. May I ask your name?

MRS. VINCENT:

Yes. I'm Mrs. Vincent.

WAYNE:

Well, Mrs. Vincent, may we step inside a moment so that we can explain our service?

MRS. VINCENT:

What type of service do you offer?

WAYNE:

How many times do you have to go to the supermarket each week?

MRS. VINCENT:

At least two or three.

WAYNE:

Do you enjoy shopping in a supermarket?

MRS. VINCENT:

Not really.

WAYNE:

Of course, you are an intelligent person. Just like my wife. She wants to get in and out of supermarkets as fast as possible. What are the hardest items to select? You know. Ah, in what section of the store do you spend most of your time?

MRS. VINCENT:

I'm not sure. Could it be vegetables or meat?

WAYNE:

You bet. It's meat. And on what item in the market do you spend most of your food dollars?

MRS. VINCENT:

Could it be meat?

WAYNE:

You're absolutely right. And that is exactly why we are here—to save you both time and money. May we come inside and give you a brief demonstration?

MRS. VINCENT:

Well, I have a house full of teenagers.

WAYNE:

Oh, we don't mind. We can do a demo in any room.

MRS. VINCENT:

All right. Come on in. We can talk in our game room in the basement.

After Mrs. Vincent gave her approval for an in-home demonstration, Wayne and Buddy moved their sales equipment and samples into the Vincents' game room. This equipment included: tripods, easels, flip charts, flyers, ice chests (containing meat and ice), frying pans, sample steaks, ribs, beef roasts, lamb chops, hamburger, aprons, chef's hats, cooking utensils, a wide variety of seasonings, and promotional booklets. Once all the sales elements were in place, Wayne began to introduce his product. He explained that his organization, AAAA Gourmet Meat Purveyors, could supply the Vincents with all the beef, pork, and lamb they could consume in a year.

MRS. VINCENT:

Well, for a commitment of a year I would like for my husband to hear what you have to say.

WAYNE:

But of course. Is your husband at home?

MRS. VINCENT:

I expect him any moment. He has been on the road all week.

WAYNE:

Oh, and what line of work is Mr. Vincent in?

MRS. VINCENT:

He is in sales.

WAYNE:

That's great. We are in the same business. Is he going to be excited when we cook him a couple of our prime-grade rib eyes tonight!

MRS. VINCENT:

You can do that?

WAYNE:

Oh, yes, with our compliments. Immediately following our presentation, we would like you both to sample our products. I'll bet Mr. Vincent has had his fill of hotel food. He is going to love having a home-cooked prime-grade rib eye.

MRS. VINCENT:

Well, he should have been here by now. His plane must have been delayed.

Mr. Vincent's plane was nearly two hours late in landing. For more than one and one-half hours, Wayne, Buddy, and Mrs. Vincent sat waiting for Mr. Vincent to arrive home. Wayne was really looking forward to making, as he called it, his "Full Prime Time" presentation. The Vincents' game room now looked like a display booth at a trade conference.

After fighting unusually heavy traffic, Mr. Vincent finally arrived home. Responding to his wife's summons, he walked down the stairs into the play room. He still had his coat on when he was warmly greeted by his wife.

MRS. VINCENT:

Honey, these gentlemen have been waiting for hours for you to arrive.

WAYNE:

Greetings, Mr. Vincent. I'm Wayne, area sales manager. This is Buddy, one of my trainees. We have been waiting for you. We have an unbelievable offer. I know what is on your mind. You're hungry, hungry for a prime-quality steak cooked just the way you like it. But first let's go through our presentation, "Prime Meat and Your Family." Then with the Missus' permission, we will cook you up a couple of our best rib eyes. Or T-bones, or New York strips. Buddy, why don't you start out with chart number one.

BUDDY:

Mr. and Mrs. Vincent, how often do you think about having the highest-quality beef, pork, and lamb at your finger tips? If you're like most of our clientele, the answer is often.

Up to this point, Mr. Vincent said nothing. He was stunned. He had envisioned coming home to the tranquility of his oasis from the rat race. But his home had been invaded. Could this be a nightmare? Was this just a bad dream, he asked himself. No, he quickly realized that two strangers, two alien beings, had penetrated the Vincents' protective barrier. Mr. Vincent's shock now turned to anger.

WAYNE:

Now, Buddy, go to the next graph on flip chart number two.

BUDDY:

Mr. and Mrs. Vincent, do you fully realize the amount of money that a family like yours spends on meat each year? Here are the facts and figures.

WAYNE:

And so often you're paying for prime quality and receiving only meat-e-ocrity. Ha! Ha! Just a play on words. I can tell by the expression on your face, Mr. Vincent, that you were shocked when you saw these figures on how much you spend on meat each year. Take it from here, Buddy.

BUDDY:

> But you feel the way that so many of our customers feel. You want better meat on the table for your family as well as for guests. I'm sure with your lovely home and this game room you entertain quite a bit. Were you fully satisfied with the meat that you served your guests at the last dinner party you had? Don't worry, we know exactly how you feel. Our customers felt the same way before they gave up serving the meat-e-ocrity currently offered by supermarkets. Wayne, did I pronounce meat-e-ocrity correctly? How'm I doing?

WAYNE:

> You're on a roll, Buddy. Go to the next chart. Mr. and Mrs. Vincent, are there any questions so far? You have not said anything.

MR. VINCENT:

> Out!

WAYNE:

> Next chart, Buddy. Quickly, Buddy.

MR. VINCENT:

> OUT! GET OUT OF HERE!

WAYNE:

> Is there a problem?

MR. VINCENT:

> [Now in a rage.] OUT! OUT! OUT! I WANT YOU OUT OF HERE NOW. RIGHT NOW. GET OUT!

In a somewhat threatening manner, Mr. Vincent moved toward Wayne and Buddy. The sales manager and his trainee then bolted for the stairs. They ran up the stairs and out the front. In just a few seconds, their vehicle shot out of the Vincents' driveway. They were in such a hurry to exit that they left without removing any of their "Full Prime Time" artifacts. The Vincents were now able to relax in the comfort of a play room decorated in full "trade show booth" motif. More than two weeks after this incident, Wayne "encouraged" Buddy to stop by the Vincents' home to retrieve the promotional equipment. He did so at a time when he was sure that Mr. Vincent was on the road. Obviously, Wayne's "Full Prime Time" presentation at the Vincents made an indelible impression on Buddy's attitude toward selling to the affluent via cold calling prospects when they are "not in the right mood." Buddy would benefit from reading Donald L. Dell's *Minding Other People's Business,* (New York: Villard Books, 1989). Mr. Dell suggests that there are times when the affluent prospect is not likely to be responsive to traditional sales messages.

An Apostle to Affluent Athletes

Donald L. Dell is considered to be one of the premier managers of top athletes in the world today. But managing talent is not the only part of this business in which he excels. Mr. Dell has the proven ability to encourage world-class athletes to become his clients. Managing and marketing skills are important components that underlie his business.

Mr. Dell has an uncanny ability to understand the needs of his targeted prospects. Other agents who will never attain his level of achievement too often focus on their own needs and not those of the athlete. In *Minding Other People's Business* (pp. 37–68), Mr. Dell discusses the concept of "getting clients." In this context, one of his more interesting discussions centers around the sales presentation he made to Michael Jordan. When Mr. Dell recruited him, he already knew a lot about him, his university, and his teammates. And Mr. Dell correctly speculated that Mr. Jordan also had a considerable amount of information about him and his offerings. Because of this fact and one other, Mr. Dell decided to alter his normal presentation. The day finally arrived for all the competing managers to "tell their stories" to Mr. Jordan. Mr. Dell was scheduled to be the last of many suitors to make a presentation during what became a very long day for the young basketball player.

Mr. Dell suspected that all the other prospective managers would spend their allotted time telling Mr. Jordan about their abilities, their track records, their talents, and so forth.

> I could see that Michael was very tired and probably sick of hearing the same sort of spiel over and over again. So I said,

"Michael, I know you already know a lot about us. So instead of telling you a lot of facts you already know, why don't we use this time for you to ask questions—about us or about anything else you've heard in other presentations today?" Immediately, he perked up, and we spent a very productive "conspiratorial" 90 minutes together, by the end of which we had already become his advisors in spirit, if not yet in fact. (pp. 48–49)

Many of the very best marketers to the affluent understand the importance of having *empathy* for the needs of the prospect/client. Obviously, Donald Dell appreciates the importance of knowing when to ask the prospect to "tell his story" so as to air his needs, concerns, and frustrations. Affluent prospects cannot help but be impressed with suitors such as Mr. Dell. They read their prospect's mind and then prove it by telling him what he wanted to hear, much as "I know how you feel." "Many of our clients felt the same way." "You're probably tired of hearing about our side of the equation." "I'll bet you're thinking, 'Oh, no, not another canned sales pitch.'" "I'm sure you would like to share your feelings about how you would like to be represented." "This will be very brief because I'm sure you have had a very long day."

For some affluent prospects, a respite from an onslaught of proposals is the most important need of the day. Too few marketers understand how to capitalize on this need.

PROSPECTING CEOS

An Antagonist of Senior Executives and Their Secretaries

Mr. JRB is known for his tenacity in selling to the affluent. For example, he attempted to make telephone contact with the CEO of a Fortune 50 corporation for more than a year. Each week he would call this prospect's office. Never once was he able to talk directly with the executive. Nor did the executive ever return any of the more than 70 calls Mr. JRB made. Of course, Mr. JRB did become acquainted with several of the executive's secretaries, receptionists, and assistants. Mr. JRB stated on numerous occasions, "It's not easy to sell million-dollar units of direct investments."

Unfortunately for Mr. JRB, he does not understand a simple rule in selling to the affluent. Mr. JRB has one major career-related need. He needs to sell direct investments to millionaires. This is essentially the message that Mr. JRB leaves with the clerical people who act as interceptors for their boss. When the executive does read the message left, he interprets it as a *statement of insensitivity*. Sensitive sales professionals understand and focus on the needs of the target. Mr. JRB conversely would leave messages about the benefits of direct investments. In reality, he was much more interested in his own product and his own livelihood. That is exactly how the messages were interpreted by the executive. And this inference, in turn, explains why the executive never was interested in speaking with Mr. JRB. Mr. JRB should have left a message that clearly demonstrated an appreciation for the executive's most pressing needs. Direct investing was never on the executive's priority list of needs. Mr. JRB assumed without testing his speculation that the executive and his interceptors would be as responsive to his canned script as some of the high-income-producing physicians and attorneys that he has as clients. The executive uses a different set of criteria when evaluating both investment offerings and the people who offer them for sale. The following case study will shed some light on how one especially gifted sales professional was able to capitalize on her knowledge of these criteria.

An Apostle of CEOs

Ms. D. C., like Mr. JRB, is tenacious when it comes to selling investment products. But she also possesses an unusual instinct for understanding the needs of prospects. Recently, she told me that she made several telephone calls to the CEO of a major corporation. Her calls to the executive were intercepted by his first layer of defense. Ms. D. C. was very polite as was the CEO's clerical/defensive staff. She called three times and left as many messages. These messages requested that the CEO return her calls. Ms. D. C. also mentioned that she was in the investment business and had something of importance in this regard to discuss with the CEO.

After making three calls and leaving three messages over the course of nearly a month, the CEO never responded. Nor did any of his staff call Ms. D. C.

Ms. D. C. was not discouraged by the lack of response generated from the CEO. Her fourth call did precipitate a return phone call from the CEO. Why did he respond, and respond so quickly, to Ms. D. C.'s fourth telephone call? The fourth message that was given to the CEO was not the same one that had been left during the first three attempts.

Ms. D. C. organized an investment fair for clients and prospects. The fair would be attended by at least several hundred investors. The securities of only three firms would be highlighted at the fair. One of these companies was headed by the CEO that Ms. D. C. attempted to contact.

SECRETARY OF DEFENSE:

Mr. G.'s office. This is Ms. S. D. May I help you?

MS. D. C.:

Yes, good morning once again, Ms. S. D. This is Ms. D. C. I would like to speak with Mr. G.

SECRETARY OF DEFENSE:

Oh, I'm sorry. Mr. G. is in a meeting at the moment. May I take a message?

MS. D. C.:

Yes. Would you please tell Mr. G. that Ms. D. C. called. Our branch is hosting an investment fair for our clients. We expect several hundred to attend. The investments of only three corporations will be highlighted at the fair. Your corporation has been selected to be highlighted. I would like to have some promotional literature about your company and its future plans for growth. I'm sure our clients would be interested in any materials that you have and, of course, a statement from your chairman.

SECRETARY OF DEFENSE:

I'll be sure to give him your message.

MS. D. C.:

I'm sure he will be very interested in helping me encourage our clients to invest in your company.

SECRETARY OF DEFENSE:

I will give him the message as soon as he leaves the conference room.

MS. D. C.:

Thank you. I look forward to speaking with Mr. G. directly. Good day.

SECRETARY OF DEFENSE:

Have a nice day.

Why did Mr. G. respond so quickly to Ms. D. C.'s fourth message while ignoring three previous ones? He likely interpreted the first three as preludes to a solicitation regarding his personal investment needs. And what type of sales professional might he expect to have authored such a message? The message was probably similar to hundreds that he had received in the past year. Authors of such common themes are often viewed as lacking originality and as telemarketing hawkers who grossly lack substance.

But the fourth message was very unique. Most CEOs have a demonstrated interest in placing the investment needs of the company ahead of their own. Ms. D. C.'s fourth message focused on this need. CEOs of Mr. G.'s stature are quick to respond to opportunities to market shares of their companies to investors.

It is likely that Mr. G. views Ms. D. C.'s investment fair as a favor for him and his company. Perhaps he will some day open an account with Ms. D. C. as repayment for the help that she gave him in carrying out his executive duties

TWO DIFFERENT ORIENTATIONS TOWARD THE CHILDREN OF THE AFFLUENT

Uncle Guido: The Antagonist of the Teenage Sons and Daughters of the Affluent

It is the dream of many married couples to own and operate their own business. One young couple hoped to operate an ice cream store someday. They picked a suitable location in an affluent neighborhood, a neighborhood that the Claritas Corporation classifies as being in the furs and station wagons category. Statistical analysis indicated strong population demographics, excellent traffic parameters. Surprisingly, potential competition was not yet even in the moderate range. The couple also discussed the possibility of obtaining a franchise with several officers of one of the major companies in the ice cream distribution business.

All the factors necessary to open the ice cream store were eventually accounted for except one. The couple did not have the amount of money needed to purchase a franchise. Several banks refused to loan the couple the money for such a purchase. The couple did not have the income or the accumulated wealth to warrant a loan of the size requested.

The couple had only one other possible solution. They would approach a wealthy relative and ask him for a loan with which to purchase a franchise. After several meetings and lengthy discussions, Uncle Guido agreed to lend the couple enough money to open the store of their dreams. Yes, Uncle Guido not only would loan them money, he would "show the kids the ropes." Since Uncle Guido was semiretired, he had plenty of time to help operate the store. Uncle Guido volunteered, in fact insisted, that he would be responsible for customer relations.

Unfortunately for the couple, Uncle Guido never attended one sales training seminar sponsored by the franchiser, nor did he bother to read any of the related literature which the firm provided to operators. Nevertheless, he was intent on helping the kids and, at the same time, protecting his investment.

Uncle Guido "allowed" the couple to work behind the counter. During peak demand periods, such as Saturday afternoons, he worked in front of the counter greeting people in his special way (for example, "Form a single line starting at the register or you won't get served"). But Uncle Guido's special greeting was reserved for teenage drivers. Any teenager that attempted to park in a space in the front of the store was personally greeted by Uncle Guido. He was out of the store in a flash whenever he spotted what he perceived to be a teenaged driver approaching a "family parking space."

UNCLE GUIDO:

Roll down you window. These spaces are for families.

TYPICAL TEEN DRIVER:

> There are not any signs that say that these spaces are reserved for families.

UNCLE GUIDO:

> We don't need any signs. You kids need to park behind the store or on the side.

TYPICAL TEEN DRIVER:

> But there are plenty of empty spaces right here.

UNCLE GUIDO:

> I don't want people to think that this is a store for teenagers. This is a family store. Park in the back. Move it. Move it right now.

TYPICAL TEEN DRIVER:

> We are just going to be here for a minute.

UNCLE GUIDO:

> If you park here we will not serve you any ice cream. You want our ice cream, you park in the back. You don't park in the back, you get no ice cream. This is a family store, not a hangout for teenagers.

What happened to those young drivers who ignored the commandment that teenagers shall not park in front of the store? Uncle Guido would quickly walk inside the store and tell the couple, "The wise guy that is about to walk in here gets no ice cream. Don't serve him." The couple reluctantly followed Uncle Guido's directive. They would have preferred to do otherwise. But Uncle Guido kept reminding the couple of his capital commitment to them and the future of the store.

Why did Uncle Guido force teenagers to park behind the store? Uncle Guido spent most of his life in the inner-city district of a major metropolitan area. During his tenure there, he witnessed firsthand how teenage gangs would "take over" small restaurants and luncheonettes. He failed to realize that there were no teenage gangs anywhere near the couple's ice cream store. He also had no understanding of the significance of the teenage market in neighborhoods classified as furs and station wagons territory.

The teenage sons and daughters of the affluent have considerable dollars to spend on ice cream. They also influence the patronage decisions of their parents. Uncle Guido not only alienated teenagers of driving age. He also damaged the image of the store in terms of families with teenagers. The family with teenagers still living at home was the number one household market within the store's trade area.

According to the law of retail gravity, more than 50 percent of the variation in revenue among competing retailers can be explained by location differences. But Uncle Guido's "customer relations" program was so strong that it overcame the law of retail gravity. The store never generated nearly the revenue figures expected given its excellent location and the strong positive image of the ice cream it sold. Businesses that target the affluent and/or the children of the affluent can ill afford to have an Uncle Guido directing and conditioning traffic.

The "Uncle Guido" experience was a bitter one for the young couple who dreamed of operating a highly profitable business. Often love and affection do not mix well with financial and management issues. One of the major reasons that small businesses fail relates directly to the concept of *other people's money*, a.k.a. *OPM*.

Owners of businesses that risk their own money often work harder and smarter in an effort to succeed. Conversely, those that are funded via OPM often feel that "their blood" is not on the betting table. It is likely that the couple in this case would not have tolerated the adoption of Uncle Guido's "selling concept" if it were not a question of OPM. But since they took very little financial risk, they never protested the manner of Uncle Guido's "selling" of ice cream to the children of the affluent.

An Apostle to Young Pizza Eaters and Their Families

Adversity often brings out the best qualities in people. This is especially true in the field of marketing. Adversity can be defined in many ways. One definition would include the competitive environment that faces John Dean and his wife, Gayle. The Deans are the owners and managers of a pizza restaurant. The retail pizza business is becoming increasingly competitive in this nation. But the Deans are literally located in "Competition City." According to a recent article (Bob Boyd, "What's Shakin' at Shakey's?", *Pizza Today,* February 1989, pp. 16–18, 21), San Angelo, Texas, has one of the highest percentages of fast-food locations per capita in the nation. In fact, during their tenure, the Deans had to compete at one time or another against a dozen or more pizza restaurants located within their trade area.

Obviously, the Deans do not enjoy the location advantages that Uncle Guido's ice cream store enjoyed as discussed above. But the Deans have overcome the laws of retail gravity. As John Dean stated in the *Pizza Today* article:

> We are now a destination pizza restaurant. Meaning customers will pass other pizza places by to come here. (p. 17)

The Deans' restaurant has ranked in the top 3 of nearly 500 in the chain for eight years. It has gross sales in the $2.5 million range or approximately four times the average for a restaurant of this type.

Competitive location/convenience cannot explain the success of this restaurant. Then what factors account for the enormous success that the Deans have encountered? In essence, the Deans are the major factor underlying the success of their establishment. And as much as Uncle Guido alienated teenagers and their parents, John Dean is an apostle to the youth of San Angelo, Texas. Consider some of the innovative promotional tactics that have been used by the Deans to stimulate patronage among young people.

- Whenever the local college's football team and its opponent score more than 50 points in a single game, a coupon in the sports pages can be redeemed for a free large pizza.
- Free tokens for the games in Dean's large video arcade are given to students who receive grades of A and B on their report cards.
- Free face painting is offered for birthday parties.
- The Deans pay the college tuition of all the college students who work for them.

What the Deans have discovered is that there is a direct correlation between these specific "youth tactics" and total patronage. The Deans's restaurant is a family restaurant that caters to all members of the family. And one certain way to attract and retain families as customers is to show respect for and interest in young people.

VARIATIONS IN SERVICE AMONG PROVIDERS OF SURFACE TRANSPORTATION

Telephone Interview Conducted by Patrick A. Hearn

The following interview was conducted by a marketing student, Patrick A. Hearn. The respondent was Dr. Thomas J. Stanley.

MR. HEARN:

Dr. Stanley, why do you use limousine services?

DR. STANLEY:

I find that it is generally easier to get in and out of a town, a hotel, or other meeting area with a known entity as opposed to a random event of finding a cab, although I often use cabs and have been impressed by many people who drive them in terms of their professionalism and the quality of their automobiles. But typically, a limo is faster and its people are more professional and more reliable. There are some security aspects involved as well. They are predictable, and generally their product is comfortable. And I think, overall, it is well worth the price one pays.

MR. HEARN:

Who would you recommend as a limousine company?

DR. STANLEY:

There are many different limousine companies that I have used in many different cities in the United States. There are several good ones in most towns. However, the one I often use in New York is the same one that chauffeurs all the Heisman Awards winners, their guests, and prospective winners of the Heisman Awards once a year in Manhattan as sponsored by the Downtown Athletic Club. Knowing several of the people associated with the Downtown Athletic Club, I came upon the firm which I often use by word of mouth. But many times in journeying to another town or city, I am not familiar with any of the limo services, nor is my reservationist. In this situation, I call the hotel and ask them whom they would recommend. Generally, hotels are a very reliable source in terms of predicting the people who are the best in providing high-

(continued)

quality limo service. Interestingly enough, even if you are not going to stay at a hotel, if you call some of the very best hotels in the town, they will recommend some of the best limo services. In fact, some of the best limo services will clean their cars every night actually down to the toothbrush stage of cleaning. I know of one instance, where a limousine company will hire what I call pseudo passengers that will test the quality of the driver unobtrusively while the driver is on the job. Pseudo passengers will enter the limo and essentially be obnoxious, uncaring, and attempt to give the driver a "hard time." Of course, the drivers who pass the tests are the ones who do not become irritated but maintain their professionalism and courtesy even though they are being verbally abused by these professional pseudo passengers.

MR. HEARN:

When did you start using limousines?

DR. STANLEY:

I am not sure. It did take a long period of time for me to make that decision. I think one of the precipitating factors took place when I flew to New York one evening and the cab driver nearly got into a fist fight with the toll collector because he felt that the toll collector was not responding to his demand for change as rapidly as he would like. After they exchanged threatening motions and cursed each other, I thought at that time it might be a good idea to use another form of transportation. I remember in Pittsburgh at one time, I was in a cab where the rear door next to me suddenly opened as we were making a turn and it would not lock, or really close. So I sat there holding the door closed with one hand and holding the seat with my other hand. It was not a terribly convenient, comfortable ride, and I did not feel really safe.

MR. HEARN:

Tell me about your most memorable experience with a driver.

(continued)

DR. STANLEY:

Well, actually there have been many memorable experiences in terms of courtesy and professionalism, but in terms of the most memorable trip that I have ever taken, and may I underline <u>exciting</u> trip, it was produced by someone named Lenny. I remember that Lenny was not driving a limousine; he was a cab driver who picked up a few of us in New York City. Lenny was driving a Chevrolet Caprice that was not in the best condition. Nor was it very clean. But I was very impressed with him for other reasons. In fact, I have to say that he really impressed me more than anyone else. I am not sure if I would want to be that impressed again. What impressed me the most about this fellow was certainly not his vehicle but the way in which he drove it and, I would say, responded to our needs. I think it is interesting in that context that so many people judge or even brag about the quality of limousine service by the size of the limousine or vehicle, whether or not it has accessories in the back, a telephone, a television, food products, or refrigerator. To me, and I think to many fellow travelers, those things are meaningless compared to the human element. I will take a small car, even an ill-equipped vehicle, with a good driver over the biggest and most well equipped limousine.

But I guess I am digressing. You asked me about the driver who gave me the most lasting impression. Lenny. I was speaking at a very fine hotel, the Westbury Hotel, which is located on 69th Street in New York City. Actually 15 East 69th Street between 5th Avenue and Madison Avenue. After my speech, two of my colleagues, Bill Moore, an executive with the firm that I was working for, and Todd Rulon-Miller, the sales manager—in fact, now the sales manager for Next Computers, another Steven Jobs innovative firm—and I, the three of us, needed to go from the Westbury to the airport. The Westbury is on a street that runs one way, I believe from west to east from 5th Avenue to Madison Avenue. We left the hotel much later than expected. My two colleagues and I had less than 40 minutes to get to the airport. Forty minutes would be very

(continued)

tight in light traffic, but we were at rush hour, and it was snowing heavily when we left the hotel, as it had been the last few hours before we finished our presentation. The three of us stood outside the hotel while the doorman blew his whistle at every cab that we could see passing on one of the main thoroughfares. I believe it was Madison Avenue. But several dozen cabs ignored his summons. And a fellow in one of the cabs attempted to slow down and negotiate a right turn on to 69th Street; however, he slid past the intersection, and we assumed that he would not be returning.

At the last minute when I thought that all opportunity was lost, this man in a yellow cab backed up the wrong way on a major thoroughfare and backed all the way the wrong way down on 69th Street to pick us up in front of the Westbury Hotel. As he slowed down, he rolled down his window and instructed us to put our baggage in the trunk. He had a trunk release mechanism which enabled him to stay in the driver's seat while we quickly put our material in the trunk. We got in the car, and he quickly sped off in the direction of Park Avenue. He was kind enough and sensitive enough to ask how much time we had before our plane left the airport. We explained to him that time was of the essence, and he said he appreciated it. And I asked, in fact, if he could get us to the airport in the limited amount of time that we had. He responded by telling me, and I quote to you, "When Naval Intelligence is trying to shake off a tail by the KGB in Manhattan, they call Lenny." I was skeptical when he told us that. I looked at my colleagues, and I'm sure they were skeptical, too. We were even more skeptical about his ability to drive quickly when he slowed down for the amber light in an attempt to cross Park Avenue. Lenny slowed down and then stopped at the red light. I was somewhat disappointed. I assumed that he might try to run the amber light and make it across. But Lenny was a man who had a mission. As soon as the light turned red, Lenny did stop. He allowed the first wave of traffic on Park Avenue to pass, and then he very coolly and very confidently went right through the red light and across four lanes of traffic without blinking an eye. We

(continued)

were beginning to believe perhaps Lenny was someone that Naval Intelligence used to shake off the KGB.

But the best was yet to come. As we approached the east-side extremities of Manhattan, he asked us what route we would prefer to take to the airport. I boldly suggested that we should take the FDR and then the Triborough Bridge. Lenny responded that he thought the traffic would be very heavy both on the FDR and on the Triborough and that he would try one of the midtown passageways. We all agreed that Lenny was in control and that his decision to take one of the midtown bridges would be the best solution to our problem. We crossed the bridge. Traffic was heavy but moving rather quickly. But as soon as we got off the bridge and into Queens, there was bumper-to-bumper traffic at a complete standstill. Gridlocked extraordinaire! And we thought we had no opportunity to get to the airport. Then Lenny turned around and pointed a finger at me and said, "Don't say a word." In essence, what he was telling me was, "Don't say a word about my decision which may now be incorrect." I didn't say a word. I noticed that Lenny was turning the steering wheel to hard right rudder. I thought that was interesting because there was no side street where we were. There was nothing there but stores and sidewalks. What Lenny did was extraordinary. He placed his car, himself, and his three passengers on top of a wide sidewalk in the Queens area of New York. He very coolly, calmly, and slowly motored down the sidewalks of New York. It was interesting driving on the sidewalk. It seemed like an eternity that we were passing by doors, up close and personal. Pedestrian traffic. People with baby carriages. I thought we would never get to the intersection. We finally made it. And ceremoniously Lenny laughed and bounced down on the street. But again, traffic was still bumper to bumper.

What would Lenny do now? Very quickly, Lenny took the car back up on the sidewalk, and we spent another several minutes in the grips of Lenny, the extraordinary cab driver. Another full block in Queens on a double sidewalk in the snow. Finally, as we broke out onto the street once again, traffic was light. We quickly negotiated back on the

(continued)

street and eventually back onto the highway. And to top the whole thing off, Lenny passed a police car while going 20 miles over the speed limit on the left side without blinking an eye. We got to the airport with 12 minutes to spare. Lenny was handsomely rewarded. It was a most extraordinary trip. Unfortunately, we were so taken by Lenny and his episodes that I failed to ask him for his telephone number or card. I hope that Lenny will have an opportunity to read this material and give me a call so that maybe we can use him once again when we are trying to lose the KGB in New York City. It is interesting about Lenny.

I was recently in a limousine in Boca Raton, and the young man who was driving was most pleasant. He asked me about the different personalities and people that I find in the cab and the limousine business. I happened to mention to him about Lenny on the sidewalks of New York. With that, the man slowed down and went on the median for three blocks. He just was trying to tell me that I can drive on the sidewalks, too. This same young man was a delightful fellow. In fact, he picked me up at the airport and then took me back to the airport. When he picked me up, he shared some of his personal interests in life which included cooking and being a part owner in a bakery. In fact, he recommended when we were driving along that I patronize the Italian restaurant located next to the hotel. He said, "They must be pretty good; they buy 80 loaves of Italian bread from us every single day." Of course, I expressed my interest in Italian food and Italian bread. On the way back he had two loaves of freshly baked Italian bread sitting in the back seat waiting for me. He was a delight because he understood the needs, both the physical and the transportation needs, of his clients and customers.

But let me contrast, and sharply contrast, some of the experiences on the other side of the equation. I remember a colleague of mine who was a sales manager having dinner with his top sales professional. The woman who was his top sales professional was somewhat irritated that she had been passed over for promotion as sales manager and

(concluded)

a younger person with less experience and actually not as much productivity in the same industry was given the job as sales manager. After a long dinner, the young man who was now sales manager seemed to come to terms with his best sales professional regarding the task that was ahead of them. So they finished their dinner. They walked out of the Waldorf Astoria and awaited the limousine that they had summoned. The limo driver, who was passing on the other side of Park Avenue, saw the couple emerge and rather than go all the way to the end of the street, made an illegal U-turn and came around quickly to pick up the couple. He opened the door and then said to the sales manager, "I made that illegal U-turn because I saw that your wife was pregnant." It is always dangerous to assume what the needs of people are based on their personal appearance. First of all, the sales manager was not married to the sales woman. And most importantly, the sales woman was not pregnant. That is one of the main reasons that the sales manager and his top sales professional never again used the limo service. Nor did they ever recommend that anyone else use the limousine service. It is especially dangerous to make assumptions about the needs of sales managers, executives, other marketing types of personnel. These people often control the budgets and transportation patronage habits of hundreds, if not thousands of people. Enough?

MR. HEARN:

More than enough. Thanks.

DR. STANLEY:

My pleasure.

Addendum on Who Controls Transportation Patronage Habits

On a recent flight to Florida, I had the privilege of sitting next to the vice president of sales of a major life insurance and annuity corporation. After spending about 30 minutes discussing airline service and food, the sales executive pointed out how he dealt with the problem of poor service on airlines.

He told me that he had repeatedly missed connections because of late flights on one national airline carrier. It got so bad that he started to write letters to the chairman of the airline. However, in spite of his complaints, things did not change. Very often flights on which he was booked were canceled abruptly. Very often flights were an hour to two or three late. These problems were dramatically affecting his business, his career, and his attitude toward flying.

So he took matters into his own hands. He finally realized how important it would be to leverage his position as vice president of sales. He sent a letter to all of his sales professionals. The letter stated in very simple terms: "Effective immediately, no longer will you be reimbursed for any flights taken on the mentioned airline." He also sent a copy of the same letter to the chairman of the airline.

Within several days, an executive from the airline telephoned the sales executive and asked if they could get together and have a personal discussion about the problem. The sales executive said that he had an open mind, and he met with two executives from the airline. The airline promised that they would assign one or two service specialists to greet him personally each and every time he was scheduled to board one of their aircraft. For six months after the meeting with the two executives from the airline, the sales executive was met by one or two service specialists every time he boarded/deplaned and was, in fact, escorted to his flights. In cases where the connecting flight was delayed or he missed the connecting flight or the connecting flight was canceled, they would deliver the executive personally to another airline and facilitate his connections.

This arrangement lasted for six months; then abruptly the service ceased. Essentially, service as usual commenced. Needless to say, this senior sales executive does not endorse the said airline.

It is, in fact, dangerous to toy with the sensitivity parameters of senior sales executives. Very often these people have a significant influence on the patronage habits that their entire sales force has regarding airline, limousine, and even hotel patronage. It is not unusual for a senior sales executive of a major company to regularly use domestic airlines. Many of them will tell you that not all sales executives use corporate jets, company limousines, or corporate apartments/suites. It is especially important that providers of service take note of the occupations and the amount of power that these executives have in controlling the travel habits of thousands upon thousands of their employees.

It would be relatively easy for airlines, for example, in the context of high-mileage clubs, to ask about the occupations of various members. It would be very valuable for service providers such as airlines to pay special attention to those individuals, as in this case, a senior-level vice president of sales, and to do everything in their power to make certain that these people are given extraordinarily good-quality service. In addition, it would be valuable for airlines and other service providers to occasionally contact these people to discuss their views about various types of services. In this way, by catering to opinion leaders of this magnitude, airlines and other service providers will find that they will dramatically increase their revenue. It is not unusual that one national sales manager controls the patronage habits regarding flying travel of 10,000 or even 20,000 sales representatives. Certainly, people who control that many dollars of travel budgets should be given very special service.

As in the case of most service providers, they never ask the occupation of their patrons. This is one of the most significant questions that can be asked of any provider of service to the affluent.

Interestingly, in discussing further the perceptions of this sales manager, I asked a simple question. "Have you ever been contacted and asked your opinion by any airline regarding airline services?" The response was: "Never contacted personally, by telephone call, nothing." He has never been contacted. But he influences the patronage decisions of thousands upon thousands of sales professionals.

It would be valuable for a senior marketing officer of the airline to contact people who are in the caliber of this senior-level sales executive and ask their opinion. A simple face-to-face luncheon once a year is likely to pay significant dividends in influencing the sales manager and, of course, thousands of sales representatives.

Extraordinary versus Ordinary Letters

An Apostle to Mr. Snack Food

Mr. William "Sonny" Brown
Big Brown's Snacks
1310 Industrial Park South

Dear Mr. Brown:

Enclosed is a copy of the latest edition of *Snacks and Chips*. You will probably need an extra copy to share with friends and relatives. You must be delighted that your peers have acknowledged your contributions to the food industry. It is not every day that a neighbor is featured in the cover story of a leading trade journal. Your success is inspirational. That is why I have ordered reprints of your story to distribute to all our dealers in the region. They will all benefit from reading about your courage and strength in overcoming all the obstacles that somehow were placed in your path.

Recently, I have personally become aware of another obstacle that you, too, may have noticed. Our family has always enjoyed eating your Big Brown Potato Chips. Your chips always seemed to be fully cooked, thicker, and more flavorful than others on the market. Your use of high-quality (expensive) oil and sea salt certainly contributes to the wonderful taste and texture of your product. Then why should our grocery bags be full of anything but Big Brown, the Big Brown brand?

Your product is becoming more and more difficult for us as a family to find. It is no longer on the shelves of the Big and Huge Supermarket where we buy our groceries. I have repeatedly asked the clerks and store manager to carry your product. However, I have not seen a bag of Big Brown chips in the store in several months.

Like you, I am a marketer and owner of a family

(continued)

business. It is absolutely amazing to me that often the products that are rated best by the consumer are not given their proper shelf space and distribution. Retailers, I feel, have an obligation to allocate space for superior products, not just products that are produced by giant corporations with almost unlimited promotional budgets.

Along these lines, I have communicated my feelings to the chief executive officer of the Big and Huge Supermarket chain. A copy of this letter is enclosed.

My own company has similar marketing problems with distribution. Many major distributors will not carry our product line. Some that do give our offerings step-child treatment in terms of floor space. Thus, in spite of the fact that our exercise equipment is superior in design, construction, and performance, our brand, like yours, is not always easy for the consumers to find. We, too, are fighting against major conglomerates that spend millions and millions on advertising.

As a consequence, our firm uses a unique form of distribution. One half of our revenue is generated from direct distribution. The other portion of our revenue comes from exclusive dealers in selected geographic regions. Most of our direct sales are made to institutions, health clubs, and corporations. However, we do sell directly to individual customers.

The article that featured you and your company in *Snacks and Chips* stated that your firm is in the process of building a new executive and manufacturing facility. I would like to propose that you consider having our exercise equipment installed in your new facility as part of your overall corporate health plan.

Also, many of the executives of the companies that we supply have several pieces of our equipment installed in their own homes. I would like to visit with you in person within the next week or two to discuss and demonstrate some of our state-of-the-art exercise equipment.

(continued)

I will telephone your office to set up an appointment. Thank you for your consideration.

Sincerely,

Dennis D. White
President and Chief Ex̱ :̱ve Officer
Health, Physics and Design

Ms. Molly S. Yelnats
President and CEO
Big and Huge Supermarkets

Dear Ms. Yelnats:

I feel it my duty as a patron of your Big and Huge Supermarket to make you aware of a recent problem I have encountered. During the last three months of shopping at your Big and Huge market on Poplar Street here in town, I have been unable to find any Big Brown's Potato Chips on your shelves. I have repeatedly asked the store manager as well as your clerks, "What happened to the Big Browns?" They were very courteous in telling me that the problem is "at headquarters." Thus, I am writing to you to bring this to your attention.

I am not sure whether or not you are aware of the fact that the owner of the Big Brown Potato Chip brand, Mr. William "Sonny" Brown, is a resident of our fine city. Interestingly, Mr. Brown, his company, and his products were recently featured in the front-cover article of *Snacks and Chips,* the trade journal for people in

(*continued*)

the snack and chip industry. In this article (copy enclosed), you will see that Mr. Brown's products and his company, as well as Mr. Brown, have been given numerous awards by peer groups in the industry. These awards were given because of his extraordinarily high-quality product as well as his outstanding leadership in the field. Isn't it ironic that Mr. Brown, who is acknowledged by his peers as having one of the most outstanding varieties of snack foods, is ignored by distributors of his product in his own backyard and neighborhood? I would urge you to consider giving Mr. Brown's products significant shelf space in all of your Big and Huge Supermarkets.

As a marketer and owner of my own business, I fully recognize the importance that businesses place on the national advertising support necessary to sell products off of shelves. However, in spite of Mr. Brown's company's small size, I believe it should be your commitment, in the spirit of entrepreneurship and family-held businesses, to give him support in terms of shelf space. He and his company have supported dozens of charitable, recreational, and civic organizations in this community, the community in which your company is headquartered. We have an obligation to support people of Mr. Brown's caliber who have made a contribution not only to his own industry but to the community where we both have our business organizations headquartered. Big Brown's Potato Chips may not be supported with heavy advertising budgets on a national basis. His products, nevertheless, have a strong following in this community and throughout the region.

I can only hope that you will seriously consider more shelf space for Mr. Brown's products as well as for other fine products made by the entrepreneurs in and around our region. Thank you for your consideration of my letter. I wish you continued success.

(continued)

Sincerely,

Dennis D. White
President and CEO
Health, Physics and Design

Too many We's, Us's and Our's, A.K.A. an Antagonist to Mr. Snack Food

Mr. William "Sonny" Brown
Big Brown's Snacks
1310 Industrial Park South

Dear Mr. Brown:

We are the finest and most innovative dealer of luxury automobiles in this metropolitan area. We sell only the finest motor cars available on the market today. All of our offerings represent the state of the art in technology, luxury, and customer satisfaction.

Because of our outstanding reputation, it is only appropriate for us to make you aware of our special blend of high-quality service and unparalleled commitment to user satisfaction. Yes, there are many fine dealers and automobiles to choose from today, but it is our unique blending of human resources with the most advanced automobiles in the world that places us at the very top in a very competitive field.

You must visit our showroom to fully appreciate our *total client orientation.* We are totally committed to our customers. We are the relationship-building dealer. We extend an invitation to you to visit our dealership. We feel certain that you will be very favorably im-

(concluded)

pressed with the atmosphere that we have created for you.

This month we are making a very special commitment to our first-time visitors. If you lease a top-of-the-line model from us during this month, we will provide you with a special price incentive. For only $995 per month you can be driving the best vehicle offered by the metropolitan area's most outstanding dealership.

Please act quickly. Our supply can run low. Obviously, you want to respond as soon as possible while a wide selection is still available. We are looking forward to greeting you when you enter our showroom.

Sincerely,

Robert J. Gregor
Sales Manager and
Chairman of Relationship Marketing

ANTAGONIST VERSUS APOSTLE OF A RESEARCHER WHO STUDIES THE AFFLUENT MARKET

Several years ago I was asked by a subsidiary of American Express to design, develop, and conduct a national study of high-income households in the United States. I recommended that we develop a representative sample of 9,000 affluent households. These 9,000 affluent households were to represent the top 5 percent of high-income households in the United States.

One of the problems in surveying the affluent is that you must provide them with an incentive to respond. This was a particularly difficult problem in this situation since our questionnaire contained over 500 items and ran 16 pages in length. What could we do to encourage these people to respond to our mail survey?

I decided that we would use an incentive. The incentive in this case was a small hand-held calculator. But we needed to have a picture and description of the calculator to include with the questionnaire to show the exact product that those who responded to the study would receive as an incentive.

I felt certain that each and every calculator company in the world would be interested in supplying us with 9,000 flyers that pictured their calculator and also provided a description. After all, these 9,000 flyers would be sent to affluent households all over the United States. I assumed, incorrectly, that all the calculator companies of the world would beat down our door in an effort to supply both the flyers and the calculators. I was certain of this since we estimated we would need to purchase at least 3,000 calculators for the people who responded to our survey.

The first calculator company that I called informed me that it was unclear whether or not they could supply us with 9,000 flyers at all. And if they could, it would take at least two to four weeks to process and deliver them. And they would charge us 50 cents for each piece that they would send us, which totaled $4,500 not including shipping. My response to this offer was in the negative. A price of $4,500 for advertising flyers seemed a little steep to me, but I was most concerned with the time horizon because we did not have two to four weeks to wait to launch the survey.

The second calculator company that I called, Canon, which was headquartered in Japan, had a very different response to my request. I spoke with their representative located in the southeastern part of the United States. He informed me that he would check into my need and return my call within an hour or two to give me an estimate of the time and cost parameters. He did call me within an hour and told me that if we wanted 9,000 flyers, they could have them delivered to my doorstep. "How long would it take?" I asked. And his response was: "I guarantee you that within 48 hours you will have 9,000 flyers."

Of course, my second question had to do with the price since they were going to fly these overnight from Japan to Atlanta. Appreciating the last quote of $4,500 that I had just received, I did ask the question about price. The response was very interesting. "There will be no charge for the flyers, no charge for the shipping. These flyers will be made available to you in any quantity that you like, free of charge." Isn't it interesting what different philosophies two companies have about marketing their products to the affluent?

In reality, we purchased more than 3,000 calculators, Canon calculators, and sent them to our respondents. Equally important, 9,000 high-income respondents throughout the United States were exposed to Canon and its hand-held calculator. While it is difficult to determine the effect, if any, on the sale of Canon products because of the mailings that we undertook, it is clear that Canon has a market orientation and understands the concepts of selling to the affluent.

SWAMP LAND OR LUXURY HOME SITES: DIFFERENCES OF PERCEPTIONS

Antagonist to an Affluent Couple from New Jersey

The affluent couple left early on Saturday morning on their way to visit the shore areas of North Carolina and South Carolina. They were excited about the prospects of finding the perfect home. They wanted a home that they could eventually occupy after tney retired.

The couple visited several different residential developments along the Atlantic coast. They were especially impressed with two developments along the South Carolina coast. However, their final choice of developments had more to do with the information and approach used by the sales professionals at these developments.

The couple first visited a very lovely residential community and asked one of the sales representatives to show them the best lots and homes offered. The sales professional in this case never asked the couple what they were really looking for, nor did he ask where they currently resided. The sales representative immediately placed this affluent couple in his automobile and sped off to lot 77C. Lot 77C was a two-acre lot that bordered what some people refer to as a salt marsh. When the couple from New Jersey looked out of the window of the car, they asked, "Is this your best lot?" And the sales professional responded that it was. The couple was shocked.

As the husband turned to his wife, he said with some laughter, "This is a swamp. Swamps are for garbage and dead bodies, not for homesites for million-dollar homes."

What the sales professional failed to do in this case was to understand the variation and perception among the affluent. To many people, this 77C lot was an ideal place for a home, especially to those who were familiar with the concept of salt marshes. They would respond favorably. However, the sales professional made a significant error when he did not ask where the couple was from and essentially what they wanted. To this couple from New Jersey, the connotations of a salt marsh translated into undesirable property, even unethical behavior and a perpetual smell from the swampland. Shortly after the couple was shown lot 77C, they said good-bye and farewell to this unfortunate sales professional.

An Apostle with Rare Earth

Why did the couple buy a very expensive lot in another subdivision not far from the first place they had visited? In this case, they encountered a young man who had an extraordinary ability to understand the needs of prospects. Although this couple was impatient to look at property and encouraged the sales professional to show them "the best lot" immediately, he asked them to spend just a few moments with him in his office. There he showed them topographical maps and other information about the property. He then spent about 20 minutes questioning the couple about where they currently lived, what they were looking for, what types of scenery and situations were best suited for them, and so forth. The couple said that ocean-front property was not absolutely essential and that something on a lagoon, river, or inlet (without a beach necessarily) would be very desirable. The young man was perceptive enough to ask the couple if they had been looking at any other property along the South Carolina coast. They responded that they had.

Then he asked them what their perceptions were of some of the competing developments along the coast. With that question, the husband responded quickly that they were just shown a $600,000 lot that was in a swamp. That immediately told the sales professional something about the needs of this couple. While more than half of the lots that were available in the subdivision that he represented were salt-marsh lots, he did not show the couple any of these parcels of land. Instead he sat down with them and showed them on the map all of the waterfront property which was available.

By the end of the day, the couple placed a significant deposit down on a lot that was, in fact, something other than a salt-marsh lot. Interestingly, the other development also contained many lovely lots along the ocean and waterfront. However, the antagonist of the New Jersey couple never considered their needs but only his perceptions and interest in the salt marsh concept.

THE REAL NEEDS OF AN EXTRAORDINARY SALESWOMAN

An Antagonist to a High-Income-Producing Saleswoman

Patricia was acknowledged recently in a trade journal as being the top-ranked sales professional in terms of income within her district. Shortly thereafter, she received several telephone calls from people who were trying to solicit "her business." These sales professionals were from the life insurance, architectural, asset management, financial planning, and securities industries.

All the callers, except one, who were clever enough to get Patricia on the telephone indicated that they had read about her in the trade journal. They pointed out that since she had such an extremely high income, it was very likely that she would need life insurance, asset management, a financial plan, a better quality security broker. Patricia did not respond favorably to any of these calls. She was annoyed by the insensitivity of these sales professionals. None of them took the time to discuss with her her own triumphs, her own successes. On the other hand, when Patricia makes sales calls, she always talks about the needs of the person that is sitting on the other side of the desk.

And Her Apostle

Several weeks after her story was printed in the trade journal, Patricia received a telephone call from a woman who was involved in selling investment products. This woman first congratulated her on her success. The broker then mentioned that she would like to send an extra copy of the article to Patricia because, as the sales professional pointed out, "You will probably want to cherish your acknowledged success by having several copies." In addition, this young woman asked Patricia to do her a favor. She asked Patricia if she would be kind enough to come to her office at 7:00 on a Friday morning and have breakfast. She also asked Patricia if she would speak to the 53 sales professionals in her branch after breakfast. The topic of the discussion would be how Patricia rose to the very top of her profession in a male-dominated environment. She also pointed out the importance of Patricia's comments. "Many of the women in my office, like myself, are struggling. We do not have a strong female role model who has, in fact, risen to the very top in sales. We would like to know how you have achieved greatness in sales so that we can better understand and benefit from your sage advice."

Needless to say, Patricia appeared at the office of the young caller and did speak about her successes.

WHAT THE AFFLUENT REALLY NEED

Antagonist of the Candy Man

In our seminars on marketing to the affluent, we often ask attendees to respond to affluent opportunities. One of these opportunities is presented in the form of a sketch and biographical profile of millionaires and multimillionaires. One of these case studies deals with the concept of marketing to "the affluent candy man."

During these case analyses, each of the attendees is given information about an affluent manufacturer of candy. Attendees are told that this candy manufacturer has a net worth of over $10 million and that he was just nominated for the "Candy Man of the Decade" award by his peers. In 95 percent of the cases, the typical response from an attendee relates directly to the attendee's needs and not to the real needs of this prospect.

We ask the attendees a very simple question. What does Mr. Candy Man need? The responses are predictable. If the seminar is attended by a group of sales professionals who sell executive clothing, they will typically say this man needs a new wardrobe. If a group of insurance specialists are present, they will usually say this man needs universal life insurance. Annuity sales professionals will say Mr. Candy Man needs an annuity. An asset manager will say this man needs his assets managed. Marketers of boats and yachts say that Mr. Candy Man needs a boat and a yacht. Those people selling exercise and gymnastic equipment for the home will typically say that Mr. Candy Man needs exercise equipment in his large home. Marketers of country club services and memberships will say that Mr. Candy Man needs a country club membership. Sales professionals who market the top-of-the-line luxury cars in the United States will say Mr. Candy Man needs a top-of-the-line model. Those who sell luxury real estate will say Mr. Candy Man needs an ocean-front home. Those who sell world tours on steamships will say Mr. Candy Man needs a world tour. And those people marketing mountain homes, mountain water, and water filtration systems will say he needs to live on top of a mountain and drink filtered water.

Affluent respondents have often told me that they are annoyed with people who approach them and immediately start talking about their problems. The sales professional's problem is to sell his or her product. But what is the major problem, the major issue, the major need of Mr. Candy Man?

Mr. Candy Man, like so many other successful people, is not only affluent but is recognized by his peers as being among the best in his chosen vocation. But interestingly enough, only a small minority of sales professionals understand how to condition, how to flatter, how to gain the affection of affluent prospects.

An Apostle to Mr. Candy Man

During the course of the seminar held in Newport Beach, California recently, a senior-level executive of one of our client firms approached me. He asked me to conduct some role playing during the course of the seminar. I mentioned to him that there were many different role-playing scenarios that could be used. And in discussing these various scenarios with him, I decided to include the scenario of the Candy Man. I asked this senior executive if there was someone in the audience who would be able to play the role of a high-quality sales professional when confronted with the Candy

Man opportunity. He said, ''I will select for you the top young rising star in our firm of over 10,000 sales professionals.''

When we reached the point during the seminar of dealing with the concept of the Candy Man, I asked this young man to come up to the front of the room. He now was going to be judged by 200 or more of his peers. I showed him a sketch and a brief profile of the Candy Man. I said, ''Young man, let us assume that you have information about this candy manufacturer. He just won an award. And let's assume that he is sitting at his desk at 7:00 A.M. as he always does. He is all alone in his office. You are about to make a cold call. When you walk into his office, without an appointment, at 7:00 o'clock in the morning, what would you say to him?''

This young, rising star showed why his senior manager put him in the star category. Let me paraphrase for you what this young star said.

> Good morning, Mr. Candy Man. I am Bob Reynolds. I just wanted to stop by and say, ''Congratulations.'' I noticed that in your trade journal you have just been nominated as Candy Man of the Decade. This is quite an achievement. In fact, I have an extra copy of the article here in my briefcase that I would like to give you. I am sure that many of your friends and associates would like to have a copy of it. It is interesting to me, Mr. Candy Man, to read about you, especially your contribution to the community, to charitable and civic organizations. I wonder if you could take a few moments and tell me how you were able to survive in such a competitive market? The reason I ask this question is that many of my clients are also independent business owners, and I find it intriguing to talk to people who have been able to pull themselves up by the bootstraps and achieve significant success in a very difficult economy.

What this young sales professional did was essentially fulfill the needs of the Candy Man. Most affluent people are high-achievement oriented. They need their achievements to be recognized. They need to be appreciated. And they need to tell their story of success. Because very often the most successful people are constantly listening to other people's problems but are rarely afforded the opportunity to tell their life history.

OPPORTUNITIES AMONG THE
BLUE-COLLAR AFFLUENT

An Apostle to Affluent Laborers: A.K.A. You Must Have Union Cards

Dozens of people were competing for the privilege of managing the tens of millions of dollars in the pension plan of this labor union. Potential managers, including brokers, insurance specialists, asset managers, and independent financial planners, were all required to submit a written proposal and to provide a copy of their credentials to the pension-selection committee. From this long list, several candidates were chosen, and their names appeared on what is called the short list.

Those on the short list were then asked to make an oral presentation to the pension committee. Following the oral presentation, the pension committee said that they would make a decision within a few days as to who would manage the money of this labor union.

All of the people and organizations that were on the short list had outstanding credentials. As the candidates waited outside the conference room at 9:00 A.M., one of the members of the pension committee emerged from the conference room. He said, "Ladies and gentlemen, please give me one of your cards. We will do our very best to have each and every one of you make your oral presentation before noon." Each of the candidates gave his card to the pension committee member. He, in turn, reentered the conference room and shut the door. Sixty seconds later the gentleman reappeared and asked one of the members of the short list group to enter the conference room. The pension committee member then turned to the other short-list members and said, "We have our selection already. Thank you very much, but the nominations are now over." The gentleman that he asked to come inside the conference room was an instant winner.

But why would the committee make a selection so quickly? What was it about this young man that convinced the committee that he should have the privilege of managing tens of millions of dollars? This young asset manager was selected, in part, because the card that he handed the selection committee member stated at the bottom, "This card was printed in a union shop by union printers." This young man obviously had studied the needs of members of labor unions. They have a need to be recognized. They have a need to deal with people who support "the home team" and appreciate the needs of labor and unions in this country.

Obviously, none of the other candidates had specified on their cards that the card was, in fact, printed by union laborers. It is likely that the cards were, but they never thought that this was important primarily because they never stopped to think of the needs of the target. These needs very often are independent of the product offered. People in unions prefer to deal with those product and service providers who are patrons of union labor.

An Antagonist to Himself

Recently, I discussed the concept of selling to the affluent with a top-ranked marketer of investment products and services. I asked this young man about the characteristics of his most important affluent client. The young man replied, "My best client is a manufacturer of fish hooks." In reality, his best client is one of the most respected members of the commercial fishing supply industry. What is interesting is that this young man's most profitable affluent client has 20,000 customers. These customers are commercial fishermen throughout the world.

After learning about the profile of this young man's best customer, I asked some simple questions. "Have you ever asked your best client to refer you to any of the 20,000 customers that he has a relationship with? Have you ever visited a trade show that contained a high concentration of affluent commercial fishing fleet owners? Have you ever read a trade journal of people in the commercial fishing industry?" And as the final question, I asked, "Are you aware that owners of fishing fleets are among the top 10 occupations in America for producing $100,000 and more annual income?"

The answers to all these questions were the same. No. He had never asked for a referral. Never visited a trade show. Never read a trade journal and did not know that people involved in commercial fishing were affluent.

While this young man has become a top producer using traditional methods of marketing, tenacity, hard work, prospecting, life could be so much easier for him if he would develop an affinity for leveraging what is called the affiliation among people within industries. All too often, people who sell to the affluent prospect strangers each and every day by making ice cold calls. They call on people in industries with which they have no affiliation; they talk to complete strangers; and they talk to prospects who have nothing in common with them.

It is only logical to suspect that the prestige and admiration affluent fishing fleet owners have for this producer of hooks would rub off on those who provide services to this respected individual. This young sales professional had something in common with 20,000 people who are in the commercial fishing business. Certainly, it would be possible to identify each and every one of these purchasers. Clearly, this sales professional could also rank these users in the context of size and potential net worth. He could, in fact, appear at trade conferences where many of the 20,000 customers of his best client appear. However, up to this point, he has used traditional methods of marketing to people with whom he has nothing in common.

PATRONAGE OPINION LEADERS: RESPONDING TO CENTERS OF INFLUENCE

An Antagonist to Selling but an Apostle to Golfers

Young John studied the game of golf. His desire was to become highly proficient in understanding the game so that he could better serve as a caddy. He watched golf on television. He took cues from more experienced caddies. He learned how to mark off distances. He developed an understanding of the relationship between club selection and distance. He even checked out various golf courses in the context of distance and strategy. He felt very strongly that he would be the Caddy of the Year at a country club for the very affluent.

What John could not figure out was why the caddymaster consistently chose other caddies for early assignments at the club. In fact, John often was not given "a loop" until late in the afternoon. He would typically arrive at the country club early in the morning and sit there and wait for the caddymaster to select him. But often the selection was not made until four, or five, or sometimes six hours after John arrived.

Then when John was let out on the course, it was often with a group of mediocre elderly golfers who shot in the 110 range. It would take six hours to go around the course, and John not only had to carry the golf bags but also two seats for the gentlemen. And John rarely received a tip from any of these people.

The best prospects for caddy services usually played in the morning, that is, the big tippers, the great golfers, the ones who could do 18 holes in just 3½ hours. John's problem was very simple. He assumed that if he developed extraordinary skills as a caddy, he would automatically be selected for the most lucrative "loops." But in essence, he was targeting golfers.

The reason John consistently failed to gain access to the most lucrative opportunities as a caddy was that he did not target the caddymaster. What could John do to enhance his image and position with the caddymaster? What were the needs of the caddymaster? In order to answer those questions, he approached another caddy, one who had a history of being among the very first caddies to be sent out on important loops.

Antagonist to Golfers but Apostle to Selling to the Caddymaster

John approached James, one of the most popular caddies at the country club. What was interesting about James? Many people considered him to be among the worst caddies at the country club. He really didn't understand the game of golf. He wasn't sure what clubs were used for what purpose. He was a disaster when it came to judging distances. He didn't particularly like golf. He didn't play golf. He did have, however, a good personality and was engaging in his discussions with golfers.

John asked James why he was always chosen for the best caddying opportunities. James replied that he had not always enjoyed such a wonderful position as a caddy. However, he discovered who was in control of the caddy's destiny. Clearly, it was the caddymaster. But James recognized that the caddymaster in this particular case was not only interested in a caddy's ability to caddy;

he was interested in other things. The caddymaster had a concession stand where he sold soft drinks, hamburgers, sandwiches, hot dogs, chips, and various sundry items to the caddies. In addition, the caddymaster maintained an accounts receivable file on caddies. He would allow caddies to buy on credit.

James pointed out to John that during the first year that he was a caddy at the club, he always brought his lunch from home and then just purchased a soft drink out of one of the soft drink dispensing machines. However, that year he made very little money, he was never selected for early loops, and he was always given some of the least desirable golfers as clients. But early in the second year, James stopped bringing his lunch from home and purchased lunch from the caddymaster. He noticed that as soon as his account with the caddymaster exceeded $20, the caddymaster developed a much different perception about his ability as a caddy. In fact, James was startled. As soon as the caddymaster realized that James had run the bill up over $20, James did not have time to sit down and wait for the next loop. Many times James was taken instantly upon his arrival and placed out on the first tee with two golfers. Obviously, the caddymaster was very interested in James's ability to generate income so that he would be able to repay his food bill.

James also informed John that he had caddied at other golf courses, but some of these had a different system. In fact, in one public course, the caddymaster had no food concession, no I.O.U. system at all. So James would wait in the parking lot for golfers to appear and then approach them before they ever got near the caddy shack and the caddymaster. He would approach them and say, "Would you be interested in having me caddy for you today, sir?" The advantage of this is that he was the first to come into contact with various golfers. He could pinpoint his targets. He could pick whom he wanted to avoid and whom he wanted to caddy for. The golfers were often interested in making an early selection of caddies for the same reasons and also many golfers did not want to carry their own bags the several hundred feet from the parking lot to the first tee.

What James had discovered was that affluent golfers, as well as caddymasters, don't always hire the very best quality caddy. Often the most financially successful caddies are those who aggressively pursue their prospects and fully capitalize on their knowledge of the needs of the target audience.

CONDITIONING PATRONAGE OPINION LEADERS

An Antagonist to the Affluent Clients of a Leading Law Firm

Gerald received a telephone call one morning from Edward, who was a senior partner in a top law firm. Edward called Gerald because he was interested in helping him obtain a new client. Gerald is an asset manager who generally is much better at managing assets than marketing his services. Edward informed Gerald that one of his clients, a wealthy widow, had $7 million that needed to be invested. He also informed Gerald that the two current providers of financial and investment advice for the widow's portfolio were "not performing up to anyone's expectations."

Gerald quickly got off the phone with Edward and called the widow. Within 15 seconds of the widow answering the telephone, Gerald suggested that she come to his office immediately to fill out papers to transfer the $7 million into his discretionary asset management account. Although the widow had a great deal of respect for Edward, the attorney, she was shocked by the callous and rather hurried approach to marketing à la Gerald. The widow told Gerald that she would like to have some more information about him and his firm. Gerald said that he would send her some information as well as references in the mail but that he would like to get this underway as soon as possible.

Shortly after the widow completed her conversation with Gerald, she called her attorney, Edward. She complained to him that Gerald seemed to be in a terrible rush, was insensitive to her needs and grief, and was making what would be considered to be an assumptive close by having her immediately sign papers turning over $7 million to the "discretion of Gerald." Needless to say, Edward was taken by surprise and never again made a referral on behalf of Gerald.

An Apostle to a Client of a Major Law Firm

Jack received a telephone call one afternoon from a senior partner at a major law firm. He indicated that one of his clients, a very wealthy widow with a net worth of over $10 million, was interested in developing new patronage habits with regard to investment counselors. He strongly suggested that Jack call the widow and discuss some of the problems that she currently had with managing her money.

Jack immediately called the widow. But before he discussed any of the financial issues, he spent over 20 minutes asking the widow about her family, her goals, how she wanted to live in the future. During the course of this conversation, the widow pointed out that one of her children, her oldest daughter, had just graduated from a top law school in this country. The widow was thrilled with her daughter's accomplishment. However, she also pointed out to Jack that she was very worried about her daughter's safety. Her daughter had taken a joo near the Wall Street district of Manhattan and lived nearby. She told Jack that her daughter had a "bad habit" of jogging before dawn each weekday morning. The widow was very concerned about her daughter's safety, especially when she heard so many bad stories about women being accosted, murdered, and raped.

Jack responded that he was a member of an outstanding athletic club in the Wall Street district. He told the widow that he would be delighted to provide a temporary guest membership at the club so that the daughter could jog within the athletic club's track and never have to chance jogging in the streets of Lower Manhattan again. He also offered to recommend her for a permanent membership. Jack told the widow that he would call his athletic club immediately and then also call the widow's daughter to invite her to the club.

Within a matter of a few hours, the widow's daughter received a temporary membership at Jack's athletic club. When Jack received confirmation of the consummation of the temporary membership agreement, he called the widow to help alleviate the tension she felt about her daughter jogging in the unprotected streets of Manhattan.

It was only after this conversation was completed that Jack began to discuss the financial service needs of the widow. And over a period of several telephone discussions that lasted sometimes over two hours, Jack eventually was given the majority of the widow's portfolio to manage. And of course, the widow, in turn, called her attorney to thank him for recommending such a quality person as Jack to manage her money. Needless to say, the attorney subsequently made many positive referrals on behalf of Jack and his professional service.

What Jack realizes is that very often the product that he sells is not the paramount issue in developing a relationship with affluent clients. In fact, in the context of affluent products and services, very often these things rank way below the top 5 or top 10 needs of affluent people. Many times, affluent people are much more concerned about the safety of their family, recognition of their achievements, and appreciation of career success than they are about boats, cars, and even asset management services.

CONDITIONING THOSE WHO INFLUENCE AFFLUENT READERS

An Antagonist to Editors and Their Review Boards

Jack spent many days researching and writing a manuscript that he intended to have published in a leading journal. Jack never let anyone else read his material. He developed the manuscript completely on his own. He never asked for advice from anyone else. He sent it to the editor of a journal, and six weeks later, the editor responded with several reviews from the editorial review board, as well as his own.

Each and every member of the review board said that this article was not worth publishing. Jack exploded with anger when he read the letter. He could not believe the comments of these people. Without hesitating, he immediately telephoned the editor. He told the editor that there was absolutely no reason why it should not be published. The editor said that it was a fair review and that it was a consistent finding among the editorial review board members that the material not be published.

Jack responded by a suggestion that the editor did not know what he was talking about and that none of the people on the editorial review board understood the real meaning of information and knowledge. Jack also informed the editor that he was seriously considering seeking advice about legal remedies to the problem about being turned down.

Not surprisingly, the editor and the editorial review board never accepted any of Jack's manuscripts for publication.

An Apostle to Editors and Members of Editorial Review Boards

Liz had a great interest in publishing articles in journals. She was very bright and had some unusual as well as original ideas. Most people felt that she could make a contribution to her field. Publishing is not easy, and very often, it is difficult to predict what will and what will not be published. But Liz was a cunning devil. She prepared various manuscripts and instead of sending them through the traditional channels, that is, to editors who, in turn, would send them to the editorial review board, she sent them directly to members of editorial review boards with a note begging them to review the material and make suggestions about how she might improve the various manuscripts. Also in the letter, of course, was a brief paragraph that paid homage to each and every one of the editorial review board members in terms of their contributions to the field and their genius for developing original ideas.

In turn, every member of the editorial review boards to whom Liz sent her manuscript responded with comments and suggestions. Naturally, Liz incorporated these suggestions into her manuscript. In addition, she would often cite the work that members of the editorial review boards had provided, either as comments and/or in previous literature. After Liz accumulated all of these reviews and, in fact, rewrote her manuscript with suggestions from the reviewers, she then submitted the manuscript to an editor of the targeted journal. The editor of the journal was the only member of the review board who had not had the privilege of previously reviewing the manuscript.

The editor, in turn, sent the manuscript to members of the editorial review board. When the members of the editorial review board got copies of the manuscript, they noticed that Liz had incorporated their suggestions into the manuscript. They were delighted. They were especially delighted that she had cited their significant contributions to the literature as well as to the industry. Then each of these reviewers would send back a favorable review of the article. Upon receiving these favorable reviews, the editor would immediately write to Liz telling her that her manuscript would be published as an article. Very often her articles were published without any changes whatsoever since she had already set the foundation stones in place for publishing the finished product.

Essentially what Liz did was to respond to the needs of the editorial review board which included ego enhancement and recognition of their achievements. In essence, if one would like to publish in various journals, he should focus not only on the needs of the readers but on the real needs of people who control the information that will be published.

THE SPALDING SCHOOL'S COUNTRY FAIR

The Spalding School Country Fair—
A perfect autumn day—
One thousand prospects cluster there
And see the prime display:
Two cars adroitly parked,
Two promos smartly penned
But a world of difference marked
The messages they send.

One sign in striking script declares:
"I'll be auctioned off today
To one who buys a ticket here
Compliments of ABC Motors." Hurray!
"We pass all proceeds to the school"—
A true apostle all perceive—
Just apply the Golden Rule
And give ere you receive.

The other sign is also clear.
Affluent prospects throng;
They read the words and stop and stare
And comment on the wrong.
"Friends and neighbors gathered here
A widow owns this car;
I'm 63 years old this year.
I want to put you on your guard.
I bought this economy compact
From Antagonist Motors, brand new,
But they charged me $1,100 (it's fact!)

For my first warrantied service, too.
This widow tells you in strongest terms
If you deal with Antagonist Motors
All you'll get will be burns, burns, burns,
But I won't allow them to gloat or
Think I might be flustered.
I plan to get even—
That firm's lost its luster—
So heed my warning given.
Please call me for details.
Here's my number for your use.
I'll tell my story, if all else fails;
I'll tell of their abuse.
Antagonist Motors, you'll regret
You brushed aside my problem.
Dear neighbors, please do not forget,
Don't buy a car from them."

Two cars were on display;
Two messages were sent
To all who ventured by that day
To all who came and went.

INDEX

A

Academic entrepreneur
  identifying, 185–87
  prospecting pro forma, 190–95
Accountants, 267
  patronage information and, 140
  seminars and, 262
  sources of information, 85
  target marketing and, 166
Achievement recognition, 4, 195
  ADWEEK and, 317
  apostolic approach to, 453–54, 456
  Asian American community and, 142
  business owners and, 7–9
  capitalizing on, 73–74
  conditioning technique and, 168
  editors/editorial boards and, 465–66
  luxury real estate and, 396, 400
  prospecting with plaque, 23–24
  sales professionals and, 11–12, 70–71
  trade journals and, 238
Active/passive investor continuum, 98–99
Adversity and career, 29
Advertising agency principles, 314
Advocate for affinity groups, 14
  Asian Americans and, 143–46
  women's issues and, 145–46
ADWEEK, 314–319, 326, 332
Affiliation groups, 177, 279–80, 283
  affluent women and, 13, 101–5

Affiliation groups—*Cont.*
  cohort groups and, 34
  imitation and, 324
  luxury car selling and, 18–19, 304–6
  marketing and, 23, 33, 172
  publishing articles and, 37
  real estate sales and, 377–78, 399
  speakers bureau and, 277–78
  success authors and, 161, 182
  varying social classes and, 61
Affiliation marketing, 313–14
Affiliation publications, 171
Affinity groups, 5
  support system and, 119
Affluence by association, 27
Affluent convoys, 33
  euphoric prospects, 331
  Garden Club and, 125–26
  luxury car selling and, 320–21
  professional athletes, 214–17
  real estate sales and, 376–78
Affluent prospects; *see also specific subgroups*
  achievement/needs recognition and, 73–74
  apostle/antagonist approach to, 20, 454–56
  developing directory of, 333
  effective approaches to, 243, 247–48
  euphoria and propensity to spend, 298
  euphoric spending frenzies, 299–300
  geographic movement and, 15–16
  letter writing and, 40–41, 45

Affluent prospects—*Cont.*
  leveraging client relationships,
    16–18
  luxury car selling and, 313
  making decisions and, 383
  needs of, 3–6
  strategies/tactics for finding, 53–54
Agresta, Anthony, 129, 133
Air travel
  antagonist/apostolic approach to,
    411–16
  controllers of patronage habits,
    441–43
American Assembly of Collegiate
    Schools of Business (AACSB), 93
American Medical Association, 94
Antagonists to affluent, 409–10
  air travel and, 411–13
  real estate sales and, 451–52
  research study case and, 449–51
Apostles to affluent, 409–10
  air travel and, 413–16
  real estate sales and, 452–53
  research study case and, 449–51
Asian Americans, affluent, 14
  characteristics of, 136–38
  education and, 130–31, 138
  family ties and, 130
  geodemographics of, 130
  growth trend of, 129–30
  insurance needs of, 138
  marketing methods for, 138–43
  medical profession and, 135
  population characteristics, 133–34
  scientific/technological professions
    and, 141
  understanding, 132–33
Asian-Indian subsegment, 132
  demographics and, 134
  higher-level education and, 132–33
  patronage opinion leaders and, 140
Attorneys, 267
  patronage information and, 140
Audit Bureau of Circulation, 182
Authors, affluent, 14
  academic entrepreneur, 185–87

Authors, affluent—*Cont.*
  best-seller concept, 348
  euphoria concept and, 178–79, 189
  key informants and, 188–89
  luxury car sales prospecting and,
    355–58
  not-for-profit scholar and, 185
  pro forma for prospecting, 154–63,
    190–95
  prospecting by defense and, 152–54
  subsegments of, 183
Avery, Robert B., 93

B

Bambenek, Greg, 334
Banking services
  antagonistic approach to, 418–20
  apostolic approach to affluent and,
    417–18
Bartering for publishing services, 239
Berger, Esther M., 101
  becoming an expert, 105–7
  designing women's affiliation group,
    101–5
  interview with, 111–19
Big league orientation, 333–35
  expertise and, 339
Bingo Card Service, 239–40
Bismarck example, 200–201
Blendstru, Gerhardt, 305
  interview with, 305–8
Blue-collar affluents, 53–54
  apostolic approach to, 457–58
Book of Challengers, 303
Bouvier, Leon F., 129, 133
Boyd, Bob, 434
Brock, David, 199
Business brokerage, 201–2
Business owners, affluent
  Asian American 140
  business valuation seminars, 263–66
  luxury car selling and, 332
  luxury real estate selling and,
    386–87

Business owners, affluent—*Cont.*
  over/underprospected, 8–9
  prospecting for, 57–58
  selling business and, 262
  status products and, 7
  themes for, 9–10
  trade organizations/journals and,
    24–25, 61
Butterfield, Fox, 130
Buy-out-plans, 138

C

Cahners Network, 59
Caller, William, 74–76
Cariseo, David, 15
  interview with, 204–12
  orientation consultant, 202–3
Carnegie, Dale, 50
Cash flow, 11, 45
  conditioning technique and, 169
  euphoria and, 299, 329, 349
CEOs, prospecting
  antagonist approach, 427–28
  apostolic approach to, 428–30
Chambers, Larry, 344
Children of affluent
  antagonistic approach to, 430–33
  apostles to, 433–34
Clancy, Tom, 181
Claritas Corporation, 131, 138, 431
Classified advertisements, 171
Clothing sales, 3
Clusters of affluent opportunities, 32,
    328
  luxury car selling and, 314
Cohort groups, 34
Cold prospecting, 46–47
Commodity brokers, 345–47
Communication campaign, 239
Computers, 48
Concerns, people's
  accessing through, 62–64
  solicitation sensitivity and, 64
Conditioning technique
  authors and, 358–62

Conditioning technique—*Cont.*
  editors/editorial boards and, 464–65
  ESPs and, 168–69
  pro forma telephone interview and,
    270–75
  prospecting by defense and, 155–63
  real estate selling and, 388–89, 400
  sales manager and, 369–72
  selling luxury automobiles and, 301,
    328, 354
Consumption luxuries, conspicuous,
    76
Courage, 27, 74
  proactive selling and, 301–2
  real estate sales and, 384–85
  selling luxury automobiles and, 303,
    328
  selling to affluent and, 28
Credibility, gaining
  enhancement association and, 233
  example cases of, 255–61
  publishing articles and, 238
  seminar programs and, 267
  talk show interviews, 267–69
Current products to current clients, 25

D

Dell, Donald L., 426
Direct mailings, 306
Directory of Associations, 334

E

Economic infrastructures, 337
Economic windfalls, 287
80/90 rule, 221–22
Elliehausen, Gregory, 93
Empathy needs, 427
Endorsements; *see also* Media
    endorsement
  affluent affiliation group and,
    216–17
  Asian Americans and, 139–40, 142
  industry opinion leaders and, 17,
    35–36, 399

Endorsements—*Cont.*
  intraindustry endorsements, 341
  marketing target and, 358
Entrepreneurial Women, 106
Entrepreneurs
  affluent women, 106
  Asian American, 140
Erhard, Werner, 62
Estate multiplier method, 98
Euphoria levels, 22
  capitalizing on, 75
  cash flow and, 299, 329, 349
  hungry fish analogy and, 298–99,
    330
  luxury car sales and, 301, 304, 317
  luxury real estate sales and, 397
  prospecting by defense and, 154,
    163
  sensitivity and, 89
  timing solicitations and, 86, 189, 358
  trade journals and, 237
Euphoric spending frenzies, 299–300
Executive and Professional Women,
    Inc, 100
Executive Women's Club, 100
Expertise
  Asian American business owners
    and, 140–41
  being perceived with, 339–41
  Esther Berger and, 112–116
  roads to, 34
  talk show interviews and, 269
Extraordinary sales professional
    (ESP), 22
  big-league orientation and, 172–73
  conditioning technique and, 168–69
  courage and, 164, 301–2
  market knowledge and, 166–67
  proactive selling and, 301–2
  sources of information and, 171–72

F

Federal Reserve Bulletin, 93
Fieldston confessions, 404–5

Financial consulting services, 3, 177
  Asian Americans and, 137
  empathy goals and, 100
  women's affiliation group and,
    101–5
  women's market and, 91
Focusing, 30
  air traveler's needs and, 413–14
  editor's needs and, 395
  needs of key informant, 351
  needs of prospect and, 153, 169,
    358, 428, 463
  real estate sales and, 375, 396
  successful authors and, 182
  target marketing and, 167, 176, 191
Forbes, 94, 172

G

Geodemographic marketing, 138
Geographic movers, affluent, 15–16
  orientation consultant and, 202–3
  premove targeting, 212–13
  temporary moves and, 214–17
Ghost writer, 368–69
Grass-roots strategy, 347
Grey haired prospects, 25–26

H

High productivity/low cost, 335
Higher education, 130
Hispanic population, 129
Holtz, Lou, 196–97
Husband-wife decision team, 386–88

I

Iacocca, Lee, 181
Identifying affluent
  sources of information, 54–55
  strategies/tactics for, 53
Image-building, 35, 140
  Asian American community and,
    142

Image-building—*Cont.*
  successful authors and, 183
Imitation behavior, 324
Income Statement Affluent, 382
Industry-specific expertise, 34
Industry taxonomy, 333
Influencers of the affluent, 16–18
  antagonist to editors, 464–65
  apostle to editors, 465–66
  conditioning for future, 227–28
  pro forma dialogue for, 222–27,
    228–32
  targeting of, 221–22
Information sources
  academic entrepreneur and, 185–88
  ADWEEK, 314–19
  Asian Americans and, 141
  expertise and, 339
  identifying affluent, 54–55, 170–72,
    202–3
  luxury car selling and, 328–29
  medical faculty, 139
  public information, 331–32
  successful authors and, 154, 179–83
Inspirational programming ideas, 270
Intelligence-based marketing, 347
  key informant and, 355
  penetrating affluent market and,
    53–54
Intraindustry endorsements, 341
Investment interview, 127–28

J

Jewelry/gem sales, 3
  affluent convoys and, 214–17
Jordan, Michael, 426

K

Kahn, Murry, 130
Key informant, 350
  authors and, 188–89
  focusing on needs of, 351
Key man insurance, 138

Kirk, Daniel F., 21
  affluent convoys and, 32–34
  courage and, 27–29
  first major league client, 23–27
  as mentor, 29–30, 32
  roads to expertise, 34–38
  sales methods, 22–23
  whole person concept, 30–31
Korean American subsegment, 132
  demographics and, 133–34
  higher educational levels and, 133
  patronage opinion leaders and, 140
Kun, Paula Keyes. 129

L

Laskis, Jeanne Marie, 302
Letter writing, 5
  extraordinary versus ordinary
    letters, 444–49
  follow-up calls and, 48
  people's concerns and, 62
  prospecting affluent women and,
    122
  targeting affluent and, 40–41, 45
Leveraging
  affluent target needs, 262–66
  client relationships, 16–18, 348, 363,
    458–59
  credibility from trade journals,
    241–42
  and proactive sales marketing, 372
  referral system and, 398–99, 464
  speakers bureau, 276–84
Life insurance professionals, 3, 6, 21
  Asian American segment and,
    129–30
  false assumptions and, 26–27
  luxury car prospecting and, 321–22
  orphan policy and, 23–24
Luxury car selling, 3
  achievement recognition and, 324
  affiliation needs and, 304–5, 321
  affinity groups and, 5–6
  big league orientation and, 333–35
  cash-flow euphoria and, 299, 317

Luxury car selling—*Cont.*
  convoys of affluents, 320–21, 343
  high-income consumer and, 18
  hungry fish analogy and, 297–98
  life insurance professionals and,
    321–22
  making house calls, 341–44
  parade method of, 344–47
  perception as expert and, 339–40
  pro-forma solicitation for, 76,
    80–84, 312–28
  real estate professionals and,
    322–23
  special editions, 306
  targeting affluent convoys and,
    308–12
  targeting by industry and, 336–37
  target market knowledge and,
    327–28

M

Magic of Thinking Big, 197
Manchester, William, 4
Marketing News, 134
Marketing to the Affluent, 166, 170,
  336, 404
Market knowledge
  extraordinary sales people and,
    166–67
  luxury car sales and, 327–28
Martin, Roland, 334
Mason, James, 405
Media endorsement
  publishing in trade journal, 236–38
  talk-show host, 235–36
Medical profession, 139
  Asian Americans and, 131, 135
Medical school faculty, 139, 141–42
Mentor, 29–30, 32, 197
  Asian Americans and, 139
  promoter and, 233
Minding Other People's Business, 426
Model minority, 131
Monday, David, 143

N

Naparst, Gene, 39–50
National Fisherman, 332
National Science Foundation, 198
Neighborhood taxonomy, 333
Network concept, 278
Newsweek, 104, 106, 115
New York Times, 130, 187, 353
Nicklaus, Jack, 393
Nicklaus/Sierra Development
  Corporation, 393–95
North, Oliver, 27
Not-for-profit scholar, 185

O

Objections, overcoming
  commodity brokers and, 345–47
  luxury car sales and, 301
  three fs and, 41–42
O'Kane, Richard, 377
Opinion leaders
  Asian American community and,
    139–40, 142
  industry-specific, 17, 35–36
  luxury real estate sales and, 399
OPM (other people's money), 433
Orphan policy, 23–24, 26

P

Parade method of selling, 344–47
Patronage habits, 73, 86, 463
  Asian Americans and, 136
  authors and, 195
Patronage opinion leaders, 139–40
  antagonist to clients and, 462
  apostle to clients, 462–64
Pension systems, 137
Personal selling, 285–88
  proactive strategy and, 300
  pro forma for mutual prospecting,
    288–96
  self-perception and, 288

Personal visit, 123–25
Plaques, 23–24, 72
  luxury car sales and, 306, 318, 324
  prospecting luxury real estate,
    403–4
  solicitations and, 83
Proactive selling, 300–302
  focusing resources and, 335
  leveraging credibility and, 372–73
  luxury car selling and, 312–13
  reactive sales and, 328–30
Professional athletes, 218–19
  apostle to, 426–27
Pro forma prospecting
  academic scholars and, 190–95
  advocate for affinity group and,
    146–51
  affluent women's market, 120–28
  letter requesting article publication
    (1-B), 250–51
  letter requesting trade journals
    (1-A), 248–49
  little-league orientation, 173–77
  luxury car selling program, 76,
    80–84, 312–28, 347–49
  luxury real estate, 402–4
  personal selling, 288–96
  prospecting by defense and, 154–59
  requesting interview with industry
    leader (1-C), 252
  sales professionals and, 76, 80–84
  targeting influencers of affluent,
    222–27
  thanking editor for publishing article
    (1-E), 254–56
  thanking prospect/client for
    assistance (1-D), 253
Program director's needs, 266
Promotional information, 326
Prospecting, 84
  by defense, 153–54
  via news stories, 84
Prospecting with plaque, 23
Public relations, 141, 225
  luxury real estate selling and, 401
Public speaking, 187

Publishers Weekly, 179–83
Publishing articles, 35
  Asian American community and,
    142
  coordinating interaction with
    audience, 37
  luxury real estate selling and,
    400–401
  opportunities for, 242
  perception as expert and, 339
  pro forma for, 367–68
  subjects for, 340–41
  trade journals and, 238
Publishing industry, 166, 183
  bartering for services, 239
  patronage from publishing, 241–42
Purchasing agents, 85

Q–R

Qualifying prospects, 401–2
Read, Robert, 14
  big-league orientation, 172
  conditioning technique and, 168–69
  courage and, 164
  information sources and, 170–72
  market knowledge and, 166–67
  prospecting by defense, 155–59
Reading, strategic, 41, 348
  sales professionals and, 347
Real estate selling, 3
  affluent and, 19
  avoiding confusion and, 391
  conditioning prospects and, 388–89
  controlling prospects, 383
  husband-wife team and, 386–88
  ideal prerequisites, 374–75
  pro forma for marketing, 395–404
  prospecting pro forma, 402–4
  qualifying prospects, 401–2
  selling inside affiliation convoy,
    376–78
  specializing and, 375–76
  timing and, 384–86
Recognition products, 38–39

Recognition service, 73
Recreational shoppers, 285
Referral system, 398, 464
   leveraging and, 399–400
Regional, State, and Local
   Organizations Encyclopedia oj
   Associations, 279
·Rejection, 285
Relationship business, 118
Retired executives, 341
Retirees/millionaires
   right message and, 201–3
   strategies/tactics for selling to,
      200–201
Retirement and Asian Americans, 137
Robbins, Jonthan E., 131
Rock and Dirt legend, 54–62
Rogers, Ken, 341–44
Role model, 409
Royalty checks, 186

S

Saavy, 94
Sales and Marketing Management,
   302, 331
Sales call, 126–27
Sales professional, affluent
   achievement recognition and, 12–13
   antagonistic approach to, 453
   apostle approach to, 453–54
   capitalizing on needs of, 70–71
   consumer patronage habits of,
      73, 86
   occupational categories of, 69
   prospecting for, 11–12
   sources for identifying, 85–86
   status symbols and, 11
Sales professionals, 3
   capitalizing on euphoria, 330–32
   five types of, 325–27
   organizing and managing of, 338–39
   profiles of, 6
   winning portfolio of, 337–39
Sales promotions, 348

Schwartz, David, 197–98
Scientific/technological professions,
   141
Self-employed individual, 287
Seminars, 262–66
Senior sales executives, 443
Service products, 7
Sierra, J. Robert, 393
Sklar, Steve, 302
Small Business Administration, 94
SNIPS, 240
Societal status, 72
Society of Extraordinary Sales
      Professionals, 77–79
Solicitation, timing of, 4
   antagonistic approach to, 420–26
   economic triumphs and, 69–70
   euphoria/propensity to spend and,
      298–99
   geographic movement and, 16
   income flow relationship to, 76. ·
      86–90
   luxury real estate sales and, 397
   marketing target and, 358
   trade journals and, 237
Solicitation sensitivity
   antagonistic approach and, 453
   euphoria levels and, 89
   luxury car sales and, 315
   luxury real estate selling and, 398
   occupational relationship and, 70
   people's concerns and, 64
   target needs and, 430
Solving current problems, 39
Spalding School's County Fair, 466
Speakers bureau, 278
Species cluster, 334
Spota, Jackie, 374–75
   client profile and, 381
   conditioning prospects and, 388–89
   courage and, 384
   fastest sale, 391–92
   focusing/specializing and, 375–76
   husband-wife decision team and,
      386–88
   marketing knowledge and, 381–82